The Catholic Counterculture

in America, 1933–1962

Studies in Religion

Charles H. Long, *Editor*
Syracuse University

Editorial Board

Giles B. Gunn
University of California
at Santa Barbara

Van A. Harvey
Stanford University

Wendy Doniger O'Flaherty
The University of Chicago

Ninian Smart
University of California at Santa Barbara
and the University of Lancaster

The Catholic Counterculture

in America, 1933–1962

James Terence Fisher

The University of North Carolina Press   Chapel Hill and London

© 1989 The University of North Carolina Press
All rights reserved

Library of Congress Cataloging-in-Publication Data

Fisher, James Terence.
   The Catholic counterculture in America, 1933–1962 / James Terence Fisher.
      p.   cm. — (Studies in religion)
   Bibliography: p.
   Includes index.
   ISBN 0-8078-1863-1 (alk. paper)
   1. Catholic Church—United States—History—20th century.
2. United States—Intellectual life—20th century. 3. Radicals—
United States—History—20th century. 4. Christianity and culture.
I. Title. II. Series: Studies in religion (Chapel Hill, N.C.)
BX1407.I5F57   1989   88-35971
305.6'2'073—dc19   CIP

Passages from the unpublished correspondence of Thomas Merton are reprinted by permission of the Trustees of the Merton Legacy Trust of the Thomas Merton Studies Center.

Passages from selected works of Jack Kerouac are reprinted by permission of Sterling Lord Literistic, Inc.

The paper in this book meets the guidelines for permanence and durability of the Committee on Production Guidelines for Book Longevity of the Council on Library Resources.

Design by April Leidig-Higgins

Printed in the United States of America

93 92 91 90 89   5 4 3 2 1

To My Parents

Contents

Illustrations

Acknowledgments

The idea for this project was born following a seemingly casual conversation I had with James W. Reed as we crossed the Rutgers College quad in the Fall of 1979. Since that time I have been extravagantly blessed by his advice and criticism: this book would not have been possible without his persistent irreverent friendship. I am likewise fortunate to have been among the multitude of aspiring cultural historians who were inspired by the late Warren I. Susman. His influence will continue to be felt for years and years. Philip J. Greven insisted that I treat religious experience as a matter of great intimate personal concern; his work provided an invaluable model of religious history. I was also very lucky to have met T. J. Jackson Lears in my final year at Rutgers, a year in which I had the privilege of working with Michael Aaron Rockland, Angus Gillespie, and Helene Grynberg in the Rutgers American Studies Department.

Anne Kenney, Pat Adams, and Kenn Thomas rendered much appreciated assistance during my visits to the Tom Dooley Papers at the University of Missouri–St. Louis. Robert E. Daggy was similarly gracious as director of the Thomas Merton Studies Center at Bellarmine College in Louisville. Philip Runkel of the Dorothy Day–Catholic Worker Papers at Marquette University is not only a fine archivist but a committed activist, whose example was a constant sign of contradiction to my historian's ambivalence toward the movement to which he is so dedicated. This work was supported in an earlier stage by a Charlotte W. Newcombe Fellowship, Woodrow Wilson National Fellowship Foundation.

Great history teachers have been the one constant influence in my life ever since my days at St. Bridget's Junior High School in Cheshire, Connecticut, in the late 1960s. For struggling to channel my nervous energy I especially thank Bill Monti, Ruth Fonken, Jason Okin, Mark Lytle, and Tom Forstenzer. And God bless my friends through all the years in New Brunswick whose support meant so much, especially Roy Domenico, Andy Koczon, Terry Radtke, John Rossi, and Susanna Treesh; Jeffrey Rosen, bookman; Bobby Albert for a place of refuge; Yun-Jae Chung, John Costanzo, Margery Fisher, Stacey Kelley, Barry Lipinski, Annette Martini, Maria Mattaliano, Ravi Misra, and each of the thousand or so students at Rutgers who helped make me a history teacher. I also appreciate the encouragement of the members of the American Studies Program at Yale. Thanks finally to Kathleen Schauble for seeing me through the homestretch.

Introduction

The situation of Roman Catholicism within American culture has always been a puzzling issue to scholars and other citizens. Many Protestants in early America were sure Catholicism was antithetical both to genuine Christianity and democracy, a sentiment manifest in much of the rhetoric inspiring both the American Revolution and the Union cause during the Civil War. In the 1850s a Republican orator and nativist proclaimed: "American civilization in its idea, is historically, the political aspect of the Reformation." The long history of American anti-Catholicism has tempted some, according to historian R. Laurence Moore, to view "everything in Catholic history, from the burning of the Ursuline Convent to the defeat of Al Smith, as evidence of Catholic powerlessness."[1]

Yet as Moore argued in *Religious Outsiders and the Making of Americans*, American Catholics began exerting significant political and social power in the nineteenth century, and their "outsider" status—far from presenting insurmountable barriers to "Americanization"—placed them at the center of a dynamic religious culture. Moore dismissed the model of an entrenched, monolithic Protestant culture jealously guarding the prerogatives of Americanism against alien incursion, and he concluded that "Catholics encountered hatred, but Catholic leaders had the relative luxury of being able to imagine more than one way to press their collective fortunes in America."[2]

The Catholics portrayed in the following pages found more than one way to pursue spiritual adventure and gain cultural authority, but their experiences all confirm historian David O'Brien's insight that twentieth-century Catholic culture can best be described in terms of "the ambiguity of success." Just as many immigrant Catholics struggled to make it in an economic system which conflicted in fundamental ways with both their largely peasant cultural inheritances and the teachings of their church, the authors and mystics who longed for a usable sense of American Catholic selfhood had to confront the Protestant tradition whether they wanted to or not.[3]

While the church enabled the immigrants to acquire the superficial emblems of Americanism, the culture of devotional Catholicism ensured that few among the laity would soon venture into the thick of a national culture which uneasily mediated tensions between communal duty and personal dreams. Historians T. J. Jackson Lears, John O. King, and others have shown how the Protestant stress on autonomous selfhood and a productive vocation in this world produced a significant crisis in middle-class culture in the late nineteenth century. The crisis was neither felt by nor relevant to the masses of Catholics, but after 1900 the *idea* of Catholicism as a potential antidote to bourgeois sterility and "weightlessness" became suddenly attractive to those, like Dorothy Day, seeking a way out of the gilded cage.[4]

This work begins with Dorothy Day's conversion to Catholicism and her invention, in the 1930s, of American Catholic romanticism. A convert from Episcopalianism and later bohemianism, the "personalism" she cultivated linked personal spirituality to the suprapersonal unity of Catholics within the Mystical Body of Christ. Her Catholic Worker movement was born at a time when many American Catholics saw their dreams of social and economic security threatened by the Great Depression, a time when the enormous popularity of the "radio priest," Charles Coughlin, indicated the attractiveness of powerful if extreme critiques of the social order. Day sought to transform the Catholic wariness of industrial capitalism from nascent theory into a permanent religious counterculture—a "sign of contradiction" to the secularizing individualism she had grown so disillusioned with in the years prior to her conversion. Though Day was essentially a devoutly Catholic separatist her movement launched a process which by the 1960s would find, much to her sorrow, millions of American Catholics exalting private conscience over the claims of the Church of Rome.

Dorothy Day's status as a convert has never been adequately treated. The attempt of a group of mostly second-generation American Catholics to establish a Catholic Worker–inspired community in Rockland County, New York, showed just how vast was the gulf between sophisticated converts and products of "ghetto Catholicism." Although I share the view of Werner Sollors and many others that "ethnicization" is a fluid process which provides the model for virtually all versions of American identity, I am also convinced that a unique

Catholic immigrant subculture generated an enormous potentiality for an alternative American ethos which only a perceptive outsider like Dorothy Day could harness, and even then with limited results. Catholicism has generated profound ambivalence within the American psyche, and I believe prominent converts have often—consciously or not—exposed Catholicism's latent nature as a "shadow side" of "Americanism."[5]

Dr. Tom Dooley, the Catholic anticommunist hero of Vietnam and Laos, was torn between a longing to express his unorthodox spirituality and dreams of triumph as a thoroughly American hero. His reluctant martyrdom signaled the end of a subculture which had deferred its irresoluble contradictions for years. Although the Second Vatican Council (1962–65) has often been conveniently cited as the cause of the immigrant church's transformation, or demise, the changes were actually rooted in three decades of an evolving sensibility I have called personalism. The Trappist monk Thomas Merton and "beat" novelist Jack Kerouac were the most gifted Catholic romantics of the postwar era. Merton moved from the convert triumphalism of the 1940s to the global mysticism of the 1960s, while Kerouac went from immigrant American romanticism to bitter parody of ethnic resentment. In the end the disparity between the genteel convert and the immigrants' son meant less than their shared literary vocation, because the unraveling of Catholic culture in the 1960s offered the burdens of freedom as their crosses to bear.

This study is primarily concerned with the self-expression of figures I have chosen as representative of the evolution of American Catholic culture between the early 1930s and late 1950s. My emphasis is on northeastern and midwestern urban Catholicism at the expense of other regions and other experiences including those of Hispanic Catholics. Nor have I attempted anything like a complete study of the Catholic Worker movement. Dorothy Day's important place in the histories of pacifism and voluntaristic social welfare has been treated at length elsewhere, as has Thomas Merton's central role in contemporary religious thought. I am strictly concerned with their meaning for the culture of American Catholics.

The Catholic Counterculture

in America, 1933–1962

The Conversion of Dorothy Day

Dorothy Day was the first American to exploit fully Catholicism's potential as a sign of contradiction. She was also "the most significant, interesting, and influential person in the history of American Catholicism."[1] Her 1927 baptism ended a flight from the "long loneliness" she had sought vainly to assuage through a fervent childhood religiosity and a reckless, romantic bohemianism. Only after the birth of her daughter in 1926 did Day embrace a uniquely Catholic Christian solution to longing and loneliness. "I wanted to die in order to live," she would later write, "to put off the old man and put on Christ. I loved, in other words, and like all women in love, I wanted to be united to my love."[2]

In 1933 Day and Peter Maurin—an itinerant French immigrant—founded a monthly newspaper in New York dedicated to fighting communism with a positive Catholic program of social reconstruction. The *Catholic Worker* was a startling phenomenon. An independent journal hailed by many priests and religious as a bold new voice of the "lay apostolate," it was feared by numerous lay people as a potential Trojan Horse for Communist infiltration, while on the Left Day's former associates scorned it as a tool of clerical fascism.

Day variously described her newspaper and social movement as personalist, anarchist, communitarian, pacifist, or radical. The whole enterprise was riddled with paradox. An enormously strong-willed woman, Day came to espouse one of the most abject brands of self-abnegation in American religious history. She published a "labor paper" to promote the views of a hobo philosopher who denounced strikes in the midst of the Great Depression. She boldly defied the United States government while preaching gentle obedience to church authority. Yet beneath these apparent contradictions lay a consistent Catholic

Worker ideology rooted in Day's convictions regarding the self and its negation. Since childhood she had been haunted by the seductive terror of darkness
as well as by a powerful conviction of God's presence in the world. From these
psychic materials she created a new religious style—as compelling as it was
bleak—which led her inexorably toward the church of immigrants' solace.

Dorothy Day was born in Brooklyn on November 8, 1897. Her father John
was a somewhat transient newspaperman from a southern background who
loved thoroughbred racehorses; he was known as "the Judge" for his astute
handicapping abilities. Dorothy's mother, Grace Saterlee Day, came from upstate New York. John Day had been raised a Congregationalist, his wife an
Episcopalian, but neither showed much interest in religion as adults, although
Dorothy Day noted in her autobiography that the five Day children (she was
the third born and eldest daughter) "did not search for God when we were
children. We took Him for granted."[3]

Nothing Day wrote can be taken for granted because, like most public
figures, she wrote with a great deal of circumspection, especially when describing her life before 1927. Her "official" autobiography, *The Long Loneliness*
(1952), is more cheerful in tone than such works as *On Pilgrimage* (1948),
which was privately printed and intended primarily for a Catholic Worker
audience. But a central theme emerges from all her work, from the bluntly
autobiographical preconversion novel *The Eleventh Virgin* (1924; "it's all true,"
she confessed to her biographer. She asked friends to buy up any remaining
copies they might discover in used bookstores), to the massive, unpublished
"All Is Grace," a distillation of retreat notes and meditations begun in the 1940s
and returned to sporadically by Day until shortly before her death in 1980. Her
fascination with "the conflict between flesh and spirit" began early in childhood and dominated the rest of her life.

Dorothy Day was an extraordinarily sensitive, lonely child. At the age of
seven she picked up a Bible and "knew almost immediately that I was discovering God." Since her parents did not go to church she attended Methodist
services with neighbors in Oakland, one of several locales in which John Day
practiced journalism during her childhood. Dorothy's initiative made her feel
"alternately lonely and smug:"

> At the same time, I began to be afraid of God, of death, of eternity. As soon
> as I closed my eyes at night the blackness of death surrounded me. I
> believed and yet was afraid of nothingness. What would it be like to sink

into that immensity? If I fell asleep God became in my ears a great noise that became louder and louder, and approached nearer and nearer to me until I woke up sweating with fear and shrieking for my mother. I fell asleep with her hand in mine, her warm presence in my bed. If she connected my fears with my religious attitude, she never spoke of it.[4]

Like the sick souls of William James's *Varieties of Religious Experience*, Dorothy was plagued by the fear that "back of everything is the great spectre of universal death, the all-encompassing blackness." But her encounter with the void was less a propaedeutic for the discovery of God than an integral part of the same experience. "Even as a little child of six," she wrote in *On Pilgrimage*, "I often awakened in the dark and felt the blackness and terror of non-being. I do not know whether I knew anything of death, but these were two terrors I experienced as a child, a terror of silence and loneliness and a sense of presence, awful and mysterious."[5]

Her fears may have resulted from a painful sensitivity to the lack of spirituality in her parent's home. Her father, in particular, was the product of a distinctly southern Protestantism which Day would later cite in characterizing her "Georgia cracker cousins" as "hard-shelled Baptists, fundamentalists, Campbellites, religious bigots and racists undoubtedly" (John Day reportedly viewed the Roman Catholic church as the province of "Irish cops and washerwomen"). The Days were also "Calvinists who lived by the work ethic, and insofar as they philosophized about life, they saw it in the light of a universe that was complete and where all the big questions had been answered."[6]

But John Day had rejected his religious inheritance, or had at least attempted to in becoming a cynically outspoken atheist. Day remembered him as a middle-brow Victorian who was "proud to have 'made' the *Saturday Evening Post* before he died." Day biographer William Miller described John Day as a self-styled "character," who "never lost his rural southern sense of the special glory of the barber shop rube."[7]

Dorothy Day was sufficiently perceptive to sense some of the bitterness behind her father's bravado (he continued to sprinkle his horse-racing columns with biblical quotations), and vulnerable enough to suffer painful alienation from him. She always believed that the hard shell of his Protestant legacy survived his apostasy. Of the unhappiness in her family life she wrote, "[W]e were like most Anglo-Saxons. . . . [W]e could never be free with others, never put our arms around them companionably as I have seen Italian boys doing."

There was no physical warmth in the family, only "a firm, austere kiss from my mother every night." Dorothy even experienced the San Francisco earthquake in solitude, skidding across the floor of her room in a brass bed while her parents rushed the other children outside.[8]

She also suffered the disparity between her parents' stern Victorian ethos and their painfully obvious human frailties. For all his bourgeois manners, her father was not always able to support the family very well; occasionally he was reduced to churning out "potboilers" from his home, between chapters of the serious novel he was sure would become a best-seller. Dorothy watched as her mother suffered a breakdown after the birth of John, her fifth child, in 1912. The elder Days were extraordinarily close, perhaps even at the expense of their children; they dined alone every night but Sunday. To John Day, "Grace was not only wife, but courtesan and handmaid as well. It was a heavy load for her, yet there is no indication she bore any resentment towards him." Yet Grace had broken at least once before, shattering dishes in a dark fit of anger and despair, after which John Day could only clumsily send the children out for ice cream. After the birth of her last child Grace was incapacitated to the point where Dorothy and her younger sister Della sometimes "wept because their home life had become so unnatural."[9]

Dorothy Day sought in God the warmth and intimacy lacking in her home. In *Memories, Dreams, Reflections*, Carl Jung succinctly recalled the nature of his childhood spirituality: "The peculiar religious ideas that came to me in my earliest childhood were spontaneous products which can be understood only as reactions to my parental environment and to the spirit of the age."[10] The grave spiritual doubts which Jung's father—a parson—suffered in silence were reflected in his son's dreams of a "subterranean God" in the shape of a phallus who reappeared "whenever anyone spoke too emphatically about Lord Jesus." Jung's problem was that his father was too much a Christian ("he did a great deal of good—far too much"). The underground God of Carl's dreams called the boy to a more integrated appreciation of the darkness and the light. No one in the Day household could explain to Dorothy why the Lord Jesus was never spoken of at all: "People were uncomfortable and embarrassed in talking about God." Thus while her experience of God in the darkness fulfilled a desire, it also threatened to sever her permanently from her family, a prospect she could only have viewed with profound ambivalence. Self-annihilation was both the promise and the price of her mystical gift.[11]

As she grew older Day cultivated a personal piety with increasing fervor. At fourteen she was still "reading the Bible with interest, but exultation was obtained only through the sermons of Wesley and the little books of Jonathan Edwards and Thomas à Kempis."[12] Thomas's *Imitation of Christ* was a late-medieval primer on spiritual selflessness, written by a monk, for monks. The work taught that "the highest and most profitable lesson" was "truly to know and despise ourselves," but it also promised that he who "established himself firmly in God" would "be dissolved and be with Christ." The author of the *Imitation* also insisted, echoing St. Paul, "you must be a fool for Christ's sake, if you wish to lead the life of a religious."[13]

Experiential Catholic piety provided Dorothy Day with the rich sensation she found lacking in Protestant worship. At age ten, shortly after the family had moved to Chicago, she grew close to a girl named Lenore Clancy ("Mary" in *The Eleventh Virgin*), the oldest of nine children in a working-class Irish family. In the novel Day describes Mary's initiation of "June" (Dorothy) into "the mysteries of her religion and her saints." Soon June and her younger sister "Adele" (Della) were playing at heroic self-denial, sleeping on the bare wooden floor of their room while "to their glowing imagination visions of St. Pelagia and the virgin with her little Christ child hovered around." Day contrasted the warm sensuality of the girls' secret devotions—"Adele snuggled her hot face against her shoulder and breathed on her neck while June narrated the trials and struggles of the early saints"—with the tragic loneliness of the faithless adult world: "And every night the smell of beer and whiskey came up in waves from the saloon below, and the Drunken Lady who lived in the flat above fell into bed and snorted and groaned with the heat all night."[14]

Day prayed in quest of "trances," "exultation," and "ecstasy," as though those states offered a permanent alternative to her family's lonely rigidity. According to William Miller, the stakes may have been growing increasingly higher: "Every time that Dorothy was threatened with a whipping, which she seemed to have gotten with fair regularity, she prayed to St. Pelagia to avert the catastrophe."[15] The victim of a barren late-Victorian milieu, Day came to sense—along with numerous older Protestant intellectuals from the early years of this century—that "independent selfhood was an illusion." But unlike such melancholics as Henry Adams and Vida Scudder, who were similarly attracted to "medieval mentalities" and "Catholic forms," Day was struggling not only with cosmic anxieties but with the stresses attendant upon an unformed identity. She had not yet developed the kind of rigid self-possession which prompted most Protestant antimodernists, for all their disillusionment, to "equate union with annihilation and retreat to autonomy."[16]

Day later recalled that during her childhood, "all beauty, all joy, all music thrilled my heart and my flesh, so that they cried out for fulfilment, for union." She also knew "it is a fearful thing to fall into the hands of the living God and I did not want to face the issue." She needed to locate a home both wholly other from her Protestant origins and receptive to her drive for self-abandonment. The dilemma would not be resolved until she was nearly thirty years old. During the final crisis before her conversion Day "thought of death and was overwhelmed by the blackness and terror of both life and death." But by then she knew where she was heading. "I longed for a church near at hand where I could go and lift up my soul."

Romancing Religiosity

When Day was twelve she joined a church, but it was Episcopalian, not Roman Catholic. A local pastor, knowing Grace Day to have been brought up in that denomination, went to her home in hopes of recruiting the entire family. Dorothy would surely not have been permitted to seek baptism into the Roman Catholic church, nor is there any evidence that she contemplated doing so. But neither could she remain for long a practicing Episcopalian, not so long as organized religion reaffirmed her parent's bourgeois evasions. In 1948 she commented on the moral tone of her family's vestigial Protestantism:

> Certainly . . . there was always an inner conviction that we were but dust. . . . [M]y early religiousness . . . included a conviction of sin, of the depravity that was in us all. The argument of conscience was always there. I was "bad" or I was "good." I was bad when I hated and quarrelled with my brothers and sister, when I stole from a neighbor's garden, when I was impure (and I felt the "dark" fascination of sex, of the physical forces in my own body very early).[17]

As an adolescent Day began to fear that her religiosity had grown "morbid"; that it sprang from the same sources as her father's apparent dependence upon alcohol. "It's because they want to escape from reality," June informs her sister in *The Eleventh Virgin*, " . . . religion, or whiskey, or dope." Yet Dorothy then turned to another source of nonreality, the world of romantic literature. Her father had instilled within his children an appreciation for the "serious" works to be found in the home of a literate, late-Victorian family: Scott, Hugo, Dickens, Stevenson, and Cooper. Dorothy, though, loved both contemporary romantic novels and poetry as well as the classics of the Romantic era. She also "loved the Arthur legend as a child and reverenced the Holy Grail and the search for it." John Day banned from his home such "trash" as Dorothy enjoyed, thus lending an even greater aura of secret pleasure to the stories of forbidden love and tragic passion which she devoured with intense fervor. In fact, "books, usually romances, continued to absorb her and to play a more vital part in her life than the talk of the boys and girls around her."[18]

The literature of romance confirmed Day in her integral identity as a writer. She had kept a diary since early girlhood, and although her brothers sometimes stole glances at it, she "never ceased keeping it, because she was lonesome and the little red book was her only comfort." Self-disclosure unleashed powerful currents of feeling within Dorothy that seemed to threaten her budding faith. Of the sanctity of the diary she wrote: "This was an emotion more sacred than God and the little Jesus." Where she had written once of "religious ecstasies," the diary now contained her "hurrying thoughts and desires" for union with a lover: desires so powerful she could entertain them only while lying under a tree in the park, "her body clutching the warm earth," or as she lay in the darkness of her room.[19]

By the age of fifteen Day was convinced that her spiritual life clashed fatally with her romantic yearnings. The "conflict between flesh and spirit" not only dominated her most intimate thoughts, it was the subject which "interested me most" as a writer. In *The Eleventh Virgin* as in *The Long Loneliness*, Day reproduced an extraordinarily revealing letter written to a friend named Henrietta, who had been her companion in preparation for baptism. She tells the girl of her unrequited, unacknowledged love for a neighbor, a married bandleader who conducted summer concerts in Chicago's Lincoln Park. She felt "happy but not in the right way. I did not have the spiritual happiness that I crave, only a wicked thrilling in my heart." She goes on to quote a line from Tennyson which best expresses her mood of exquisite despair: "Oh death in life, the days that are no more." She continues:

How weak I am. My pride forbids me to write this and to put it down on paper makes me blush, but all the old love comes back to me. It is a lust of the flesh and I know that unless I forsake all sin, I will not gain the kingdom of heaven. . . . I have so much work to do to overcome my sins. I am working always, always on guard, praying without ceasing to overcome all physical sensations and be purely spiritual. It is wrong to think so much about human love. All those feelings and cravings that come to us are sexual desires. We are prone to have them, at this age, I suppose, but I think they are impure. It is sensual and God is spiritual. We must harden ourselves to these feelings, for God is love and God is all, so the only love is of God and is spiritual without taint of earthliness. I am afraid I have never really experienced this love or I would never crave the sensual love or the thrill that comes with the meeting of lips. I know it seems foolish to be so Christlike—but God says we can—why else His command, "Be ye therefore perfect." Oh, surely it is a continual strife and my spirit is weary.[20]

In *The Long Loneliness* Day self-effacingly noted, "I was writing self-consciously and trying to pretend to myself I was being literary." She was also attempting to prove that Christian asceticism had always been rooted in her character, thus making her later flirtation with unbelief appear a temporary, if significant, aberration. But thirty years earlier, before she had become a Catholic, Day wrote in the *Eleventh Virgin* that, as a fifteen-year-old, "she felt that her attitude in the letter to Henrietta was a backyard and dingy attitude, strangely lacking in beauty." "She realized that the conviction of sin which is so vital a part of religious feeling was ignoble, and that it was wicked to spend an hour on one's knees in contemplation and repentance of one moment's ecstasies which had to the girl's budding womanhood the aesthetic value of a symphony or a beautiful poem."[21]

Instead of going to church she wanted to explore natural beauty and human feeling: "to bask in the sun on a warm spring day, or walk in a snowy park when the twilight made deep blue shadows behind the trees, or to read beautiful poetry." The poetry she liked best was that which evoked the dark undercurrents of Western romanticism, the poetry which voiced its seductive danger: "When she thought of poetry she thought of Swinburne's 'Tristram' which she had been reading and which was hidden back of the bookcase for safe keeping. With the thought she picked up her diary and defiantly wrote: I should like to lie on the grass in the woods with a lover all night just like Tristram and Iseult."[22]

Here Day's self-understanding found its limit. She was sure that romance and religion were mutually exclusive: in the wake of increasing sexual feeling, she turned toward romance. But as William James wrote, "[T]he true opposites of belief are doubt and inquiry, not disbelief." Dorothy Day's struggle was not so much between religion and doubt (or, as would often later be supposed, between religion and the "heresy" of communism) as between two varieties of mystical experience, inextricably bound up one with the other. Tristram and Iseult were, after all, more than just the archetypal figures of romantic literature and art (whose passion would echo through time, to the Wagnerian opera Day loved all her life); their romance, as Denis de Rougemont argued in *Love in the Western World*, was "an adulterated and sometimes ambiguous expression of courtly mysticism." Against the brutal marriage customs of the feudal age, the myth's creators—troubadours inspired by the Cathars' Manichean denuncia-tion of the visible world and the flesh—poised a "purer" love, but a love which, according to de Rougemont, "requires death for its perfect fulfilment and triumph. . . . [I]n the innermost recesses of their hearts, they have been obey-ing the fatal dictates of a wish for death; they have been in the throes of the active passion for darkness." De Rougemont argued that the myth was progres-sively "degraded" after its creation in the twelfth century until its sacred origins grew totally obscure.[23] In late nineteenth-century America, according to histo-rian T. J. Jackson Lears, popular romantic literature exalted suffering and death "as urgent necessities in a modern culture where personal meaning had dis-solved in comfort and complacency, where experience seemed weightless and death a euphemism."[24]

Day's precocity led her to the heart of this issue. Death was such a consum-ing mystery to her that she often lost sight of the distinction between physical death and the terrors that haunted her imagination. As a child she once watched as the bodies of two young children were taken from the lake in which they had drowned: "Here was death in the concrete and yet it did not touch me so nearly as those forebodings of death which came to me at night after I had closed my eyes in the dark room and the universe began to spin around me in space."[25]

Day's receptivity to the underlying menace of romantic literature proceeded from her obsession with death. There is also an aspect of self-punishment in her fascination with the literature of suffering, prompted by the continuing gulf she felt between her father and herself. She sensed her power to assuage the pain in her family; her painful failure ultimately to do so was consoled by the language of self-dissolution. According to Mario Praz, romantic literature was characterized above all by the sadomasochistic aesthetic of many of its creators, especially Swinburne. The concluding lines of his "Tristram of Lyonesse" suggest one solution to the suffering of the lonely:

> Here once, or here, Tristram and Iseult lay:
> But peace they have that none may gain who live,
> And rest about them that no love can give,
> And over them, while death and life shall be,
> The light and sound and darkness of the sea.[26]

No religion could appeal to Dorothy Day unless it promised just such an experience of self-abandon and dissolution from loneliness toward darker seas. She wanted to merge with the infinite, not commune with it in the world. Day rarely alluded in her body of writing to the kind of "ineffable" mystical experience in which all sensual analogies are negated in the depths of encounter with an Absolute. Day's account of her brief career as an Episcopalian—though intended to convey the awkwardness of adolescence—illuminates her spiritual temperament: "Going to the Communion rail was an agony. Fortunately one did not have to do that more than a few times a year. What I did love were the Psalms and anthems; the rubrics of the Church. When the choir sang the Te Deum or the Benedicite my heart melted within me."[27]

Dorothy Day was thus deeply religious as a young woman. The conflict of her youth was between a type of Christian devotion which—by the time she reached adolescence—was equated with the stifling middle-class milieu of her parents, and a more strictly mystical way of knowing in which "suffering and understanding are connected; death and self-awareness are in league." She had already glimpsed, as one among those de Rougemont would call "the best romantics," that "sufferings, and especially the sufferings of love, are a privileged mode of understanding." Day left home at age sixteen to begin her search for the vocation most inspired by that insight.[28]

The City

By the time Dorothy Day entered the University of Illinois as a scholarship student in 1914, she had discovered a new object for her romantic quest. She was now fascinated by the lives and struggles of the urban, immigrant working class. After reading *The Jungle* she began to explore the world of Chicago's West Side, "going up and down interminable grey streets, fascinating in their dreary sameness, past tavern after tavern, where [she] envisaged such scenes as the Polish wedding party in Sinclair's story."[29]

The discovery of the immigrant poor lent a direction to the intense feelings of compassion and sorrow which had been bottled up amidst the nervous silence of her parent's home. Day's shadowy tours of the immigrant precincts left her convinced that "from then on my life was to be linked with theirs, their interests were to be mine; I had received a call, a vocation, a direction to my life." For as long as she lived Day would express a palpable sense of unity with the poor. After becoming a Catholic she invoked the ancient doctrine of the Mystical Body of Christ as the model for this supernatural solidarity. But even as a college student she suffered deeply any separation from the objects of her feeling. As she told her brother John (for whom she cared during the illness of her mother), "I suffered because I was separated from you. It was as though I had been torn from my own child." Day even claimed that she had rejected "all the gentle things of life" and sought "the hard" because she was hurt at being "torn from you, my brother and my child."[30] Yet it was precisely "the hard" that aroused her emotions and imagination.

The first story Day submitted to her college literary magazine was on the "experience of going hungry." She did not have much money but tended to make things more difficult for herself than they need have been. "I felt a sense of reckless arrogance and with this recklessness, I felt a sense of danger and rejoiced in it. It was good to live dangerously." She also discovered her ability to arouse within others a view of hardship and strife similar to her own. After witnessing Dorothy's fervent interest in labor struggles, her mother told her "how she had worked in a shirt factory in Poughkeepsie when she was a girl. She had seen no romance, no interest in those few hard years of her life, until she saw it through [Dorothy's] eyes."[31]

Although Day's college years coincided with a period of intense Christian Social Gospel activity—in which such Protestant ministers as Walter Rauschenbusch boldly proclaimed "the revolutionary consciousness in Jesus"—she remained much more deeply interested in a personal identification with the victims of industrialization and social dislocation. She resented the hypocrisy of ordinary Christians, who had built a world in which "Christ no longer walked the streets," but her radicalism remained strictly mystical. She responded less to ideological discussions than to dramatic calls to battle such as the Marxist's "workers of the world unite," which "was to [her] a clarion call that made [her] feel one with the masses, apart from the bourgeoisie, the smug, the satisfied."[32]

Day followed her family to New York after two years of college and quickly became a "rebel girl" of Greenwich Village. She acquired a job on the socialist *Call* by promising to move to the Lower East Side and live on five dollars a week—in mockery of the middle-class reformers who considered that an adequate sum for "working girls." "I am taking the decisive step," she wrote. "I am suffering the tortures of the condemned." She had a good time in so doing. "I enjoyed that winter in the slums and I have never lived any place else," she later wrote. If one had to be poor, there was no better place than the Lower East Side, with its "streets of pushcarts and public baths, and the colorful costumes." But she remained hounded by familiar demons. Despite her outward gaiety in the face of slum life, she knew that the tenement atmosphere evoked "not the smell of life, but the smell of the grave." Yet she was drawn inexorably toward that world: "As I walked these streets back in 1917 I wanted to go and live among these surroundings; in some mysterious way I felt that I would never be freed from this burden of loneliness and sorrow unless I did."[33]

The editors of the *Call* expected Day to highlight the misery and suffering capitalism had wrought: "To picture the darker side of life, ignoring all the light touches, the gay and joyful side of stories as I came across them." But even her "light touches" scarcely hid a seemingly inconsolable sadness at the impermanence and fragility of life in the world. Of the children of an impoverished, diseased East Side family she wrote: "Little Maurice, with the smoochy face, is three, and the cuddly baby with the big dark eyes was sentenced to life only five months ago." Whether writing about imprisoned prostitutes weeping for their infant children, or birth control crusaders heroically enduring hunger strikes (she covered the theatrical prison saga of Margaret Sanger's sister, Ethel Byrne), Day's urgent tone indicates that—by the time she was twenty—the mystery of human suffering had become her consuming passion.[34]

Dorothy Day became a central figure in "the drama of Village life" during the war years because she embodied many of the traits—an air of reckless abandon, a vaguely self-destructive romanticism—that appealed to her fellow exiles from Main Street. Floyd Dell hoped Day might become a heroine of the new paganism, but she rejected his offer to personally initiate the process, probably sensing the undertone of midwestern circumspection which he and many fellow rebels never quite overcame. In *The Eleventh Virgin* Dell ("Hugh") tells

June, "you make me furious with your pose of cool indifference, I know you're an exotic person." June remains unimpressed by his modernist gospel of free love, yearning instead for "someone who would tempt me very insidiously to give up my virtue, persuading me to wickedness just because it was wickedness."[35]

As a woman in bohemia, Day had reason to doubt the authenticity of her male counterparts' rebellion. Radicals like Dell were often shackled with traditionally sentimental attitudes toward women. For the men around *The Masses*, "the romantic notion that women lived primarily for love" was a shared assumption. The exaltation of women and the mystical, creative principle they were expected to embody (Dell said, "One must have seen Isadora Duncan to have died happy") tended to make even the most radical women prisoners of sex. Of Duncan, Emma Goldman, and Mabel Dodge, the historian Leslie Fishbein wrote: "All these women would disregard their other accomplishments when they felt themselves failures in love."[36]

In a book review for *The Masses*, Day decried the "modern attitude towards love," in which "the idea of permanence is dismissed as old-fashioned." She endorsed *Helen of Four Gates* (by "An Ex-Mill Girl") because "it tells the story of a man and woman who love each other, in spite of everything, to the end." But in rejecting the free-love abstractions of the Village philosophers, Day remained deeply vulnerable to a vision of love which linked romance and suffering. Her first sexual relationship was with a man who, according to Malcolm Cowley, "used to quote Nietzsche—something to the effect 'goest thou to woman and forget not thy whip.'" In *The Eleventh Virgin* Day described the affair as "a fatal passion." "You are hard," June tells "Dick" (in real life, Lionel Moise; he was a newspaperman admired by Hemingway whose "specialty was getting women to commit suicide over him"). "I fell in love with you because you are hard." She adds, "women love to be victims." Day, like June, was truly victimized, suffering through an abortion after her loutish boyfriend threatened to abandon her. William Miller suggests that Day also attempted suicide during this period.[37]

The Eleventh Virgin showed that Day was not a novelist, but it is a much more significant document than has been acknowledged. Misread by a literary historian as "an example of how 'Back to Normalcy' was operating in the sphere of the emotions," and by the historian of the Catholic Worker movement as evidence that Day recognized quite early "the great dilemmas of reconciling personal happiness with serious social commitment," the book was above all a reflection of Day's persistent, if unconventional, religiosity. By the time the novel was written (in 1921, in Europe), the remnants of her Christian sensibility and her more purely romantic mysticism had merged into a single potent force, both strains informing her journey along "the downward path to salvation." That Baudelarian phrase was often invoked by Day to describe both her preconversion excesses and her postconversion experience with poverty. But in *The Eleventh Virgin* the distinction disappeared. In one crucial scene, June sits brooding in a cafe. She had just been cruelly rebuffed for yet another time by her lover. She recalls that her friend "Billy" had called her a fool for becoming involved with such an irresponsible and destructive man, yet defiantly concludes: "So she was. A line of Scripture flashed through her mind. We are all fools for Christ's sake. She suddenly laughed and Dick took hold of her hand which was hanging by her side." Day has June—in a moment of desperate self-abandonment—invoke her girlhood religiosity in order to integrate the light and dark facets of her "downward path." In becoming a Catholic, Day would make the fateful assumption that the dark aspect of her imagination could be left behind.[38]

Conversion

Dorothy Day was received into the Roman Catholic church on December 18, 1927. She was baptized in a church overlooking Raritan Bay on Staten Island, New York, near the small beach house where she lived with her common-law husband, Forster Batterham. Accounts of Day's conversion have suffered from a tendency to search for causes rather than meaning. Day's "turning" was—given her lifelong religious experience—an illustration of Philip Slater's theory that "an individual who 'converts' from one orientation to its exact opposite appears to himself and others to have made a gross change, but actually it involves only a very small shift in the balance of a focal and persistent conflict."[39] It is also true, as Day wrote in 1938, that "a conversion is a lonely experience. We do not know what is going on in the heart and soul of another. We scarcely know ourselves."[40]

Day's interest in Catholicism began to increase at the height of her chaotic life in Greenwich Village. Eugene O'Neill's second wife, Agnes Boulton—who was for a time Day's rival for the playwright's affections—recalled that a major element of Day's legendary "desperate quality" was her inability "to resist those sudden and unexplainable impulses to go into any nearby Catholic church." Boulton believed Day was a "sort of genius" whose religious impulse sprang from a need to dramatize herself during those times when "she was not singing 'Frankie and Johnny' . . . which she sang in a way it was never sung before."[41]

But this talent for self-dramatization was always matched by an imposing detachment which enabled Day to exploit—as a creative person, a writer— experiences which might have debilitated others. She "surrounded her person with a no-man's-land of distance that shielded her from a too-ready vulnerability of feeling." Just as the conflict between flesh and spirit was the subject that both "interested" her as a writer and haunted her as a budding mystic, her adult identity revolved around an unusual axis of detachment and desperation. After the well-known Village personality Louis Holladay died of a drug overdose in January 1918, Day breathlessly informed friends, "[H]e died in my arms." Yet she was also sufficiently composed to hide from police the vial of heroin she found in Holladay's pocket.[42]

Her entire life might be viewed as a response to the tensions generated by this dialectic. Although she knew what suffering felt like, her attraction to the truly destitute and oppressed betrayed an oddly serene quality, as though the poor represented that death in life she could only experience vicariously. She loved the world of the Lower East Side because down there she could reap her fantasies about dispossession, could resonate with the spirit of romanticism's heroes and heroines who, as Michael Hoffman wrote, needed to be "the outcast, the exploited outsider who is violated by an unsympathetic, impersonal society." Yet Dorothy Day was—in fundamental ways—the antithesis of the stereotyped consumptive romantic. She was five feet nine inches tall and very sturdy. Her ancestors were among those who conquered the forbidding American wilderness (and in the process made her eligible for membership in the Daughters of the American Revolution). Her downward path was longer than most, beginning, as it did, with a flinty Protestant-American inheritance.[43]

The detached style Day affected undoubtedly resulted in part from an effort to render herself invulnerable to her father's remoteness. For all her rebelliousness, she was in sufficient need of her family to leave college after two years and move with them to New York. In a book review for *The Masses*, she admitted that her father had destroyed the novel under review before she could even finish it, having put it "immediately in a class with Havelock Ellis and Greenwich Village and short hair and other radical things." John Day could not have gotten his hands on the book had not Dorothy brought it to her parent's home, perhaps hoping to provoke some gesture of approval or understanding from her father. A sense of mutual disappointment and pain remained for the rest of each of their lives. In the late 1930s, shortly before John Day died, he wrote to a relative: "Dorothy, the oldest girl, is the nut of the family. When she came out of the university she was a Communist. Now she's a Catholic crusader. She owns and runs a Catholic paper and skyhoots all over the country. . . . I wouldn't have her around me."[44]

In turning toward Catholicism, Day found an autonomous realm where her father would never dared have tread. But since her religiosity was largely a reaction—to loneliness, to middle-class, Protestant sterility, to her father—it often appeared merely a dramatic "pose," a charge her sister made while Dorothy was still a girl. Despite the admission, in *The Eleventh Virgin*, that such was the case, she continued to feel pursued by God. Catholicism would increasingly appear as the resolution of these conflicts. Radically other, it provided the vehicle for her exploration of the terrain lying between the remnants of the Christian ascetic ideal and the darker will to self-abasement.[45]

"For a long time I thought I could not bear a child," Day wrote in *The Long Loneliness*, "and the longing in my heart for a baby had been growing." Her biographer even suggested that Day's casual sexual behavior during the early 1920s can be attributed to this powerful impulse (it was a time, according to her occasional host Malcolm Cowley, when she was "almost contemptuous of the flesh," by which he meant she was "promiscuous"). She moved to the Staten Island beach house with Batterham in the spring of 1925 and gave birth to a daughter, Tamar Teresa, the following spring, not, as has been persistently reported, in 1927. Day's celebrated *New Masses* article on the experience of childbirth recalled familiar themes:

> Where before there had been waves there were now tidal waves. Earthquake and fire swept my body. My spirit was a battleground on which thousands were butchered in a most horrible manner. . . . Never have I known such frantic imperious desire for anything. And then the mask descended on my face and I gave myself up to it, hurling myself into oblivion as quickly as possible. As I fell, fell, fell, very rhythmically, to the accompaniment of tom toms, I heard, faint above the clamor in my ears a peculiar squawk. I smiled as I floated dreamily and luxuriously on a sea without waves.[46]

In the aftermath of this extraordinarily emotional and creative moment, Day decided to have the child baptized a Catholic. "I knew that I was not going to have her floundering through many years as I had done, doubting and hesitating, undisciplined and amoral." Batterham, a naturalist and anarchist often depicted as a listless misanthrope who preferred fishing to the company of humans, declined to endorse the move. He, too, loved the child greatly. The final eighteen months of his relationship with Day saw angry conflict, temporary reconciliations, beach house doors slamming in the night, and finally, Day's conclusion that "no human creature could receive or contain so vast a flood of love and joy as I often felt after the birth of my child." Day decided to join her daughter in the church while Batterham—embittered by the executions of Sacco and Vanzetti—increasingly withdrew from human contact. But when she was finally baptized the day after she broke off with Batterham for good, she felt little joy, only the pain of doubt arising from her persistent self-consciousness:

> I had no particular joy in partaking of these three sacraments, Baptism, Penance, and Holy Eucharist. I proceeded about my own active participation in them grimly, coldly, making acts of faith, and certainly with no consolation whatever. One part of my mind stood at one side and kept saying, "What are you doing? Are you sure of yourself? What kind of affectation is this? What act is this you are going through? Are you trying to induce emotion, induce faith, partake of an opiate, the opiate of the people?" I felt like a hypocrite if I got down on my knees, and shuddered at the thought of anyone seeing me.[47]

Day's conversion seemed to require a relentless affront to her self-esteem. The nun who instructed her in basic Catholic doctrine humiliated her regularly: "And you think you are intelligent," she berated the New York sophisticate. "My fourth grade pupils know more than you do." She criticized Day's housekeeping and, in dread of encountering Batterham, waited outside their cottage until he angrily fled out the back door. Day explained that "she would probably have regarded any husband so, no matter how exemplary. She knew little of the world of men."[48]

Sister Aloysia typified Day's experience with Catholics, the one group Day felt was fundamentally estranged from the culture which had only offered her loneliness and despair. "Catholics were then a nation apart," she wrote, "a people within a people, making little impression on the tremendous non-

Catholic population of the country." She would later note appreciatively that "in America the Catholic immigrants have been the despised." Although she had once found herself amidst a group of Catholic college students disrupting a meeting of "Jew radicals" in Baltimore, she remained drawn to the gentle spirituality and wounded innocence which seemed to mark so many of the faithful. The woman who shared Day's hospital room just prior to Tamar's birth was an Italian who

> had a very serious and obscure heart condition which led every physician who examined her to declare that she should not have children, that death was certain if she did. But she had three, and, day by day, doctors gathered around her bed to examine her . . . and expostulated with her for bringing children into the world. Several times they stood there giving her information on birth control and she listened with her eyes cast down, not answering them. They assumed she was stupid and repeated in the simplest phrases their directions, speaking in phrases as they spoke to foreigners who cannot understand English. Then when they looked on her chart and saw she was a Catholic they expressed their impatience and went away.[49]

When Day tried to refuse the woman's gift of a medal of the Little Flower, St. Thérèse of Lisieux, her reply was disarming in its simplicity: "If you like someone, you like to have something to remind you of them." Several years later, when a priest asked Day to describe the influence of Catholic social thought on her conversion, she confessed that she had no idea, in 1927, that the church even had a social doctrine: "I had never heard of the encyclicals. I felt that the Church was the Church of the poor, that St. Patrick's had been built from the pennies of servant girls, that it cared for the emigrant."[50]

Although Day knew as well that the church was too often allied with the forces of wealth and privilege, this only stimulated her growing attraction to signs of contradiction. In America, the church was the church of the poor. She intuitively sought a means of turning Protestant-secular America inside out, aware that this demanded that the nation's middle-class mythology be challenged where it really counted on the altar of the self. As early as in *The Eleventh Virgin* Day had written, of a lonely train ride toward the prison to which she had been sentenced following a Washington suffrage march: "[T]his bleak countryside made me feel that I should struggle for my soul instead of my political rights." Her alienation recalled a tradition begun three hundred years earlier by the New England Puritans—through which those first white Americans saw the barrenness of their spirits reflected in the wilderness; only then could they "externalize their experience, attributing their spiritual reform to the exigencies of a satanic new land." But where those before her had usually—in their obsessive Protestant rigor—fashioned a mode of discourse in which the building up, or conquest, of the wilderness mirrored the making new of their selves, Day sought to merge her self, in a literally organic sense, with a "body" as contrary to the American spirit as could be imagined.[51]

At the moment of her conversion Dorothy Day became the most sophisticated Catholic lay woman in America. Although she later recalled a conversation between Kenneth Burke (Batterham's brother-in-law), Malcolm Cowley, and John Dos Passos which "stood out especially in my memory because I could not understand a word of it," she was anything but naive. The literature which drew her toward the church resembled the popular devotional works favored by the masses of Catholics only in its exaltation of suffering. She had always loved Dostoyevski's tales of grotesque mysticisms and starving ascetics, but after her own tragic experience she began to read him with "an appreciation of men and suffering." Even more important in the months preceding her conversion were the strange works of the Dutch-French Decadent novelist, J. K. Huysmans. She read *En Route*, *The Oblate*, and *The Cathedral*, "and it was those books which made me feel that I too could be at home in the Catholic Church. . . . [T]hey acquainted me with what went on there."[52]

Huysmans's work encompassed many of the themes which later emerged from the Catholic Worker movement. He belonged to the tradition of "aesthetic Catholics" which included Baudelaire and others who "savoured above all in religion the charms of sin, the grandeur of sacrilege. . . . [T]heir sensuality caressed dogmas which added to voluptuousness 'la suprême volupté de se perdre.'" Huysmans created a sensation with his art-for-art's sake novel *Against the Grain* (*A rebours*, 1884); its hero, Des Esseintes, became the prototype for the languid, vaguely misanthropic Decadent personality. In one celebrated scene, Des Esseintes sets out on a journey from Paris to London only to conclude—after visiting, still in fog-shrouded Paris, an English tavern and bookstore—"it would be a fool's trick to go and lose these imperishable impressions by a clumsy change of locality."[53]

Yet beneath Huysmans's detached fascination with artifice lay an unrelenting obsession with spirituality, which, given his taste for the bizarre, led him into episodes with "hysterical mysticism, erotomania, scatology, sadism, and Satanism." A Catholic by baptism, Huysmans experienced "religious atavisms" and began "lurking around churches" in search of a sympathetic priest. In 1891 he finally confessed to a cleric, "I have just published a Satanic book [*Là Bas*], full of black masses. I want to write a white book, but for that I must be white myself. Have you anything that will bleach my soul?"[54]

He then went on to write the books which helped guide Day in her move toward the church. Huysmans offered a peculiar conversion narrative. He retained his weary contempt for ordinary Catholics and their uninspiring devotions. His solution to the problem of the Fatal Woman (in his case a creature named Florence, with whom he regularly performed unnameably perverse acts) is to partake of the spectacle of young women being entombed, while still alive, into the deathlike body of the Church. After witnessing the investiture of some Benedictine nuns, "Durtal" (Huysmans' literary persona) remarks: "Well, this scene is to my mind the most touching alibi of death that it is possible to see, this living woman, who buries herself in the most frightful of tombs—for in it the flesh continues to suffer—is wonderful."[55]

As the literary historian Mario Praz succinctly characterized this sort of writing: "Sadism and Catholicism, in French Decadent literature, become the two poles between which the souls of neurotic and sensual writers oscillate." Critic Richard Gilman sought—in his book on *Decadence*—to rescue Huysmans from that pejorative epithet by insisting that his was a "prophetic voice"; arguing that his garish accounts of blasphemies actually "afford a sense of the self such as the merely pious and conventionally moral can never know," and claiming that Huysmans testifies, "the way darkness does to light, to the possibility, even the imminence, of its opposite." Gilman viewed Huysmans's reconversion in terms of this "dialectic": "[T]he movement is neither forward nor backward but around a center."[56]

But Huysmans's return to the church signaled a continuing descent more than a dialectic. He became a connoisseur of tortured, self-abasing saints and martyrs: "He liked his saints to be sick and was fond of repeating the remark of St. Hildegarde that 'God does not inhabit healthy bodies.'" He wrote a biography of a fifteenth-century saint, a plague victim who offered up her own sufferings as a mystical substitute for those of others "[T]he lungs and liver decayed; then a cancer devoured her flesh; and finally, when the pestilence ravaged Holland, she was the first victim, and was afflicted with two abscesses. 'Two, that is well,' she exclaimed, 'but if it pleases our Lord, I think three in honor of the blessed Trinity had been better!' and a third abscess formed in the cheek."[57]

He also celebrated St. Benedict Joseph de Labre—later to become one of the patrons of the Catholic Worker movement—who was known to "pick up the vermin that fell out of his sores and put them back." When Huysmans was stricken with cancer he told a priest, "[I]t was necessary for me to suffer all this in order that those who read my books should know that I was not just 'making literature.'"[58]

Huysmans found a home for his asocial spiritual interests in a French church that could never fully recover from the assaults unleashed during the Revolution; soon the refrain "the working class has been lost to the Church," would be heard throughout that country. His retreat from secular France to a purely imaginary universe centered around suffering was a typical pose for late nineteenth-century Decadents. As Dorothy Day noted, "a friend of mine once said it was the style to be a Catholic in France, nowadays, but it was not the style to be one in America." The church's unpopularity in America—especially among intellectuals—activated her interest in mystical self-abnegation and surrender. In Huysmans she found a spirit really quite like her own. For both of them, art was a residual and irreducible product of experience, but the distinction between the two was never clearly established.[59]

Day was often perceived as an ominously "dangerous" personality. In *The Eleventh Virgin* she has June's lover admit that her "decadent flavor" was a major source of her attractiveness. Huysmans' work is significant for an appreciation of Day not only because it clearly served as one of the textual models around which she ordered her conversion, but also because to underestimate the "dark side" of her preconversion psyche is to promote the same sort of confusion Day generated when she presented herself to the Catholic community. Like the church itself, Day was unprepared to acknowledge or understand the continuing claims her shadow side made upon her. Some of Day's friends—in writing about the period of her conversion—would reveal a continuing interest in her life before Catholicism, as though half-consciously concerned to restore some continuity of meaning. There is a passage, for instance, in Malcolm Cowley's celebrated *Exile's Return* which initially appears to be both gratuitous and—in precisely the phrase Day later used to describe it—"told out of context." Writing of an after-hours club in Greenwich Village, Cowley claimed: "The gangsters admired Dorothy Day because she could drink them under the table;

but they felt more at home with Eugene O'Neill, who listened to their troubles and never criticized." Day is mentioned nowhere else in the book. Writing shortly after she first gained notoriety as the founder of a religious movement, Cowley may have well been uncomfortable with the notion of Day as dramatically "converted" from a past he had shared in.[60]

Of much greater significance is Caroline Gordon's novel *The Malefactors* (1956). Ostensibly concerned with the events which prompt an estranged, intellectual couple to move, separately, toward a Catholic Worker spirituality, the work is haunted, as are its characters, by the presence of "Catherine Pollard" (Day), a Catholic convert. In the novel (set in the late 1940s or early 1950s), Pollard presides over a Bowery bread line and a rural commune. But none of her former friends can dismiss their memories of her as a young woman in Paris who partook of alchemical experiments with the blood-crazed homosexual poet "Horne Watts" (Hart Crane), drank to frenetic excess, and finally abandoned her husband and infant daughter (Day's casual reminiscences of 1920s legends would become a source of great appeal, years later, to young Catholics raised far from bohemia. Michael Harrington recalled, "Dorothy startled me over coffee one morning when I mentioned one of my then favorite poets, Hart Crane. 'Oh that Hart,' she said. 'I used to have breakfast with him all the time when I was pregnant with Tamar'"). The original version of the novel included a scene in which Pollard is linked to a Black Mass purportedly held in Huysmans's Paris during the 1920s, but the scene was excised at Day's insistence and at least one of Day's friends from the period asserted that, though a Black Mass had been held by acquaintances in Greenwich Village, Day had not taken part.[61]

Dorothy Day was in Paris in the early 1920s; no period of her life is more shrouded in mystery. She went there with a man who married her on the rebound from Moise; she subsequently returned to New York alone. When a woman sent Catholic Worker Jack English money to visit Paris in 1949, Day intercepted the check and

> ran to the bathroom and locked herself into the bathroom and said, "I'm going to tear this up and flush it down the toilet." We had a real commotion then. She came out and gave me the thing and said, "You are going to wind up in the sewers of Paris someplace. . . ." Because she told me at this point that she had made a trip to Paris with no passport, no money. She

just happened to get on a boat with someone. She said she got out of there by the skin of her teeth.[62]

In the 1950s Day told an editor of the *Catholic Worker* that she had suddenly grown disgusted with her life in Paris and had secretly pawned her jewelry to finance passage on the next ship out of France. "There was much weird business in the air those days," Geoffrey Wolff wrote of the expatriate Harry Crosby, whose suicidal obsession with the "black sun"—rooted as it was in Huysmans and the occult—was but another manifestation of the Parisian avant garde's obsession with spirituality. The cultural historian Henry May was surely mistaken in dismissing the influence of Huysmans and his "overrated, languid, black-mass foolishness," on the rebel generation. Strange and powerful things were happening in that transoceanic bohemia of the 1920s. This was a world Day was more than casually acquainted with.[63]

Caroline Gordon was a friend of Day's and a fellow convert. *The Malefactors* is a text which works to restore some coherence to Day's conversion experience. Gordon contrived a highly unlikely scenario in which a nun-scholar discovers startling similarities between Watts's poem "Pontifex" (Crane's "The Bridge") and the *Divine Dialogues* of St. Catherine of Siena. The alcoholic homosexual's quest for blood is reinterpreted as a desire to share in the Passion of Christ. "Sister Immaculata" thus provides the link between Pollard's dark past and her current state of grace (of the black magic the nun insists: "She was a wild young girl in those days and had no notion of what it was they were after.") In their blindness, that is, they struggled confusedly for redemption.[64]

The nature of Day's conversion would be of relatively little interest had she been a European like Huysmans, reduced to private cultivation of an increasingly peripheral faith. But she was to exert profound influence over that segment of American Catholicism which followed her after 1933: "It was the Irish of New England, the Hungarians, the Lithuanians, the Poles, it was the masses of the poor who were Catholics, in this country, and this fact in itself drew me to the Church." The possibility that Day's religiosity was tinged with sadomasochistic impulses is not so important, in itself, as the role her conversion played in permanently excluding this level of discourse both from her own effort at self-understanding as well as from the effort of those who would seek to understand her and her community of faith. It is certainly possible that Day's encounter with darkness, the void, evil, or sin was cushioned with the same quality Edmund Wilson ascribed to Huysmans's similar temperament: "We always feel that the wistful student of Satanism has too much Dutch common sense really to deceive himself about his devils." But the Catholic immigrants—and their children—who embraced her lacked the kind of detached sophistication such an insight required. They knew only that Day had joined them in their alienation from such haughty figures as Wilson (who Day always referred to as "Bunny"—in sarcastic tones mingled with sadness—when telling young Catholic Workers of the old days).[65]

When Day quoted from Eric Gill to show that "it is a strange fact—man cannot live on the human plane; he must be either above it or below it," she spoke with the vested authority of a priest or priestess delivering the literal truth about the nature and destiny of men and women. Such was the encounter of Dorothy Day and the immigrant church. It produced one of the most remarkable movements in American religious history: the Catholic Workers.[66]

"Fools for Christ"

Dorothy Day and the Catholic Worker Movement, 1933–1949

Before there was a Catholic Worker movement there was the *Catholic Worker*, a monthly tabloid first distributed in New York's Union Square on May Day, 1933. The paper was inspired by Peter Maurin and produced by Dorothy Day: as Maurin was fond of saying, "Man proposes and woman disposes." They had met late in 1932, shortly after Day returned from covering a Communist hunger march for the *Commonweal*, an elegant, liberal Catholic magazine. Day later recalled a deeply emotional moment experienced at the end of her trip. On December 8, 1932, the young journalist in search of a vocation visited the National Shrine of the Immaculate Conception in Washington. She was troubled at the thought that

> there was social justice in the demands made by the Communists—they were the poor, the unemployed, the homeless. They were among the ones Christ was thinking of when he said, "Feed my sheep." And the Church had food for them, that I knew. And I knew, too, that amongst these men there were fallen-away Catholics who did not know the teachings of their Church on social justice—that there was a need that this message be brought to them. So I offered up my prayers that morning that some way be shown me to do the work that I wanted to do for labor.[1]

Day's tearful prayer for a direction was answered when Maurin appeared in the doorway of her apartment. He had been a frequent if not always appreciated visitor at the *Commonweal's* New York offices. That journal's learned editor, George Shuster, suggested that Maurin might enjoy speaking with Day, who was becoming widely known in Catholic intellectual circles as a former social-ist (perhaps even Communist). Rather than obtain her address from Shuster, Maurin simply took to the streets, asking priests and radicals alike as to Day's whereabouts, until finally "a red-haired Irish Communist" told him where she lived.[2]

Shuster sensed that Day was looking for something more than a conven-tional Catholic activist could provide. "I still believe," he wrote in 1974, "that Dorothy was the only person to whom I could have sent Peter. . . . John A. Ryan would not have known what to do with this strange little man." Ryan was a liberal social thinker whose enthusiasm for Franklin Roosevelt prompted Fa-ther Charles Coughlin to dub him "the Right Reverend New Dealer." Day was in need not of a political theorist but a spiritual master, and in Maurin she found the exemplary peasant Christian to embody her hopes for a community founded upon suffering and self-sacrifice.[3]

This was a mysterious calling. As late as 1929 Day was in Hollywood writing scripts for Pathé Films, when she suddenly decided to visit Mexico with her daughter. She described the trip in *Commonweal* articles which were devoid of the brash, Anita Loos style of wit which had endeared her to the film company. Dorothy Day was on the verge of becoming a powerful religious writer. Of a pilgrimage to the Shrine of Our Lady of Guadaloupe she wrote: "As Our Lady of Lourdes revealed herself to the poor peasant girl, so did our Lady again reveal herself to the poor peasant Juan Diego, filling his tilma with roses that he might convince the bishop—it was so long ago that it was the first bishop of Mexico —that his appearance was indeed true."[4]

Day's Mexican writings reflected her struggle to overcome natural feelings of strangeness toward a faith so alien to her inheritance. The presence of her daughter—baptized in infancy—helped bridge the void. Dorothy compared Teresa's innocent faith (the Hebrew name "Tamar" was not restored until the girl reached her eighth birthday) with the humble persistence of the peasants who struggled on their knees toward the hillside shrine. Teresa brought some saving light-heartedness to the experience: "After Teresa had blessed herself with holy water, and made her rather lopsided genuflection, she skipped out of the church again that she might lean over the low walls and peer into doorways at the chickens, pigs, lambs, and pigeons. . . . 'These are all Mary's babies,' she said. 'The little pigs and the chickens and the boys and the girls. And these are all little baby houses, and that,' pointing to the church, 'is the mama house.'"[5]

Teresa's response to the pilgrimage mirrored Day's own faith in its infancy and revealed some residual anxieties over the cost of her conversion. After returning to New York, Dorothy and Teresa lived near an Italian church and frequently witnessed dramatic funeral processions:

> To Teresa, this glimpse of death with massed flowers, its dignity and its solemnity, has lent a new aspect to heaven. A year ago she had said, "I do not want to die and go to heaven. I want to stay where there is plenty of fresh air." And this evident impression of a stuffy heaven which she had in some way or other visualized, dismayed me. She was thinking of the grave, I assured her, and not of a heaven which was filled with not only all the present delights of her life, but many more. "Beaches?" she wanted to know. "And many little crabs and pretty shells? I do want to live on a beach in heaven." And I assured her there were indeed beaches in heaven.[6]

Since Day had complained in her journal that three-year-old Teresa was "inarticulate and unresponsive," she was very likely speaking through her daughter in much of her early writing as a Catholic. She had rejected a youthful, somewhat pagan romanticism for an adult commitment to a faith whose own downward path demanded a disciplined self-denial. Teresa's resistance to death hints at Day's final doubts about surrendering herself to the church. She later often told the story of St. Teresa's jaunty appearance at the convent walls just prior to her induction, clothed in a bright red dress: the symbol of her free-spirited girlhood. The stark contrast between the red dress and the selfless mystic Teresa was to become represents the poles of Day's poignant rejection of worldly pleasures in favor of sainthood. That remained the goal even though Day understood—as did St. Teresa, who sometimes served steaks to young novices struggling with the Carmelite regimen—that the flesh made claims on humans. This recognition was a source of Day's rare talent for spiritual writing, but even her "light touches" continued to betray some unutterable melancholy, some bitter disappointment with the world.[7]

Day's discovery of peasant Catholicism in Mexico intensified her equation of suffering with salvation and heightened the contrast between the spiritual community she sought and the loneliness of American life. She marveled at the nonbourgeois, non–Anglo-Saxon character of Mexican Christianity, especially after assisting at Easter Monday mass "at the altar of the Black Christ, blacker by far than any of the Indians in the congregation."[8]

Unlike such non-Catholic intellectuals as Stuart Chase, who perceived in Mexico's organic culture an echo of Jeffersonian democracy, Day was far less interested in reviving American culture than she was in seeking a more exotic route to self-dissolution than was available in her culture of origin. She needed premodern Mexican Catholicism in the same way she would later invest more deeply in alienated American immigrant Catholicism to bolster her interior self-exile. Several years after becoming an absolute pacifist, Day wrote of the "civilizing" efforts of the anticlerical Mexican leader Rodolpho Calles: "When I contemplate civilization which offers us silk stockings and playgrounds and electric ice boxes in return for the love of God, I begin to long for a good class war, with the civilizers and the advertising men for those same civilizers, lined up to be liquidated."[9]

Peter Maurin

Peter Maurin very quickly became the personal symbol of Day's quest for pilgrim sainthood. One day in December 1932 she returned to her apartment to find him indoctrinating her brother and his anarchist wife. The Frenchman then turned to Day, explaining that it was up to her as a journalist to popularize his program for Christian social reconstruction. The plan comprised three parts: round-table discussions for the "clarification of thought"; the establishment of hospices in which Catholics would reproduce the charitable essence of primitive Christianity by offering food and shelter to the destitute; and a back-to-the-land scheme Maurin termed the "Green Revolution." Agrarian utopianism was by far the most important element of Maurin's program. Like many antimodernist intellectuals of the 1930s, he urged a complete rejection of urban industrial society.

"The Maurin that others came to know," wrote historian Mel Piehl, "was in large part Dorothy's image and interpretation of him." Piehl emphasized the contrast between Day's native American common sense and Maurin's bewildered eccentricity, and suggested that—as a highly driven social radical and religious reformer—she readily employed Maurin as a kind of figurehead: "It was therefore personally comforting to Day, as well as strategically useful to her as a woman leading a social movement in the sexually conservative Catholic Church, to be able to point to the male cofounder of the movement and to emphasize that she was merely carrying out Maurin's program."[10]

Catholic Worker ideology grew out of the tension between Maurin's desire to see his program taken literally and the largely symbolic role to which he was relegated by virtue of his personality and appearance. Maurin was born in 1877 in a tiny village in the southern French province of Languedoc (the site of the Albigensian heresies whose romanticism would be echoed in Maurin's later interest in recruiting "troubadours for Christ").[11] He was the eldest of twenty-three children in a peasant family whose roots in the local soil were said to extend back over a thousand years. Peter was educated by the Christian Brothers and later entered their order, working for seven years as a teacher until the government of Emile Combes, an ex-seminarian and "anti-religious monomaniac," suppressed Catholic schools in 1902. Maurin then turned to Marc Sangnier's Christian Republican movement, Le Sillon ("the furrow"). Sangnier followed in the tradition of such French Catholic democrats as Lammenais and Montalembert. Through the Sillon he cultivated a charismatic, authoritarian mystique of personal piety and devotion to the ancient traditions of Catholic France. Members of the Sillon, like their bitterly rightist enemies in the Action Française, fancied themselves messianic crusaders against irreligion in France. But Sangnier also favored rural cooperatives and communal ownership of property, and when he engaged the Sillon in electoral politics after 1907, the royalist French clergy lobbied for a papal censure. When Pius X condemned the movement in 1910, he noted, "[W]e have hardly to point out that the advent of universal democracy is not the concern of the Church's action in the world." A leading royalist cleric explained, "[T]hey had to be condemned. They would have made Breton priests accept the Republic."[12]

Peter Maurin apparently grew disenchanted with Sangnier's decision to involve the movement in politics. In his only published reference to the Sillon, Maurin indicated his agreement with the condemnation:

"The Sillon," says Abbé
    Leclerq
editor of *La Cité chrétienne*
"was a Christian
democratic movement
founded by Marc Sangnier.

It was full of enthusiasm
and generosity
but lacked deep thought.

It had allowed itself
to present democracy
as the only political regime
in conformity
with Christianity."[13]

Maurin's suspicion of democracy reflected his formative years amidst the intensely anticlerical atmosphere of early twentieth-century French politics. But his affinity for the rural utopianism of the Sillon as opposed to the militantly royalist Action Française was rooted in a gentle, apolitical nature. Even his superiors in the Christian Brothers were concerned—despite his obvious devotion—that his restlessness and aversion to authority made him a dubious candidate for final vows. Unwilling to serve again in the French army, and having learned of homesteading opportunities in Canada, Maurin left France in 1909 to continue his life as a pilgrim.[14]

Although Maurin never published anything while in France, his later thought descended directly from the French Catholic milieu. As the author of the only (and unpublished) nonhagiographical study of Maurin concluded, "[T]here was little in Maurin's Green Revolution that was not present in French social Catholic thought at the end of the nineteenth century."[15]

Maurin's journey from theorist to symbol began on May Day, 1933, when Day paid fifty seven dollars for twenty-five hundred copies of the first issue of the *Catholic Worker*, which she then distributed in Union Square, aided by a sickly convert named Joe Bennett and two "commission workers" from a local parish who disappeared after hearing the taunts of Communists gathered in the park. Day's first editorial was one of the most moving pledges ever uttered by an American Catholic:

For those who are sitting on park benches in the warm spring sunlight. For those who are huddling in shelters trying to escape the rain. For those who are walking the streets in the all but futile search for work. For those who think that there is no hope for the future, no recognition of their plight—this little paper is addressed. It is printed to call their attention to the fact that the Catholic Church has a social program—to let them know that there are men of God who are working not only for their spiritual, but for their material welfare.[16]

On the first page of that issue, alongside an exposé of the working conditions faced by blacks toiling on the Mississippi Flood Control project, appeared a polemic in free verse by Peter Maurin. This first "Easy Essay" began:

Jean Jacques Rousseau says:
"Man is naturally good, but institutions
make him bad, so let us overthrow institutions."
I say man is naturally bad, but corporations,
not institutions, make him worse . . .
If the Catholic Church is not today the
dominant social dynamic force, it is
because Catholic scholars have failed to
blow the dynamite of the Church . . .
It is time to blow the lid off so the
Catholic Church may again become the
dominant social dynamic force.[17]

Maurin's message was similar to that expressed in the landmark social encyclicals of popes Leo XIII ("Rerum Novarum," 1891) and Pius XI ("Quadre-gesimo Anno," 1931). The pontiffs had condemned both liberal capitalism and socialism in favor of a neomedieval social order where class conflict would be eliminated through the establishment of hierarchical, "functional" classes. The encyclicals boldly denounced the injustices suffered by workers under indus-trialism but reserved their harshest criticism for socialism, which the popes considered the greatest threat to the church's survival. They thus called for the creation of Catholic labor guilds designed to win back the allegiance of the alienated masses (in a concise analysis of Social Catholicism, historian Joshua B. Freeman argued that "in the end it was a sometimes noble quest for the impossible, capitalism without its logic, its morality, its necessity").[18]

Maurin's aggressive posture and conservative view of human nature ("man is naturally bad") suggested an orthodox espousal of Vatican policy, but in the same issue of the *Catholic Worker* Dorothy Day introduced her own special vision of Maurin and the type of Catholicism she hoped to promote through him. She noted that Alfred E. Smith, "one of our most prominent Catholics," had refused her request for an interview, and she went on to conclude: "So we must content ourselves this issue with contributions from a more humble Catholic whose address, when he is not employed outside of the city in manual labor, is Uncle Sam's hotel, the Bowery."[19]

Day thus contrasted the symbol of acculturationist, upwardly mobile Catholicism with her peasant mentor. Smith's combination of personal charm and pragmatic political expertise had gained him the 1928 Democratic presidential nomination, but by his defeat many Catholics were reminded that "they and their church were an object of mistrust and suspicion to an uncomfortably large number of their fellow citizens." Whereas Smith represented the slow struggle of Catholics toward acceptance within a Protestant culture, Maurin forever remained the recalcitrant foreigner, speaking with an impenetrable accent after more than twenty-five years in North America. He rarely bathed, owned but one shirt, and slept with his trousers rolled up under his head. At a time when many Catholic intellectuals were upholding (precisely because disillusioned Protestants had left them an opening) the genteel American tradition, in its "exquisite intuitions of innocence," Maurin doggedly invoked European-style "tradition."[20]

Day had begun to create the gently antitriumphalist mode of American Catholic expression which would resonate with startling effect through the 1930s and, especially, the 1940s. She provided the textual model without which it might never have existed. As historian John King argued in his study of the structure of American spiritual conversion, "textual expressions are in themselves capable of creating a person's character," and can be "considered to be in themselves efficacious for giving shape to reality." (King's study revealingly concluded with an analysis of perhaps the final testament to America's Protestant origins: Max Weber's *The Protestant Ethic and the Spirit of Capitalism*.) The Catholic Worker movement was founded at the start of what scholars would later call the post-Protestant era. As historian Donald B. Meyer and others have shown, mainstream Protestant leaders of the early twentieth century found themselves increasingly isolated from the sources of social tension in America—not the least of which was the clear majority of Catholics within the great working masses.[21]

Day's genius resided in her ability to reverse the trajectory of the conventional American conversion narrative. Unlike King's protagonists, for instance, who painfully affirmed a vision of the self as working doggedly through a world of machines and counters—building upon the ruins of private melancholy as the only means to salvation—Day offered deconversion, or breakdown, as a permanent state of grace. Protestants could assail the self only to discover that it was all they would ever have to work with. As Sacvan Bercovitch wrote of the origins of American selfhood: "We cannot help but feel that the Puritan's urge

Peter Maurin, September 1934. Courtesy Marquette University Archives.

for self-denial stems from the very subjectivism of their outlook, that their humility is coextensive with personal assertion. . . . [T]he very intensity of that self-involvement—mobilizing as it did all the resources of the ego in what amounted to an internal Armageddon—had to break loose into the world at large."[22]

Unlike earlier American Catholics, Day knew something of this tradition, and she fervently sought a new version of Catholic selfhood as though she were adhering to a national requirement. She worked throughout her life on a never-published biography of Peter Maurin; the book could almost be received as her response to Weber's maniacally productive, worldly yet ascetic Protestant. Maurin was the first real Catholic she had ever met because he seemed so innately devoid of self: "He never comments on the weather, whether it is hot or cold; whether it is wet or dry; whether he feels well or ill; hungry or thirsty. . . . He was another St. Francis of modern times. He was used to poverty as a peasant is used to rough living, poor food, hard bed, or no bed at all, dirt, fatigue, and hard and unrespected work. He was a man with a mission, a vision, an apostolate, but he had put off from him honors, prestige, recognition. He was truly humble of heart, and loving."[23]

The essential difference between Maurin and the classical model of American selfhood was in his acceptance of poverty as a goal in itself, even as one to be worked toward. Where American heroes had often been compared in their struggles with Old Testament figures or an authoritative Christ, Day introduced American Catholics to a prophet in their own midst who emulated not the leadership qualities or moral excellence of Christ but his vocation to suffering. She made the connection explicit in writing:

> While I write these pages my heart glows within me and I feel joyfully how happy this book is going to make many of our friends. "They will thank me, they will be grateful," I say to myself as I write, "just as I am thankful and grateful to Peter." The infant John leaped with joy in the womb of Elizabeth at the salutation of Mary, bearing the Lord. So we feel when we encounter Christ in our brother. . . . Peter has taught us to know each other in the breaking of bread, to see Christ in each other in the breaking of bread. . . . He has brought to us Christ in the poor, as surely as the Blessed Mother brought Christ to Elizabeth. He has shown us the way, with his poverty and the works of mercy and that way is Christ.[24]

In the late 1930s other Catholics adopted Day's figural method in discussing Maurin. Joe Breig's 1938 *Commonweal* article, "Apostle on the Bum," began: "Everyone calls him Peter, perhaps more wisely than they know; for Peter Maurin of the Catholic Worker, like another Peter, is laboring to reconstruct a civilization that is collapsing under the weight of its sins."[25]

Breig was a German-American Catholic whose interests in labor and politics were both more conservative and more reformist than Day's; his comparison of Maurin with St. Peter indicated his taste for masculine religious role models. But he also presented Maurin as a challenge to the status aspirations of *Commonweal*'s sophisticated Catholic audience. He noted that Maurin was "gnarled and shabby and somewhat disreputable, and seems to enjoy being called an agitator and a bum, because he regards activity and poverty as two indispensable qualifications for his particular apostolate."[26]

Like Day, Breig stressed the pilgrim character of Maurin's life in such a way that Peter's often opaque, profoundly un-American philosophy acquired a rustic tone of childlike wisdom. He described Peter's restless wanderings in search of manual labor, including his brief stint with the H. C. Frick Coal and Coke Company near Brownsville, Pennsylvania. "Peter got $1.50 a day, and lived in a coke oven with a Negro. He liked it, he says, because 'the Negro was a gentleman. There was no housework to do.'" Breig was one of the few journalists fortunate enough to obtain usable quotes from Maurin, but rather than lessen his otherworldly quality, they merely highlighted the rehearsed quality of his speech, the better to discourage intimacy. Of the dramatic religious experience Maurin underwent while giving French lessons in Woodstock, New York, in the late 1920s, he would say only: "'I gave up the idea of charging for lessons. The world had gone crazy, and I decided to be crazy in my own way. They didn't let me starve.'"[27]

Maurin had read Marx during his years away from the church but "was much more inclined to anarchy." His "Easy Essay" technique was designed to baffle the expectations of the ordinarily pious. When a Kingston, New York, Rotarian invited Maurin to a meeting of his group so that they might "have a good laugh," Peter simply stood before them and declaimed:

The other fellow says that I am queer:
and that he is normal.
When he says that I am queer

he means that I am queer
to him.
I may be queer to him,
But he is queerer to me,
and he being queerer to me
than I am queer to him,
he hasn't a chance
to make me normal.[28]

Breig was so enchanted by Peter's peculiar genius that he nearly lost sight of Maurin's own view of his apostolate, a major part of which involved combating the enemies of his church. During the late 1920s—his Woodstock period—Maurin began "his career as an agitator. He travelled the night boats between Kingston and New York, and made speeches in Union Square. 'Union Square,' he says, 'was in the process of becoming Red Square. So I went there to keep Union Square Union Square.'"[29]

Maurin's essays and sayings often resembled Zen koans; he loved puns and American idioms, and used language to suggest a mode of consciousness beyond the reach of ordinary discourse. Dorothy Day pursued Maurin as one would a guru, but in the early days of the movement she strained to attain the detachment which for him seemed effortless. She wanted more Catholics to act like him, but when she pleaded with them—as she did in dedicating the first issue of the *Catholic Worker* to the policemen of New York—her profound urgency sounded almost derisive: "If the police don't want to buy this paper we will give it to them. As so many of them are good Catholics, prominent and resplendent in Holy Name processions and at Communion breakfasts, we feel sure that they will give this issue, which is dedicated to them, their sympathetic and intelligent attention."[30]

Maurin was the most natural fool for Christ Day would ever know. A Catholic Worker testified, "[H]e was the most detached person I ever met." At the height of the depression, Day had found a man who ignored poverty in his imitation of Christ. Her vision of him as a Christ figure spread rapidly. Breig wrote: "He carries his apostolate all over the country, travelling by bus, and trusting to the donations of friends to pay his fares. . . . [H]e remembers that 'the foxes have holes and the birds of the air their nests, but the Son of Man has no place to lay his head.'"[31]

Day even admitted that Maurin was not very "likeable" in the conventional human sense, as if to show that his appeal was rooted in a transcendent realm far removed from her middle-class bohemian standards: "I was sure of Peter—sure that he was a saint and a great teacher—although, to be perfectly honest, I wondered if I really liked Peter sometimes. He was twenty years older than I, spoke with an accent so thick it was hard to penetrate to the thought beneath, he had a one track mind, he did not like music, he did not read Dickens or Dostoievski, and he did not bathe."[32]

The equation of Maurin with the spirit of poverty and suffering meant that his worldly failure could never be separated from whatever positive message he hoped to convey. To belong to the Catholic Worker movement during the 1930s and 1940s was to share in Maurin's humiliations as in those of Christ. There was a familiar litany of Maurin lore: mistaken by the wife of the distinguished historian Carlton Hayes for a plumber, he uncomplainingly sat in their basement for hours until the professor came home. A representative of a woman's college sent to meet Maurin at a train station called the Catholic Worker house in New York to report that no one was waiting at the station but an old bum. "That's Peter," was the knowing reply. Maurin became Day's child as well as her master—just as, having been rescued by Catholicism, she now sought to nurture her vision of it as a pristine community. Richard Deverall, later active in the Catholic labor movement, recalled that Maurin "was obviously a foreigner and a man who was more than detached from the world. In the middle of a discourse on St. Francis Peter stopped talking and just walked out of the door. Dorothy smiled: 'He's just like a child, you know.'"[33]

Maurin often resembled one of the great tragicomic figures of the depression. In 1934 he opened a storefront office in Harlem to convince blacks to emulate St. Augustine rather than the downtown white bourgeoisie. For hours he and a friend would sit in the dark, or by the light of a single candle, waiting for visitors who never materialized. Maurin once decided to take the stage of the famed Apollo Theater on amateur night, in search of a wider audience. The pathos and low comedy of the ensuing scene foreshadowed the tragic vision of a Samuel Beckett: "He was announced as a comedian, and when he began reciting his essays, catcalls filled the theater. Maurin was escorted off the stage. Later he recalled that he really 'got the hook that night.'" He also conceived the idea for a "moving billboard" in which student volunteers would each carry a sign bearing a part of his message. But the marchers were "abruptly dispersed by a barrage of insults and garbage hurled at them by members of the Harlem community."[34]

In his biography of Day, William Miller did not make clear whether his analysis of her attraction to Eugene O'Neill applies also to her postconversion relationship with Peter Maurin. "O'Neill had a quality common to all the men with whom Dorothy was ever seriously involved," he wrote. "He was, as a personality, a maladjusted egocentric, a type to which she was drawn as some people are to stray dogs."[35] Maurin embodied the stripped personality type around which Day ordered her Catholicism. But as her summary appraisal of his life indicates, his achievement entailed the legitimation of suffering and self-humiliation as the foundations of spiritual excellence:

> Peter had been insulted and misunderstood in his life as well as loved. He had been taken for a plumber and left to sit in the basement when he had been invited for dinner. He had been thrown out of a Knights of Columbus meeting. One pastor who invited him to speak demanded the money back which he had sent for carfare . . . because, he said, we had sent him a Bowery bum, and not the speaker he expected. "This then in perfect joy," Peter could say, quoting the words of St. Francis to Friar Leo, when he was teaching where perfect joy could be found.[36]

In such a thirst for a short downward path to the absolute lay the essence of Catholic Worker spirituality during the 1930s and 1940s.

The Movement Unfolds

Peter Maurin was, by his own lights, a reactionary who viewed Western history since the fifteenth century as a disastrous mistake. He told Day: "I did not like the idea of revolution. I did not like the French Revolution, nor the English Revolution." Against this legacy of rebellion he poised the church, which stood, as "Rome used to stand, for law and order." "I am peasant, a medievalist," proclaimed Maurin: "Call me anarchist or what you will but never call me a socialist. My family has had farmlands for fifteen hundred years. I come from that Catholic Mediterranean tradition." Maurin preferred the corporatism of Frederick Kenkel's Central Verein and the medievalism of Edward Koch's *Guildsman* to liberal Catholicism.[37]

Maurin biographer Anthony Novitsky convincingly argued that "the ideology of the Catholic Worker . . . is understandable only in the context of French Social Catholicism and other movements." Novitsky rooted Maurin's harsh rejection of Reformation, Enlightenment, and American thought in the bitterness French Catholics suffered after the decline of the church's temporal influence. But Novitsky, like several others, insisted upon contrasting Maurin's traditional Catholicism with the left-wing reformism Day purportedly brought to, and through, her conversion. Day, he believed, "seemed chiefly interested in the work of assisting the downtrodden. . . . [S]he was not much concerned with the philosophical premises of the movement." This is true only insofar as the content of that philosophy is concerned. The form of Maurin's thought was of the nature of a sign of contradiction, and was received as such by Day. She could occasionally soften the tone of his polemic—as when she revised "I say man is naturally bad," to "I say man is partly good and partly bad." But Maurin's status as a European philosopher and fool for Christ enabled her above all to forge a new spiritual posture from traditional symbols.[38]

Day described the *Catholic Worker* as a "labor paper"; one of her most vivid articles described her dramatic entrance through a window of the locked-out General Motors plant in Flint during the monumental 1937 strike. Yet Maurin had written, "strikes don't strike me. . . . [W]hen the organizers try to organize the unorganized, then the organizers don't organize themselves." Day could thus call the workers to a more authentically Christian commitment than unions could ever offer. In 1936 she had written:

> The *Catholic Worker* does not believe that unions, as they exist today in the United States, are the ideal solution for the social problem, or any part of it. We do believe that they are the only efficient weapon which workers have to defend their rights as individuals and Christians against a system which makes the Christ-life practically impossible for large numbers of workers. We believe that Catholic workers must use unions in their efforts to heed the exhortations of the Popes to "de-proletarianize the workers."[39]

Whereas Maurin abstractly rejected the industrial wage system outright, Day personalized the issue, seeing workers primarily as victims whose sufferings pointed to the collapse of the entire bourgeois ethos. Many early members of her movement were genuine victims of the depression. Among the recruits were "a former Franciscan who had decided he had no vocation and had left the seminary before ordination, and, jobless, had taken to sleeping in Central Park; a former real estate man who had become a janitor."[40]

These were not unusual misfortunes for that era, but it often seemed that the mark of a Catholic Worker was a general unfitness for the competitive marketplace. Day welcomed especially the "undeserving poor," whose superficial unattractiveness enhanced their status as "ambassadors of God." Among those "who have gone off the deep end and whose poor brains have collapsed completely" was "C," a poet

> who wrote poems like Poe . . . who stood for hours in the middle of the floor, "caught in a cold air pocket" he used to say. Peter brought him to us one evening and for several years he lived with us, deranged though he was. . . . But the hardest of all to deal with are the mad men who come with panaceas for the social order in their pockets. Perfectly serious, they will sit down beside your desk and take out of their brief cases curious scrolls, and unroll them before you and start to tell you that theirs is the mighty brain which has been waiting to direct the work.[41]

Day divided the movement into "workers" and "scholars," the former referring to "the offscouring of all": Bowery alcoholics, drifters, the homeless elderly. Scholars were generally lower-middle-class Catholics who were unsure as to their vocations, or who had rejected their families' expectations. After 1940 the movement came increasingly to serve as a kind of halfway house for men on their way into or—as was much more often the case—on their way out of seminaries and monasteries. The movement was committed above all to performing works of mercy in a nonproselytizing atmosphere which blurred the distinction between volunteers and afflicted so radically that evangelical programs such as the Salvation Army and professional social service agencies seemed patronizing by comparison. Day described herself as the movement's "housekeeper," though she was rarely involved in the actual preparation of meals or other manual labor.

She strongly encouraged the scholars to emulate her penitential attitude toward the "workers" no matter how unpleasant that task might be. Among the more trying of the latter was a Mr. Breen, an irascible former newspaperman who had taken up residence in the New York house (during the 1930s dozens of Catholic Worker "houses of hospitality" were established in American cities, and the paper's circulation exceeded one hundred thousand, much of it in the form of bulk mailings to parishes). Day wrote to the Baroness Catherine de Hueck—a Russian émigré who led the Worker-inspired Friendship House in Harlem—that thanks to Mr. Breen,

I am at my wit's end. He sits at the lower window like a Cerberus and growls and curses at everyone who comes in for a bite of food or some clothing. He hates us all, he hates this place, he says that he is going to die, yet he won't have the sacraments, etc. He won't bathe. He won't dress. . . . And he, after all, is Christ. . . . I know that if we send him to a hospital, he will, with his present temper and shoutings and cursings, land in the psychopathic ward. Can you imagine Christ in the psychopathic ward.[42]

Day's continuing identification of Christ with suffering and failure determined the outcome of the Catholic Workers' effort to realize the "theoretical heart" of Maurin's program: his "Green Revolution." Her qualified support for labor unions contained a wish that they might serve as "'organizations of workers wherein they can be indoctrinated and taught to rebuild the social order. . . . [W]e stress the back-to-the-land movement so that the worker may be de-proletarianized.'" Her ambivalence was reflected in a promise not to "leave the city to the Communist," whose advocacy of class struggle was in fundamental opposition to the Workers' gentle spirituality. Against charges that her passive strategy was doomed to failure, Day reiterated the central theme of her apostolate: "[W]e admit that we may seem to fail, but we recall our readers to the ostensible failure of the Christ when he died upon the Cross, forsaken by all His followers. Out of this failure a new world sprang up." Day asserted, in announcing the opening of a Catholic Worker farm commune in Easton, Pennsylvania, in 1936, that agrarianism was the key to the survival of America's Catholics. "Four fifths of the Catholic population is in the city," she wrote, explaining that industrialism had imperiled fertility and produced a middle-aged society.[43]

Peter Maurin steadfastly argued that there was "no unemployment on the land," a peculiar assertion in light of the severe agricultural depression of the late 1920s and 1930s, but his romantic agrarianism was echoed in a broad movement among antimodernist intellectuals in both Europe and America. Maurin was well versed in the distributist, decentralist thought of the Englishmen G. K. Chesterton and Eric Gill and the French-English Hilaire Belloc, all of whom believed that "the spiritual values of Christianity . . . were expressed in the hierarchical guild society of medieval times." In America Maurin discovered an affinity with neo-Christian thinkers like Ralph Adams Cram, whose program he approvingly quoted in an "Easy Essay":

> "What I propose
> is that Catholics
> should take up
> this back to the land problem
> and put it back into operation.
> Why Catholics:
> Because they realize
> more clearly than any
> others the shortcomings
> of the old capitalist
> industrial system . . ."[44]

The decentralists were attracted to medieval Catholicism because it allegedly featured a timeless social order founded upon artisanal values and small landholdings. This was a vision of unity for a fragmented world. As Gill put it, "If there be God, the whole world must be ruled in its name." Such a search for unity often found the decentralists in league with antiurban, anti-Semitic, and fascist ideologues. Although Maurin sometimes spoke of "the pluralist state," he explicitly sought the complete re-Christianization of the West. He concurred with Pope Pius XI that "secularism is a pest." As he concluded his paraphrase of Cram:

> And there is
> no sound
> and righteous
> and enduring community
> where all its members
> are not substantially
> of one mind
> in matters of the spirit—
> that is to say,
> of religion.[45]

Maurin was unburdened with the ruggedly Protestant heritage which rendered the medievalism of Cram or Henry Adams so poignant, but his extreme eccentricity profoundly mitigated his affinity for triumphalist, authoritarian Catholicism. His idea of a farm commune was apparently satisfied by the Workers' one-acre garden on Staten Island, where he happily indoctrinated workers and scholars alike while they planted seeds. Day, for her part, was not nearly so interested in the abstractions of the "Chesterbelloc" as in the radical distributism of the English Dominican Vincent McNabb, who "wore hand-woven clothes, refused to use a typewriter, and travelled nearly everywhere on foot." The residents of the farm communes were expected to act like fools for Christ: Maurin even thought the farms would make a good place for prostitutes and alcoholics to marry and take care of one another. But the radical self-abandon promoted at the communes had a dark side as well; by historian Mel Piehl's rather conservative appraisal, "most . . . failed to provide even a subsistence living and exacted a hard toll on those who tried to keep them going." The farm communes simply became rural houses of hospitality: flophouses in the country.[46]

William Miller also alluded to the "discordancy and confusion that occasionally turned the ideal community into something that was ugly." More than crosses to bear, the recalcitrant individuals harbored at the farms were viewed as vehicles to salvation. Day suffered in almost ritual fashion the abuses of the likes of Mr. O'Connell, an elderly gentleman who complained to visitors that he was deprived of food and clothing, while in truth he owned "a dozen suits of underwear" and stole farm tools to finance his drinking. The farm communes, like the urban houses of hospitality, offered abundant opportunities for Catholic Workers to replicate the folly of the Cross.[47]

Personalism

The complex relationship between Maurin's reactionary social theory and his symbolic importance for the movement created an impression of confusion and inconsistency. The Communist *Daily Worker* (edited by Day's former boy-friend Mike Gold) could thus cite the contradiction in the Workers' claim that while the church was not "anti-revolutionist," it condemned class consciousness and upheld property rights. But leftists who scorned the Workers' traditionalism failed to see that ideology, in the conventional 1930s sense, played a decidedly secondary role within the movement. Inconsistency was but another sign of contradiction. In fact, the movement's guiding ideal—personalism—had less in common with the European philosophy of that name than with the pressing need to define a new American Catholic vision of selfhood.[48]

Personalism emerged from out of the chaos of European thought between the world wars. Though originally promoted by a group of non-Catholic intellectuals inspired by Nietzsche's triumphalist "defense of the human person" against both the claims of bourgeois capitalists and Marxist collectivists, Personalism was ultimately identified with the devout Catholic Emmanuel Mounier and the group which helped him launch the journal *Esprit* in 1932. Mounier, like Marc Sangnier, sought "to plant in French soil the seeds of reconciliation between the ancient opposing traditions—the France of religious faithfulness and spirituality—and the France of human emancipation." Mounier was thoroughly unimpressed by the politics of the Third Republic; he hoped instead to infuse human affairs with a "mystique" worthy of his idol, Charles Péguy, whose prose works helped Mounier fuse "Bergson, socialism, anti-theological Christianity, and hatred of the Sorbonne into the 'spiritual revolution.'"[49]

Personalism was implicit in the romantic milieu of early twentieth-century French Catholicism and its heroes: the bourgeoisie-hating "ungrateful beggar and author," Léon Bloy; the Maritains, Jacques and Raissa, who dramatically converted on the brink of carrying out a double suicide pact; Péguy; and later Gabriel Marcel. Mounier was of Grenoble's middle class; he grew to hate both his own background and the lifelessness of secularist worldviews. He dreamed of "remaking the Renaissance" by creating an exalted new "person," distinguishable from the "individual" by its inviolable link with the Absolute. Mounier revived the ancient Pauline doctrine of the Mystical Body of Christ, less as a sign of the visible church than as a potent metaphor for each person's rights to spiritual wholeness through social unity.[50]

Although Mounier's Personalism encouraged a heroic imitation of Christ over docile obeisance to religious or temporal authorities, he concurred in the judgment of the leading Catholic social thinkers of the 1930s—as well as the popes—that "the person could only fulfill himself in 'organic communities.'" He was thus susceptible to the various movements for "national spiritual revolution" then underway throughout Europe, and he was for a time greatly enamored of the Nazi left wing. As John Hellman explained, "Many *Esprit* partisans betrayed admiration for the German National Socialist's spirit of Gemeinschaft." Like Dorothy Day, Mounier despised both the bourgeoisie and the vestigial bourgeois spirit within himself. "On the altar of this sad world there is but one god, smiling and hideous," he wrote, "the Bourgeois." But unlike Day, Mounier saw little consolation in victimhood; in his hope of restoring spiritual unity to France he participated in the Vichy leadership school at Uriage. There France's elite youth had their "individualism broken so their person might develop." The "elitist, totalitarian, and gnostic" character of the training prompted a former Mounier ally to ask, "[W]hat is this operetta for the enemy?"[51]

Mounier was arrested and jailed in 1941, probably because of the influence at Vichy of his enemies from the ultrarightist Action Française. A devout Catholic and Christian above all, his career typified the fate of the 1930s "spiritual revolutionaries." As a more militant activist told him before the war, "[W]e are leaving, go and make your spiritual meditations."[52] Although Mounier turned to the Left after the war, his influence on Peter Maurin was confined to the early campaigns for organic spiritual communities. Maurin persuaded the Benedictine monks at Collegeville, Minnesota, to translate Mounier's *Personalist Manifesto*, and he wrote, in an "Easy Essay":

> The Nazis, the Fascists
> and the Bolshevists
> are Totalitarians.
> The Catholic Worker
> is communitarian.
> The principles of Communitarianism
> are expounded every month
> in the French magazine *Esprit* (the Spirit).

Like Mounier, Maurin believed that only the church had a legitimate claim to universal authority and loyalty. As Mounier's Belgian ally, the Catholic Actionist and mystic Raymond de Becker had put it, only Christianity had the right to be totalitarian. Maurin approvingly quoted from de Becker:

> "the social task of the laity
> is the sanctification
> of secular life
> or more exactly
> the creation
> of a Christian secular life."[53]

Maurin accepted the standard definition of Catholic Action during the 1930s: "the participation of the laity in the apostolate of the hierarchy." He insisted that Catholic Worker houses of hospitality only became necessary upon the failure of America's bishops to initiate their own programs. But the tone of Mounier's Personalism bore little resemblance to that of the Catholic Worker movement. A Mounier essay on war which Day reprinted in 1937 reveals just how alien his spirit was to the antitriumphalism of his American counterparts: "We want a peace that nourishes the grandeur of the soul, the virile virtues. . . . [O]ur peace is not the peace of the bourgeois. . . . Our peace is not an appeasement; it is a call to struggles more heroic, more difficult, than the call to arms. Our peace, in a word, is not a weak state."[54]

By 1941 Mounier could actually believe that his vision was about to triumph in France. Nationalism of any kind was totally rejected by the Catholic Worker movement. Maurin had fled France in large measure to avoid reconscription. While Mounier trained the future leaders of his country at Uriage, Day and Maurin presided over an obscure slum dwelling and a commune in which a lone farmer arose early each morning to ritually drive his tractor through the fields. Peter Maurin's theoretical evolution ceased after 1933. He had actually stormed out of the New York house after discovering that the first issue of the *Catholic Worker* was not devoted entirely to his writings. By 1941 he had stopped writing, though readers continued to believe he took an active part in the movement.

Maurin's decline gave witness to the true nature of Catholic Worker personalism. Day's search for suffering Christs overshadowed an interest in abstract, "Third Stream" philosophical nonsystems like Personalism. Her commitment to the concrete and personal evokes Alfred Kazin's assertion that "theology in America tends to be Protestant. The self remains the focal point of American literary thinking." Her cultivation of worldly failure resided more within the shadows of the Protestant ethic than in a viable program for a Catholic culture. An air of deconstruction and even death hung over the movement. As if on cue, Peter Maurin continued to provide the exemplum. In 1948 Day dramatically announced, "Something has happened to his mind."

> We must say it again because of its tremendous significance. It reveals more than anything else his utter selflessness, his giving of himself. He has given everything, even his mind. He has nothing left, he is in utter and absolute poverty. The one thing he really enjoyed, exulted in, was his ability to think. When he said sadly "I cannot think," it was because that had been taken from him, literally. His mind would no longer work. He sits in the porch, a huge old hulk. His shoulders were always broad and bowed. He looks gnomelike, as though he came from under the earth.[55]

In the lengthy, rhapsodic obituary Day wrote for Maurin in the *Catholic Worker* of June 1949 (which shared the front page with stories of the deaths of two other Catholic Workers, one a young man who died attempting to start a Catholic farm in Missouri), she explained that "he had stripped himself throughout his life": "He had put off the old man, to put on the new. He had done all that he could to denude himself of the world, and I mean the world in the evil sense, not in the sense that 'God looked at it and found it good.' . . . He had stripped himself, but there remained work for God to do. We are to be pruned as the vine is pruned so that it can bear fruit, and this we cannot do ourselves. God did it for him." It was not unusual for a Catholic to write, as Day did, that "we are sure he welcomed Sister Death with joy, and that underneath him he felt the Everlasting Arms," but the overall tone of the eulogy is startlingly jeremiadic. Day was proposing self-dissolution as the goal and essence of Catholicism rather than as a phase of watchful preparation for eternal life. She asked for an unprecedented acceptance of personal responsibility in the struggle to estrange Catholicism from America's spiritually barren wasteland. Victims of the long loneliness were to become as "pilgrims and strangers on earth."[56]

The Mystical Body of Christ

"The truth about Dorothy," the Catholic publisher Maisie Ward once remarked, "is that she is a great poet." On another occasion Ward was more precise. "Dorothy Day is a poet and a seeker after perfection." Day was undoubtedly much more than a dour ascetic espousing a Catholic way to suffering and self-humiliation. She remained—in the years following her conversion—a charming, charismatic woman who anticipated by several decades the style potential of second-hand clothing. She was not unaware of her charms: a former Catholic Worker insisted that she was a natural master of the Stanislavsky method of self-dramatization. Sometimes she could use it against people—when she was angry, she could disorient a disciple for days at a time with a single stare. Perhaps her behavior was shaped by the towering migraine headaches she occasionally suffered, which threatened to erupt at any time. Still, she conveyed as great a "presence" as any Catholic figure of the twentieth century and provided a celebrity ideal for immigrant Catholics wary of the evolving secular "culture of personality."

Day's celibate grandeur was an enormous source of appeal to men and women alike. A young Italian-American woman who joined the movement in the 1930s "compared her to Greta Garbo who was very popular then—Dorothy's beautiful jaw and her features and her coloring, beautiful bone structure." Unlike most of her followers, Day knew about opera, modern literature, poetry, and painting, which perhaps helps to explain part of her appeal to people who were complete strangers to the world of the ordinary American Catholic: W. H. Auden, Robert Lowell, the shipping magnate Michael Grace. Her list of friends included the names of wealthy capitalists who often rescued the movement from disaster with generous contributions.[57]

Yet her focus never shifted from the poor and powerless. As late as 1973 she continued to insist, "I first became a Catholic because I felt that the Catholic Church was the church of the poor and I still think it is the church of the poor." She also made explicit the historical relationship of immigrant Catholics to their Protestant host culture: "I think it's the church of all immigrant populations that came over or [were] brought over for prosperous Puritan, money-making, developers of this country, ravishers of it, you might say." Her search for a way to make that condition the foundation of Catholic selfhood brought her to a dramatically new appreciation of the symbol of the Mystical Body of Christ.[58]

St. Paul described the church as "the body of Christ." While his location of Jesus at the head of that body and the faithful as its members became a model for later hierarchical authority, he also alluded regularly to "this mystery, which is Christ in you." Although some of the early Fathers of the church spoke of the mystical union between Christ and the communicant, this central image lay dormant for centuries. In 1938 the Belgian Jesuit Emile Mersch admitted, in his historical study of the Mystical Body: "We had expected the doctrine to be very much in evidence, but found it for the most part only dimly visible." Mersch suggested that the doctrine was only revived in response to the challenge of Protestantism, with its emphasis on the intimate personal relationship of Christ and the individual. But the seventeenth- and eighteenth-century French theologians who popularized the idea of the church as the Mystical Body veered perilously close to the twin "poisons" of Protestantism and Jansenism, the celebrated heresy which was a kind of Catholic Calvinism without the profit ethic.[59]

By the late nineteenth century the doctrine of the Mystical Body had come to symbolize the church's aggressive solidarity against its multitude of secular

Dorothy Day and Dorothy Weston, a Catholic Worker *editor, with unidentified child, September 1934. Courtesy Marquette University Archives.*

enemies: naturalism, socialism, liberalism, and modernism, to name but a few. Before the First Vatican Council was interrupted by the Franco-Prussian War in 1870, a schema was drafted which identified the church with Christ's Mystical Body and warned there was no salvation outside of the visible church: "[M]embership in the Church is not a matter of option, . . . it is a matter of necessity. . . . For in the economy of salvation which providence has established, none can receive the communication of the Holy Spirit, and none can partake of the truth and life except in the Church and through the Church, whose Head is Christ."[60]

This triumphalist, authoritarian, and juridical view of the church predominated in the 1930s among both European and American theologians. The most influential among them, such as Fulton J. Sheen and the German, Karl Adam, carefully distinguished between the *union* of Christ and the believer within the church, and the mystical *equation* of Christ in and with men and women. The church was anxious to give the laity a greater sense of importance and belonging, but not at the expense of the very authority figures Protestantism had rejected. Mersch thus warned of the heresy of seeking personal "dissolution" into Christ.[61]

Pope Pius XI frequently referred to the Mystical Body, "this beautiful doctrine that shows us the Person of the Word made flesh in union with all His brethren," but the doctrine was not formally promulgated until 1943, when Pius XII issued the encyclical "Mystici Corporis." The pontiff carefully limited the connotations of the term "mystical," in warning against that "false mysticism" which "in its attempt to eliminate the immovable frontier that separates creatures from their Creator, falsifies the Sacred Scripture." Pius XII insisted that—although Christ had died for us all—the church remained the sole source of salvation. He also linked the doctrine of the Mystical Body with the responsibility of lay people, especially those involved in Catholic Action, to execute the mission of the hierarchy in "the building up and increase of His body."[62]

Whereas the theologians viewed the Mystical Body as a symbol of the church's resistance to paganism, Dorothy Day interpreted it as a summons to share in Christ's crucifixion, and she boldly identified the victims of suffering with Jesus Himself. The term "worker" was almost becoming synonymous with sufferer. She sought to dissolve the barriers between sufferers just as the distance between Christ and persons was dissolved in the Mystical Body. "We wish to assure our readers," she wrote in 1934, "that most of the people who are writing for, and putting out this paper, have known poverty. . . . [S]ome have slept in city lodging houses, in doorways, in public parks, have been in the wards of city hospitals; have walked the city with their feet upon the ground searching for work, or just walking because they had no shelter to go to. The *Catholic Worker* is edited and written by workers, for workers."[63]

The Mystical Body was thus a symbol not of triumphalist exclusion but of Christ's invitation to all to share in His passion. In 1934 Day provided an interpretation of the concept which set the suffering and compassionate—regardless of outward belief—against the comfortable and affluent. Radicals and Communists especially, she argued, "should realize more readily than the great masses of comfortable people, the mystery of the tremendous sacrifice of Christ, who suffered in His agony in the garden, not only His own agony, but the agony of all others, the agony of those who suffered and the sins of those who inflicted suffering and death upon them."[64]

Day's reinterpretation of the theology of the Mystical Body was far more "radical" than any one of her social convictions, especially since the doctrine functioned as a conservative organizing symbol for the "official" Catholic culture of the 1930s. As historian Philip Gleason argued: "The Church was the authoritative teacher and embodiment of salvific truth, and the growing emphasis on the theology of the Mystical Body unified the Church and the faithful as members of Christ Himself."[65] But it is not accurate to claim that Day's affinity for the doctrine demonstrates the "traditionalism" of her movement, as Mel Piehl did in asserting that she "never attempted a theological reconstruction to take account of modern circumstances, but simply drew on the existing body of Catholic social teachings and elaborated such basic Catholic doctrines as the Mystical Body of Christ."[66]

Day's vision of the ideal Catholic community differed greatly from that offered by the mostly male, mostly clerical figures who dominated Catholic journals of opinion in the 1930s and 1940s. As such scholars as William Halsey and Alden Brown have shown, the superficial vitality of Catholic thought in that era actually masked an unwillingness to embrace experience over abstract dogma—an especially glaring weakness as far as Americans were concerned. Halsey argued that Catholic intellectuals could naively embrace the genteel tradition of the nineteenth century because they were not "extremely alienated from bourgeois culture. . . . In fact, Catholic culture, as conceived by Americans, was an attempt to save middle-class culture from its own decadence." Alden Brown's thesis is more fundamental. The Catholic Action movements of the 1930s and 1940s were simultaneously fervent yet insular, he argued, because shibboleths like "'integral Catholicism' and 'Christian culture' functioned more as a substitute for, rather than a transforming influence within, American culture."[67]

The neoscholastic corporatism which dominated Catholic thought was virtually ignored by Day. In 1934 she issued a striking editorial criticizing the corporatist basis of Pius XI's celebrated encyclical, "Quadregesimo Anno." She characteristically began by noting the objections of her resident European philosopher:

> Peter's message is that "Forty Years After" does not hold up the ideal of personal responsibility voiced by the encyclical on St. Francis of Assisi. It is as though a sad and weary father said to his children who warred continually on one another: "Very well—you will not follow the ideal for the sake of Christ. I will present to you still another program of action— organization—the organization of some that others may be coerced thereby."[68]

The encyclical on St. Francis was actually a relatively insignificant commemoration of the saint who, Pius noted, was "rightly spoken of as another Jesus Christ." But even this letter concluded with the pope's triumphalist call for vocations to the Franciscan order, which he termed "this immortal band of soldiers." Day's personalism offered Catholics an unprecedented opportunity for religious *experience*, the experience of intimate union with Christ. "When we pray," she wrote, "we pray with Christ, not to Christ." But if her Catholics were to be soldiers of anything, they were to be soldiers of self-abnegation. So while she freed her followers from the sterile piety of the neo-Thomists, she could really only offer them resignation to suffering and death as the essence of experience. Her celebrated pacifism was thus explicitly linked to the imitation of Christ in his martyrdom. In May 1936 she wrote: "A pacifist must even now be prepared for the opposition of the mob who thinks violence is bravery. The pacifist in the next war must be prepared for martyrdom. We call upon youth to prepare." After a seminarian was attacked at a Young Communist League antiwar rally in 1934, she indignantly refuted arguments that Catholics avoid such confrontations. But rather than strike back, she thought that "it is a good thing to be struck sometimes. It makes it a bit easier to meditate on the Passion of Our Lord. One can feel more keenly the blows and jeers He received from the mocking soldiers."[69]

Images of dissolution, breakdown, pain, and martyrdom pervaded the Catholic Worker movement. Day's controversial status within the church itself merely provided another opportunity for mortification. Her most enthusiastic clerical supporters often adopted a similar tone in consoling her for the scorn her movement often received. The Benedictine Virgil Michel assumed she must remain outwardly unsuccessful, despite her talents. "If people slander and calumniate you," he wrote, "so did they Christ. You are indeed an eyesore and a scandal, even to Catholics." Day's social views were usually created from this perspective. Her hostility to the autonomous self was mirrored in a constant anticipation of social breakdown. Although the *Catholic Worker* had vigorously condemned the National Recovery Act (while other Catholics jubilantly claimed—and Roosevelt concurred—that it was partly inspired by "Quadregesimo Anno"), the front page headline for June 1935 exclaimed, "Capital and Marxists Applaud as Supreme Court Kills New Deal; Strikes and Violence Imminent." At the same time her exaltation of pacifist martyrdom often found her in league with such rabidly isolationist, right-wing prelates as the Archbishop of Cincinnati, James McNicholas, who issued a cry in 1938 for "a mighty league of Catholic objectors" to the impending war against fascism.[70]

The Catholic Worker movement was, of course, not the only place where men and women looked for a new sense of selfhood and belonging during the 1930s. The era witnessed the birth of a host of decentralist, communitarian, and distributist movements led by Americans disillusioned by individualism. The search extended from the quest of intellectuals for "culture and commitment" to the plaints of impoverished citizens seeking a way out of the suffering wrought by the depression. As one man wrote to Franklin Roosevelt, "I think the people need to get together, and feel as a body [sic]." In perhaps the most famous passage of literature from the period, Tom Joad provided another definition of a mystical body: "I'll be everywhere. Wherever you look. Wherever there's a fight so hungry people can eat, I'll be there . . . why, I'll be in the way guys yell when they're mad an'—I'll be in the way kids laugh when they're hungry and they know supper's ready. An' when folks eat the stuff they raise an' live in the houses they build—why, I'll be there."[71]

As the 1930s drew to a close, Dorothy Day was still searching for a vehicle to authenticate her own experience with just such powerful authority.

On Retreat

Day's continuing quest for "a hard contest, a war" with herself culminated with her discovery of "the retreat" in the late 1930s. A Lay Retreat movement had been gaining popularity in America since 1900. Retreats complemented the older, more common parish missions which, since the early nineteenth century, had provided American Catholics with their own variety of evangelical piety. Retreats were by nature more elitist than missions: "The mission was aimed at the masses, but the retreat was more limited in scope, appealing to a particular class of people who could afford to take time off from their usual occupations . . . and spend the time sealed off from the world in prayer and recollection."[72]

The *Ecclesiastical Review* for October 1930 reported that over twenty-four thousand men had attended retreats during the previous year and confidently asserted that "the Lay Retreat Movement in the Catholic Church is, therefore, fundamentally spiritual and supernatural and is intended to bring refreshment and peace to the soul that would know and love God and live bravely according to His law."[73] The retreats featured a muscularly triumphalist, Loyolan theology which offered, at most, an ambivalent critique of Catholics' material aspirations. Day attended a conventional retreat in 1933 and did not care for it. Several years later her friend Maisie Ward (heiress to a distinguished English Catholic family and partner, with her husband Frank, in the leading Catholic publishing firm of Sheed and Ward) showed her the notes from an austere, silent retreat given to workers in Canada. Day remained unmoved. It was not until she met Father Pacifique Roy, a practitioner of the Canadian retreats, that she first recognized the special brand of devotion which soon effected her "second conversion." Father Roy, like Peter Maurin, "talked as long as there was anyone to listen." He told Day and her compatriots at the Mott Street Catholic Worker House of Hospitality about "nature and the supernatural, how God became man so that man might become God, how we were under the obligation of putting off the old man and putting on Christ. . . . [W]e had to aim at perfection; we had to be guided by the folly of the Cross."[74]

The creator of the retreat, Onesimus Lacouture, a French-Canadian Jesuit, placed great emphasis on the Christian's duty to mortify the natural faculties so that God could fully inhabit one's self. His disciple, Father Roy, once visited "a poor crippled sister" who lay in a hospital bed with only a radio by her side. "Sow everything, take up your cross, do not try to escape from it," he urged her:

"Mortification, penance, that is what we need. You are being mortified; you are dying little by little, but not fast enough. Die to the things of the sense. Don't use that talcum there; you are indulging your nose. And your ears with the radio, and your taste with that pudding. And when you get rid of mortifying all your exterior senses, there are the interior senses, the memory, the understanding, and the will."[75]

The first Lacouture retreat was held at the Easton farm over the Labor Day weekend, 1940. The Jesuit had written that, if the retreat was to be successful, the master must "exact absolute silence all day. Give them no recreation at all." Father Roy, sensing that he could not do full justice to the retreat, introduced Day to John Hugo, a Pittsburgh priest with a much more scholarly understanding of mysticism and the retreat theology. Just as Peter Maurin had been the first genuine Catholic she ever knew, now the retreat masters became the first clerics to direct her conversion toward its final logic: "Eric Gill had written, 'man cannot live on the human plane, he must be either above or below it.' And Peter Maurin had been saying these things to us for years, but here were a group of priests saying them again and again, over and over, on days of recollection, on retreats."[76]

Father Hugo was in search of lay people willing to accept the perfectionist rigor of the retreats. He and Father Louis Farina had been limited to giving retreats to nuns in a Pittsburgh orphanage when suddenly, "Providence intervened in a most remarkable way." He was introduced to Day and gave a retreat for Catholic Workers in Oakmont, Pennsylvania, in August 1941. Hugo knew precisely what Day was after: "While much concerned with contemporary social and economic problems, she has gradually become convinced—would that the conviction would spread—that only totalitarian Catholics, that is, men and women who accept in full the practical implications of the Gospel, are capable of creating a genuinely Christian society or could feel at ease in such a society should it ever be established."[77]

Day took careful notes during the retreats of the early 1940s; she later began compiling them into a manuscript entitled "All Is Grace," an account of her spiritual odyssey which survives as loose fragments of prayers and reflections. "All Is Grace" provided the source material for most of her spiritual writing after 1943. The retreats, above all else, introduced Day to an interior landscape which vindicated her withdrawal from the American demand for measured productivity in the world. She was pointing toward a reversal of the process Weber saw as central to the Protestant ethic: "When asceticism was carried out of monastic cells into everyday life, and began to dominate worldly morality, it did its part in building the tremendous cosmos of the modern economic order."[78]

The Catholic Worker retreats provided spiritual analogues to the deconstructivist ethos of the houses of hospitality, which were themselves a living refutation of the buoyantly Progressive optimism of Jane Addams and the earlier generation of settlement house workers. Addams had written of Catholic immigrants, "to change suddenly from picking olives to sewer extension is certainly a bewildering experience." She proposed that they be taught "the fascinating history of industrial evolution . . . to illuminate for them the materials among which they will live." Day encouraged the destruction of those very materials.[79]

The retreats liberated Day in another sense too. Fifteen years after her Mexican pilgrimage had provided her with a peasant model of Catholicism, Day could finally admit her estrangement from the American church, which had come to resemble nothing so much as a place for bourgeois social ritual: "The average Catholic is baptized, instructed for his first holy communion, then confirmation, and then Sunday after Sunday the short masses repeat themselves, with inadequate sermons, all the announcements, appeals for money. The shepherds are not feeding their sheep."[80]

Fathers Roy and Hugo shared her bitter hostility to middle-class religiosity, to the exaltation of what the world seductively proffered. In his privately published explication of the retreat theology Hugo mockingly reprinted the menu from a reunion dinner for a group of recently ordained priests: "Manhattans, crabmeat cocktail, soup, celery, olives, roast chicken and dressing, hot rolls, rum eggnog parfait, cordial (chartreuse), coffee, brandy, cheese and crackers, cigarettes and cigars."[81] The retreats featured a consistent jeremiad against the worldly ambitions of Catholics. Day noted in "All Is Grace," "Half the children in juvenile court are Catholic. Yet population is only one-third Catholic. You will say 'Catholics are poor.' But Catholics should be helped by poverty. They should love poverty. It is a privilege. It should be easier for them because they have less of the world. But they want more world, more money, to gain recognition, power, the esteem of the world."[82]

The retreat masters drove the point home repeatedly: salvation would only come through an assent to the suffering and folly of the Cross. "Accept all suffering," Day reminded herself in "All Is Grace," "people, sickness, calumny, injury. Lives of saints filled with it. Our enemies are the galley slaves that row us into heaven. Say a rosary for them. Love your enemies. They make us into saints." The retreats enabled her to assimilate fully the venerable message of one version of Christian self-abnegation. "We should be grateful," she noted. "[W]hat are we—a bundle of original sin. Dirt."[83]

The retreats coincided with "the critical juncture in the history of the Catholic Worker movement." The 1940 gathering in particular has been described as "the high tide of the movement." This was due partly to the imminent onset of the Second World War, which saw roughly 80 percent of male Catholic Workers reject Day's absolute pacifism in favor of various forms of wartime service. Many houses of hospitality were either closed or purged from the movement. But the retreats offered far more than ritual lamentation over the movement's impending decline. Hugo and his associates fostered a radically personal spirituality unlike anything ever encountered by the American laity. Nineteenth-century mission preachers had highlighted Christ's awful sufferings and the forgiveness which flowed from His precious blood, but their teaching instilled far more fear of God than warmth and intimacy with Him. Dorothy Day was the first American Catholic who could have written: "God is a sensitive lover. . . . Think of world only in terms of Him. . . . We are in love with God. . . . In the Mystical Body, Christ changes us into Christ. The higher takes the lower. . . . I'm selfish when I pray. All I want is God. . . . I become a fool for Christ. If you are not a fool, you are not a Christian."[84]

The retreats created a Christ who needed the sufferings of others to complete His own. The faithful were now invited to become—in Day's favorite image— victims alongside of Christ, to whom, she said, "I am united as a victim every moment." Day's account of the last days of Father Roy, like her obituary of Peter Maurin, showed that a devotional style could even influence the manner of dying. Roy had been found wandering in Montreal and was subsequently placed in a mental hospital. When Day visited him he told her that the other patients were hitting him and that an attendant called him "a dirty old pig." "I sat there weeping, and then I thought and said aloud, 'Did you offer yourself as a victim? Had you offered yourself as a victim soul?' To suffer as other men suffered, the neglect, the cruelty, the loss of all goods in this world, especially those of the mind."[85]

Day was not just being poetic when she wrote of wanting to meet "the kind of people we were reading about, who really felt that God was a devouring fire, and that they were ready to cast themselves into the flames in search for him." She truly believed that life could follow the art of the retreat experience. A priest named Father Judge once begged her to write about the retreat and "what it did for us." "I kept remembering that promise, just as I remember him, and what the retreat did for him. He died of it. That is, he grew in the love of God so steadily that he got to the point that he offered his life for his people in that little parish far out in Minnesota."[86]

The retreat was so intense in its otherworldliness, in its emphasis on mortification and the cultivation of suffering, that "it has split the Catholic Workers in two." Day had insisted on attendance at the early retreats, arguing that "no excuse, such as 'we have taken a wife'—'we have bought a farm,' 'we have a new yoke of oxen' is a valid one. . . . We are only anxious that you get the full benefit of the conferences and that Brother Ass does not revel before the week is out." Many of the Workers simply could not fathom the austere theology of the retreat, while others were repulsed by the priests' continual denunciation of the world and the flesh. Stanley Vishnewski, a Lithuanian-American from Brooklyn who joined the movement in 1934 at age seventeen—and remained intensely loyal to Day until his death—bluntly voiced his objection to the retreat's life-denying message:

> It seemed to open up a lot of words in the Bible that I didn't understand but at the same time there was a sort of coldness to it, a feeling that what kind of a religion is this where God creates beautiful samples of the world, beauty, and tells you you can't have it. I was thinking, what kind of a God is this. My own opinion was that it was [a] sort of mystic retreat where the best world would be the shortest possible world where a baby would be baptized and then put to death right away, instead of living through it all.[87]

The retreatants' commitment to mortification was severely tested in 1943 when Hugo was silenced by ecclesiastical authorities and Father Lacouture was banished to the nomadic Indian territories of upstate New York. The theological issues raised by this controversy were exceptionally complex, but centered essentially around Hugo's private battle with "the entire theology faculty of the Catholic University" and their organ, the *American Ecclesiastical Review*. The circulation of Hugo's printed retreat notes prompted an attack by the theologians on his apparent total subordination of nature to grace; they railed especially against the "false mysticism" and "quietism" which his extraordinary emphasis on God's divine action encouraged. The critics foundered, revealingly, over the very paradox at the heart of Dorothy Day's personal theology:

the retreats smacked both of Jansenism (too much concern with mortification of the rotten flesh) and of Protestantism (Day's notes on the "four great truths" of the retreats were headed by "The Priesthood of the Laity"). The theologians clearly were more anxious over the question of authority than with the excessive scrupulosity fostered by the retreats. One of the ongoing, hair-splitting debates within the pages of the *Ecclesiastical Review* during the early 1940s concerned the true definition of the Mystical Body with respect to membership within the visible church. Day's conviction went far beyond the most liberal clerical stance. The retreats only confirmed her belief that the Mystical Body was not only a

reality in the moral order, but a genuine reality. Whom does Christ include? What does the Mystical Body include? Only Roman Catholics? That is heresy. Only one nationality, one color, one social status? Heresy. The Mystical Body is the union of the human race through His redemptive will, from Adam to the last man. . . . Can I have any animosity towards any Japanese, German, Italian, Negro or white? If we have prejudices we are liars in Christ. There is no nationality. The only foreigner is he who has not Jesus in him.[88]

This was precisely the sort of antinomianism over which barrels of theologians' ink had been spilled in dreaded anticipation. Hugo had to be silenced, especially after "Mystici Corporis" reaffirmed the priority of church membership to salvation. Hugo's critics could now proclaim, "[A]t this time there is no excuse whatever for teaching that a man is constituted as a Christian by the possession of the theological virtue of faith."[89]

The retreat controversy exposed the genius as well as the peculiar limitations of Catholic Worker personalism. When Hugo was silenced Day declined to speak out, explaining, "[I]t was the old controversy of nature and grace, and not being a theologian I cannot write about it." The condemnation of her mentor was actually consistent with her antitriumphalist posture. Hugo's ordeal was a reminder of "that New Testament teaching, 'unless the seed fall into the ground and die, it remains alone, but when it dies it bears much fruit.'" Hugo compared the persecution of Lacouture with Christ's own suffering. "So the enemies of Father Lacouture are triumphant," he wrote. "So, likewise, were the enemies of Him who hung upon a gibbet."[90]

Hugo had learned his retreat theology from French-Canadian priests imbued with the bitterly mystical, "gloomy Catholicism" which wedded the

Jansenism of Port Royal to the harsh struggle for Catholic survival in Canada. In Catholic Quebec, "nationality had been identified with suffering, defeat, and martyrdom since the English conquest." Hugo shared Peter Maurin's intense hostility to Anglo-American liberalism, to the point of suggesting that the English (and the now-heathen French) deserved the punishment of World War II because "they had been faithless to Christ." The ethnic Jansenism of the priests blended potently with Day's aesthetic Jansenism. As Denis de Rougemont wrote: "Jansenism is the kind of morose mortification—self-punishment, Freud calls it—most appropriate to the romantic temperament."[91]

Day's relationship with the hierarchy was quite complex. As an "unofficial" Catholic journal, her paper generally operated independently of the church's censorship apparatus, although she was summoned several times to the chancery office to be advised on controversial issues (such as Hugo's silencing). She was often quoted as saying, "If Cardinal Spellman ordered us to close down tomorrow, we would." The Worker's obscure position within the church was a persistent stumbling block to those interested in assessing the movement's relationship to American radicalism. In *The Communal Experience*, historian Lawrence Veysey cited the contradiction which seemed to place the Worker outside of his dualistic typology of communal experiments as mystical or anarchist. "Definitely anarchistic, they insisted on retaining a tenuous tie to the Catholic Church." Dwight Macdonald wryly argued that the Workers were tolerated because "there are many mansions in the Church of Rome, an ancient bureaucracy that rules with a sophisticated tolerance not yet achieved by its Communist rivals, and the Catholic Workers have been allotted if not a mansion at least a hall bedroom."[92]

Day actually paid a high price for becoming a celebrity within such an intransigent, male-dominated institution. Spellman's biographer noted that the cardinal "shrewdly realized that censuring Dorothy Day would create more problems than it would solve," and that he also once remarked: "She might be a saint." But in practice Day's tenuous status within the church required that she tell the priests what they wanted to hear. "I was taught," she told Bill Moyers in 1973, "that a woman had to write sob stuff and whenever I tried to write serious things, like the revolution in Mexico when I was living down there in 1929, and the closing of the churches and the martyrdom of Catholics and so on, these stories would be rejected and the stories that would be accepted would be the stories of the wanderings of myself and my four year old daughter."[93]

During the first year of the Catholic Worker movement, the Jesuit Wilfred Parson wrote to Day explaining his decision not to publish an article on anti-Semitism she had submitted to *America*. He offered to define her proper role within the life of the church: "If I may venture a bit of advice, as I know I may without fear of hurting you, I think that your best line, in which you are really supreme among our Catholic writers, is observation and comment on what you see and know personally. There are dozens of such things in our New York life which have a universal significance, and I do hope we will be able to get you going along that line."[94]

Unlike her editors at the socialist *Call*, Catholic intellectuals were anxious for Day to concentrate on the "light touches," but Day continued to seek Christ in the lowliest. Her instinctive appreciation for suffering often led her to interpret authoritarian dictates as occasions of grace. When the French worker priests were forbidden from participating in union activities in 1953 (thus ending the church's boldest attempt to win back the working class), Day told a magazine editor that it was all for the best:

> I would like to bring out the fact that by this act of the hierarchy they are being providentially pushed still lower in the social scale. . . . [I]f the priests cannot belong to them [the unions] they will be the ragpickers like Abbé Pierre, or dishwashers, or hospital attendants (who are recruited so often among the drunks who are brought into the hospitals). They will become the casual laborers, the migrants, the ones without respect or status, or sense of strength that union and unity gives. They will be truly the suffering.[95]

The church had nothing to fear from Day as long as she viewed authority as another sign of contradiction lighting the path to self-abnegation. It is in this context that Mary Daly's analysis of the "tomb-like" quality of the Mystical Body bears some validity. To Daly, that doctrine (along with the Bhagavad-Gita, the Talmud, Plato's *Republic*, Calvin's *Institutes*, Hobbe's *Leviathan*, and the Constitution of the United States) served the ends of "androcracy: to find a final resting place for the living dead (the unlead)." Just such a haunting echo of Huysmans at the nunnery continued to reverberate throughout the Catholic Worker movement. Day promoted self-immolation even against clerical supporters who wanted a more conventional crusader. She wrote to Catherine de Hueck:

Just had a long blast from Father Sullivan in which he bawls hell out of me and tells me that those who are holding up the procession (meaning me and Peter) ought to get off the road, that he had wanted to follow a St. Joan, but that she would not get in the saddle. . . . I do know exactly what I am doing . . . with the very poor human material God sends. Just look [at] the kind of disciples he chose for himself, and how little they understood him, how they wanted [a] temporal kingdom. . . . Why should we expect to be anything else but unprofitable servants.[96]

Like many Catholics of the 1930s, Day believed that women were designed as special instruments of God's grace. This attitude was particularly evident in the literature of the "Catholic Revival" of that era; most of it European, much of it translated and published in the United States by the publishing firm of Sheed and Ward. Male writers such as Claudel, Bloy, and Bernanos, and such women as Gertrude von le Fort and Caryll Houselander, generally "chose as instruments of redemption the young woman, a suffering and sacrificial victim." The idea of women surrendering themselves to God's will, was, as Dolores Elise Brien wrote, "enormously appealing . . . reinforcing in them what they had been told was 'natural' to them anyway, to give themselves in love and surrender." Peter Maurin liked to point out that "woman is matter, man is spirit." Dorothy Day often portrayed herself as the harried mother of a large and unruly family. Not surprisingly, she felt a mother's special duty was resignation to suffering and physical decay. "A mother's children cause her terrible suffering of mind and body," she wrote in "All Is Grace:" "One may say her husband, good though he may be to her, causes her suffering. Yet would she be without it? She looks at her body, deprived of beauty, her flesh sagging, her hair, her skin losing its color and she is delighted to be so used, by love, by life. There may be occasional regrets, but casual ones. In general she will be happy to have fulfilled the job she was put here for."[97]

In *The Long Loneliness* Day wrote that she had missed married life in the years after her conversion, that at the age of thirty-eight she still sometimes wished she "were married and living the ordinary naturally happy life and had not come under the dynamic influence of Peter Maurin." But she then realized that she was of course a mother, not only spiritually, to the Catholic Workers, but physically, to her daughter Tamar. "Being a mother is fulfillment, it is surrender to others, it is Love and therefore it is suffering." Day hinted at the difficulties of choosing a celibate vocation for one who had known sexual experience. She did, however, take a very active interest in the family life of Tamar, who married Catholic Worker David Hennessy shortly after her eighteenth birthday. Hennessy was an ardent disciple of Chesterton and Belloc and their back-to-the-land philosophy, but he and Tamar were unequipped for a life of poverty in the wilderness, especially with nine children to raise. Day conceded the family's hardship and instability but opposed most worldly strategies to lessen their burden. When her sister Della died in 1980, Day recalled that, upon witnessing the Hennessy's plight, Della exhorted her "not to urge, as a Catholic, Tamar, my daughter, to have so many children. . . . I got up firmly and walked out of the house, whereupon she ran after me weeping, saying, 'Don't leave me, don't leave me. We just won't talk about it again.'" Seriously ill, Hennessy eventually left the family, whose care was entrusted to the Catholic Workers.[98]

Day's attitude toward birth control reflected both a sensitivity to the feelings of the poor as well as an ambivalent stance toward sex and life itself. Historian Penina Migdal Glazer argued for Day's compassion: "To ask people to refrain from having children was, perhaps, to cut them off from the only genuine satisfaction available to them in a cruel world. The family was highly sanctified in the Catholic Worker's ideal society."[99] Yet the Hennessy's were not the first of many families who found that the world-denying abandon of fools for Christ could produce a traumatic, sometimes truly horrifying result. A large measure of responsibility must rest in Day herself, because her pronouncements on family life were accepted without examination of the dark ambiguities they contained. She was deeply suspicious of sexuality considered apart from eternity. The retreats stressed the seemingly advanced view that marital sex offered a "foretaste," or "sample" of union with God, but it could never be enjoyed for its own sake.

In the war of Day's imagination between the forces of darkness and light, it was "only by denying satisfaction of the flesh that we strengthen the spirit." Though this was a conventional, if (for a layperson) rigorous view, Day was possessed by an unusually powerful sense that "wisdom of flesh is death." She was so preoccupied with death that she fashioned a spirituality which raced to meet it. She was lavish with analogies between sex and the beatific vision which—unlike the passing ecstasy of sex—would become permanent at the moment of death. "I don't know which of the retreat masters," she wrote, "went so far as to compare beatific vision to the orgasm. A few decades ago such a word was never used." She feared that this bolder sexual language of mystical experience offended some clergy and religious because they "had perhaps never quite grown up." But in 1948 she confessed that, upon first reading Havelock Ellis as a young woman, "an ugly tide rose in me, a poisonous tide, a blackness of evil." She would not read the Kinsey report, but denounced it just the same as a "sample of hell" because its statistics testifying to the overwhelming reality of sexual experience in America would only encourage people to "cease to regard themselves as the least of all, the guiltiest of all, as the saints say we should."[100]

On Pilgrimage

The Catholic Worker movement truly stood as a sign of contradiction—not only to the materialism of American culture but also to the rigid conformism of the American Catholic church itself. Day and Maurin saved the faith of many disillusioned Catholics because they showed, as Catholic Worker Tom Sullivan wrote in 1949, "that Catholicism was something more than a police code and that it could and should be integrated with our everyday life." In an industrial civilization where the leading Catholic prelates had enthusiastically "put the weight of their influence behind thrift, industry, temperance, and Protestant Sabbatarianism," Day spoke passionately against the dehumanization and exploitation of workers. When the celebrated Canon Cardijn of Belgium visited the United States in 1946 to promote his strategy for "Christianizing" the factories by establishing small "cells" of Young Christian Workers, Day wrote: "We are anxious . . . to talk to him about machines that turn men into machines, about decentralization, about striking at the roots."[101]

Day's personalism was modeled after a type of reverse pilgrimage in which rugged American individualism would be deconstructed by the sufferings of Christians (in 1946 "On Pilgrimage" became the permanent title of her monthly *Catholic Worker* essay). Like the Puritans, her emphasis on personal piety made the self the focal point of all discourse, and like the Puritans' successors (and unlike the neo-Thomists) she recognized the necessity of fashioning the story of one's soul out of plain speech. In 1938 Donald Powell wrote in the *Catholic Worker* that the church would make no real progress in America until Catholics began to "write the living language, the American language, the language of the people."[102]

As though in response to Powell's exhortation, the *Catholic Worker* introduced a new contributor to its readers in the summer of 1939. Day described

Ben Joe Labray as a victim of the depression who rediscovered the Gospels while serving time in jail for supporting a strike of shipyard workers. In a passage mixing Scripture and Steinbeck, she wrote: "No more would he be alone. He could walk with a Friend. And he and all those others would be stronger because of the presence of that Friend. And whether any of the others knew it or not, He would be there, lying in the next bed in the Municipal Lodging House, walking with them on the picket line, working beside them in the factory, in the fields, along the highways."[103]

Labray's dispatches—filed from along his lonely road between 1939 and 1943—represented the first attempt to wed Catholic romanticism with a distinctly American tradition. He self-consciously retraced Peter Maurin's legendary wanderings through the heartlands, adding a native feel Maurin lacked. Ben Joe wrote of fellow apostles who were "full of zeal and spreading the word . . . on freights, in jungles, in Hoovervilles . . . so tell Peter not to worry about his troubadours of God. They are being raised up around the country."[104]

Ben Joe's narratives were an extremely popular feature of the *Catholic Worker*, attracting a broader audience than the more strictly sectarian material. Carl Sandburg was said to have "liked particularly their American folk lore quality, telling of the lives of men working in railroad gangs, in lettuce fields, and other itinerant jobs, always on the raw edge of poverty, yet with a great zest for living." But Ben Joe's urge toward self-dissolution belied his superficial vitality. His exaltation of suffering lent a discordant note to the pieces; anyone who actually underwent the experiences he described would not likely cultivate additional self-abasement. To Ben Joe, it was all part of his initiation of Christ: "Suffering is ugly, grotesque, ridiculous, unless you look at it as sharing Christ's. You see a man with a couple of shiners and his face pushed to one side and he looks pretty funny. Everybody thinks he's probably been out on a drunk, or starting a fight with a policeman. There's no noble beauty about such suffering. Yet Christ must have looked like that when the soldiers got through with Him."[105]

Ben Joe's quest for religious experience always ended with a vision of death. Although he once boldly led (in the absence of a priest) his own retreat for fellow prison inmates, he also recalled "the nuns in parochial school, telling us to practice dying every night when we went to sleep." The message of his pilgrimage was: "[W]e've got to strip off the old man, die to ourselves, and if we don't, we'll be stripped: life and suffering will do it for us." He ultimately hoped to "be dissolved and be with Christ."[106]

If Ben Joe sounded much like Dorothy Day, it was for good reason: she invented him. In 1946 Day reported that she had envisioned Ben Joe as "a present day working class saint . . . one of the lumpin' [sic] proletariat who recognized not only the misery of his state, but the sin it led to." Day used some of her own travel experiences in the stories (by the 1940s she spent as much as six months out of each year on the road, speaking to Catholic groups and offering encouragement to fledgling Catholic Worker communities). The articles had been discontinued after a Brooklyn pastor complained they disgraced his parish's patron, Benedict Joseph Labre, the ragpicker hero of Huysmans and Catholic bohemians. "I wonder," she wrote of the Brooklyn parishioners, "if they would have sat next to him, in his filth and vermin, in these days when dirt and sin are synonymous in people's minds and unless you have hot and cold running water, flush toilets, daily baths, and other plumbing appurtenances, you are either slovenly poor white trash, demented, a medievalist, a loafer with no self respect, or a machine smasher."[107]

The Ben Joe series demonstrated Day's power to create texts which determined the outlooks of her followers. After writing the initial installments, she encouraged other Catholic Workers to describe their own experiences in Ben Joe's name. They all came out sounding the same. Day had thus created both a literary genre and a model of personality which was defined by its ironic rejection of the American ethic and its central tenet: the necessity to work in a productive calling in the world. "Remember that article about Peter Maurin that came out in *Commonweal*, called 'Apostle on the Bum'?" Ben Joe wrote in 1940. "That gave me an idea when I read it. I decided I'd be an apostle on the bum, too. After all, I was on the bum, what with being unemployed, and I thought to myself—why not make a vocation of it. I like that word vocation. A calling."[108]

Day continued to seek an end to "the personality that defined—most particularly, Weber thought, the ethic of America." She clung to a vision of Catholicism which demanded not a monastic respite but a field upon which to dramatize the ongoing cruelty in the world, where fools for Christ could convert the taunts of the respectable into unmistakable signs of their election. I have focused primarily on Day's romantic spirituality in order to adjust a commonplace view that estranges her social concerns from her more intimate convictions. Very few Catholic Workers from immigrant backgrounds fully perceived—by the 1940s—the ultimate trajectory of Day's message, but they were beginning to. In 1936, for instance, the Belgian-born artist Ade Bethune drew a front page figure for the *Catholic Worker* depicting "St. Dorothy, Martyr"; her strong jaw and prominent cheekbones bore a startling resemblance to the real-life Dorothy. The saint is shown being led to her death by a grim-visaged executioner while she smiles under the glow of her halo.[109]

On one occasion during the 1930s Day took pains to assure an admirer, Catherine de Hueck, that she was really not pursuing an excessive degree of ascetic heroism. Day explained: "[T]hough I slept on the floor I haven't ever shared my bed. I know that most assuredly, so when you tell the tale that I took a syphilitic into bed with me, you make me out one of those creatures fantastical and quite lacking in common sense."[110] The stories had been spread by young Workers, awestruck by the convert leader who, far from encouraging their Americanization, anxiously vindicated their own lonely, holy pilgrimage.

The Catholic Worker ideal resonated with unique power among some of Day's highly sophisticated fellow refugees from Protestantism. She had written in 1941, "[T]he revolution is indeed upon us, and we had better prepare to go underground." By 1945 Robert Lowell, recently converted, would similarly relate his newfound faith to a desire to burrow under, dig right through the roots of his Brahmin inheritance: "His sense of Catholic mission was sustained, he said, by a vision of a postwar world dominated by the totalitarian threat: 'there will be more wars, a universal materialistic state [and] Christians will be driven underground.'"[111]

Lowell coerced his wife, Jean Stafford, into doing "Catholic work." After she described a mortifying day bundling *Catholic Workers* at Mott Street, "he immediately wanted to go down and live there." Stafford claimed that Lowell's quest for Catholic self-dissolution was so intense that he declined to have sex with her after his conversion.[112]

Caroline Gordon was likewise drawn to the self-abandonment of the Catholic Workers but, like Lowell, she had less experience with the movement itself than with its textual structure. In her novel *The Malefactors*, a poet seeking both wisdom and his estranged wife finds himself on a farm closely resembling the Worker commune at Newburgh, New York. Gordon's depiction of Peter Maurin ("Joseph Tardieu") horrified Dorothy Day, but she was merely extending Day's own text on self-humiliation as the key to salvation. Her poet does, after all, experience an epiphany on the farm, but not before a disturbing encounter with the aged Frenchman:

The old man staggered as he came up the bank, clutched at a willow bough and, regaining his balance, stood, swaying a little, staring at the man and the woman out of bloodshot blue eyes. He was barefooted and wore nothing except a pair of earth-stained trousers and a medal that hung from a chain about his neck. He seemed unaware that his trouser fly was open and his withered, sagging member protruding, but tore at the waistband of his trousers and then, as the clasp eluded him, bent forward, muttering. Vera cried out, "Oh Joseph!" in the same instant that Claiborne, seeing the bright drops spatter on the leaves, went forward, saying: "Here, old son! Can't have that. Ladies present!"[113]

Gordon's account of Maurin's final days was consistent with the antitriumphalist ethos of the Catholic Worker movement. Day invested deeply in the humble estrangement of American Catholics from the centers of cultural power. She once argued with Edna Ferber at a luncheon for American writers given by the National Conference of Christians and Jews. Ferber's critique of Catholic anti-Semitism reaffirmed Day's conviction that she belonged to a despised and separate community. "I don't wonder Catholics keep to themselves," she wrote. "No wonder they are a group within a group, almost a state within a state."[114]

Day, like Lowell and Gordon, sensed that Catholics—for all their superficial patriotism and confidence—remained uniquely beyond the pale of secular American culture. That Catholics, according to American theory, should have been the least likely group to win national acceptance was indeed true. As Sacvan Bercovitch wrote, in his study of the rhetoric of America's middle-class consensus, a place could be found within the culture for all those who demonstrated "that [they] wanted to fulfill (rather than undermine) the American dream. On that provision, Jews and *even Catholics* [my emphasis] could eventually become sons and daughters of the American Revolution." But since that consensus was born of the belief—as a nineteenth-century orator put it— that "American civilization, in its idea, is historically, the political aspect of the Reformation," the immigrant church remained a most potent sign of contradiction.[115]

Still, Dorothy Day's relationship with American Catholicism was a problematic one. In responding to Ferber's taunts, for instance, Day noted that the author sounded, in her hostility, "like those Catholics [here she crossed out a more pointed reference to 'the Brooklyn Irish'] who went around with a chip on their shoulder being 'militant Catholics.'" There was a more significant issue. Like Puritanism, the Catholic Worker movement was designed—unlike a monastic order—to be in but not of the world. But unlike the Puritans, the Workers were led by a woman convert moving in precisely the opposite direction from most of her coreligionists. They were really just discovering America; she had known it and found it wanting. Day wanted to raise up fools for Christ to expose the sin of secular materialism, but eventually each of them would have to discover that America's seductive appeal lay precisely in its power to offer a great deal more than mere materialism. Catholics would have to discover that America was a religion unto itself. The Catholics of the 1940s who tried to construct their own cities on hills would have to discover for themselves the meaning of John King's remarkable insight into America's founding spirit:

> Protestantism has given itself a structure by declaring that it has no structure at all; it has provided itself identity by saying that it has no identity at all. Protestantism, as protestation, or as a bearing witness in protest—an antinomian or "mystical" strain that may hardly be a sect at all, let alone an ism, has demanded a deconstructed universe: the burning of a text (post-structural erasures), the removal from a cabin—but only after those texts, chambers and cabins have in themselves been well constructed, built as exercises in useless mechanics.[116]

King was discussing the primacy, in American culture, of experience, of the requirement to work through and give a name to one's estrangement before any conversion can occur. The Catholic radicals and communitarians of the 1940s and 1950s—seeing self-denial as their primary responsibility—would have to struggle against an inclination to build cabins just for the sake of seeing them fall, or seeing themselves fail.

The Catholic Workers

and Catholic Culture, 1933–1949

The Catholic Worker movement was radical only so far as it was radically Catholic. In the 1930s Catholicism remained as foreign and obscure to other Americans as it had been to Dorothy Day prior to her conversion. Aside from attacks on Father Charles Coughlin, sophisticated non-Catholics rarely showed any awareness of the church in the 1930s. It was only with the emergence of the genteel nativism associated with Paul Blanshard in the late 1940s that Catholicism was recognized once again as a "problem" for American culture. Yet even more sympathetic observers than Blanshard remained befuddled. In 1946 Willard Sperry, the dean of Harvard Divinity School, remarked: "The average Protestant householder knows Catholicism only outwardly; by its substantial churches; by the crowds pouring from its doors at the end of a Mass . . . by the arrangements which must be made to allow maids to attend Mass."[1]

Not until the 1950s could many Catholic intellectuals squarely face the special yet obvious character of their church's history in America. Writing in 1956, a period when Catholicism had finally been embraced within an American culture of "consensus," the priest-sociologist John L. Thomas noted: "Of course, there are those who argue that since immigration has ceased in the 20s and the second and third generation ethnics are becoming rapidly acculturated, the problem of minorities in the Church is no longer significant. But this is to ignore the facts of history. The Catholic Church in the United States is largely an immigrant Church and it bears the stamp of its origins to this day."[2] At the same time, few now argue with the conclusion (proclaimed repeatedly in the many works of Andrew Greeley and his associates since the early 1960s) that the descendants of Catholic immigrants have, if perhaps more gradually than others, generally made their way into the American middle class. It is precisely this model for the progressive evolution of the Catholic commu- nity—from isolation to engagement, from defensiveness to a level of self- confidence sufficient to generate social criticism at once Catholic and Ameri- can—which has guided students of both the Catholic Worker movement and the broader history of the church since 1930.

This view of the Catholic Worker movement as a sign of the Church's security in America obscures Dorothy Day's original intent, which was radically separatist. Day struggled mightily against the process by which immigrants and their children pursued the elusive yet rewarding emblems of American belong- ing. The fundamental significance of her movement was disclosed within the relationship between an idea of the church which Day "finally manufactured for herself" and the actual community to which she addressed her appeal. Hers was indeed a radicalism unlike any which had come before. Although Day's unwavering commitment won the grudging respect of many former associates, they generally regarded her brand of religious radicalism as impossibly anoma- lous. As Emma Goldman wrote to Day's (not yet baptized) admirer Ammon Hennacy in 1939: "I confess that it is a new one on me, for I have never heard of Catholics being radical."[3] Catholicism thus remained beyond the ken of most Americans during this period, but the strain of maintaining that separate reality was increasing as ordinary Catholics sought better lives. The Catholic Worker movement was but one volatile fragment in the explosion of activity within the church during the 1930s. The Workers indeed must often have felt like lonely prophets of the wilderness when poised against the awesome power of the radio priest, Charles Coughlin. Alan Brinkley has vividly described one of the most familiar city scenes of the 1930s: "In urban neighborhoods throughout the East and Midwest—not only Irish communities, but German, Italian, Polish; not only Catholic areas, but Protestant and, for a time, even Jewish—many residents long remembered the familiar experience of walking down streets lined with row houses, triple deckers or apartment buildings and hearing out of every window the voice of Father Coughlin blaring from the radio."[4]

Years before he first heard of Dorothy Day, a future editor of the *Catholic Worker* witnessed just such a scene each Sunday in Taunton, Massachusetts. Kieran Dugan listened to the radio priest and was spellbound, along with his family and Irish neighbors, "by his indoctrination on Depression issues"

(Dugan also recalled that Coughlin faced stiff competition from the Boston Red Sox during the summer. Andrew Greeley similarly claims that, in his Chicago Irish home, the priest was often switched off in favor of "the much better entertainment of the then fabulous Chicago Bears").[5]

Although Coughlin was fervently admired by millions of non-Catholic victims of the depression, he was claimed most avidly by Catholics as a prophet out of their own ranks. In towns and cities like Taunton, or Boston, or Brooklyn, those Catholics who took their religion seriously were generally among Coughlin's most vocal supporters. And contrary to the conventional assertion that his Social Catholicism represented a force "on the Right" during the 1930s, while "on the Left the major voice was the Catholic Worker," Catholic culture was in truth so unified in its separate sphere that Coughlinites naturally assumed that the Worker—as Catholic—could not help but be their ally.[6]

The *Catholic Worker* was quietly supportive of the radio priest until July 1937, when it rejected his equation of neutrality toward the Spanish Civil War with sympathy for Communism. Since both the Catholic Workers and the Coughlinites claimed to be inspired primarily by recent papal teaching, there was vast room for agreement on basic issues. In September 1934 the *Catholic Worker* approvingly quoted from a speech in which Coughlin had warned the American Legion: "[I]f the Legion attempts to crush out radicals and Communists without first crushing the evils of capitalism which have given birth to those radicals, the American Legion will find itself smashed against the rock of its own shortsightedness."[7]

Peter Maurin set the tone for the Workers' attitude toward Coughlin in an "Easy Essay" of February 1936:

On my last trip west
I was asked several times
what I thought of Fr. Coughlin.

My answer was
that Fr. Coughlin
was rendering
a great service
by taking from the bankers
a prestige
that was not due to them.[8]

Despite, or more likely partly because of Dorothy Day's unwavering hostility to capitalism and the secular state, the Catholic Worker movement was enthusiastically received into the church by a broad variety of priests, religious, and lay people, all of whom saw the work as encouraging Catholic solidarity. A radio reporter–priest wrote, "I think the inception of the Catholic Worker is about the first real piece of Catholic Action we've had hereabouts," while another cleric exclaimed: "The Catholic Worker is a fine example of splendid Catholic effort—to put within the reach of the Catholic Worker the motive, the means and the method of the Catholic church, in her solution of the problems that vex us all."[9]

A garment worker testified to the importance of such an apostolate for Catholics who "are employed in industries, organized or unorganized, where the Socialist and Communist struggle for supremacy." Even the *Brooklyn Tablet*—Coughlin's staunchest ally and perhaps the most influential diocesan paper in America—noted approvingly in a front-page article that the *Catholic Worker* "particularly serves to counteract the influence of radical sheets which aim to mislead the unemployed and defraud the present workingman."[10]

Since Day had joined the church precisely because it contradicted the spirit of the secular age, she readily contributed to demonstrations of Catholic solidarity. She joined a committee which sought to erect a statue of Christ, "The Light of the World," in Washington, D.C.; as she explained, the statue would symbolize the opposition of American Catholics to the Communist philosophy "which denies Christ, makes man subject to the state rather than to Christ." She added, in the more characteristically personalist mode, that the statue would exalt "the gentle Galilean who never coerced, but persuaded by love and example."[11]

A critical division within American Catholicism did occur in the 1930s, but it was less the result of differences over social doctrine than of underlying conflicts over the nature and destiny of Catholic identity amidst a largely unsympathetic society. The issue was best defined in the conflict between Day's increasingly absolutist antitriumphalism and Coughlin's much more ambivalent if not downright confused posture. This was not initially a source of tension between the two sides. In the early months of the *Catholic Worker's* existence readers often voiced their support for the paper in stridently militant terms. "All power to the instruments of God," wrote "A Knight of Social Justice" in the spring of 1933: "The crusaders for social justice are instruments of God. Therefore, all power, moral and financial to the Catholic Worker. . . . The

Catholic Worker, when supported by loyal Christians, will crush the forces of social injustice."[12] As late as May 1935, a former chaplain of the Knights of Columbus applauded the paper's anticommunism and asked: "How many Catholics realize that they belong to a militant Church, or know the difference between modern Communism and Catholic Communism?"[13]

The tone of Coughlin's National Union for Social Justice was similarly triumphalistic during its most expansive period (1934–35). Coughlin's appeal to disgruntled non-Catholics notwithstanding, his sixteen-point program was modeled explicitly after the social encyclicals, especially the recently promulgated "Quadregesimo Anno." Pius XI had issued the call for "valiant soldiers" to fight "this good and peaceful battle of Christ" against atheism, socialism, and secular materialism. In 1934 Coughlin promised that the sixteen principles represented "the solid ground on which the majority of us will march to victory." Like Dorothy Day, like the pope, and like James Gillis, editor of the Paulist Fathers' widely read *Catholic World*, Coughlin was as hostile to capitalist individualism as he was to bolshevism. "The outworn creed of capitalism is done for," he bellowed in 1934. "The clarion call of communism has been sounded. I can support one as easily as the other. They are both rotten! But it is not necessary to suffer the slings and arrows of modern capitalism any more than it is to surrender . . . to communism."[14]

Coughlin's solution to these twin ills was contained within the exceedingly vague definition of "social justice," the term most often invoked by Catholics of all persuasions during the 1930s to suggest their ideal social order. "Social justice" blended elements of medieval corporatism with modern distributist theory; its proponents generally called for the widest possible ownership of property and the primacy of human labor (and personality) over capital and the profit urge. More incantation than ideology (it even provided the name for the Mott Street Catholic Worker cat) "social justice" was a rallying cry signifying the utopian, third-stream ethos Catholics poised against those more familiar antitheses, capitalism and socialism. Conflict arose only over the manner in which the ideal would be borne unto the world by actual Catholics. Coughlin, for his part, did not view self-inflicted poverty as an ennobling prelude to eternal life. "It is not Christianity to teach that men and women are supposed to live in poverty," he informed his radio audience. "Poverty is the breeder of holdups, brigandry, immorality, and vice." This apparent concession to materialism has misled numerous scholars into overlooking the distinction in Catholic (and Coughlin's) thought between capitalism as a system and the person's inherent right to property. Brinkley could thus argue that Coughlin "remained committed to a determinedly capitalist, middle class vision. . . . [A]s if material acquisitions were a part of Catholic religious dogma, Coughlin told his radio audience that 'the Church is anxious for the workingman and the farmer to own his own home.'"[15]

That was precisely the message of "Quadregesimo Anno." There was, however, a persistently gnawing underside to all of Coughlin's triumphalist rhetoric. He seemed haunted by a grim awareness that the road to social justice offered only pain and sorrow. "All I ask," he implored the members of his radio league in 1934, "is that those who apply for membership will be men and women of courageous heart and intrepid spirit willing and ready to suffer." Like many Catholics of the 1930s—including the Catholic Workers—Coughlin was profoundly tormented by the persecution of his coreligionists living under the anticlerical Mexican regime. He cried out: "Mexico is today pleading on her knees and asking us in the name of the Infant Jesus who we revere at this moment to have pity on her and cease associating ourselves with her crucifixion."[16]

He thus likened the Mexican's sufferings to those of Christ—whose sacrifice had been necessary for the salvation of the world—while pleading for an end to the torture. The broadcast's conclusion offered a jarringly cheerful reminder that the way of Christ "is the path which leads to progress, to prosperity, and to happy eternity."[17]

The Mexican crisis was the last time Coughlin's message paralleled that of Dorothy Day. In March 1937 the Catholic Worker echoed his equivocal lament in paying tribute to the "two, and some say three, martyrs to religious freedom killed during the last month," and in providing a similarly upbeat conclusion: "If Catholics can maintain their present level of Christian heroism, and if we support them with our prayers, Christ will surely grant them the victory."[18] This ambivalently triumphalist message would soon yield, in the pages of the Catholic Worker, to a univocal rhetoric of suffering, martyrdom, and self-abnegation, while Coughlin increasingly embodied the large contradiction he never directly confronted: if the spirit of suffering was intrinsic to Catholicism, what then was the true nature of American Catholic success?

Catholics indeed remained susceptible in the 1930s to the same ambivalence historian Jay Dolan located in the spiritual guidance they received during the late nineteenth century, a period marked by growing middle-class aspirations if not achievements. Mission preachers of that era alternately espoused the "gospel of acceptance"—the traditional consolation to immigrants whose lack of riches would be rewarded in heaven—and the "gospel of success," which promoted an ethic of the self-made Christian. The latter was employed especially for encouraging Catholic temperance. According to Dolan: "Preachers continually espoused the materialism of the United States, where the itch for profit seemed to permeate all society. They also noted that Catholics liked this aspect of American society too much for their own good. What revivalism encountered then was the dilemma of making the traditional gospel of acceptance meaningful in a society that championed the aggressive, self-made achiever."[19]

The dualistic mode of preaching resisted integration because, Dolan argued, "the revivalists did not notice the anomaly, since each ethic appeared to have its proper place." The church's financial needs surely also motivated the preachers to work a perilously self-contradictory field of discourse. The confusion and bitterness expressed by many German and, especially, Irish-Catholic Americans during the first half of the twentieth century was the legacy of this unrelieved tension. Somewhat more advanced economically than their counterparts from central and eastern Europe, and generally more conversant in the encyclical-based teaching of Coughlin and others, they suffered more of the intangible costs of Catholic identity (or were at least better equipped to voice their pain, however confusedly). A 1935 letter to the *Brooklyn Tablet* serves as a vivid illustration of the self-contradiction engendered by the clash of Catholic values with American opportunities. R. L. Magee wrote in complaint over a series of articles from the *New York World-Telegram* which had linked depression poverty with the need for improved contraceptive technology. To Magee the issue was entirely spiritual, not social. Not poverty but "too much money and prosperity lead people away from God and His teaching." As a Catholic, Magee confessed his shame in subscribing to the materialist, secularist *World-Telegram*, but he added that the paper was the only one "that gives final prices on stocks, etc., that can be had at my post office, otherwise I would not have it in my home."[20]

Out of such confusion grew the especially rabid support Coughlin enjoyed from German and Irish Catholics following the humiliating defeat of his National Union Party at the hands of the patrician Franklin Roosevelt in the 1936 presidential election. The destruction of Coughlin as a political force vindicated the fears of many Catholics who had sensed all along that they would remain victims of an irreligious American culture. Coughlin readily supplied them with the material for increasingly paranoid and violent fantasies after 1936. But who, or what, was the real object of Coughlinite fury? Jews and the international Anglophile banking establishment were the most conspicuous target of the priest's wrath. Yet as James Shenton astutely observed in 1958, Coughlin's later supporters included many Catholics also alienated from "their own church and priesthood." Coughlin had indeed been among the few priests in American history to openly condemn a member of the hierarchy. In 1934 he shouted: "For forty years William Cardinal O'Connell has been more notorious for his silence on social justice than any contributions which he may have give either in practice or in doctrine towards the decentralization of wealth or towards the elimination of those glaring injustices which permitted the plutocrats of this nation to wax fat at the expense of the poor."[21]

Coughlin was a *priest* who respected the economic aspirations of Catholics while recognizing that they could not easily be reconciled with America's acquisitive capitalism. He could not even admit that his own speculations in the silver market demonstrated sound business sense. Instead, when this seeming hypocrisy was exposed, "he resolved instead to play the role of martyr, the man whom the international bankers had decided to victimize because he was too dangerous to them." Yet Coughlin ultimately blamed religious authorities for his demise: "I didn't succeed because I could not get bishops to support me. Bishops with their sanctified collars have been my bane all through my life. I knew the futility of the whole thing. I knew that my days as a prophet had come to an end."[22] Coughlin's resentment of the antimaterialist dogma he had adhered to since his days at the Basilian seminary was persistently evident throughout his career. He once remarked that if he did not believe in the afterlife, he would have surrounded himself with "the most adroit hi-jackers . . . [and] avail[ed] myself of the laws under which to hide my own crimes. . . . [B]elieve me, I would [have] become the world's champion crook."[23]

Irish Catholics surely had grounds—however obscured by embarrassment— for resentment of the church's claims on their pocketbooks as well as their souls. As Daniel Patrick Moynihan argued in *Beyond the Melting Pot*, the Irish had indeed built an imposing American church, but not without paying a significant "price": "In secular terms, it has cost them dearly in men and money. A good part of the surplus that might have gone into family property has gone to building the church. This has almost certainly inhibited the development of the solid middle-class dynasties that produce so many of the important people in America."[24]

Coughlin brought to the surface the smoldering resentments many ordinary Catholics harbored toward prelates and others who preached resignation while enjoying the very fruits they counseled their flocks to disdain. An irate Coughlin supporter wrote to Msgr. John A. Ryan: "the likes of Cardinal O'Connell of Boston a Cardinal unfit for such high office a money mad Cardinal owns about half of Boston. Father Coughlin hurt him because he was in with the bankers." Another woman asked Ryan, after comparing Coughlin to the crucified Christ: "Judas betrayed our Lord for thirty pieces of silver. How much did you get from the moneychangers for misleading and deceiving the people?"[25]

Letters from Coughlin supporters to Dorothy Day and the *Catholic Worker* reveal the bitterness of many Catholics as well as the anguish they felt in criticizing members of the church establishment—even one so allegedly radical as Day herself—and indicate the degree to which Coughlin was idolized. A woman from Syracuse admonished Day in 1937: "You don't like Father Coughlin do you? Why didn't you answer him when he took up the subject of combatting communism and your method of doing so, you didn't, you are just an ordinary lay person . . . and as such have no right to sign yourself 'yours in Jesus Christ.'" The woman thus demonstrated the hesitation lay Catholics often felt in asserting themselves against a priest-dominated church. More importantly, she sought to diagnose the essential difference between Coughlinism and the Catholic Worker philosophy: "I might mention here that Father Coughlin is trying to change legislation, so that the working man can have an annual living wage, he is about to prevent the suffering you are trying to alleviate, then who is doing the greatest work."

She concluded by virtually pleading with Day to prove her views incorrect, if she could do so. The tone of the letter blends grudging deference with jealous resentment, as though Day, a convert, had enjoyed and continued to enjoy freedoms denied ordinary Catholics. "If you want so much to be a Catholic," she wrote, "why do you associate with such dangerous radicals as Harry Bridges . . . we, who have always been Catholics, and careful where we go, and with whom we associate."[26] A workingman from Los Angeles bore witness to Coughlin's appeal in the simplest terms: "Money is scarce as we all know. I have 7 to support on 24.00 a week. I am still hoping God will touch those rich selfish hearts, I am for Father Coughlin's Plan the Bankers exact too much interest and the companies take it out off the poor laborer."[27]

People like these were more drawn to Coughlin than to Day during the 1930s because he was willing to press for dramatic, quixotic remedies for poverty while sustaining a commitment to Catholic tradition. Dorothy Day's more complex attitude was rooted in her equation of actual poverty with the *spirit* of poverty and mystical suffering. "I condemn poverty and I advocate it. . . . [I]t is a social phenomenon and a personal matter. Poverty is an illusive thing, and a paradoxical one." Strangely, some non-Catholic intellectuals—in condemning or ridiculing Coughlin—seemed to share that vision and were thus offended by the priest's this-worldly appeal. Jonathan Mitchell wrote, in a condescending *New Republic* article on "Father Coughlin's Children": "He has told them, crudely and flatly: 'God wants you to have more money.'"[28]

If Coughlin's status as a cleric lent him sufficient authority to challenge the gospel of acceptance during the 1930s, his inability to transcend the grammar of suffering resulted in an equivocal message which mirrored the tension within Catholic culture itself. For just as Catholics sought escape from the conditions which brought them hardship, the *ritualization* of suffering became an even more pervasive feature of their world. One of the most familiar institutions of parish life in urban Catholic neighborhoods of the 1930s was the "passion play" staged by amateur theater companies. Every Wednesday and Sunday evening in Queens County, New York, for instance, Catholics flocked to the auditorium of Our Lady of Sorrows for "the Passion Play of Queens." The *Brooklyn Tablet* reported on this highly emotional spectacle in 1936: "The drama becomes awe inspiring as we behold the betrayal by Judas, the denial by Peter and the suffering and agony of Jesus. These scenes are so heart stirring that the audience is moved to tears."[29]

The grammar of suffering reflected a disposition inherent within immigrant Catholicism. But just as Dorothy Day sought to move the Catholic Worker movement closer to the sources of this impulse—in the belief that it promised authentic resistance to the middle-class ethos—other Catholic leaders, such as Coughlin, groped to discover the promised land on the far side of suffering. The ritualization of suffering offered triumph as a future possibility, because it was usually built around a tripartite scheme in which the original innocence and beauty in life was crucified, only to reemerge in glory. Fulton Sheen's statement of this theme in *The Mystical Body of Christ* is but one particularly classic illustration from among many. He wrote, of Christ: "The footprints of the Eternal Galilean were soon to fade from the sands of the seashore and the dust of Jerusalem's streets; even the beautiful body which He took from His mother would be so tortured by men as to lose all its comeliness before assuming that glorified state in which men could no longer touch it."[30]

More than a mere reassertion of faith in the Resurrection, this language evoked the ritual passage of Sheen himself, from grandson of poor Irish immigrants to doctoral work at Louvain to triumphant return as a leader of the American church. The promise of eternal glory worked as a ritual expression of more tangible, if less acceptable, dreams of worldly success.

The finest study of Catholicism in a twentieth-century immigrant community provides substantial evidence that the grammar of suffering played a central role in both easing adaptation to a new world and encompassing almost unspeakable aspirations. In *The Madonna of 115th Street*, Robert Orsi argued that the structure of the festas the Italian Harlem community raised in honor of Our Lady of Mt. Carmel recapitulated the immigrant's ordeal while holding the key to transcendence of those very sufferings. The religious life of the community centered around a repertoire of penitential rites, from the dragging of a woman down the aisle of the church (as she licked the floor with her tongue), to the carrying of a Jesus-figure around the church by young women prior to His being placed "in glory on the altar" on Easter Sunday. (The identification of women with a special vocation to suffering, discussed in Chapter 2, was a major legacy of nineteenth-century European Catholicism. It passed directly from the immigrants to the Catholic Worker movement and other romantic postimmigrant apostolates.) The festas were especially poignant celebrations for a community in continual transition. The Italians' traditional loyalties to family and God were besieged by the powerful lure of American opportunity. Much more than wealth was at stake in the immigrant's pursuit of success: "The compulsion of this materialism—although this is not precise enough a word to convey the complexity of hopes the Italians nurtured—reflected in part the immigrants' expectations that by defeating poverty they would achieve a new dignity. It was this dignity and self-respect that startled and impressed southern Italians when their paesani returned from America for a visit."[31]

The same forces that lured the Italians away from the domus could provoke rage and guilt as well. A woman of Italian Harlem remarked of married relatives who had left the old neighborhood: "If there's a God, he'll be the one to punish them. It's the air of this damn country." The festas reinforced the Italian-Americans' bonds of shared suffering while providing a means of denying their permanence through the voluntary owning of the ordeal. As Orsi explained: "The movement from suffering to sacrifice during the festa was a movement towards freedom: by embracing suffering on the day of the festa and on behalf of their families and the Madonna, the men and women of Italian Harlem were declaring their human freedom and dignity. . . . In this new world document, sacrifice means triumph—it is what is required of the immigrants if they would prevail in their struggle against adversity in their new home, a struggle which, it is emphasized, they undertook themselves."[32]

Finally, the festas reminded the Italians that the church itself stood as an irreducible sign of contradiction against which their temporal desires were judged. But this was much less apparent to recent immigrants than to the Vatican leadership and to convert intellectuals like Dorothy Day. For the adoration of the Madonna was "a distinctly and embarrassingly obvious non-American devotion," endorsed by Pope Leo XIII in the wake of his condemnation of "Americanism" (1899). The church, along with the immigrants, had suffered greatly in modern history, yet clung doggedly to its leader's dreams of a triumphant restoration. Popular devotions to the Madonna were approved by the church because they "found their meanings in the interstices between what the Church wanted for itself and for history and the degradations it had to endure." The church thus paradoxically endorsed the antitriumphalist symbols its own decline had generated in peasant cultures.[33]

Although the depression heightened Catholic insecurities, the grammar of suffering spoke to a broader condition: the gradual but persistent transformation of American Catholicism from a defensive subculture to a widely diffused body, vulnerable to the insecurities freedom and mobility produce. Rituals of suffering enabled Catholics to cling to a familiar aspect of their religious experience (outside of the liturgy itself, which was obviously the central rite) in the face of changing circumstances. Catholics of more secure footing than the immigrants of Italian Harlem were deeply receptive to a similar, if more sophisticated message. In March 1932, for instance, the Passionist Fathers' *Sign* magazine offered a response to a reader's familiar question: "What sort of trial . . . is comparable to the heroic acts of the early Christians?" An anonymous cleric wrote that while primitive Christians suffered tangible persecutions, "the trials which beset Christians nowadays are more subtle and, we might say, domestic in nature. The avoidance of birth control, and the patient bearing of the hardships which the raising and educating of children entail, with the concomitants of poverty and social ostracism, are an insistent challenge to faith in Christ. . . . The martyrs overcame once; modern Christians must overcome times without number."[34]

Most of the *Sign*'s readers had left abject poverty behind, as their generous support of the Passionists' extensive missionary enterprises demonstrated. Yet just as the missionaries cultivated daily suffering in their efforts to convert the pagans of Asia, so too were American Catholics inclined to interpret their growing mastery of a non-Catholic culture against an intimate expectation of suffering. Charles Coughlin was the great Catholic hero of the 1930s because his oratory conveyed both the grandeur of suffering and the promise of ultimate triumph. But he was so possessed by resentment and hostility that he never grew fully conscious of the source of his own power. His confusion was the perfect mirror for the experience of Catholics struggling against an anti-triumphalist tendency so much a part of their inheritance they could not part with it, though it was their worst demon. Coughlin was neither the first nor the last prominent Irish-Catholic American to unravel from lack of self-knowledge. At the same time, the ubiquity of the grammar of suffering seemed to vindicate Dorothy Day's original vision of the church. During the 1930s and 1940s she worked to make the language of sorrow the normative and unequivocal mode of Catholic expression.

Catholics and Jews

The relationship of the Catholic Worker movement to Catholic culture can be determined more fully through a final comparison with Coughlinism. The radio priest was openly, rabidly anti-Semitic after 1936; apparently he had been that way in private for years. Dorothy Day, just as surely, harbored little if any of this bitter prejudice (she nearly married a Jew, Mike Gold, during her time at the socialist *Call*). But the underlying attitude toward Jews that emanated from the Catholic Worker movement—and in particular from Peter Maurin—exhibited less concern with pluralism or tolerance than with discovering the proper role for the Jew within the new Catholicism. Maurin was profoundly influenced by the views of the French novelist Léon Bloy (1846–1917), the "ungrateful beggar." In 1942 the *Catholic Worker* published a versified compilation of Bloy's vision of Judaism that Maurin had adapted from the memoir of Raissa Maritain (the wife of Jacques and a convert from Judaism).[35]

Bloy argued that Jews had been unfairly stereotyped as greedy usurers and middlemen. The stereotype, he maintained, only contained truths so far as it applied to "the dregs of the Jewish world." As a Catholic in self-exile from Republican France, Bloy linked the Jews' travail with his own alienation from a world that no longer exalted the grandeur of suffering. Since Judaism bore "the miseries of all centuries," Jews suffered infinitely. Bloy insisted that the church had always protected the Jews from their enemies out of respect for their dogged, inscrutable, yet principled inability to accept the sacrificed Christ as their Messiah.[36]

This bizarre form of philo-Semitism formed an integral part of the rabidly antibourgeois worldview of the French-Catholic avant-garde. Peter Maurin never failed to blame not the Jews but John Calvin for the growth of usury in early modern Europe. He sought an end to Protestantism and the conversion of the Jews, quite different things. One of Maurin's disciples recalled his attitude: "I think he would have loved to have seen them become converted, because he felt that the Christ was the Messiah, and if the Jews became Catholics, they became 100% Jews." Maurin was anxious to explain to the Jews the nature of their tragic incompleteness, a condition he thought aggravated by their grow- ing tendency to behave according to stereotype:

Three thousand years ago
when a Jew
met a Jew
he asked him
"What can I do for you?"
Now, when a Jew meets a Jew,
he asks him
"What can I get out of you?"[37]

By converting, the Jews would surrender to the wisdom of the Cross and fulfill their ancestor's prophecies. Of the six Jewish-American converts who became priests, Maurin wrote:

As priests,
they announce
the good news
that the Messiah,
announced by the
Prophets,
died on Calvary.
As priests of Christ
they again offer

Christ's sacrifice
on the altars
of the Catholic Church.[38]

Maurin began an apostolate to the Jews which—like his Harlem storefront—was greeted with derision or indifference. The essence of Maurin's belief, derived from Bloy, was that Jews were not authentically Jewish until they accepted their natural vocation to suffering. This in turn would lead them directly into the arms of the church. Bloy could sound at times like the most rabid of anti-Semites: "Anyone who is not instinctively disgusted by the Synagogue is not worthy of a dog's respect." He also promoted an idea never far from the sources of Catholic antitriumphalism: the Jew's conversion would effect the world's atonement for the murder of Christ. Only then would they accept what they could not have known at the time. "It is true that these miserable children," Bloy wrote, "did not know that they thus accomplished the transfer of figures and prophecies, and that through their crime without measure they inaugurated the bloody reign of the Second Person of their God, succeeding the First which brought them out of sorrowful Egypt." Christ was thus held hostage by the Jews: "They nailed Him powerfully, so He might not come down without their consent."[39]

Maurin invoked Bloy to condemn the assaults against Jews committed in Brooklyn and other cities by members of the Coughlinite Christian Front. His objectification of Jews as authentically spiritual—if superficially materialistic—was intended to counter the Front's charge that the Jews were simply exploiters of humble Christian working men and women. Here again the conflict between Coughlin and the Catholic Worker movement was suffused in irony. The Christian Front was supposed to represent an aggressive force against the enemies of the church, but the futile hatred it generated—and the self-hatred it was fueled by—merely reinforced the Catholics' bonds of suffering. At the same time, the Catholic Worker movement, which promoted victimhood and a sophisticated version of the gospel of acceptance for both Catholics and Jews, emerged from the controversy as a voice of enlightenment.

Urban and especially Irish Catholic anti-Semitism was born of a persistent tendency to posit "an extravagant picture of Jewish success in a setting of exaggerated Christian failure."[40] Correspondents to Patrick Scanlan's *Brooklyn Tablet* (whose pages reveal an absolute obsession with Catholic-Jewish conflict in the 1930s) expressed envy and admiration of Jewish success as often as hostility; they also displayed an unfocused bitterness toward Catholic leaders and their own impotence as lay people. "We hear it said on all sides," wrote Kieran Devlin. "'The Jews get everything they want.' Yes they do because they are loyal to each other. Can Catholics say as much? . . . Hardly had Hitler begun his cruel persecution of the German Jews when American Jewry, always alert, intelligent, courageous and resourceful, staged what will certainly be an effective counterattack [sic]." Devlin repeated the familiar charge that Catholics had failed to mobilize support for their persecuted brethren in Mexico. He concluded that "Catholics could do an even better job [than Jews] if they started at it. Why don't they start. I think I know why; in fact, I'm sure I know, but I would prefer to have the *Tablet* state the reasons for our supineness when millions of our faith are robbed of the consolations of our religion."[41]

Anti-Semitism was one of the responses of Catholics to angers they dared not examine directly. When the *Catholic Worker* finally called Coughlin to account for his bigotry in a 1937 "Open Letter," his aggrieved supporters clothed their protests in the rhetoric of betrayal, confusion, anxiety, and self-hatred. The Catholic Worker movement suddenly became the focal point of grave concerns over the borders of Catholic identity. The appositely named Harry Guiltinan wrote to Day: "I know you were formerly active as an open member of the Communist Party and claim to have been 'converted' to Catholicism. . . . I know further that you are now engaged in a 'smear' campaign against the greatest living exponent of Catholic Action and social justice in this country, in an attempt to show him anti-semitic. . . . I think you are still a dirty Communist parading as a Catholic." Guiltinan demonstrated the potent mixture of rage and self-hostility so common to Coughlinites in his concluding remarks: "Scallions to you, D. Day and to all your fellow travellers—Jewish or gentile. I hope I meet you in the dark some night, when you are accompanied by some of your 'Red' butcher friends, as I have a burning desire to achieve martyrdom for the faith."[42]

The letter provided Day with an opportunity to ridicule the Coughlinites. She noted that the "Open Letter" was actually written by Bill Callahan, a Catholic since the age of five days (shortly after writing the letter, Callahan went on to edit a short-lived Catholic publication dedicated to opposing anti-Semitism). Day chose to remain above the battle, confining her remarks to a letter to the *New Republic* in which she chided Coughlin and Patrick Scanlan for their "bad manners." She reminded them of the Pope's recent assertion that

"spiritually, we are all semites." Scanlan fumed that Catholics were not supposed to contribute to such irreligious publications.[43]

Behind the anti-Semitism issue lay a struggle to define the boundaries of
Catholic identity amidst a period of great changes. Coughlin's followers were
too emotional to propagate organized Nazi-style terror; the Christian Fronters
were generally bullies who pursued into adulthood the neighborhood battles
they had fought with Jews during adolescence. Sometimes they assaulted Jews
on subways and street corners. But their most notorious achievement was
being indicted on conspiracy charges: several Fronters allegedly planned to
overthrow the United States government by blowing up Jewish-owned busi-
nesses; the ensuing chaos would usher in the final battle between Catholics and
Communists, after which the victorious Front would "set up a right-wing
dictatorship, and eliminate the Jews." One of the defendants committed suicide
during the lengthy trial; the others were acquitted or had charges dropped after
mistrials were declared on several counts.[44]

The bitterness of many Catholics in the 1930s reflected anxieties over real
threats to their social status as well as their ambivalent attitude toward economic opportunity. Stephan Thernstrom's contention that the Irish in Boston
demonstrated a higher rate of "slippage"—or downward mobility—than other
groups bolsters the argument that powerful forces within Catholicism cast a
shadow over economic aspirations. The obverse of Catholic anxieties over
middle-class standards was a species of Catholic nativism, particularly in cities
such as New York where Catholic political leaders were often toppled by
reformers after 1930. The election of the allegedly anti-Catholic Fiorello La
Guardia as mayor in 1934 "ended an era of Irish control of New York politics—
or at least this is how some of the Irish began to feel."[45] Many of the letters from
Coughlin supporters to the *Catholic Worker* during the anti-Semitism crisis
contained a nervous charge that the movement had betrayed the community
just as it was going under siege. John P. Weber wrote, in response to the "Open
Letter": "So the Catholics are woefully ignorant and incapable of thinking for
themselves! Rot! Rot! Rot!" After assailing the Communists who had recently
marched in New York, carrying an effigy of Coughlin alongside those of Hitler
and Mussolini, Weber cried: "You can perform a great mission with your
Catholic Worker but don't throw a monkey wrench into Father Coughlin! We
believe he is a prophet sent by God to lead us into the promised land. So let us
all work together against the common enemy and then our effort will be well
spent."[46]

A member of the New York City police force complained to the *Brooklyn Tablet* that Catholics received enough abuse from society at large without having to face additional criticism from within. Responding to a *Catholic Worker* story which referred to the policemen who arrested strikers outside Ohrbach's department store as "Thugs in Uniform," "A Patrolman" wrote: "If this is a Red publication, well and good, or if the article was written by a Communist, that's all right too, for this is their racket. But to find such dirty and mean attacks in a paper calling itself 'Catholic' and supposedly being for religion, is rather galling."[47] The policeman implied that the Catholic Workers misperceived the practical Christian spirit that pervaded the Irish-dominated force: "I will gamble any Catholic in my stationhouse has done more for social justice, has relieved more genuinely poor souls, has fanned hope in more down and outers hearts than the whole crowd of 'would-be champions of the poor' put together."[48]

Such complaints revealed more about their authors than about the Catholic Worker movement, since Day was not especially involved with labor issues. The Ohrbach's protest was actually led by Michael Gunn of the Catholic Labor Guild, one of several Worker offshoots which quickly grew independent of the movement. At issue was was the resentment of a number of Irish Catholics toward the seemingly disembodied, abstract Catholicism of the Catholic Worker movement and its denigration of the informal but well-developed institutions which characterized Irish-Catholic communities. An Irish ditch-digger named Tom O'Brien derided the movement's apparent condescension to genuine "workers" and raised a prevalent fear about the its affiliation: "What is the matter with those Ohrbach employees who write to your paper? [the *Tablet*] Don't they know that they are not the ones to decide as to whether their wages or hours are satisfactory? Those who are to rule on the question are those who are outside the firm—preferably red pickets, most of whom hate work like they do our flag."

In his final paragraph O'Brien displayed the attitude which had broken the hearts of countless Protestant reformers for decades. In his pledge of loyalty to the homegrown Father Coughlin over the suspect Catholic Worker movement, he evoked the resistance of the Irish to the non-Catholic outer world: "To clear all doubts I confess I am a laborer who earns by pick and shovel $1,400 a year—ten of which goes to his reverence, Father Coughlin. In digging a trench last month, we were working near a large excavation. Mike Mahoney, the boss, yelled: 'always keep your balance, my lads.' I recommend this to the champions of this and that, who rush into history and philosophy, to denounce everyone and everything with which they disagree."[49]

To such a man as O'Brien, the *Catholic Worker*'s persistent anticommunism was insufficient proof of loyalty (and was indeed overlooked by most) because the leadership did not wear the true colors of immigrant Catholicism. Coughlin was the folk-hero of that community partly because he was one of their own. That an individual so prone to irrationality and violent rages could capture the allegiance of so many indicates the level of tension within a group still torn between the demands of the gospel of acceptance and the gospel of success. Coughlin was one of those leaders who, according to Erik Erikson, "somehow know how to exploit our unconscious without understanding the magic reasons for their success."[50]

Coughlin himself became a victim of the realistic materialism he slouched toward when the great majority of Catholics helped reelect Franklin D. Roosevelt to the presidency in 1936. But the New Deal would also create sharp new tensions: on the one hand Catholics applauded the ascendance of men like James Farley to unprecedented levels of influence, while on the other they resented Roosevelt's indifference to Catholics in Mexico and the intrusion of government into their family lives.

If Coughlin encouraged economic aspirations without abandoning the familiar rhetoric of suffering, Dorothy Day—perhaps half-consciously—derided the first half of the equation while exalting the latter. Yet it is equally clear that they toiled in the same rhetorical field, though on different sides. Her favorite saint—Thérèse of Lisieux, the patroness of bourgeois manners mortified—was also the inspiration for the priest's crusade. Few Catholics during the 1930s could readily ascertain the often subtle distinctions between them. The poignant appeal of Howard Meeks of Jamaica, New York, to Day in 1939 probably rang truer to the experience of many Catholics than abstract speculations over social justice and the necessity of suffering. "Enclosed please find one (1.00) dollar," Meeks wrote, "to help your job of feeding and housing the less fortunate than myself, and all I ask in return is Our Lord will make my estranged wife speak to me which she hasn't for over five years, and still proclaims a devotion to the Little Flower of the Sacred Heart." Three years later the same Howard Meeks wrote to Day of the radio priest's tribulations: Coughlin had been silenced by his bishop and his paper suppressed. Meeks showed no awareness of the conflict between Day and the priest: "Too bad *Social Justice* was stopt here. I got mine from a 72 year old man who sold 650 here. I wonder how

Father Coughlin will make out. The nerve of Archbishop Mooney of Detroit, giving in to the antis to smear Coughlin's good work, which is plenty."[51]

The New Apostles

While Father Coughlin drew most of his support from Catholics who saw their community threatened by forces from without, many of the Catholic Worker recruits during the 1930s and 1940s were seeking a departure from those same ethnic precincts. They yearned for the richer, more universal spirituality of the European Catholic renaissance, which spread to America in 1933 with the opening of Sheed and Ward's New York office. The Sheeds specialized in translations of works of continental Catholic authors while also publishing an impressive list of original English works. Maisie Ward and Frank Sheed became close friends of Dorothy Day, and the *Catholic Worker* fervently promoted such previously obscure authors as Jacques Maritain and Georges Bernanos. The Mott Street House of Hospitality became an essential stop during the American tours of European intellectuals. Maritain likened the romantic atmosphere of the Catholic Worker movement to the exalted milieu of the Parisian Catholic avant garde in the years following his conversion: "It seemed as if I had found again in the Catholic Worker a little of the atmosphere of Péguy's office in the Rue de Sorbonne. And so much good will, such courage, such generosity."[52]

The movement's intellectual aura appealed to many bright young Catholics who were anxious to shed their immigrant inheritance yet could not imagine life apart from the church. The 1930s were marked by enormous devotion on all levels of Catholic life, from the dockworkers huddling in lines awaiting the next hourly Mass at St. Veronica's on the Lower West Side of Manhattan to the seventy thousand faithful who lined up outside the Servite Church in Chicago each Friday afternoon for the Novena to Our Sorrowful Mother. For budding intellectuals, the Catholic Worker movement provided—in Chicago and Boston as well as New York—both adventure and piety. Dorothy Day exuded a mysterious charm which attracted many who might have otherwise felt torn between the looming romance of America and the thick claims of their faith. In 1934 future Catholic Worker Jack English witnessed her visit to the Jesuits' John Carroll University in Cleveland: "The next day, down in the cafeteria . . . she was being discussed at great length. But apparently no one got the message. They were talking about how beautiful she was. She talked the entire lecture

Dorothy Day at Saint Benedict's Convent, St. Joseph, Minnesota, about 1937.
Courtesy Marquette University Archives.

with a cigarette hanging out of a corner of her mouth, with a beret on, and someone said that she looked as though she needed her neck washed."[53]

Day and the priests who supported her—including the sociologist Paul Hanly Furfey and the Benedictine liturgist, Virgil Michel—combined the tradi-traditional condemnation of secular paganism with a vision of a new beloved community. Many Catholics grown disenchanted with the compromises of their immigrant forebears looked to this supernatural absolutism as the key to an authentic life. Furfey and Michel encouraged a literal imitation of Christ, and the Benedictine created a new approach to the Mass which promised a much richer personal spirituality (and directly anticipated the reforms of the Second Vatican Council). In 1926 he wrote: "We are not aiming at a cold scholastic interest in the liturgy of the Church, but at an interest that is more thoroughly intimate, that seizes upon the entire person . . . [and] affects both the individual spiritual life of the Catholic and the corporate life of the natural, social units of the Church, so properly called the cells of the corporate organism which is the entire living Church, the Mystic body of Christ."[54]

Michel's rejection of rigid neomedievalism in favor of a community-centered spirituality inspired the founding of numerous experiments in midwestern rural living. (He taught at St. John's College in Minnesota. One of the Christian farming experiments was launched by a young St. John's graduate, Eugene J. McCarthy, and his wife Abigail.) The new personalist and communitarian Catholic ethos quickly won converts from among those who had left urban communities to attend Catholic colleges or seminaries, where the values of a business civilization were often challenged by studies in Catholic Social Doctrine. The Catholic Worker idiom gained widespread currency. A seminarian wrote to Day: "From the bourgeoise [sic] mentality, O Lord, deliver us."[55]

Catholics disenchanted with the race to success identified Day with Christ's travail just as readily as aggrieved factory workers likened Coughlin to the Christ who drove the money changers from the temple. A woman wrote to Day in 1941: "I do feel you are an honored member of Christ's disciples and that your weary feet are pressing the holy dust that His own trod." Despite the Workers' avowed intention to build a new society within the shell of the old, the movement was perceived by some as a place of refuge from an unrelentingly brutal world. The spirit of poverty and suffering was indeed seen as identical with the mission. A Catholic lawyer wrote: "I would consider it an honor to be listed as a cell of the Catholic Worker organization. . . . I feel quite at home with hoboes, whether ambassadors of God, or just plain hoboes." The farm communes in particular seemed to promise emotional shelter. "Do any of the Catholic Worker farms have a place for single people?" Day was asked in 1946. "Specifically for a young woman recovering from a breakdown, needing plain food, a chance to work some but not feeling able to take responsibility or a regular job."[56]

The downward path Day had chosen for herself and her movement symbolized the Catholic path to authenticity amidst an unreal bourgeois culture. Her "unofficial" status within the lay apostolate added to the air of danger and self-abandon which hung thickly over the movement. The nun whose contribution of a single dollar helped launch the Worker movement in 1933 later recalled: "Dorothy would say to me that the Worker was a step down the ladder from what I was doing—that being in a religious order I could not identify to the depth of what Dorothy was doing, but that was not my calling."[57] An Irish-American graduate of a fashionable Sacred Heart convent school in Connecticut applied for Worker membership on these compelling grounds: "I feel strongly the need to submerge myself in this work in order to know and feel more than the mere superficialities gleaned in the past. We live in an unreal world, who know this other life only through Orwell's 'down and out' books, etc., and brief forays teaching religion to Puerto Rican children."[58]

The Catholic Worker movement's romantic personalism distinguished it from the more organized branches of Catholic Action which proliferated throughout the 1930s and 1940s. Catholic Action was originally defined as "the participation of the laity in the work of the hierarchy," and had, as such, been encouraged by Pope Pius XI as part of his struggle against communism. Whereas in Italy the *Azione Catolica* was directly commissioned to do such work as the hierarchy deemed suitable for lay people, in America the situation was more complex. Since the end of the First World War, the National Catholic Welfare Conference (NCWC) had represented the bishops, but it was a voluntary organization without canonical jurisdiction, and "it did not and could not give to the Department of Lay Organization the 'mandate' which, according to papal doctrine, was one essential characteristic of 'Catholic Action.'" Local dioceses were free to sanction Catholic Action groups within their own jurisdictions.[59]

This prompted a battle between proponents of the Belgian JOCISTE movement—which featured an aggressive "like-to-like" method of evangelization: workers to workers, students to students, and so on—and the NCWC's more conservative approach, with its stress on study clubs to protect the faith of

Catholics. But this remained basically a conflict among clerics who shared a critical assumption: Catholic Action should be directed from the top down.

The leading proponent of the JOCISTE technique, Msgr. Reynold Hillenbrand, was a charismatic, rather authoritarian figure who hoped to unleash highly motivated lay zealots toward the ultimate "conquering of society for Christ." His Young Christian Workers and Young Christian Students sought to convince the masses that, in Pius XII's words: "They could find real consolation and peace only in the church and in Christ."[60]

In 1940 a third approach to Catholic Action—much closer in spirit to the Catholic Worker movement—appeared when Bishop Bernard Sheil of Chicago invited the Dutch "Ladies of the Grail" to establish an American outpost on farmland owned by his archdiocese. The Grail had been founded by Jacques van Ginneken, a Dutch Jesuit, and was modeled after the Jesuit-inspired, noncloistered "institute of Mary" founded by Mary Ward in the seventeenth century. Van Ginneken was sure the salvation of the world lay in the hands of Catholic women who—by embracing their natural vocation to suffering and sacrifice—would effect the re-Christianization of a hardened world. In 1932 he wrote: "And what is, after all, your task? To counterbalance in the world all masculine hardness, all the angles of masculine character, all cruelty, all the results of alcoholism and prostitution and sin and capitalism, which are ultra-masculine, and to Christianize that with a womanly charity. Well, what is that than the conversion of the world?"[61]

The Grail was brought to America by Joan Overboss and Lydwine van Kersbergen. As a "pious union" rather than a "lay institute," they required only the approval of the local bishop before establishing their farm and school, which aimed to prepare women for the lay apostolate. The women of the Grail cultivated a highly personal spirituality. Their bold claim that "together we will celebrate the Holy Mysteries" through the liturgy drew a rebuke from Chicago's Cardinal Stritch; by 1944 they had resettled to a farm near Loveland, Ohio.[62]

Van Kersbergen called Dorothy Day "the John the Baptist of the lay apostolate in the United States." Like Day, the women of the Grail believed their freedom as Catholics lay in direct proportion to a commitment to mystical victimhood. In 1943 Overboss reflected upon

> what I think might be called the woman's viewpoint in the manner of suffering, woman in a very special way being made to bear that suffering. . . . Our experience as Ladies of the Grail with the young women in

America is that once they discover the beauty of suffering, their whole lives seem to change. . . . [T]hey found they were not happy at all; whereas once they really understood how everything that happens, not only the beautiful things, but also the hard things, could be made an act of praise to God, they really found happiness and peace.[63]

The women of the Grail rejected the "specialized" Catholic Action techniques of the male-dominated church. Van Kersbergen felt that Hillenbrand lacked a "cultural dimension"; that his "rigid adherence to 'see, judge, act,' also revealed him as a 'very masculine type' . . . successful mainly with priests."[64]

But the separatist position espoused by the Grail and the Catholic Worker movements also estranged them from sources of power within the church as well as the world. A woman who became a Grail vice-president recalled that the goal of conquering the world for Christ was never more than a romantic fantasy. Ironically, many women were attracted to the movement because it evoked the romantic spirit of such popular Hollywood films as *The Song of Bernadette* (1944). The Grail's medieval exoticism was very unlike the urban Catholic world of its member's origins (Brooklyn was an especially fertile recruiting ground) and the spiritual sterility which loomed should they be fortunate enough to make it into the middle class. The Grail engendered an organic spirituality: "babushkas and molasses bread." A former Catholic Worker recalled that the liturgies there—with their homespun altar linens and coarse Communion bread—were designed to create a "foretaste" of the natural life of heaven.[65] In the end the Grail offered an undiluted vision of womanly self-surrender which could inform only one-half of the sexually integrated Catholic Worker movement, but it was closely akin to Day's guiding spirit: "Woman's 'innate tendency to inwardness and repose, her spiritual intuition, her sense for symbolism, and above all the receptivity and capacity for surrender so deeply rooted in the feminine psyche' suits her for contemplation. Her naturally 'profound realization that life is only borne out of suffering' enables her to respond intuitively to the vocation of victim."[66]

The common thread linking all of the romantic, otherworldly, and separatist Catholic discourse of the 1930s and 1940s was rootlessness. The reason is simple: the leading fools for Christ all came from someplace other than the mainstream of American Catholicism. Day was a convert, Maurin an unreconstructed French peasant; the Ladies of the Grail were Dutch. Virtually all of the era's literary inspiration was European. But since many second-generation

Catholics were beginning to view the old neighborhoods with disdain, the Catholic Worker movement was often seen as the most authentic source of genuine Catholicity in America. Dorothy Day had taken the grammar of suffering out of its spatial confinement and elevated it to a central position within the universal, Mystical Body of Christ. Her movement thus appealed to something deeper than the idle romanticism of Catholic eccentrics; it provided an emotional and spiritual shelter for people every bit as vulnerable as the Bowery destitutes they came to serve.

The evolution of this new Catholic temperament was brilliantly illuminated by two of the most important works of Catholic fiction from the era. The first was Myles Connolly's novella, *Mr. Blue*. Originally published in 1928, the work aroused little notice; in one year during the 1930s only seventy copies were sold. But after 1940 the book was reprinted almost annually until, by 1954, over one quarter of a million paperback copies were in print. *Mr. Blue* became the great classic for the first generation of native-born lay apostles. The story concerns a young man who squanders an inherited fortune on balloon factories and reckless charity. He does almost everything one can do with a great deal of money except prudently invest it. Blue is ultimately reduced to the poverty of Boston tenement life, but it is a poverty joyously embraced. Most of his friends are derelicts. A classic fool for Christ, Blue's life stands as a challenge and indictment to those who, like the narrator, enjoy money and warm, clean rooms.

Even more so than Peter Maurin, Blue's background is shrouded in mystery. "There are some people who say that no such person as Blue ever existed," Connolly wrote. "I hope after the publication of this document others will come forward, possibly even some who knew Blue in his early years, and volunteer their aid to some fitting memorial."[67] Of one thing the narrator was sure: "[I]t was Blue's philosophy which kept him from getting along in the world." Mr. Blue is an enchanting character. He dreams of starting a Catholic motion picture company to produce his visions of Christ returning to destroy the slavishly conformist world (at the end of his first imagined film, "the sun blew up like a bubble. The stars and planets vanished like sparks . . . through the vault of the sky ribbed with lightning came Christ as He had come after the Resurrection. It was the end of the world!"). Between fantasies Blue pursues "the cross God gives His friends." He is eventually run over and killed while saving the life of a Negro companion. At the hospital the narrator overhears a man saying, "[W]ell . . . what good end can such fellows come to with their gin and bad companions."[68]

Mr. Blue was written in the antitriumphalist style that was becoming de rigueur for lay apostles. Connolly supplied all the familiar symbols: "Lady Poverty," the "Providence of God," along with pervasive imagery of suffering and self-abnegation. Connolly was a witty writer, but for all his whimsical effects, *Mr. Blue* is an exceedingly grim and melancholy work. The hero pursues his self-dissolution with an awesome passion. He is sexless, rootless, and ageless. Like many of the lay apostles, Blue is happiest when pursuing mortification or suffering. Permanently cut adrift from the home of his youth, he never quite attains adulthood either. His life scarcely lends credence to his motto: "Through suffering only can one attain the greatest understanding."[69]

Harry Sylvester's *Moon Gaffney* is, on the surface, as far from the spirit of *Mr. Blue* as can be imagined. This 1947 novel presents a relentless condemnation of Irish-Catholic life in New York as Sylvester experienced it in the late 1930s and early 1940s. Moon Gaffney is a Lower East Side Ward heeler and son of a deputy fire commissioner (a powerful position in the Tammany hierarchy). The novel depicts a Catholic milieu wildly comical in its hypocrisy. The chaplain at a local woman's college intentionally gives students the wrong information about the rhythm method so that they will become pregnant. The most esteemed lay people are invariably criminals and perverts. Many of the most pious young men are secret, if repressed, homosexuals. One such individual is described as "not so much the intellectual end product of the clerical schools as their symbolic product, subject to all false restraints, to all specious and convenient misunderstandings; to all half-truths, to truth watered or etiolated; to ecclesiastical caprice and priestly confusion; mawkish, mock-serene, forever fatuous; smiling and fearful; gilded, gelded, and glad; your true spiritual androgyne, the intellectual capon."[70]

The book's raging anger made for quite a controversy in the pages of the *Commonweal* and other Catholic publications; the author, a Notre Dame alumnus from Brooklyn, was alternately praised for expressing the unutterable truth or damned for his one-sided portrait of urban Catholicism. But amidst all the furor few recognized the book's real theme: ghetto Catholicism was hopelessly corrupt, Sylvester argued, but the genuine faith was being preciously guarded in a shabby tenement on Mott Street. *Moon Gaffney* was dedicated to Dorothy Day and three other "Catholic radicals."

Gaffney's sister loves Ed Galvin, the sickly editor of the *Catholic Worker*. Moon is initially disgusted by the movement and its dedication to the "nigger saint," Blessed Martin de Porres, but over the course of the novel he undergoes a second conversion to a purified spirituality. He discovers that "Dorothy" and "Linford Thomas" (John Cort, who as founder of the Association of Catholic Trade Unionists was, according to that movement's historian, "dedicated to the point of asceticism") have attained a state of perfection. They have totally overcome the hate which burns within Moon and his Irish friends. Moon turns down Thomas's offer of a job with his reformist union, but gives it instead to "McGuffey," as part of his patronage. McGuffey's infuriated wife promptly abandons him for working with "Communists."

One day McGuffey and another of Moon's friends, Schneider, are walking home together after commiserating in a bar. On the wharf they spot two thugs beating another man they recognize as Linford Thomas, the convert ascetic. He is offering no resistance. Sylvester's description of the ensuing scene is the most powerfully cathartic statement of Catholic rage and grim hopes for redemption that exists for his generation. Schneider and McGuffey run for the hoods, with all the abandon they had shown as Notre Dame football teammates: "Schneider yelled formlessly, perhaps in warning—he could never remember later—saw the curving run begin to come back on itself, saw McGuffey's body leave the ground in what at school they had called a dive-and-roll block—saw the body, parallel to the wharf, at right angles to the men, cut knifelike across their knees, the knees break, the bodies crumple, the hands flung in gestures that could have been those of despair." While Thomas watches in horror, Schneider and McGuffey drag the men into the water and begin beating them to death. Suddenly they both hear

> the same voice. "In Christ's name, stop. You'll be murderers." And each of them, drowning with his enemy, knew it for Thomas speaking and was filled with a sorrow more terrible than anything yet felt in those moments, as though for the first time they had knowledge of the full nature of sin; and so in that water were sustained: without knowing why. Somehow, near them, too, their enemies appeared, also sustained, seen—although not Thomas, they remembered later—and again time was without dimension and they remembered, each of them, his own sorrow.[71]

This remarkable scene symbolizes the passage of American Catholics: from crude victims of their own rage to purified, authentic Christians. Catholic

Worker theology would provide the vehicle for the new dispensation. Sylvester has Schneider marvel at Linford Thomas's "constant negation of self."[72] Moon himself achieves this enlightenment by the conclusion of the novel. Yet this is a highly problematic transformation. Sylvester did not understand that the Jansenism of the Catholic Worker retreats more than rivaled that of ghetto Catholicism in its antisexual severity. There is an almost tragic irony in Sylvester's dramatic leap from the neighborhood to the Catholic Worker movement: just as Day went looking for a new home in the immigrant church, the children of that same community now came to her for a way out of their dilemma. Her unsettling strategy for being in but not of the world was the best they could find without leaving the church. The central motif of *Moon Gaffney*—the bitter hostility of the Irish poised against the Worker's eerie perfection—brilliantly delineated the struggle of Catholics with their own passions. The Catholic Worker movement offered to reroute that passion through a process of self-dissolution. By the late 1940s a number of Catholics from out of the ghetto felt sufficiently infused with that spirit to build their own movement and their own community. They would struggle with and, ultimately, inadvertently help topple the sign of contradiction.

The Limits of Personalism

Integrity and the Marycrest Community, 1946–1956

In October 1955 *Integrity* magazine published an article on "Responsibility in Christian Marriage," in which the anonymous authors, "Mr. and Mrs. X," wrote: "We have come to wonder if perhaps one might well gain heaven by not having more children than is prudent, given the setting and circumstances of particular marriages."[1]

The article signaled a major shift in *Integrity*'s posture toward family planning—from bitter condemnation of America's pagan, antinatal culture to a frank recognition of "the problem of marital chastity." This dramatically changed attitude toward sex and sanctity could be viewed as symptomatic of a drive for lay autonomy and personal freedom within the church, anticipating the spirit of the Second Vatican Council by nearly a decade. As a Redemptorist priest wrote in the following issue, the magazine's evolution was akin to "the growth of a person through childhood to adolescence to adulthood."[2]

Yet the signs of liberation which emerged across the Catholic landscape during the 1950s exposed the paradox at the heart of radically Catholic efforts to resolve the dilemma of selfhood. *Integrity*'s founders pursued self-dissolution with a passion that even Dorothy Day occasionally found disconcerting. Their identity as fools for Christ depended upon the scorn of materialistic non-Catholics and an embarrassed rejection by their increasingly bourgeois coreligionists. Under new leadership by the early 1950s, *Integrity* outgrew its debilitating hatred of secular culture, but it failed to generate an equally compelling vision of Catholic selfhood. Somehow autonomy and personal choice were not sufficient bases to sustain a journal devoted to "the integration of religion and life for our times." *Integrity* ceased publication less than a year after the contro-versial "Marriage and Virginity" issue.

Integrity was born in 1946, shortly after Dominican Father Francis Wendell introduced Carol Jackson to Ed Willock. Wendell was a leader of the lay apostolate in New York and the author of an inspirational manual for such zealous groups as the Young Christian Workers, who sought, under the direc-tion of the hierarchy, to "restore all things in Christ." Carol Jackson, a Wellesley graduate, had converted in 1941 after hearing a lecture on Catholic Action in New York. Ed Willock was an alumnus of the Worcester, Massachusetts, Catho-lic Worker House of Hospitality, where he had met Dorothy Day and Peter Maurin as well as his future wife Dorothy. By 1946 Willock was back in Boston, trying to support a growing family by unloading trucks of Planter's Peanuts and publishing articles and cartoons in the *Torch*, a Dominican magazine edited by Wendell, for which Jackson also wrote.[3]

Integrity reflected the painful contradiction at the heart of Catholic culture during the 1930s and 1940s. Jackson and Willock combined a blisteringly triumphalist enthusiasm for "integral" Catholicism with a raging pursuit of self-abnegation. The latter force was a direct result of Willock's career in the Catholic Worker movement, but his evaluations of the movement's impact on his thinking always stressed the constructive aspects. In a 1953 *Commonweal* article on "Catholic Radicalism" he wrote: "We established a policy which made us dependent for our very survival upon the efficacy of Catholic Worker indoctrination. We counted heavily upon the fact that the movement's ideas had caught on. We appealed to a Catholic audience on a national scale, and the generous response was a surprise even to us. Had not the ground been pre-pared for us, the plea of *Integrity* for self-criticism by American Catholics would have been laughed out of existence."[4]

Willock once told Dorothy Day: "I count myself as a . . . spiritual god-child of you and Peter." Like Day, Willock viewed Catholic radicalism as proceeding directly from the experience of suffering; from "a renewal of Christian sympa-thy for the massed victims of industrial society." Life among the poor and outcast enabled Catholics to "be themselves the victims." Willock, a third-generation, working-class Boston Irishman, was the first Catholic from an immigrant ghetto to launch his own lay apostolate. The significance of this was not lost on Dorothy Day, who derided, in the third issue of *Integrity*, "the blind and idiotic attitude to our brothers who have come from countries far away and who have brought with them, and lost, a culture far superior to the brash, materialistic pagan culture of the kingdom of this world." Day was often explicitly referred to in maternal terms by members of the *Integrity* group. Elizabeth Sheehan, an Irish American, promised, in her review of Day's *On Pilgrimage*, that the book would "be welcomed by Dorothy Day's spiritual children to whom she has preached better than any other in contemporary America the doctrine of the Mystical Body of Christ, not only in her many wonderful writings but by sharing intimately and lovingly the life and hardships of the very poor."[5]

Willock was clearly transformed by Catholic Worker spirituality in the late 1930s. Although his own father lost his job during the depression, he was even more concerned with helping truly destitute victims. Other members of the Worcester House of Hospitality marveled at his apostolicity, his willingness to treat others as Christ. He also adopted the rhetorical style favored by Day and others who paid the price of social ostracism in order to wildly cultivate God's providence. After Willock decided to move his family to New York in 1946, he placed an ad in a Catholic newspaper which read: "Undesirable tenant wishes to rent apartment. Have four children and will probably have more." Behind the wit lay an intense if not always focused determination to, as Day put it, "spend" himself for the church.[6]

Carol Jackson later wrote that Willock's sense of humor tempered "my own nakedly apocalyptic view of the situation." Jackson was the product of a "mixed" marriage; though she was baptized, she received no religious training as a child. Her father was a corporate lawyer and she was raised in such affluent suburbs as Pelham Manor, New York. Like Dorothy Day, Jackson joined a Protestant (Presbyterian) church at the age of fifteen, becoming "fervently religious for a year or more among nice people who were innocent of any doctrinal knowledge."[7] Again like Day, she soon grew attracted to an agnostic brand of socialism.

Jackson was always less instinctively detached than Dorothy Day, so that when she began to pursue self-abnegation as a Christian goal her writing crackled with a brittle, nervous tone. After a very unhappy career at Wellesley (where she composed a sample magazine called "The Atheist"), she traveled around the world only to return to "more unhappy, frustrating years in the business world." She recalled her alienation with painful acuity: "During those years I lived in Greenwich Village (New York) with a lot of other college graduates seeking refuge from the bourgeois world. We were idealists going sour, and sickening even of ourselves."[8]

Jackson's conversion was more dramatic and immediately transformative than Dorothy Day's. After hearing a lecture by Paul McGuire, an Australian propagandist for Catholic Action, she began taking religious instructions from Father Wendell. In 1941, at the age of thirty (the same age as Day, the same age at which Erikson's "great men" [sic] most often underwent conversion experiences), Jackson was baptized. She now saw the church as "the first positive thing in my life. I saw it as the answer to everything." Unlike Dorothy Day, Jackson was interested to the point of obsession in the relationship between religion and mental health. She insisted that compared to the ordinary candidate for conversion, "I started considerably below scratch, misshapen and neurotic." Conversion seemed to effect a cure. "Gradually," she wrote, "my neurosis unwound itself (courtesy of grace, and without benefit of psychoanalysis), and my ideas straightened out and I started writing."[9]

Her articles for Wendell's *Torch* were published by Sheed and Ward under the name Peter Michaels with the titles *Designs for Christian Living* (1947) and *This Perverse Generation* (1949). (Jackson had used this male pseudonym for the first several years of *Integrity*'s existence, primarily in order, she explained in 1952, "to prevent people from confusing my good ideas with my [then] belligerent personality.") With often violent rhetoric, Jackson pitted the culture of despair she had recently escaped against an imagined Christian culture of infinite purity. In *Designs for Christian Living* she even proposed a Catholic restaurant apostolate, in hopes that establishments with names like "The Refectory" might provide wholesome alternatives to the defiled fare offered at secular eateries. Food themes would continually appear in Jackson's work; she railed endlessly against the denatured white bread ethos of supermarket America. Her obsession with pure nutrition was more rooted in a radical separatism than in traditional Catholic morality. As historian Lawrence Veysey argued of a pervasive theme in American radicalism: "In an important sense, ideas are imbibed (or vehemently rejected) like foods; in each of these forms of nourishment, 'impurity' is a constantly feared enemy."[10] Jackson, like Willock, discovered her vocation at a time when Catholic Action had reached its peak in galvanizing the resistance of lay zealots against secular culture (one indication of the Dominicans' far-flung activity is found in the subtitle of the *Torch*: "the official publication of the Third Order of St. Dominic, the Angelic Warfare, the Rosary Mission Society, the Blessed Martin Guild, and the Blessed Imelda Confraternity").

Jackson's conversion transformed her dramatically. As a visitor to *Integrity*'s

New York office during the magazine's early days remembered: "There was Carol Jackson: slim, young, immaculately groomed and, well, 'spiritual looking.'" In the summer of 1946 Jackson engaged a group of female Catholic college students to meet in her $18.50-a-month New York tenement (virtually unadorned but for a crucifix) "to discuss one of the Catholic Masterpiece Series then being published by Sheed and Ward and sold at a dollar a copy." The group studied the Desert Fathers, Newman, Belloc, and the *Confessions* of St. Augustine. At least one of the women moved on to a full-time career in the lay apostolate. But Jackson wanted more than simply to be a mystical inspiration. Unlike Dorothy Day, she was greatly impressed with the highly ordered system of St. Thomas Aquinas, especially as interpreted by her Dominican mentor. She now proposed to unleash the Thomistic synthesis on a social order reeling from the sudden return to peacetime.[11]

Thomism posited a hierarchical universe founded on timeless, natural distinctions, one of which was the ineluctable difference between men and women. Jackson, a single woman, believed that manhood had been progressively degraded, first by the Reformation, then by "the ignobility of an industrial-commercial civilization." Along with virtually every other Catholic intellectual of the twentieth century, she found the modern world wanting in comparison with medieval Christendom. Nowhere was this more true than with respect to manhood: "An interesting subject for meditation would be the coming into manhood of the medieval and the modern youth: the appalling contrast between the armored knight, pledged to Our Lady, who kept an all-night vigil before the Blessed Sacrament, and the huckster, who spends his last thirty dollars on the hand-painted necktie which will give him entry into his first million."[12]

Jackson perceived in Willock a kindred spirit and concluded he was destined to become the American Chesterton. Against the blandly optimistic "armchair" Thomism of most clerical philosophers, the pair openly talked of tearing down the existing social order and replacing it with a Christian one. In the beginning they relied upon a feisty Thomism to a comical degree. Jackson's lengthy essay on "A Christian Abnormal Psychology" (published in the January 1947 *Integrity*) was so literally freighted with the categories of medieval psychology that one subscriber responded: "The informed reader feels disposed to advise the author to resort to bleeding in the hopes her mind will clear" (he knew something other readers did not, that "Peter Michaels" was really Carol Jackson). Willock's accompanying drawings contrasted "The Hierarchical

Man"—depicted in a pyramid-shaped house, kneeling in prayer at the top, studying and lifting weights on the next level down, sleeping peacefully, working at a tool bench and eating on the lower levels—with "The Disordered Man," whose prie-dieu gathers dust in the attic while his passions rage out of control in the basement.[13]

Yet while *Integrity* featured aggressive polemics—"Nothing short of total revolution can restore our world to Christ," Willock wrote in the first issue—the magazine's founders privately pursued lives of humble poverty. A writer recalling "the *Integrity* era" evoked the journal's spirit by symbols unconsciously listed in ascending order of passive simplicity: "Pio Decimo, Encyclicals, Liturgy, laity, poverty, Mariology, Advent wreaths, whole wheat bread, the Grail." At *Integrity's* communal lunches (in an office which had served as the front half of a coal cellar) "the lights were put out and a candle was lighted in front of a statue of the Blessed Virgin, and a long and elaborate grace followed, as at the Catholic Worker."[14]

The editors embraced voluntary poverty, not that any of them could have grown wealthy from the proceeds of a monthly which sold for a quarter and whose circulation never exceeded fourteen thousand influential and zealous readers. During *Integrity's* early years, its authors did not emphasize private self-abnegation as strongly as did Dorothy Day, who was increasingly under the influence of Catholic Worker retreat theology. But their shared hostility, as radical Catholics, to a culture which promoted godless self-expression prompted an intense desire for social deconstruction, in preparation for the reemergence of primitive Christianity. In October 1946, Jackson wrote, in deadly earnest:

> It might conceivably happen that presently, under the terror of atomic bombing, and urged by holy and fiery preachers, possibly over the radio, several million Americans would take to the traditional sackcloth and ashes. It would be an edifying sight. Imagine an army of Franciscan-like penitents filling the highways from coast to coast and refusing to eat anything more tasty than the scraps of old hot dogs left by the Sunday picnickers. Converted psychiatrists might form a special elite of flagellants, scourging themselves constantly for their sins, the while repenting their foolish talk about masochism.[15]

Ed Willock was somewhat less lyrical but more direct in prophesying the end time for Western capitalism: "A careful look at the foundations of our society (which are the family and the consciences of men) indicates that total collapse is not far away." In his "Hints for Converting America," Willock outlined the only truly Christian program for the new world:

> If the apostolate is not a penitential movement, then it is not an apostolate. . . . The spirit of poverty should be so strong in the hearts of those who seek for Christ's kingdom on earth, that it would necessarily be reflected in the appurtenances of their surroundings. A pagan world dedicated to the accumulation of shiny new gadgets would be halted in its tracks by a dignified but obvious return to frugal living by Catholics. Every unnecessary possession is an obstacle on the road to Calvary. Both our hands should be so busy with the Cross not to allow for any other impedimenta.[16]

Integrity thus encompassed the two poles of Catholic expression in the 1930s and 1940s: an aggressive neo-Thomism which slashed through unpleasant realities, and a subterranean, unacknowledged antitriumphalism. Jackson and Willock were sure they were charting a wholly constructive course. When a seminarian criticized their "negative" approach, Jackson replied: "We don't think we are using it but only doing the necessary diagnostic work." This issue was of crucial significance. Jackson and Willock began as Thomists and ended as personalists because they learned through painful experience that America was not about to return to "the merry middle ages." Jackson, in particular, experienced wild swings of mood and tone between 1946 and 1951. In 1949 she brashly predicted that the world would be re-Christianized and that "the Mystical Body will be coterminous with the human race." She blithely minimized the difficulty of such a task: "Just how civil and temporal affairs will be synchronized with the ecclesiastical Church structure remains to be worked out, but, from what is going on now in the Church and from what the Popes have said, it looks as though this harmony will be attained through the maturation of the laity in the Mystical Body."[17] But in bleaker moments Jackson hinted at the futility of serious hopes for social reconstruction. Amidst the most seductively post-Christian culture in Western history, the temptation to don the sackcloth was always great. "What matters it now if the system is finished," she had written in 1947. "So are we. We are all ordered to Mammon too."[18]

Still, they refused to give up without a fight. Between 1946 and 1951 *Integrity* published some of the most caustic critiques of American culture ever to issue from a Catholic journal. The magazine's most persistent argument was that bourgeois capitalism had produced a sensate culture which perverted the "natural" faculties of humankind beyond recognition. For radical Catholics the most obvious sign of decadence was the promotion of sexuality apart from procreation. *Integrity* was positively obsessed with the sin of birth control, so much so that Jackson once admitted with amazement that "people who regularly subscribe to *Life* and the national women's magazines say that *Integrity* is the sexiest magazine they have ever seen." To her that only proved that "Catholics are involved in every step of this Christ-less civilization," where sexuality had become so degraded that "many people cannot see a tall building or vegetable stand without sex associations."[19]

Jackson and Willock felt isolated both from conservative Catholics whose "Jansenist" upbringings made even the mention of sex a scandal, and post-Freudian secularists who saw sex as the wellspring of all human consciousness. Jackson struggled to make the point that birth control was bad not because the pope forbade it but because it violated immutable natural law. She forgave non-Catholic contraceptors who sinned from ignorance, but ominously warned: "They can, however, be guiltless in the sight of God without the slightest sympathy from nature, which always takes its toll. So if their practices are against nature, unnatural, they can expect to suffer natural consequences, the grief or the loneliness of the nervous disorders which they bring upon themselves. Birth control, for instance, is a much greater threat to mental health than a nursery full of children is to physical health."[20] She and Willock believed that God had divinized sex by making it subservient to the rational will and the intellect. So did most intellectual clerics. But Willock could scarcely separate this conviction from an unbridled scorn for a class of non-Catholic "experts" who knew what the (still) largely Catholic working class really needed. He summarized his complaint in a memorable jingle:

The working man of all his troubles
the social worker rids.
Freud relieves him of his soul.
And Sanger takes his kids.[21]

Both Jackson and Willock were faced with the virtually unprecedented task of publicly defining a Catholic vision of sexuality which applied to themselves rather than simply to their flock, as had been the case for the generations of male clerics assigned the task. Although they occasionally deferred to priests, as in the case of a 1948 article which unequivocally condemned even the rhythm method of contraception, their own identities remained at stake. Once again they felt themselves caught between a largely unsympathetic Catholic laity and a secular culture which sneered at such traditional ideals as consecrated virginity. Jackson argued that pre-Reformation Christianity had sanctified single women by allowing them to become "brides of Christ, women who were impatient of reaching their final goal of divine love through the intermediate channel of human love and so chose a direct route of total and immediate self-giving to God." Modern Catholic women who chose to remain single but in the world seemed particularly vulnerable to the depredations of a manipulative consumer culture in which, as one *Integrity* writer put it: "[A]dvertising is one long aphrodisiac designed to end in an orgasm of buying. Not conception, but consumption, is the fruit of our caresses." According to Jackson, the lay apostolate was the place for women to "bring Christ, purity and happiness to a dispossessed younger generation."[22] But like Mr. Blue, they would still carry the cross of social, even parental ostracism.

Ed Willock's situation was more complicated. He needed to support a wife and family which ultimately included twelve children. During the depression he had spent a great deal of time in his parish library studying Catholic social thought. He grew particularly enamored of the English Distributists, especially Chesterton, whose fondness for paradox provided Willock with a useful tool for analyzing the role of radical Catholicism within a culture obsessed with productivity and tangible results. By the time Willock helped launch *Integrity*, he was convinced that the re-Christianization of America could not begin until apostolic families gathered together in rural communities. He viewed the postwar housing crisis not as a temporary problem but as the result of generations of selfishness on the part of banks and insurance companies: "[I]nevitably the financial interests of these parasitic bodies ran counter to the needs of the families who used the property. The cause of the family went undefended." Since Americans had forgotten that "the family is a garden of souls," and an integral part of the "unity of the Incarnation," families were now shamelessly crowded together; the "sin of birth control" was consequently encouraged.[23]

To Willock, as to Jackson, the problem with modernity lay in its perversion of the natural: "Christ came to restore order to the universe." The Christian in a pagan state was now faced with an awesome responsibility, because "as Christ becomes one of us, we are given the awful privilege of becoming one with Him." Willock's enormous desire to rebuild the ideal social order resulted in a burst of creative ideas between 1946 and 1949. He constantly sought ways to bridge the void between faith and life. Catholics living in integral communities, he argued, would come to realize not only that birth control was evil; they would discover "what a beautiful thing sex is," seen in the light of the Incarnational order. But first the proper roles of men and women had to be redefined. In "The Family Has Lost Its Head," Willock rejected both the companionate and romantic marriage models in favor of "a concept of life that finds order and beauty in diversity." This diversity was again founded upon a presumably eternal order in which "the man is head of the family." "The restoration of all things in Christ must include," he wrote, "the restoring of the man to his proper position within the family economy."[24]

Willock's polemic against the "feminization" of American culture was not in itself unique or original, especially in a period in which the alleged growth of "momism" was regarded with dread and concern. But his search for the feminine ideal went well beyond traditional Catholic notions of the chaste woman. His exaltation of Mary was familiar enough: "She is a virgin, and yet a mother. She is an active housewife and yet a contemplative, a mystic. She walks upon the stars, and yet it is her delight to be with the children of men." But he then went on to link Mary with sexuality in a wholly new way: "Manliness in husbands can never be measured apart from their conduct as lovers, and a failure to see the relevance of Mary to this act lies at the root of current marital unhappiness." In an effort to distinguish between "prudence and prudery," Willock struggled toward a theory of sexuality which encouraged Catholic men to transcend the dichotomy which estranged Mary as the unattainable model of purity from real women. Willock never resolved the central contradiction: Mary was, after all, a virgin and a mother, a role not many women could realistically aspire to. But his inconsistency was less significant, and ultimately less debilitating, than his inability to recognize the naked power of the complex forces—long submerged in Catholic culture—he was helping to uncover.[25]

Integral Catholicism

Carol Jackson hoped that Willock would become the American Chesterton. But he had almost nothing in common with G. K. or the other partner in the vaunted "Chesterbelloc," Hilaire Belloc. Chesterton was a foppish and in many respects ineffectual and even slightly ridiculous character, a well-bred convert who poised his considerable bulk against the daily outrages of modern European life. Willock was a high-school graduate from South Boston whose family, as Jackson cryptically put it in 1962, "had vicissitudes of its own in addition to the great depression through which it suffered in his youth." Having assumed the responsibility for being the chief male theorist for a controversial religious periodical, Willock sometimes assumed the role of militant, authoritarian defender of the one true church, as when he wrote: "There is only one opinion worthy of respect, and that is the *right* one. It is to the end of spreading the truth that Christ our Lord founded the Church." But beneath Willock's aggressive pose lay a profound desire to break loose from his inherited shackles, to wildly court the disfavor of respectable society, even the church, in return for the warmth of intimacy with the victim Christ.[26]

Even within the "official" church-controlled lay apostolate of the immediate postwar years, signs of similar tensions were beginning to emerge. In Wilmington, Delaware, the Young Christian Workers (YCW) met weekly to pray and discuss ways to restore a pagan culture to Christ. They were but one of numerous local groups inspired by the Belgian Canon Cardijn, Msgr. Reynold Hillenbrand, and Father Francis Wendell to combat the enemies of the church by proselytizing to their peers in the workplace. The records of the Wilmington group reveal a profound anxiety over the fate of Catholic identity in America, an anxiety fueled by clerical charges that the group lacked the genuinely selfless spirit of the true apostles. The members of the group hounded their less zealous peers with a prissy, overscrupulous fervor: "When Phyllis mentioned to a girl in her office that the next day was a holy day of obligation, the girl said she was sorry Phyllis had reminded her. Phyllis will keep an eye on this girl." *Integrity* was a major source of inspiration for the YCW. Carol Jackson felt a special affinity for these young, mostly female, mostly Irish, Catholics. As one of them recalled: "My own first meeting with Carol certainly shook me up. I was a recent graduate of a Catholic college and worked as a secretary for a prestigious advertising agency. A friend had brought me to a meeting of the Young Christian Workers. Carol was there and when she learned where I was working she said I was 'prostituting my talents' by working at an advertising agency. I had never heard of the lay apostolate—but she changed my life."[27]

Members of the Wilmington group viewed with suspicion married Catholic women who failed to become pregnant shortly after marriage. The threat of a lost Catholic identity was prevalent. A bowling team was chided because "you could not tell they were Catholics from their clothes." Yet this pettiness was in contrast to the genuinely personalist spirituality promoted within the group.

One night a member made a presentation on the Mystical Body of Christ and concluded: "Our religion is more than a set of truths; we must live as Christians and become other Christs!" Reflecting on the apparent failure of the group to achieve its temporal goals, the group resolved: "Perhaps we are too much of the world and should make retreats so that we can hear Our Lord speaking to us." Like all Catholic romantics, they rejected the "smugness" of many Catholics out of a conviction that "the sign of Christ at the end of the world is the sign of the Cross. Only those who have taken up the Cross during their lives will recognize it at that time."[28] They thus declared themselves captives of the sign of contradiction.

One of the major problems of the Wilmington group was endemic to the lay apostolate: there were not enough male zealots. Partly in response to that situation, an Ohioan named Carl Bauer began, in 1947, a male counterpart to the Grail movement. His Center for Men of Christ the King, located in Herman, Pennsylvania, was designed to prepare apostles "for their new role of action and conquest." Bauer was a mysterious figure, a kind of romantic technocrat who spoke in the modern idiom of "leadership techniques" (and went on to become an ardent supporter of Adlai Stevenson in 1952). But his center had less impact on the real world than even the Grail. In a remarkable fragment of American Catholic autobiography, the poet Ned O'Gorman recalled his brief stint at the Center:

> In 1950, in an apostolic fervor that ravaged all my friends, I left college and joined—for I saw it as a kind of religious calling—"The Center for Men of Christ the King," in the coal mining hills of Western Pennsylvania. Three men, one girl and the "head" gathered together in an old farm house to find out if the Church had selected us to begin, in the midst of the modern world we all found wanting, a new life. . . . It was a madhouse of sexual, liturgical and aesthetic bedlam. In the air the lust for power and an obsession with religion that if it were not bogus was so personal, so intricate, so bound to the unfulfilled heart that disaster of the most abominable kind would have demolished us were we not young and had the angels on our side.[29]

The illusory desire for conquest was swept away by a raging desire for freedom from authority and adult expectations. O'Gorman was a most unusual American Catholic in that he carried the blood of both Puritans and European noblewomen. But his "apostolic fervor" was shared by many members of the postwar Catholic avant-garde. In the case of a working-class Irishman like Willock, even more was involved in a desire to emulate the path advised by the eighteenth-century French Jesuit who authored *Abandonment to Divine Providence*. Willock embodied both Bauer's dreams of Christian conquest and O'Gorman's howling antinomianism. *Integrity* urged Catholics to boldly abandon their desires for social status and place all confidence in the merciful God. In a piece of thinly veiled autobiography, Willock wrote of a family without money or prospects, a family whose very existence was a sign of defiance to medical authorities who warned the couple not to have children. ("[A]n earnest doctor warned them that their combined blood factors were unfavorable to the birth of healthy babies." Willock had also nearly died from a kidney injury suffered in his youth.) It was impossible for Willock to discuss his family life without negative reference to a culture that oppressed them all: "[T]his family has turned up its nose at every one of the modern security axioms."[30]

Willock felt spiritually poisoned by American culture. In 1949 he wrote: "Catholics in ever-increasing numbers are coming to realize that the Faith in our times is being asphyxiated by an insidious gas called the bourgeois spirit." His quest for poverty and mortifications represented a drive for catharsis and ultimate purification from the ravages of secular materialism. In 1948 he and Carol Jackson had editorialized: "Perhaps the Christian convulsion going on today, that has been gaining force throughout recent years, is a sort of vomiting out of tepidity." This wrenching out of the bourgeois spirit was no easy task because it had fostered an all-enveloping ethos. What horrified Jackson and Willock the most was their recognition of precisely that American characteristic which so astonished Max Weber. America was a middle-class culture, they wrote, not by some objective economic criteria but "because of its spiritual orientation."[31]

Willock was destined for tragedy of a sort Dorothy Day would never have to face, simply because he felt doubly alienated, doubly betrayed. In a searing critique of "The Catholic Politician—Alas," Willock condemned not only Yankee capitalism but the urban-Irish culture he had grown up with in Boston. The immigrants, he argued, handed their souls to the Irish machine politicians who preceded them because "they were not fitted by temperament, experience, or education for any more democratic or representative form of government." In a grotesque parody of their social betters, the Irish substituted faith in the ward heeler for reckless trust in God. They yearned for comfortable civil service appointments (as Carol Jackson had written earlier) "to the point of indecency for Christians who have been assured that under certain circumstances all things will be added unto them."[32]

Gradually the Irish came to emulate "the carriaged Protestants, in their clean, trim propriety, in their facility for gracious living." To Willock the greatest scandal of all was the church's abdication to Yankee standards. He recalled one sermon which concluded with the priest imploring the young people in the congregation to "raise their hands in a none too solemn pledge that they would seek out and capture a civil service position." Willock's attitude toward the church was never the same after that. Carol Jackson recalled that "he used to tell us about the night he discovered some priests weren't interested in religion." *Integrity* owed its existence to Jackson and Willock's incredulity "that even one priest should be more interested in baseball than the apostolate."[33] Willock was thus highly receptive to the message Dorothy Day had been spreading among disaffected Catholics since 1933. In a society which saw nominal Christians unabashedly pursuing wealth and status, the only genuine alternative was to contradict the worldly spirit as dramatically as possible. Day's inspiration was like a jolt of transforming power to Willock. In 1949 he wrote: "We have been witness in the past twenty years to a revival of the spirit of holy poverty. It has been spread like a crusade by Dorothy Day and the Catholic Workers." But as a married man, Willock was in a position to make a much bolder gesture against secularity. Perhaps the most striking feature of the *Integrity* group was its absolute commitment to procreative sexuality unbound by the slightest concession to family planning. In an editorial on the family for the May 1947 issue, Willock wrote: "As a blow to our pride we must admit that the sum total of children represented in this issue is a paltry fifteen." It was becoming clear how radically he had embraced the rhetoric of contradiction. His ideal was "not a niggardly penny-pinching economy of scarcity," he wrote, in derision of capitalists who limited their productivity in children, "but an economy of abundance. Each new child is a further guarantee of prosperity." He obviously had in mind a type of prosperity not measurable in terms of dollars. He knew and welcomed the tangible price to be paid. The apostolic Christian must, he wrote in 1950, "shoulder all the extra burdens that go with sustaining unproductive children, and rather than receiving help he is considered foolish, ostracized."[34]

Willock sought to challenge American decadence by bringing new life into the world. "It is the desire of these parents that the old order die with them," he wrote, "and in their children will be the resurrection of the new Christ-life."

Beneath this stirring rhetoric lay two extraordinarily important themes. Willock dismissed ethnic identity as contradictory to the spirit of Catholicism, yet his ideal community resembled nothing so much as the peasant life of pre-famine Ireland, where men and women married young and had enormous families because, in a subsistence economy, deferred gratification was a meaningless concept. As historian Hasia R. Diner argued, it was only after the famine that the rural Irish became concerned with property and status. As Catholics they obviously could not use birth control but they could delay marriage and foster an intensely negative view of sexuality in order to defuse the tensions arising from a new worldview. In 1949, when Willock and several friends began making plans for a rural Catholic community, their vision evoked the idealized old world village, complete with pigs and goats nuzzling against the multitudes of children contentedly working and playing in the fields. Willock's dogged resistance of the cash nexus and selfish calculation recalled Henry David Thoreau's encounter with the impoverished Irish farmer, John Field. To the Walden philosopher, the Irish fought "at an overwhelming disadvantage,—living . . . alas! without arithmetic, and failing so."[35]

The rhetoric of abandon also unleashed in veiled form a critique of the church itself, surely the last obstacle to Irish-American autonomy and self-expression. In an *Integrity* article entitled "Six Aren't Enough," Bill Morgan credited the magazine with introducing his wife and himself to the spiritual glories of the large family. Morgan also paid tribute to a "Family Renewal Day" (known elsewhere as Cana Conferences) in which a priest had extolled the beauty of parenthood. But other than on that one occasion, Morgan complained that "neither of us has heard one word from the pulpit on the glory and the joy and the grace that God reserves for the parents and the children in a big family living His way." Willock, who was often mistaken for a seminarian, privately held a dim view of the celibate priesthood: "He didn't think that a seminary was a good place to educate a young man for the priesthood. He thought priests should be chosen from among the mature and responsible and formed men of the community. He had someone like himself in mind; and said so."[36]

To be a radical Catholic thus meant to be more boldly apostolic than the church's appointed officials. The family was the obvious symbol of this new spirit since it represented a sphere of unique lay spirituality. The family apostolate was enshrined in a remarkable book edited by publisher Maisie Ward, who was to figure prominently in Willock's communitarian experiment. *Be Not*

Solicitous: Sidelights on the Providence of God and the Catholic Family (1953) included many essays originally published in *Integrity*. In "Plea for the Family," a lengthy introductory essay, Ward captured in summary the romantic appeal of cultivating none but God's providence. All the essays, she wrote, shared one element in common: "It is just, and only just, before breaking-point is reached, that God comes to the rescue, sometimes almost visibly. On the strongest and most courageous He seems to put a burden that the rest of us could never carry."[37]

But for a number of the authors, the desire to experience that saving grace was so powerful that they actually courted insecurity and disaster as if in fulfillment of a spiritual requirement. The awful tension between the gospel of acceptance and the gospel of success was still very much in evidence. In "The Joy of Poverty" (an essay which originally appeared in *Integrity*), "Mrs. J." wrote in gratitude of the five dollar gift presented her by Jackson and Willock following the birth of her fifth child. Mrs. J. and her family had been going hungry on a diet of oatmeal and potatoes when the check arrived. She was reminded once again of how often God "gives you things like this. Surely I must be the most spoiled child in the world. I have the most indulgent Father." Life careened from emptiness to sudden bursts of grace, just as Mrs. J hoped. "I can't even think about poverty any more without being joyful." She also knew that her behavior would give scandal to those less reckless, especially if they knew she had actually prayed that her husband *not* obtain the civil service job he had applied for. Getting the job would mean "no more surprises, no more unexpected incidents." Her husband took a part-time job instead.[38]

"Poverty in Marriage" was a transitional narrative, because Mrs. J. describes two sympathetic priests who encouraged the couple in their pursuit of sanctity. But the genre found its apogee in an astonishing essay (Maisie Ward assured the reader that these were all true stories) by William Walsh, "The Young Familiar Faces." There are no priests in this story. Walsh and his wife Avis spend most of their time in Saliman's Grill in Denver, where he works on his doctoral dissertation while Avis helps prepare him for his foreign language examination. They are both thirty-eight years old, and the parents of twelve children. Bill occasionally sells books from out of his briefcase, but otherwise they are apparently without means of support. One day they spot a poor family from Appalachia struggling through the Denver streets. Separately, they give the family all of their money, leaving no money to feed their own family or even pay for bus fare home. As dusk gathers around, they begin a ten-mile pilgrimage to their home in the foothills. Upon arriving home, they discover that the children have been enjoying a day-long celebration, thanks to three separate groups of friends who each suddenly decided to do something for the overburdened Walshes. They have received so much food that one of their sons decides to give the three dollars he earned that day to "the poor." Bill and Avis return in prayer to the railroad tracks where he had stumbled and fallen along the journey home.[39]

"The Young Familar Faces" recalls Carol Jackson's argument as to why modern Catholics seemed so vulnerable to nervous breakdowns. They were victims, she wrote, of the hopeless disparity between "the nobility of their religion and the sordidness of their economic aspirations." The Walshes' solution was to adapt their grandiose spiritual desires to the mundane everyday milieu of a family desperately struggling not to become middle class. Walsh was oblivious to the moral absurdity of a doctoral candidate playing existential Russian roulette with the well-being of his children. But the story brilliantly captures the extraordinary longing of radical Catholics for the kind of religious experience seemingly denied to them in a civilization of machines and insurance. The journey home of Bill and Avis becomes a 1950s American version of Christ's ordeal to Calvary, complete with a fall and an anguished, near-blasphemous expression of despair. Walsh invoked the antitriumphalist tradition in citing Léon Bloy's explanation of Christ's embrace of suffering: "Man would never have been saved if Jesus had not sweated blood from fear and boredom. He began to be dismayed and distressed. What a text!" The Walshes, fools for Christ, vowed to order their lives to the realization that "the suffering of Christ is in the air we breathe. We accept only part of it normally, but we drag it to us in desperation."[40] The inhalation of suffering had become the essential breath of life, or death in life.

"The Young Familiar Faces" embodies all of the central themes which emerged from *Integrity* between 1946 and 1950. There is the sanctimoniousness bred by the lay apostolates, with their separatist anxiety and fear of strangeness. Of a hard-shelled, non-Catholic waitress he knew to be a decent woman, Walsh quotes himself: "'They know about God but they do not love Him, and they hate injustice but they do not love justice, and they hate meanness, but they do not love the practice of charity.' He was about to enlarge on the familiar theme, but he saw his wife's lips moving in silent prayer, so he too fell silent." Walsh also revealed the personalist's characteristic attitude toward women, and the women's attitude toward themselves. Peter Maurin had said—"contrary to modern feminism"—that "the man must strive to discover and understand his 'mission' in life, and that woman's vocation is to be a help-mate to man in striving to realize his vocation." While Bill Walsh grandly elaborated his philosophy of suffering, Avis "walked along, saying little, nodding occasionally, and making little sounds of assent." She had embraced what Dorothy Day extolled—after Thérèse of Lisieux—as woman's "little way": the daily mortifications experienced by a dutiful wife and mother. As Mary Reed Newland explained in *Integrity*, "[D]eath comes in little ways daily, in silence, in endurance, in grinding, uninspired effort, in all the things we don't want to do, the particular things He has given us to do."[41]

In some respects this attitude converged with what has been called the "sexual counter-revolution" of the cold war era. Willock's claim that "we would be astounded to discover how many kept women decide the policies of our nation" was a direct echo of charges made in Jack Lait and Lee Mortimer's enormously popular *U.S.A. Confidential* series. His concern that birth control would increase "the natural tendencies of sexual promiscuity and feminine coquettishness" was shared even by the avowedly Freudian authors of the cold war's most influential study of women. Ferdinand Lundberg and Marynia F. Farnham were no less certain than Willock and Jackson of the only proper purpose of sex. "For the sexual act to be fully satisfactory to a woman," they wrote in *Modern Woman: The Lost Sex*, "she must, in the depths of her mind, desire, deeply and utterly, to be a mother."[42]

But women's special vocation to suffering was both the source of their appeal and the basis of marital relationships. Since childbirth was viewed as the most significant single act in life, women were naturally elevated to a plane which brought them closer to Christ than men. As Newland wrote of a woman giving birth: "Her pain must really have approximated what Christ felt, at least part of the time. And it was the most ravishingly beautiful baby I have ever laid my eyes on." Though similar in spirit to nineteenth-century Protestant attitudes toward women, the personalist vision was unique in that the marriage partners' roles as "co-creators" bound them together against a skeptical culture and ensured their child's "re-birth in the waters of Baptism into the Mystical Body of Christ."[43]

Be Not Solicitous was significant in another critical sense. Maisie Ward was a sophisticated Englishwoman and co-proprietor, with her husband Frank Sheed, of an important publishing firm. Her occasional poverty, such as it was,

was entirely voluntary. She was very friendly with Claire Booth Luce and other wealthy Catholic luminaries. Although her husband was Irish-Australian, it would not be unfair to note that, like Dorothy Day, Ward was always a bit befuddled by American immigrant Catholicism. Here there were imposing class barriers not present in her dealings with Belloc, Chesterton, and Waugh. On the one hand she fully endorsed the wild abandon demonstrated by the authors included in her anthology: "As long as we are quite clear on the Church's teaching in the matter, we can joyfully and with fullest admiration read the story of those heroic people who have responded to what in their case was doubtless God's call to a reckless trust and acceptance of an enormous family." But she seemed a bit uneasy with the ferocious literalism in at least one of the stories, in which she detected "a slight tendency to throw stones in the general direction of fellow-Catholics who may well be guided by God in a path of continence, no less heroic." The personalists thought continence was for the unmanly nascent bourgeoisie. They yearned to build at least a small city on a hill to demonstrate the power of their alleged foolishness. Not surprisingly, perpetually short of funds, they eventually went to Maisie Ward for the money with which to build it.[44]

Marycrest

In 1949 Ed Willock was sent by a Catholic speakers' bureau to a meeting of the Boyd Council, a Knights of Columbus chapter in the Highbridge section of the Bronx, New York. Willock was filling in for a Catholic newspaper editor who could not make the meeting. Although the Boyd Council was New York's largest Knights of Columbus chapter, with over three thousand members, only seven men were in attendance the night Willock spoke. Among them were several Irish Americans from the local community: John Dermody, his close friend Alan Hudson, and John Hogan. Dermody recalled that he was "baptized" that night into truly apostolic Catholicism. A commercial graphic designer from a very poor family, Dermody was an intensely devout Catholic who, like Willock, had been a sickly, solitary child, and later became deeply involved in Catholic Action work. But whereas Willock was initiated into Catholic Worker radicalism while still practically in his teens, Dermody had been involved in the more conventional work of distributing official Catholic literature. Willock exposed him to a much richer Catholic universe, and Dermody—who had considered himself incapable of disciplehood—became Willock's ardent ally.[45]

The men, along with Hudson, Hogan, and several others from the Bronx, spoke often of finding a piece of land in the country where they could raise their families in apostolic fashion. They were soon in contact with several other Bronx Catholics who had participated in cooperative stores and credit unions in various parishes. The newly formed Christian Family Movement supplied additional couples anxious to put their convictions to the test. The severe postwar housing shortage combined with ideological motivations encouraged roughly one dozen families to forsake the only neighborhoods most of them had ever known. Through the Catholic Action network they learned of an Irish-American lawyer in Rockland County, New York, who shared their interests and had located a large parcel of land in West Nyack, approximately twenty miles northwest of the Bronx in a then-rural section of Rockland County. The attorney, Charles Neill, took title to the property and agreed to form a Marycrest Association (as the community would be named), which heads of families could join for $600. That sum entitled them to private ownership of a one-acre homestead site and pro rata ownership of a large common field where "a member may herd cattle, raise grain, and so on." The men were to raise the financing for home construction themselves. Maisie Ward loaned two of the families $4,400. Others similarly received financing assistance from private individuals. The men decided to hire an architect and a master builder for periodic advice, but they did all the contracting and virtually all of the construction work themselves. Since each home took approximately three years to build, there were only three families settled at Marycrest by 1952. Since there was no access road to the property, the men were forced to park an old school bus half a mile from the building sites and transport all their tools and materials by hand. By the late 1950s twelve homes had been completed.[46]

Marycrest can best be approached not so much as an actual commune but as a sign, perhaps the ultimate sign, of contradiction. Willock wrote that "it matures a man to drive hundreds of nails, lay hundreds of bricks, erect hundreds of studs, apply hundreds of shingles, all to an end of his own choosing . . . persons who create together will learn to re-create together and even pray together." Yet none of the founders' dreams of a self-sufficient Christian community came close to realization. In September 1951, Willock suffered a cerebral hemorrhage, and was never again a well man (although he fathered four more children). He died in 1960 at the age of forty-five. For much of his illness he was unable to speak and had to use a chalk slate to communicate. Willock's profound suffering seemed to fit the demands of antitriumphalist Catholicism, in that his intense desire to be apostolically constructive was always in conflict—largely unconscious—with the claims of another text, that supplied by the Catholic Workers. That movement's rural experiments had been virtually unmitigated disasters, and it is now clear that Dorothy Day's policy actually encouraged the pursuit of worldly disorder. In 1942 a woman wrote to Day from the Easton farm: "The day after you left and for several days everybody was drunk. . . . We have to suspect that you gave Mr. O'Connell some money. It turns out the same way every time. I know how hard it is to refuse it, but for the children's sake it makes me feel so rotten, when they all are like beasts."[47]

On an earlier occasion a man had written to Day, informing her that he would not obey her order for him to leave the farm. "When you trust the management of the farm into the hands of habitual drunks," he wrote, "then you can't blame me for disagreeing. Every week you send money to the farm for groceries and feed for the animals, but a good part of it goes for liquor and the payment of fines to the police. . . . What would your subscribers do if they knew what their money was being spent for; such as road-house patronization."[48] In a letter to a priest who was horrified with conditions he found on the farm, Day made a crucial admission. Rather than achieving purification through separation from society, the Catholic Worker movement, by its very antitriumphalist nature, seemed only to magnify existing social and personal problems: "We work with the poor human tools," she wrote. "Maryfarm is certainly a failure and always has been a failure. . . . It seems to me in dealing with the terrible problems of today in our paper, we have them exemplified in our mistakes."[49]

Day eventually abandoned hope of establishing a family component for her movement. Several families had settled at Easton, but she soon discovered they were practicing what she termed "the peculiar heresy of the family." According to her biographer William Miller, a man who had reminded Day of her beloved Dostoyevskian hero, "Prince Myshkin" (*The Idiot*), suddenly turned against her. "Emphasizing the 'priesthood of the laity,' he gathered about him a group . . . and then proceeded to bedeck his person with symbols of authority, insisting on the performance of solemn obeisances from others." Day bought another farm in 1947.[50]

Willock thus lacked a constructive model for establishing a rural Christian community. Although some of its members shared certain goals with Ralph Borsodi's nearby decentralist community, Van Houten Fields, Marycrest always suffered from the profound uncertainty of its founders over the nature of Catholic success. How could, or should, people pledged to Christian poverty run an efficient community? Despite the existence of a highly reasoned constitution, arguments raged at weekly meetings over whether or not it was appropriate to use power tools in the construction of homes. For a time it was even proposed that homes be built from mud tamped into bricks by the women of the community. A wildly antinomian spirit thus clashed with a need to provide shelter for enormous families (the twelve original families included seventy-nine children). Marycrest was occasionally the scene of rich paraliturgical ceremony: the fields were blessed by local priests; the entire community gathered for Christian folksinging under the light of the moon; bonfires were lit on St. John's Eve. But the rejection of worldliness exacted a profound cost. One of the original members, William Cobb, was a convert from Judaism. He never lived at Marycrest because the other residents disapproved of his attitude toward manual labor, and he was asked to resign from the association. But during the time he was involved, Cobb proved himself to be the best truck driver in the group. He was subsequently told to do something else, something which would better develop his own reliance upon God's providence. Not surprisingly, Cobb thought the Marycresters were Irish Calvinists, as well as "the most lovable band of misfits you could ever hope to meet."[51]

The community attempted for a time to live as much like primitive Christians as possible. Instead of displaying jockeys on their front lawns (which didn't exist in any case), they planned to construct the Stations of the Cross in the unpaved road. Each member was supposed to repay the time donated in constructing his own home (wet masonry or wood-frame construction: several were architecturally striking, while others were basic structures, reflecting the extent to which their owners applied the spirit of poverty). The unit of currency was a stone, each of which represented one hour of work. What was most striking about Marycrest's assault on the "bourgeois spirit" was that none of the homesteaders had ever *known* a bourgeois existence. They were not middle-class reformers. They were lower-middle-class Catholics: firemen, railroad agents, roofers, bus drivers, none of whom had ever owned property before. Nor of course were they Communists. They took their cues from either European reactionary Catholicism—whose critique of bourgeois culture was wholly irrelevant to the American situation—or from the Catholic Worker movement, where the reliance upon God's providence had never been quite so literally tempted.

Alongside faith in divine providence there existed a lack of faith in the future of the world. As Dorothy Willock wrote: "The threatening spread of communism, the prospect of atomic warfare, the terrible unrest of whole nations, all these make our faith in the continuance of life as we have known it seem rather silly." But it soon became apparent that the real needs of individual families could not easily be reconciled with the somewhat apocalyptic goals of the community. Gradually, the dreaded symbols of modernity began to appear. When one couple bought an electric washing machine, they were nearly ostracized. Several families abandoned completely the commitment to voluntary poverty (which had not been required by the constitution). These families tended to have fewer children and sought to avoid having their children treated as misfits by their schoolmates. Whereas Willock refused to apologize for the "runny-nosed, dirty-faced children at Marycrest," one mother explained that her children arrived in muddy shoes each day at the local parochial school because the road was unpaved, not because they were sent off that way.[52]

Willock and some of his neighbors often felt abandoned by the church, but they had actually been struggling for autonomy from the start. Marycrest, like Integrity, had no meaning outside of its status as a wholly lay enterprise. Willock was particularly adamant in his refusal to approve an official chaplain for the community, although a number of Dominicans, including Carol Jackson's former confessor, Father Wendell, were sometimes consulted by Marycresters. The residents there were surely an embarrassment to the more worldly priests in the area as well as to the nuns who taught in the local Catholic school. The children were often chided for—of all things—having too many brothers and sisters. Fertility was the community's most conspicuous sign of contradiction. And yet Marycrest was, as one of the women of the community put it, "for the men." Few of the wives had looked warmly toward a future of rising before dawn to feed the goats and chickens (fortunately for them animal husbandry never took root at Marycrest). In later years the women would sometimes use the term "brainwashing" to explain their apparent willingness to bear so many children and go for years without new clothes. Miscarriages and extremely difficult pregnancies were a prevalent feature of life there. It would be difficult to determine how well personalist spirituality survived the ravages of experience at Marycrest, but from the standpoint of the development of a

Scenes from Marycrest, West Nyack, New York, early 1950s.
Courtesy Alan Hudson.

Catholic culture, this much could fairly be said: the original character of
the community could not possibly have survived beyond one very short
generation.

But the point had been made. Marycrest, at least in Willock's view, represented a self-exhaustive denunciation of bourgeois materialism and its sexual

manifestations, from the "spermatic economy" of the nineteenth century to contemporary interests in birth control and eugenics. While the Protestant perfectionists at the mid-nineteenth-century Oneida community demanded strict male continence and carefully planned breeding, Marycrest made unplanned and prodigious reproduction the most visible sign of its antirationalist convictions. This in no way indicated an unusually high rate of sexual activity, since even at Marycrest a woman could only become pregnant about once a year. Yet these Catholics may well have been had a critical insight about the connection, in middle-class America, between sexuality and the spirit. It was no accident that the leading anti-Catholic of the era, Paul Blanshard, was also an ardent eugenicist, and that his "interest in eugenics was closely bound up with [his] interest in Catholicism." Blanshard's concern with "the qualitative overproduction of inferior types" seemed to reflect a rather parsimonious nature and fear of the nonrational and spontaneous which Catholic personalism fostered, however tentatively. The Marycresters seemed almost to sense that their community was a Blanshardian's worst nightmare, but their patriarchal authoritarianism, and the lack of a *positively* Catholic communal model, contributed to the demise of their original ideals. Conservative Irish Catholics for the most part, they shied away from their community's genuinely antinomian potential with some fear if not embarrassment.[53]

The Subculture Cannot Hold

Ed Willock was about to leave *Integrity* when he suffered his first stroke. Carol Jackson thought Marycrest was a waste of his valuable time and energy, especially since the community was "started without capital of any sort, including knowhow and group formation." Yet both of them, in their separate ways, moved in the 1950s toward a posture much more like that of Dorothy Day. They dropped their militant, frenzied Thomism in favor of a more mystical personalism. Jackson never surrendered her hostility to non-Catholic culture, but she increasingly withdrew into a melancholic recognition that militant Catholicism was a contradiction in terms. She came to agree with the English mystic Carryl Houselander that "twentieth-century sanctity is child-like sanctity and the sufferings of pure and innocent children are needed to reform a world sunk in vice and pride." During her last year as editor of *Integrity* she finally indicated her understanding of the true orientation of her apostolate:

"We must accept not only the authority of the Church but also the mystery of the Church, which like the Cross can be a sign of contradiction." The years of struggle had taken their toll on her. "The final result of 'trying to give what we didn't have,' was the revolt of our brains. . . . [I]t was several years before I could even read a book."[54]

In one of Willock's last *Integrity* pieces he urged readers to "see the clown in Christ." He invited the judgment of a world which "sets the true Christian apart not as hero nor as seer but as fool." What remained for Willock was to interpret his illness in the light of his religious beliefs. In "Suffering and Spiritual Growth" he made a final attempt to define the relationship between the human spirit and the awesome reality of God's Providence. There was now less distance between the militant Catholic who talked of conquering a pagan world and the defiant mystic who often drew cartoons of a smiling man lying atop a bed of nails. The "mystery of pain," he wrote, could only be understood in terms of Christian revelation, which suggested to him that "all striving for a better life involves our having to do violence to the life we presently possess, and the pain follows as part of the regenerative process."[55]

Willock surely did not invite his own illness and premature death. During the 1950s he spent many evenings with John Dermody, still discussing future projects for Marycrest. It was a heartbreaking experience for his old friend. Yet Willock had entered a special tradition during his days as a promising young member of the Catholic Worker movement. His friend Dennis Howard wrote: "Ed, who preached the failure of 'Success,' succeeded—like Christ—through failure. . . . In the end, we must still confront the cross—like Christ—and embrace it. Because Ed Willock did this, he was and will remain a sign of contradiction to our own comfortable lives and a symbol of reassurance for all who suffer." It was finally left to Dorothy Day to place his sufferings in the tradition she had helped define in the 1930s:

Ed Willock was, in a way, a Job. He exemplified the mystery of human suffering. . . . The only way to explain it, of course, is the Fall. Without the doctrine of original sin, the evil in the world would be an unbearable mystery. . . . We all felt Ed was suffering for us all. If one looks at all men all over the world as members, or potential members, of the Mystical Body of Christ, Ed had been chosen among those worthy to suffer . . . to take some of the suffering of families today upon himself, willing or unwilling though he might be.

Day went on to virtually repeat what she had written of Peter Maurin more than a decade before: "It is all very well to talk of mounting the Cross joyfully, with Christ, singing. Suffering is not like that except perhaps for a woman bringing new life into the world. But Ed died daily. He was literally putting off the old man, and putting on Christ, as St. Paul said, 'and there was no beauty in him.'" Day had never sounded so much like the leader of some obscure gnostic cult, intoning the formula for the ritual passage to the next world of one who was an elite member of the fellowship of suffering; who, as Day concluded, "was tried as though by fire, in the crucible of life itself."[56]

Integrity was dramatically transformed under the editorship of Dorothy Dohen. Having witnessed the ordeal of Jackson and Willock, she pursued a more moderate editorial and personal course. Dohen was younger than her predecessors; as a student at the College of Mt. St. Vincent during the early 1940s, she grew deeply impressed with the spirit of the European Catholic Renaissance then underway, particularly its emphasis on personal spirituality and its charitable embrace of much modern thought. A single woman, Dohen also worked out for herself a theory of vocation within the lay apostolate which did not require the immolation of her entire being as rigorously as it sought to curb the excessively worldly spirit. In 1967 she would write a moving letter to the Trappist, Thomas Merton, describing the difficulties several of her friends had experienced after "leaving" the world for contemplative vocations. She now believed that the "contemplative must be open to the anguish of the world." That anguish was real enough, there was no need to go looking for it. Dohen lacked both Carol Jackson's born-again antipathy to the self and Ed Willock's resentment of the Irish-American inheritance they shared. In April 1952, in her first editorial, she wrote, "A certain amount of destructive work is necessary to make way for construction. But we feel there comes a time when we have an obligation to give plans for a constructive program, for a positive apostolate." With these words she was, in effect, bidding farewell to an era in which Catholic lay people viewed the relationship between themselves and secular culture in radically adversarial terms.[57]

Yet the way had actually been prepared, if unintentionally, by her predecessors. The personalism of *Integrity* had followed in the Catholic Worker tradition: the self was denounced, but only after being painstakingly examined it all its manifestations. Willock had revealingly written: "You can't expect the family spirit to survive in a society where everyone is concerned with self-expression, self-aggrandizement, and even the religious people solely concerned with self-improvement. This is especially true when the idea of self-improvement is divorced from the traditionally Christian notion that the way to self-improvement is self-sacrifice."[58] He had thus fought a consumer culture's version of selfhood with the personalist alternative: not rugged individualism but rugged self-abnegation. But from what Dorothy Dohen saw at Marycrest, this was not a viable strategy for life in the kingdom of this world. She adapted the personalist initiative to a more modest project of evangelization.

"To be centered with Christ in God is the aim of the Christian," she wrote, invoking a spiritual language now, by the early 1950s, strikingly appropriate. "The trouble is," she noted, "that we are often so busy combatting the contemporary error that we fail to strive for wholeness." Dohen erased any doubts that she was intent on reshaping the Catholic posture toward the self and the world in an editorial disavowing the entire fools for Christ tradition: "The Christian chooses neither failure nor success as his primary aim, but to further the coming of Christ's kingdom. In accepting temporal responsibilities, if his efforts are crowned with success—God's be the glory; if after striving he fails—again—God be glorified. That is all there is to it."[59]

Yet once the door to the world was opened, Catholics rushed quickly to embrace precisely those secular standards Jackson and Willock spent themselves condemning. The authors of the controversial article on birth control referred to at the beginning of this chapter expressed the new concern in writing: "We are impressed at the irony of the best secular graduate schools being filled overwhelmingly with non-Catholics, married, practicing birth control, winding up at the top of their fields, while we Catholics place ourselves outside in many cases by our unwillingness to sacrifice, whether in or outside of marriage."[60] That birth control could be viewed by Catholics as a sacrifice—the sacrifice of losing the exquisite reliance on God's mysterious providence—indicates the power of the traditional personalist ideal.

But after *Integrity*, few Catholics would ever be so torn between the urge to build and the urge to destroy; between an innate resentment of the gospel of acceptance and a peculiarly virulent strain of the gospel of success. For the radical personalists of the 1950s, children of the Catholic Worker movement, success demanded a wild abandonment to the providence of a God whose ways had become more mysterious than ever. The intensely practical, driven man who wanted his house to be the layman's equivalent of a beautiful sermon watched, helplessly stricken, as his house fell apart. Few Catholics had ever tempted providence so boldly; few had ever learned the meaning of authentic

American experience, naked in a wilderness whose mystery was its own sign of contradiction: a mockery of the tired formulas of the comfortably sheltered neo-Scholastics. Will Herberg thought Americans in the postwar era had replaced their ethnic identities with a safer, blander, sectarian commitment. Willock and his colleagues did precisely the opposite, gambling on a purified Catholicism which required a radical severance from those all-too-secure ethnic precincts. They were the last Catholics to risk everything while still insisting on their rightful place within the church. After *Integrity*, Catholic romantics would have to travel alone.

Thomas A. Dooley and the

Romance of Catholic Anticommunism

Dorothy Day was a Catholic and a separatist. Beyond her genuine interest in social issues (which caused her to be egregiously mislabeled a "liberal Catholic") lay the unchanging vision of a woman seeking a beloved community for the inconsolable. For a self-proclaimed "radical Catholic," her language found a deep space within the discourse of a postimmigrant culture. But it was a space in the shadows. The self-expression of apostolic Catholics during the later 1930s and 1940s was redolent with suffering because they had become critics of American culture without first surmounting the pain born of their alienation or "uprootedness." After 1950 all but the most radical grew more conversant in the rhetoric of American opportunity. It was no coincidence that at Marycrest the most tragic figure—Ed Willock—was also the most rooted in Catholic Worker ideology. His more cautious Bronx-Irish compatriots survived to see their land skyrocket in value, and although this unexpected prosperity created new tensions, several of the founding families learned to enjoy a measure of hard-earned suburban comfort.

There was another cause for the transformation of the personalist ethos after 1945: the dramatic convergence of Catholic anticommunism with both the imperatives of American foreign policy and the domestic mood. The personalist, romantic impulse was too deeply rooted within Catholic culture to simply disappear once the cold war elevated the special international concerns of ethnic Catholics to public prominence. Between the meteoric emergence of the popular symbol of Catholic anticommunism—Sen. Joseph R. McCarthy—and the ascendance of John F. Kennedy, yet another individual worked within and beyond the spaces of a culture still bedeviled by the conflict between suffering and triumph. He was the fabled jungle doctor of Laos, Thomas A. Dooley.

Tom Dooley first gained fame as the young Navy doctor who aided in the transit of nearly a million refugees, most of them Catholic, fleeing from North to South Vietnam after the Geneva accords of 1954 divided that country in two. He actually *made* himself famous by authoring a book, *Deliver Us from Evil*, which artfully mixed images of torture and religious persecution—familiar to readers of the Catholic anticommunist press—with the compelling tale of a young Irish American imbued with the feisty "can-do" spirit of American overseas adventure. A self-made saint, Dooley died a martyr's death in 1961. But he was also a mystic, a romantic, and a poet whose experiences in Southeast Asia gradually neutralized the reflexive anticommunism responsible for his initial celebrity. In his ultimate loyalty to a personal vision as against national or sectarian identities, Dooley exemplified a shift in Catholic life later identified by the historian William Halsey: "[I]ncreasingly after 1945 personal egoism would begin to swell, while institutional egoism would slowly shrivel." A rich American, an Irish Catholic, a jungle doctor, a socialite and social critic, a sexual renegade, Dooley was a one-man sign of contradiction, as much to himself as to those who would try to understand him. A frightfully unintegrated personality to begin with, Dooley finally left only the fragmentary testimony of a self seeking wholeness, dying early in the decade which saw Catholic culture itself fly apart in shards.[1]

Dooley's background and early life made him a most unlikely candidate for sainthood. Born in St. Louis on January 17, 1927, he was, as he later noted, "a rich man's son." His grandfather, Thomas A. Dooley, Sr., an immigrant from County Limerick in the west of Ireland, made a fortune by designing and building the first all-steel boxcar just prior to America's entry into the First World War. His employer, the American Car and Foundry Company, shortly thereafter received war contracts in excess of over $100 million. The elder Dooley's creation was used to transport ammunition. Thomas A. Dooley, Jr., graduated from the Jesuit St. Louis University and became an executive and major shareholder in American Car and Foundry. In 1925 he married a young widow, Agnes Wise Manzelman. Her husband, Earle Manzelman—a pilot in the "Cracker Box" Air Force—was killed in flight just after the First World War ended, three months prior to the birth of their son, Earle. As 1st Lt. Earle Dooley, he too would die young, in the battle of Hurtgen Forest, November 18, 1944.[2]

Tom Dooley often claimed that he owed his success to a central tenet of Americanism: the belief that "ordinary men can accomplish extraordinary things." His mother believed that the thousands of young people who wrote to her in the years following her second son's death wanted, "most of all, assurance that he was an ordinary boy, with whom they could share ordinary experiences." But the attempt of his family and followers to reconstruct Dooley's childhood after the ideal of red-blooded American boyhood collapsed under the strain of building a legend from unpromising materials. Young Tom Dooley, it is reported, demonstrated precocious "self-confidence and the will to lead." The evidence for this assertion comes from Tom's response to boys who jeered at him for playing with dolls and doing embroidery with his best friend, Patsy Morrissey: "[C]riticism like that never troubled him. Later, when someone remarked on his ready skill with a surgeon's needle, Tom said he had learned quite young to set stitches." Even his stern father dropped his objections upon learning that Tom did not just play with dolls, he cured them. "In this way he played at being a doctor long before he became one." Yet, it was hurriedly added, "this phase was brief; suddenly the dolls got better and they were given away." Or, "he was not interested in them except to 'doctor' them."[3]

Dooley's father ran what Tom later described as a "taut ship . . . dictatorial—with much love, but dictatorial nevertheless." His mother clearly favored him over her three other sons (when she tried to explain to the boys "the real meaning of charity," "as usual, it was Tom who responded most keenly," by soliciting charitable contributions from his wealthy neighbors). Winning the approval of his father required Tom to perform acts which upset his highly protective mother. The narrator of a Dooley memorial record album solemnly reported: "[A]lthough not considered a 'good athlete,' he was a sports fan and intensely pursued his one sports love, that of being an outstanding horseman." Dooley's younger brother Malcolm remembered that "mother was always upset when Tom was riding, and was alarmed when he would go galloping into the wooded trails without a guide or adult companion, but she could not stop him, nor did Dad want to stop him. Tom's horsemanship pleased Dad, who had been quite an equestrian in his day. He would virtually beam through his stern Victorian face, as he saw Tom speed off."[4]

Where members of Dooley's family understandably sought to deny the significant distance between myth and reality, many of his admirers were given to even greater flights of fantasy. Thus Barbara C. Jencks could write: "In high school, he was a track and swimming star. In St. Louis, he soloed with famous orchestras."[5] Dooley was a man whose greatness and goodness many people needed very badly to believe in, and the often frantic quality of the Dooley myth reflected in part an attempt to surmount the obstacles his character and background presented along the path to American heroism.

The Dooleys lived in an affluent, mainly Catholic St. Louis neighborhood. Tom Dooley's mother, a member of an old Pennsylvania Protestant family, had become a Catholic because her husband's "devotion to his religion so impressed me. My parents also became Catholics." Daily prayers and attendance at Mass were perhaps the central activities of their family life. Dooley attended a Catholic grammar school and the Jesuits' St. Louis University High School. One of his classmates was Michael Harrington, who—before discovering his ultimate vocation as a democratic socialist—would help edit the *Catholic Worker* in the early 1950s. In his memoir, *Fragments of the Century*, Harrington explained that Catholic life in St. Louis differed from that in the eastern cities whence the familiar image of the defensive, anti-intellectual "ghetto Catholic" had emerged. In St. Louis, "the living Irish Republican tradition of the East Coast cities was missing and social class and national origin were not as intertwined as in New York and Boston." St. Louis had even been founded by French Catholics, and thus solidly middle-class families such as Harrington's (as well as decidedly upper-middle-class families like the Dooleys) experienced virtually no social discrimination. And yet, Harrington concluded, "even that happy, secure and relatively unresentful world was a ghetto." That the St. Louis Irish "still lived in a pale of our own making" suggests "how deep rooted the ghetto tendency in America was." The church had institutionalized its ongoing "struggle against the modern world" to the extent that efforts toward achieving an "integral" Catholic culture during the 1930s and 1940s took firm root in even the most assimilated Catholic communities. For Harrington the "neat syllogisms" through which his Jesuit educators (in St. Louis and at Holy Cross College) derided secular thought and experience were symptoms of cultural impoverishment masked by triumphalist rhetoric.[6]

The influence of this culture on Tom Dooley would only gradually become apparent. As an adolescent he was considered more of a "debutante" than a Catholic crusader: "In high school, Tom belonged to two dancing clubs and was one of the most popular beaus in St. Louis society." Harrington recalled: "[H]e arranged my first date and we and the young ladies went to the movies in his family's chauffeur-driven limousine." A gifted pianist (but far from a concert soloist), Dooley became adept at obtaining the backstage autographs of such

high-culture luminaries as Maurice Evans and Artur Rubinstein. He was becoming a highly refined aesthete, yet within a distinctly Catholic aesthetic
idiom. Travelling in Mexico after his graduation from high school, Dooley
visited the shrine of Our Lady of Guadaloupe where, just over a decade earlier,
Dorothy Day had initiated her pilgrimage toward peasant Catholicism. He was
most impressed with the church's ornamentation, the "pure gold-leaf work and
a profusion of gargoyles, animals, and angels. All of this adds to the almost
pagan opulence and creates an atmosphere of joy." After visiting the nearby
Floating Gardens of Xochimilco, he wrote, "[F]or once in my life I had all the
flowers I ever wanted."[7]

Dooley graduated from high school at sixteen and, in January 1944, enrolled
in the accelerated premedical program at the University of Notre Dame. He
enchanted his less sophisticated friends with his dancing prowess and talk of
his plan to become a "society doctor" specializing in obstetrics. But in October
of that year he enlisted as a hospital corpsman in the wartime Navy, shortly
before learning of the combat death of his older brother, Earle. Although his
mother wrote that Dooley "really 'came of age' during 1943 and 1944," there is
little evidence of any significant changes in his outlook during this period.
Although he helped treat wounded soldiers at the Marine Hospital in San
Diego, his most memorable accomplishment as a corpsman involved sneaking
into the Plaza Hotel dressing room of Hildegarde, the popular chanteuse, and
convincing her to visit the Long Island Navy Hospital where he was then
stationed.[8]

Dooley returned to Notre Dame in 1946. That institution had been a major
source of Catholic-American pride since long before 1913, when undergraduates Knute Rockne and Gus Dorais perfected a football technique of Coperni-
can significance: the forward pass. In the 1940s Coach Frank Leahy revived the
lagging tradition of Fighting Irish football glory: for millions of Catholics
(including the masses of "subway alumni" who had never been anywhere near
Indiana), the gridiron Irish embodied their own bold aspirations amidst a
somewhat unfriendly society. Notre Dame also symbolized the fortuitous wedding of triumphalist Catholicism and militant patriotism. According to a professor from that era, the university's faculty appointment agreement required
that "God, Country and Notre Dame were not pious abstractions, but facts that
governed our lives."[9]

Yet there was a great deal more to Notre Dame than athletics and patriotism
during the 1940s. As the best-known Catholic college in America, Notre Dame

took seriously its mission to inculcate its students with religious values. In the
the 1940s Catholic educators generally remained devoted to the special task
they had defined for themselves in the previous decade, when they had "not
only promoted papal social teaching and Catholic Action, but also insisted . . .
on the organic wholeness of Catholic truth and contrasted it more sharply to
the prevailing secularist order that was plunging mankind headlong to destruction."[10] Father (later Cardinal) John O'Hara, Notre Dame's president from 1934
to 1940, recruited a number of prominent European intellectuals to his faculty.
They brought the Catholic Revival along with them; since their numbers
included Jacques Maritain and Etienne Gilson, it could almost be said that they
were the Catholic Revival. These men "brought to Notre Dame a sense of other
worlds, other cultures, other versions of the Universal Church." Since most
considered themselves either victims or opponents of both nazism and bolshevism, they personified the tradition of Catholic civilization in flight from
ruthless totalitarianism. As such they provided a model of academic life wholly
distinct from the increasingly vocational orientation of secular institutions. At
the same time, they inspired the continuing estrangement of budding Catholic
intellectuals from their own national culture.[11]

Yet the university's triumphalist aura—undeniably bolstered by football suc-
cesses as well as by such haughty continental exiles as political theorist
Waldemar Gurian (who was once seen reclining his bulky physique in the back
seat of a car while his elderly wife struggled to repair a flat tire)—mitigated the
potential for alienation. Along with being a "holy priest," Father O'Hara was "an
incomparably shrewd man" who grounded Notre Dame's religious mission in a
muscularly pragmatic approach. He created the famous Notre Dame *Religious
Bulletin*, a publication slipped under students' doors thrice weekly which,
among other things, "correlated fifty years of football scores with communion
statistics . . . reported 448 genuflections in Sorin chapel on Tuesday morning
. . . [and] threatened personal interviews with students who failed to make
their Easter duty."[12]

Yet by the time Dooley arrived at Notre Dame some strains in the facade of
militant Catholicism were already apparent. The innate antitriumphalist strain
of American Catholic culture was embodied in several of the school's most
renowned personalities and institutions. The best loved humanities professor
at Notre Dame between the 1940s and the 1960s was Frank O'Malley, an Irish-
Catholic native of Massachusetts. The journalist Kenneth L. Woodward wrote,
"[O]f all the legendary figures of Notre Dame, none captured the spirit of the

place like Professor Frank O'Malley." O'Malley was an English teacher and one of Notre Dame's "bachelor dons"; he lived in a residence hall for over forty years and profoundly influenced many hundreds of students (including such future prominent Catholic Workers as Ned O'Gorman and Kieran Dugan). O'Malley shared with most Catholic educators of the period the desire for an integral religious culture; he was in the vanguard of those at Notre Dame who generated, as Philip Gleason put it, "the thrust . . . toward an organically unified Catholic culture in which religious faith constituted the integrating principle that brought all the dimensions of life and thought together in comprehensive and tightly articulated synthesis." (This was precisely the goal of the editors of *Integrity*, founded during Tom Dooley's second year at Notre Dame.) By night O'Malley extended his vocation into what he called his "evening colloquia": favored students were encouraged to pursue him at any of "a dozen or so watering holes he frequented." Once engaged, he would deliver "pungent monologues spiked with wit," while gradually drinking himself to death. This was not in itself so unusual for a legendary academic, but O'Malley differed from his counterparts at secular institutions by providing his students less with scholarly knowledge than with a "religious vision, one even of sanctity." As a colleague recalled: "Frank's real subject was religion." At a time when Notre Dame religion courses offered rote catechisms, O'Malley, like other avant-garde Catholics, romantically defined the church as the "corporate community of the faithful, saints and sinners alike, united in the Mystical Body of Christ, living in time and under the liberating shadow of the cross." But in offering a powerful countervision to secularism he characteristically promoted the literature of suffering at the expense of more complete accounts of human experience. A former student remembered O'Malley as "the most charismatic teacher I ever had" but also recalled that "Frank was hooked on redemptive Christian suffering. He often ignored the work of major writers while exalting that of minor ones. Léon Bloy was enshrined, while Thomas Hardy ('that agnostic who repudiated the efficacy of human suffering') was relegated to the scrap heap."[13]

This tendency to define Catholic culture's distinctiveness in terms of its greater appreciation of suffering suggests that, to the extent Catholicism resisted the dominant culture, it did so from a source rooted in a melancholic passivity. From this perspective some new light might be shed on the highly provocative but unsupported assertion made by Richard Hofstadter in *Anti-Intellectualism in American Life*: "American Catholicism has devoted itself alternately to denouncing aspects of American life it could not approve and imitating more acceptable aspects in order to surmount its minority complex and 'Americanize itself.'" The aggressive triumphalism evident at Notre Dame during the 1930s and 1940s was complemented, and finally contradicted, by its antithesis. This was manifest more clearly in the special loyalty of the students and faculty to the school's honoress, Our Lady. That the devotional center of the campus was a lovely shrine explicitly modeled after the Grotto at Lourdes revealed the depth of influence antitriumphalist piety enjoyed there. The two forces could interact quite harmoniously: students at the Grotto might pray for good grades and a win over Southern Cal one day, something much more profound and elusive the next. So long as the boundaries of Catholic culture maintained their inviolability, the harmony could be preserved.[14]

Only in retrospect is it clear that the synthesis was already beginning to unravel by the late 1940s, almost as quickly as it was being spun together in classrooms and chapels. Frank O'Malley, in his own "apostolic fervor," decided to found a new college in 1948, "where mystery would triumph over bureaucracy." Like Marycrest, this was to be an entirely lay-controlled institution. But the thought of leaving Notre Dame was apparently too much for him; in the midst of an all-night planning (and drinking) session, O'Malley "broke down and cried, saying he couldn't do it." Perhaps even more poignant, and closer to the heart of Notre Dame, was the plight of Frank Leahy, the football coach. A disciple of Knute Rockne, Leahy produced some awesome teams at his alma mater, at one point going four consecutive seasons without a defeat. Yet his success came at the expense of his health and his family. While that in itself failed to distinguish him from other, similarly driven coaches, Leahy, en route to his subsequent decline and resignation, constantly invoked the Blessed Mother as though she held the key to his success. When Notre Dame tried to de-emphasize football in the early 1950s, Leahy refused "to believe that Our Lady wanted anything less than perfection." But he also admitted that he finally "left Our Lady because I had to in order to stay alive." Was Our Lady the symbol of chivalric triumph or did she activate unconscious yearnings for martyrdom? Leahy's collapse during halftime of the 1953 Georgia Tech game (when he was given Extreme Unction, the last rites of the church) might be viewed without too much exaggeration as the moment when the Notre Dame—and American Catholic—contradiction exhibited its first dramatic breakdown (Notre Dame has since enjoyed only one era of gridiron success similar to that of the Leahy years. It occurred under an Armenian-Presbyterian coach and was greatly abetted by black, largely non-Catholic, athletes).[15]

Notre Dame students of the 1940s were thus trained at the epicenter of American Catholicism. The extent of the school's "influence" on Tom Dooley, though, raises complex questions. He already possessed the personality of an outsider but lacked the theory to transform circumstance into virtue. At Notre Dame he annoyed many students by constantly referring to his wartime exploits (as late as 1957 he listed "Pacific Theater of War from 1944 to 1946" on a passport application. A Notre Dame classmate who recalled that Dooley rarely took off his SeaBee's jacket was surprised to learn that his tour of duty was confined to stateside naval hospitals). A premed major, he showed no interest in the various lay apostolates that were springing up at the time. The only campus organization he seems to have belonged to was the Inter-American Club, a group devoted to improving understanding between the Americas; his Mexican trip had made a strong impression upon him. In the club's 1947 yearbook photograph a nattily attired Dooley appears slightly ill at ease amongst his largely Hispanic colleagues (including a Salvadoran named José Napoleon Duarte who had followed his brother, Rolando, to South Bend. Rolando chose Notre Dame over Harvard and Yale because "I had seen Notre Dame in a film, a short which showed Knute Rockne"). Dooley, who did not do very well either academically or socially at Notre Dame, actually left without graduating after gaining acceptance into St. Louis University Medical School, a practice not so uncommon during and just after the end of the War.[16]

Yet throughout his career Dooley worked to define his own Notre Dame myth as though adhering to a Catholic requirement, exalting its gentle spirit over its rugged athleticism. He alluded to Notre Dame frequently in his books and lectures, crediting the university with having first impressed upon him the reality of "the brotherhood of men under the fatherhood of God." And, in a letter of December 2, 1960—written virtually from his deathbed—to Notre Dame's president, Father Theodore Hesburgh, Dooley movingly paid homage to what he now claimed had always been his true spiritual home. "How I long for the Grotto," he wrote: "Away from the Grotto, Dooley just prays. But at the Grotto, especially now when there must be snow everywhere and the lake is ice glass, and that triangular fountain on the left is frozen solid, and all the priests are bundled in their too large, too long old black coats and the students wear snow boots. . . . If I could go to the Grotto now, then I think I could sing inside.

I could be full of faith and poetry and loveliness and know more beauty, tenderness and compassion." Dooley admitted his sentimentality and went on to suggest why his love of Notre Dame was only belatedly realized: "Do the students ever appreciate what they have, while they have it? I know I never did. Spent most of my time being angry at the clergy at school: 10 P.M. bed check, absurd for a 10-year-old veteran, etc., etc., etc."[17] "That Grotto," he concluded, "is the rock to which my life is anchored." The letter affirmed on the one hand the thoroughly romantic quality of Dooley's Catholicism. In calling Notre Dame his "favorite Lady" Dooley showed his affinity for the neochivalric Marian piety that formed an important component of personalist antitriumphalism. His own life ultimately comprised a search for a Grail beyond the ken of Catholic culture. Since he had strayed well beyond the boundaries of the American Catholicism engendered at Notre Dame, he was seeking through the letter not only consolation but reconciliation and perhaps forgiveness for some unnameable transgressions as well. Notre Dame itself was the Grail of millions of American Catholics; Dooley had made it there but, as was so often true of his life, its meaning for him was obscure and elusive. In the gulf between expectation and experience he fashioned a myth for himself, whose resonance among American Catholics would reveal a great deal about the their own elusive dreams.

"The Passage to Freedom"

Dooley returned to St. Louis to begin his medical studies in 1948, after a summer spent studying French at the Sorbonne. A trip to Lourdes left him feeling somewhat estranged from popular Catholicism and uneasy about his future:

> I joined in the candlelight procession, Mass, Communion, litanies, songs, flowers, stations of the Cross, and Benediction because I wanted to be a *pilgrim*, not just a tourist. But for me the last four letters of that word will always apply to Lourdes, "grim." I did have a sort of peaceful feeling while looking up, but was torn apart when looking around me. A doctor must, to a certain extent, be cold and calculating. I do not yet possess those attributes. To acquire them will be the hardest part of my medical studies.[18]

That November his father was stricken with a fatal heart attack outside the rectory of Our Lady of Lourdes Church in St. Louis. Dooley "felt lost without Dad," though he may also have felt a sense of liberation from his father's stern expectations, for he quickly developed, among his fellow students and professors, "a reputation for being a non-conformist." According to a Navy publication, "from all accounts, he partied his way through med school, drove a flashy red convertible with a full-size, cigar-store wooden Indian as a passenger and ended up repeating his final year." He probably would have been expelled altogether but for his family's prestige in the St. Louis Catholic community, and his friendship with the school's dean, Dr. Melvin Casberg, who later gingerly described Dooley's character and behavior as a student: "Even at this stage of his development I recognized a heart which could not be restrained within the boundaries of the routine things of life. . . . [I]nstead of attending required classes he often became absorbed in unscheduled medical activities. The faculty reaction to such unorthodoxy made it necessary for Tom to meet me occasionally in the Dean's office."[19]

Dooley became more flamboyant than ever. "He adapted his piano playing to the modern idiom, earning extra pocket money by playing at supper clubs." He took paraplegics from local clinics on outings in the "posh" automobiles of his socialite friends. He was particularly fond of young people: on his frequent visits to St. Louis hospitals, "all around him they crowded—like the Pied Piper's children." Dooley's more emotional and adoring chroniclers tended to unwittingly reveal more about the nature of his unorthodoxy than they meant to. Lucille Selsor, in her children's biography of Dooley, detailed his enthusiasm for reforming teenaged boys of the streets. After being told by one such youth that he didn't need a doctor, Dooley was said to have replied: "You're right, young fellow. You look like you'll keep a lot of doctors on the unemployment list." According to Selsor, Dooley "began a day after day effort to know such boys." He found jobs for them and rented an apartment in his own name for six of them to live, despite the objections of neighbors. Another account of this period is more succinct: "Tom was . . . interested in Father Dunne's Newsboy's Home for waifs of the streets, many of them with reformatory records." The narrator of "Portrait of a Splendid American" intones, "There were some people who disliked him, there were others who were charmed by his Irish wit and intelligence. . . . Tom Dooley only turned an ingratiating smile towards his detractors." His mother, having endured years of anxiety lest her son's fame collapse in scandal, recalled simply: "[H]e was a nonconformist. That made trouble for him in school; we couldn't be sure how things would turn out." Dooley's rocky career in medical school confirmed his belief that his prospects for a glamorous career as a society doctor in St. Louis were rather dim. Upon graduation he rejoined the Navy and was assigned to serve his internship at Camp Pendleton, California.[20]

After a year's internship Dooley was granted an overseas transfer to the United States Naval Hospital in Yokosuka, Japan. During a stopover in Guam in May 1954 he told his brother Malcolm (who was a navigator in the Air Force) that he hoped to be sent with a Military Advisory Group into Vietnam to fight against the Vietminh. He also indicated his desire to make "the Navy his life." By the time the brothers met again in Yokosuka three weeks later, a truce had been signed between the Vietminh and the French, and "Tom appeared disappointed that he would not get to Vietnam." But on July 14, Lt. Dooley received Temporary Additional Duty orders to take part in amphibious exercises and practice landings on Philippine beaches. In August his ship, the USS *Montague*, was ordered to North Vietnam, to aid in the evacuation of those who—under the terms of the Geneva accord—were to be free to move south of the 17th parallel before the border was closed in May 1955.[21]

Dooley was initially ordered to supervise the creation of medical and sanitary facilities aboard the ships destined to move the evacuees from Haiphong to the South, and to educate the crew members as to the nature of the tropical diseases they would encounter among the Vietnamese. But his remarkable facility with languages—he not only spoke French fluently, but quickly acquired a basic understanding of Vietnamese—made him extremely valuable to the rather perplexed line officers responsible for executing the evacuation. In September he was reassigned to a special task force centered in Haiphong, "to do preventative medical studies, and epidemiology work in Haiphong."[22]

The makeshift tent hospitals the Navy built at Haiphong—which delivered treatment to many of the over eight hundred thousand, mostly Catholic refugees fleeing south in what became known as the "Passage to Freedom"—provided the locale for the self-legend Dooley created in *Deliver Us from Evil*. Accounts of his heroism stressed the voluntary, above-the-call-of-duty quality of his achievement: "Although never specifically authorized to do so, Dooley began to treat them. . . . [W]ith the help of only four enlisted corpsmen, Dooley sometimes treated as many as 300 patients in a day. . . . [H]e drove himself, pouring out his energy and ruining his health." In reality, Dooley blithely wrote his mother (at a time when the swaggering faith in America's world mission swept many cautions aside), "[M]edical intelligence is really what I spend most of my time doing." He was, for the most part, a spy. "Under the heading of medical aid to the refugees we are able to seek out the intelligence information needed." His most important role was in relaying information from Vietnamese military officers to the Americans, who had decided to covertly support the Catholic mandarin, Ngo Dinh Diem, in his attempt to create a South Vietnamese government. "I take it, usually at night, and then with everything except a cloak and dagger, give it to the nearest ship for coading [*sic*] and forwarding to the command ship." During the mission Dooley withheld some information from his mother, but when it was over he credited her with a degree of common sense he must have assumed was lacking among the millions of readers of *Deliver Us from Evil*:

> I knew all along that you fully realized what my job was for those last six months in Indochina. The Viet Nam government in Saigon had doctors, the U.S. Public Health had doctors who are specialists in Refugees. And dozens of other organizations such as the International Rescue Committee, Care etc. all have doctors to work with refugees all over the world. Yet the Navy saw fit to keep me there, who had not training whatsoever in refugee work. The reasons must have been obvious to anyone. In fact they were, to the Viet Minh.[23]

Dooley was but a bit player in the drama of exodus being conducted in Vietnam; the fact that he shared the faith of the refugees would assume great significance only later, to American strategists as well as to American Catholics. In the meantime sophisticated American intelligence operatives led by Maj. Edward Lansdale mounted an intensive propaganda campaign designed to discredit the North Vietnamese government by encouraging large numbers of Catholics to flee South in advance of the May 1955 deadline. Although exile made sense for a number of reasons—many of the Catholics had fought for the French under the papal flag in the 1946–54 war, while others were sure to become victims of Ho Chi Minh's increasingly brutal land reform program—Lansdale feverishly promoted the immigration by flooding the North with leaflets proclaiming that "'God had gone South' and that Mary, the Mother of God, had also left the North." One of the studies comprising the Pentagon Papers suggested the largely secondary role Dooley played in the immigration campaign: "Dr. Tom Dooley found refugees with a Vietminh pamphlet showing a Hanoi map with three concentric circles of nuclear destruction—conceivably, an example of Colonel Lansdale's handiwork."[24]

Tom Dooley left Haiphong on May 12, 1955, one day before it was formally turned over to the Vietminh, but not, he claimed, before being detained overnight by the Communists. He assured his mother, "I was never touched." He was, he reported, deprived of toilet facilities and subjected to persistent interrogation, during the course of which he was asked, "Sir, do you own an automobile? And is it not true that this car cost the equivalent of many people's yearly salary?" After receiving a special decoration in Saigon from Premier Ngo Dinh Diem, Dooley left Vietnam for Yokosuka to begin writing, with the Navy's encouragement, his account of the "Passage to Freedom." From Japan he asked his mother to send him all the specifications on a 1955 Oldsmobile 88 Convertible, "including the colors (could you get me one of those beautiful color charts that show them in their real depth?)." He had not been brainwashed.[25]

Dooley headed home with his manuscript in November 1955. He spent two weeks in Hawaii with Navy commander William J. Lederer, who "made suggestions for revising the book" and arranged an appointment for Dooley with the editors of *Reader's Digest*. The magazine decided to run a condensed version of the book in April 1956, just prior to its publication by Farrar, Straus and Cudahy. Sales for the hardcover edition quickly approached one hundred thousand. More than half a million paperback copies were eventually sold, making Dr. Tom Dooley an American hero and celebrity.[26]

A friend and admirer once issued a classic understatement about Dooley's career: "Interpretations vary strangely."[27] *Deliver Us from Evil* is a bizarre and fascinating work which raises questions of maddening complexity. How much of the book is "true" and how much is it brazen anticommunist propaganda? In light of what was to come for Dooley, the book rings false less from his infidelity to the "facts" than from his willingness to subordinate the meaning of his own unique experience to the exigencies of American foreign policy and American Catholic mores.

Deliver Us from Evil was successful in large part as a testament to the power and majesty of Catholic anticommunism, no longer confined to the pulpit and Knights of Columbus hall but confirmed in the cauldron of experience:

Yes, cocky young Dooley, whom the profs at medical school had ticketed as a future "society doctor," was learning things the hard way, but he was learning at last. At Notre Dame they had tried to teach me philosophy. Now out here in this hell-hole I had learned many profound and practical facts about the true nature of man. . . . I had seen inhuman torture and suffering elevate weak men to great heights of spiritual nobility. I know now why organized godlessness can never kill the divine spark which burns within even the humblest human.[28]

Dooley's faith lent an aura of expertise and authenticity to this work concerning the valiant sacrifices Vietnamese Catholics made in order to escape communism: "[A] Young Navy doctor, himself a Catholic," was the way the *New York Times* reviewer identified Dooley. Yet on the surface, at least, Dooley never invoked the Catholicism of the refugees in a triumphalist or self-congratulatory fashion; he managed instead to place their struggle in the context of American freedom of worship, making their Catholicism seem as natural and familiar as it claimed to be back home, in the great new era of interfaith consensus: "They had made a wholly free choice in tearing up century-old roots and abandoning revered ancestral graves. For the right to continue to worship their God—the decisive motive in nine cases out of ten—they had given up their rice paddies, their homes, their beloved native villages."[29]

Dooley quite literally, if unconsciously, blended Americanism with Catholic ritual in winning the loyalty of the refugees. American pharmaceutical companies had provided the Navy with large quantities of pills. "With every one of the thousands of capsules of terramycin and with every dose of vitamins on a baby's tongue, these words were said: 'Dai La My-Quoc Vien-Tro' (This is American Aid)." Yet even this wealthy would-be sophisticate often proclaimed astonishment that he was so privileged as to actually speak *for* America to the Vietnamese. According to Dooley, when he thanked the corporations, "[T]hey responded with letters thanking *me*. Imagine that! Every person from whom I requested aid responded wholeheartedly. It gave me a feeling of nearness to all the people in my country. It was as if all the wealth of America were in my own medicine chest." He breathlessly reported: "[R]est assured, we continually explained to thousands of refugees, as individuals and in groups, that only in a country which permits companies to grow large could such fabulous charity be found." Dooley's awe at his own power was a genuine response to his newfound cultural authority. As Nicholas von Hoffman wrote, in a cynical 1969 article for the *Critic* (as if in retribution for the illusions with which Dooley had seduced a generation of Catholic idealists): "He had a touch of the American Catholic urban peasant about him." To von Hoffman, *Deliver Us from Evil* was written "the way you might expect a Notre Dame boy of the previous decade to write." It is not surprising then that for all his apparent worldliness Dooley was, as of 1955, a ripe target for manipulation.[30]

One of the Americans in Vietnam who took an interest in Dooley's work was Edward Geary Lansdale, an Air Force officer who went to Vietnam as an operative for the Central Intelligence Agency in 1954. Lansdale, a former advertising executive with roots in the Maryland gentry, had recently helped suppress the procommunist Huk rebellion in the Philippines. One of the more mysterious and legendary figures in American military history, Lansdale—a master of psychological warfare ("psywar")—carried out counterinsurgency operations ranging from pouring sugar in the gas tanks of Vietminh trucks (which David Halberstam called "a gesture of no small amount of mindlessness") to such "blacker" activities as hiring Vietnamese soothsayers to fabricate direful predictions for the fate of Catholics in North Vietnam should they remain behind after 1955. Although he was the first great American champion of Ngo Dinh Diem, Lansdale's actual degree of influence during the early days of American dominance of South Vietnam is a matter of major debate. Frances FitzGerald argued that, in late 1954 and early 1955, "he was almost single-handedly to reverse the whole course of events in Saigon," while Stanley Karnow claimed: "[H]is clout has been exaggerated by both his admirers and critics."[31]

Although Richard Drinnon created a fascinating interpretation of Lansdale as a classic figure in the evolution of American racist expansionism—"a sort of twentieth century incarnation of Johnny Appleseed, warning folks in the back-country against modern merciless savages and handing out the seeds and saplings of American democracy"—no one has yet provided the insight into Lansdale's character which might explain the special role he envisioned for Dr. Tom Dooley. Lansdale was, above all, an American Protestant who sounded remarkably like the moral reformers of the nineteenth century. His invocation of that tradition's rhetoric was completely unabashed. The leader of the Huk movement in the Philippines, he explained in his memoirs, surrendered to the government in large part due to the "moral suasion" generated in negotiations carried on over seven years with the Philippine president ("I had helped establish this relationship originally with President Roxas"). Lansdale had an invincible conviction of his nation's transcendent mission: "In sharing our ideology, while making others strong enough to embrace and hold it for their own, the American people strive toward a millennium when the world will be free and wars will be past."[32]

Critics of American involvement in Vietnam would identify in Lansdale's naive rhetoric the spirit that "has made you nice Americans the most dangerous people on the face of the earth." But Vietnam was hardly ripe for the direct transplantation of the Protestant ethic and the spirit of capitalism. It was one thing for Lansdale to play cowboys and Indians with Diem's nieces and nephews on the floor of the presidential palace; it was quite another to market and promote back home this Catholic, self-styled mandarin whom he had decided to anoint the George Washington of Vietnam. In *The Quiet American*, Graham Greene lampooned the innocent faith of "Alden Pyle" (an American of indeterminate mission in Vietnam, widely believed to be based upon Lansdale) in the "Third Force" solution to the Vietnam crisis. As "Fowler," the world-weary British journalist explains to Pyle, while the casualties of his counterinsurgent activities mount: "This Third Force—it comes out of a book, that's all."[33] But to Diem the Third Force was no abstraction. It was the political expression of the one good idea modern French culture, in his estimation, had produced: Personalism.

The relationship between Diem and American Catholicism provides a superb case for arguing that even this most "universal" faith can only be properly appreciated in terms of the vagaries of local practice and expression. Tom Dooley had no idea what Personalism was. He had almost certainly never heard of Emmanuel Mounier. Even in the Eurocentric Catholic Worker movement this French philosophy, such as it was, exerted little formal influence over Dorothy Day and her followers, other than to lend additional encouragement to the new search among Catholics for a fuller sense of the self. Day's confrontation with Catholic culture produced a lowercase "personalism" which can only be understood in the context of a dominant Protestant host culture. Dooley would grope—in an even more intuitive, theory-bare fashion—for a romantic spiritual identity which, in its critical distinction from American individualism, was likewise "personalistic." Diem and his brother Ngo Dinh Nhu shared a much more straightforward and practical view of the uses to which an exotic mystique could be put. "After the war," wrote Frances FitzGerald in *Fire in the Lake*:

Nhu had been impressed by the works of Emmanuel Mounier, the Catholic thinker, and misinterpreted them as a doctrine of the corporate state in which the alienated masses would find unity through participating in certain authoritarian social organizations, and through leaders of superior moral fiber. Always a highly abstract affair that lacked the rigorous analysis of Marxism, the doctrine in Nhu's hands grew into an incomprehensible hodgepodge having something to do with state power, the dignity of the Person (as opposed to the individual), and the virtues of humility, renunciation and sacrifice. Whether or not Nhu had a clear idea of what he meant by Personalism remained questionable, for, when once pursued by an American graduate student hot for dissertation material, he said that no written statement on the subject perfectly expressed the true philosophy of the regime.[34]

One of the leading experts on the Diem regime, the Frenchman Bernard Fall, wrote in *The Two Viet-Nams*: "This writer will candidly admit that repeated readings of Mounier's prose have not brought him closer to a clear understanding of what exactly Personalism is in the European context, let alone in the Vietnamese context."[35]

Diem's ideology was obviously fluid enough to appeal to non-Catholic Americans. According to Drinnon, Edward Lansdale admired Diem's puritanical asceticism (a bachelor, Diem had contemplated joining a monastic order). Moreover, "even the vacuities of personalism—Diem's personal philosophy that was an amalgam of papal encyclicals, Marxism, and Confucianism—struck responsive chords in his own sonorous sermons on Paul of Tarsus and Tom Paine, though he did urge the premier toward broader ideological formulations." Yet Lansdale found it difficult convincing his bosses in Washington that Diem was worth the investment the protection of his regime would require. In the spring of 1955 Gen. Lawton Collins, President Eisenhower's personal military representative in Saigon, lobbied for an end to support for the weak and inefficient regime. But on April 28, the day after Secretary of State John Foster Dulles decided to jettison Diem, Lansdale persuaded his protégé to ignore the puppet emperor Bao Dai's order that he return to France, and strike quickly instead against his enemies in the Binh Xuyen, a Saigon sect heavily involved in organized crime. The ensuing victory provided Diem and Lansdale with a temporary reprieve. It was in the wake of these events that Diem was photographed exchanging champagne toasts with the young Navy doctor he had just presented with Vietnam's highest honor, the medal of "Officier de l'Ordre National." Unbeknownst to Dooley, Lansdale had "inspired" Diem to make the award; Dooley was simply told that "it was extremely unusual for a junior officer to receive a decoration of a foreign country. And to have it personally awarded by the country's president in the middle of the internal strife he has in his country . . . this was most extraordinary."[36]

Lansdale was surely impressed with Dooley's zealous efforts in selling Americanism to the refugees, and he could not possibly have missed the rich propagandistic value suggested in the clink of champagne glasses between the Vietnamese Catholic—sworn to supplant European imperialism—and the Irish-Catholic American whose achievements shone glory on America's pluralist democracy. Dooley had a natural fondness for the Vietnamese: he was a favorite of the children at the orphanage of Madame Ngai, a wealthy Tonkinese Catholic widow who moved to Saigon in 1955. Lansdale was a somewhat anachronistic figure in his stiff crew cut and mustache: "In person he sometimes appeared to be a curiously disappointing, almost simplistic man"[37] (aside from a brief reemergence during the administration of another Irish-Catholic adventurer, John F. Kennedy, Lansdale would never again enjoy the prominence he attained in the early days of the Diem regime). Lansdale's relationship with the Vietnamese was rather like that of the Christian Social Gospel ministers working with the urban working classes earlier in the century: all the good intentions in the world could not overcome disparities of sensibility. The Catholic convert author of *The Quiet American* has the Lansdale figure, Alden Pyle, killed off, as though the lethal innocence of his kind had run its final course. But the real-life war had only just begun.

Tom Dooley became a legend primarily because he was useful in promoting American interests in Vietnam. The Pentagon Papers indicated his essentially propagandistic role: he "dramatized the misery and fearfulness of the refugees for American audiences." He need not have been a Catholic to play that part. Yet almost in spite of Dooley's desire to become a transcendentally American hero, *Deliver Us from Evil* held an undeniable fascination for Catholics. The book served both to confirm and reshape the ferocious anticommunism which had unified their community—across ethnic lines, for a change—since the end of the Second World War. The contents of the book heightened the religious experience of many. One middle-aged Irish-American woman from New York City brought the book along on a vacation to the Catskills in the summer of 1956. She read it over and over until one day, just after leaving Mass, she sat on a bench and wrote a letter to Dooley, by this time working in Laos. Although Teresa Gallagher later became Dooley's most trusted stateside assistant, her response to the book was no different than that of thousands of Catholics: "The book made a deep impression on me, and Dr. Dooley's vivid picture of the frightened refugees remained with me long after I closed the book. His sense of compassion, his deeply rooted faith, his patriotism, his ability to make you see the Vietnamese as real people and suffering human beings who needed help, made me re-read the book again and again."[38]

Dooley was less interested in becoming a professional anticommunist than in vindicating himself and becoming a hero. After being honored by President Diem, he wrote to his mother, "[I]t's a long time since I flunked my senior year." The medical school authorities "didn't think I was adequate yet the president of Indo China thinks I am." Yet since he still lacked any strong convictions, Dooley's writings often glibly reflected the type of Catholic anticommunism he was familiar with from St. Louis and Notre Dame. And even before he had written anything, while still in Saigon, he was interviewed about his mission by a reporter from the St. Louis *Post-Dispatch*. Never one to disappoint a journalist, Dooley claimed that the Vietminh had recently burned a young Catholic leader at the stake. Dooley also reported that priests were being routinely tortured in the North. This was not inconceivable; priests were invariably the leaders of Vietnamese refugee groups. Conversely, the Vietminh used friendly priests to dissuade Catholics from fleeing. A priest of the Diocese of Haiphong wrote, in the *Catholic Patriot* of February 24, 1955: "Arriving in the south, the young men are put into the Army by force, the young girls, pure children of Notre Dame, are sold to houses of prostitution, boys are being sent out to the rubber plantations."[39]

Catholics thus became pawns in the Vietnamese power struggle. For the most part, though, they were better off moving to the South than continuing to face the hostility of their northern compatriots, a sentiment that long antedated the birth of Vietnamese communism. The reliable Bernard Fall concluded: "The Tonkinese Catholics fled because they had had a long experience of persecution at the hands of their non-Catholic fellow citizens." *Deliver Us from Evil* was therefore a dishonest book not because it engendered sympathy for the Vietnamese Catholics but because Dooley incited their American coreligionists to view their plight solely in terms of communist savagery and Catholic suffering. The most memorable passages in *Deliver Us from Evil* concerned tortured priests Dooley claimed to have treated, including one whose head was matted with pus and there were eight large pus-filled swellings around his temples and forehead. Even before I asked what happened, I knew the answer. This particular priest had also been punished for teaching "treason." His sentence was a Communist version of the Crown of Thorns, once forced on the Saviour of whom he preached. Eight nails had been driven into his head, three across the forehead, two in the back of the skull and three across the dome. The nails were large enough to embed themselves in the skull bone. When the unbelievable act was completed, the priest was left alone. He walked from his church to a neighboring hut, where a family jerked the nails from his head. . . . The old man pulled through. One day when I went to treat him, he had disappeared. Father Lopez told me that he had gone back to that world of silence behind the Bamboo Curtain. This meant that he had gone back to his torturers. I wonder what they have done to him by now.

Dooley was so moved by this episode that in its wake, he wrote to his mother: "I vomited and vomited until my guts turned upside down. That was the only time I had ever gotten sick at my stomach over a medical thing. But it wasn't just medical, it was something sort of the soul and heart and very nature of man."[40]

Again, the question is not whether atrocities were committed but whether Dooley was correct in placing all the blame on an ugly situation with the Communists, who, he said, "have perfected the techniques of torture, inflicting in one moment pain on the body and in the next pain on the mind." Journalist Robert Scheer, an opponent of America's escalating involvement in the war in the early 1960s, claimed that "often these atrocities were the result of bandit gangs (tearing an ear is their traditional mark)." Lansdale himself referred in his memoirs to the leader of one of the noncommunist Vietnamese sects and "the novel torture method he used for forcing farmers to disclose their hidden valuables—a steel nail pushed slowly into the victim's ear." Another letter Dooley wrote to his mother suggests he believed he was telling the truth, though he sometimes lied to her, and that by 1955 he was a young man light years removed from understanding himself or that part of the world about which he claimed great expertise: "I am not writing this to nauseate you or make you feel bad, as I know it does, but in hopes that you will let others read this, and understand the nature of this enemy that we are fighting. Let them know that it is these same peoples, these same officers and soldiers who are a threat to our security."[41]

While Dooley's revelations promised personal vindication, his images of torture and suffering provided powerful ammunition for the well-organized pro-Diem, anticommunist lobby in America, led by Francis Cardinal Spellman of New York. The front pages of diocesan newspapers were dominated throughout 1954 and into 1955 with headlines such as "Vietnam Church Now in Tragic Period." While secular newspapers duly reported the exodus of Catholics, and some, including the New York Herald Tribune, recounted accusations of torture (Homer Bigart, the Tribune's man in Vietnam, obtained much of his information from Lieutenant Dooley), the Catholic press isolated the religious issue as the cause of the conflict. According to Spellman's biographer, "many Americans came to believe that Vietnam was a preponderantly Catholic nation."[42]

At the same time, some secular agencies were becoming concerned by the nature of Dooley's claims. Six American functionaries who participated in the Haiphong operation wrote a critique of Deliver Us from Evil for the United States Information Agency in Saigon. They "did not accept the thesis of his book that the success of the evacuation of the refugees was entirely his work." They also characterized Dooley's tales of atrocities as "non-factual and exaggerated . . . not the truth." The report concluded by urging that "any further U.S. Government support of ventures by Dooley be terminated."[43] The report signaled the beginning of an uneasy relationship between Dooley and his government, which would continue for the rest of his life. Like it or not, by 1956 it was clear that his most steadfast constituency would be found among the Catholics of America.

The Culture of Catholic Anticommunism

Although American Catholic anticommunism has long been routinely cited as integral factor in the cold war, it remains a puzzling issue. One thing which can be said for certain (that could definitely not be said with respect to other Christian denominations) is that no one in the American church of the 1940s and early 1950s believed it was possible to be at once a Catholic and a Communist, socialist, or self-styled Marxist of any flavor. As historian Donald Crosby explained, both liberal and conservative Catholics "were passionately, even obsessively, opposed to communism, profoundly convinced that it represented the greatest of all possible dangers to both church and Republic."[44]

Dorothy Day was a staunch anticommunist, although her concerns, as ever, were more spiritual than political. Even this purportedly avant-garde Catholic was greatly concerned with shoring up the bulwarks surrounding Catholic identity in a period of intense anxiety. In 1946 she wrote of the repentant ex-leftist labor leader, Joe Curran of the National Maritime Union:

> Joe is a Catholic, a baptized Catholic, so I ask our readers to pray for him, the head, as he is, of one of the biggest and most powerful unions in the country and one which has done great work for its men. He is married for the second time, being divorced from his first wife. On one occasion he was advertised as a Catholic when he was running for political office on the west side, and when I telephoned to ask him about it, to pin him down as to whether he was a practicing Catholic, he told me of his second marriage. . . . I have already asked many a convent of holy nuns through the country to pray for Harry Bridges, another former Catholic and another great labor leader. And there will be results of that, I am sure. Prayer is a weapon that they cannot combat.[45]

Aside from whatever merits it may have possessed at the time, anticommunism was thus the key to consensus in a church confronted with a variety of potentially divisive issues. The American Communist party, for its part, was fully conscious of the propaganda value of winning converts from Catholicism (the reverse pilgrimage was, of course, much more common by the 1940s). In *The Romance of American Communism*, Vivian Gornick reported an interview with a female graduate of Boston College who became a Communist at the height of the depression. The party had come after her "full force. 'You see, darling,' Maggie says, her voice richly edged with laughter, 'I was Irish. That was the key. That was always the key. They wanted me because I was Irish.'"[46]

Catholic anticommunism in the cold war years has also been seen as providing opportunities for social mobility and increased prestige; anticommunism was an article of national faith, and Catholics were supposedly the most zealous and experienced of all its proponents. Catholics had led the fight against American recognition of the Soviet Union in the 1930s, and their hostility to the anticlerical regime in Mexico led to uneasy relations between many Catholics (overwhelmingly Democratic in those days) and the New Deal. Now, in the postwar "era of security clearances, to be an Irish Catholic became prima facie evidence of loyalty. Harvard men were to be checked; Fordham men would do the checking." The Irish were far from alone among Catholics in their preoccupation with communism. Historian David Caute wrote that "although the war inevitably tended to discredit Fascism among American Catholics, the rapid spread of Communist hegemony in Eastern Europe only intensified the traditional fear and loathing of atheistic Communism. The diocesan papers were full of the sufferings of the East European Catholics; Yalta had been denounced by the bishops. Tensions increased following the arrests of Archbishop Stepinac in Yugoslavia and Joseph Cardinal Mindszenty in Hungary."[47]

The meaning of images of suffering in the Catholic anticommunist worldview has been generally overlooked by historians of the cold war period. This is due in part to the misleading, superficial vitality of the church at a time when "Catholics were enjoying a population boom that made them by far the largest single denomination in the land. This remarkable growth in numbers, plus their success in winning converts from Protestantism, did little to endear Catholics to Protestants, especially since they seemed to delight in bragging about their unparalleled success."[48] Catholics became increasingly visible in organizations such as the FBI, where J. Edgar Hoover had actively recruited agents who were "young, aggressive, and—not coincidentally—alumni of Catholic colleges, particularly Notre Dame. They were holy terrors." They fought gangsters and Communists alike. A tough Catholic priest was immortalized in the film "On the Waterfront" for his courageous battle against the corrupt (Irish, in this case) leaders of the International Longshoreman's Association. In the minds of many, Catholics seemed to specialize in occupations which valued obedience, discipline, and self-sacrifice. Englishman David Caute sarcastically asserted that "the American Catholic Church remained, at that time, under Irish domination: it produced not so much poets, scholars, scientists and artists as security officers, immigration officers, policemen, customs officers and prison wardens." From this point of view, the step up to the FBI would thus merely represent a logical progression for college men.[49]

One such recruit, G. Gordon Liddy, offered in his autobiography some insight into the nature of Catholic character formation during the 1930s and 1940s. "So the nuns," he wrote, "introduced me to authority. First God. And then: the flag. After morning prayers at school, we all pledged allegiance to the flag. This too was led by the nuns and required dignity and precision. We stood at rigid attention, facing the flags in lines straight enough to rival those of the massed SS in Leni Riefenstahl's *Triumph of the Will*."[50] Liddy described himself as a fearful youth with a sharp sense of his failure to fulfill the promise of a sterling genetic inheritance. He claimed that the church's emphasis on self-abnegation actually helped save him: it laid the foundation for the ultimate triumph of his will: "I knew what I had to do, and I dreaded it. To change myself from a puny, fearful boy to a strong, fearless man . . . but I knew from the priests the price would be terrible. God gave us a free will, but to strengthen that will to meet the temptations of life required denial, 'mortification,' suffering. Suffering. That was the key."[51] As an upper-middle-class youth, Liddy may have been more in touch with secular influences than most Catholics. He drew inspiration not only from Jesus suffering on the cross but from the once-crippled track star Glenn Cunningham, Franklin D. Roosevelt, and Adolf Hitler. The pagan streak which exhibited itself early in his life also makes dubious any claims for Liddy as a representative Catholic, but his language neatly captured one prominent strain in the Catholic ethos in the era of the Second World War and beyond. Liddy was a Fordham graduate; although his memoirs at times achieve the level of black comedy, he continued to believe in the triumph of the will (but not the Christian God).

The post-Watergate period witnessed the birth of a new confessional genre, as former agents of the CIA renounced their former allegiances in an effort to expose the excesses of the "Company." Two of the most notable works were by Notre Dame graduates, Philip Agee and Ralph McGehee. Agee began his narrative with a reminiscence of his senior year at Notre Dame and his recruitment there by the CIA. As a first-year law student at the University of Florida, he already missed the unique discipline of his alma mater: "No more bed checks or lights out at midnight. No more compulsory mass attendance and evening curfew. No more Religious Bulletin to make you feel guilty if you didn't attend a novena, benediction or rosary service." Where before he had chafed under the restrictions, life in the secular world seemed aimless by comparison. "It is the discipline and religion that makes Notre Dame men different," he thought at the time. It was a view bolstered by speeches given at Notre Dame by men like Air Force general Curtis Lemay and Adm. Arleigh Burke, Chief of Naval Operations, who proclaimed, at Agee's 1956 graduation ceremonies: "Notre Dame symbolizes many virtues. It blends the virtues of religion and patriotism—service to God, service to country. Notre Dame stands for faith—faith in self and faith in country. . . . Self discipline and determination and fighting spirit are an integral part of the curriculum."[52] In 1957 Agee joined the CIA.

Ralph McGehee was another Notre Dame man who, in 1983, offered a public confession in *Deadly Deceits: My Twenty-Five Years in the CIA*. But McGehee was no Catholic; he was a Baptist football star from Chicago who was convinced by two high school teammates to join them in South Bend. He played for Frank Leahy during the glory years, 1946–49, when the Fighting Irish lost not a single game; three times they were crowned national champions. McGehee's account of his early years suggests that the Americanism promoted at Notre Dame blended perfectly with his earlier training:

> I was raised to believe in the American dream—the Protestant work ethic, truth, justice, freedom. I had lived through World War Two with its clear black and white heroes and villains and the stirring messages of fighting for God, country, and democracy in the world. . . . I believed in the basic lessons of life that my legendary Notre Dame football coach, Frank Leahy, had drilled into us—work hard, do your best, and victory in the game and in the larger game of life will be yours. . . . My proudest, happiest, most patriotic moments came before the games as the starting teams lined up in the kick-off formation in the center of the stadium, surrounded by Notre Dame's loyal fans.[53]

Liddy, Agee, and McGehee all stressed the masculine component of their patriotic religiosity. Catholic anticommunism indeed exhibited a militant, highly aggressive aspect during the cold war years. Yet there was an another important strain which worked dialectically against this triumphalism. At first glance, it might appear to derive from the difference in Catholic gender roles. Numerous memoirs of Catholic girlhoods of the 1940s and 1950s offer a counterpoint to Liddy's remembrance. In *Home before Morning*, a nurse-veteran of the Vietnam War presented a flippant yet representative account of a devout pre–Vatican Two girlhood:

> Those were the days when I had no other desire than to grow up to be a martyr, although I'm sure that if I'd ever talked about it with my father, he would have discouraged me. Of course, at the time, there was no way to talk me out of the notion. While good Catholic boys usually fantasize about becoming major league baseball players . . . good Catholic girls usually harbor, at least once in their lives, a secret desire to become martyrs. If I couldn't make it to martyrdom, there was always sainthood, which was kind of like being on the second string of an athletic team . . .

but the martyrs were the real heroes. I wasn't sure exactly what had to be done to become one, but I knew it had something to do with being burned at the stake or pilloried. . . . My hero was Catherine of Siena. . . . [S]he finally ended up being killed for the faith, which was the Catholic girl's equivalent of growing up to be Babe Ruth.[54]

Yet the cultivation of martyrdom transcended gender distinctions in the 1940s and 1950s, although, as usual, suffering was linked generically with the feminine. Certainly the most striking aspect of Catholic anticommunism in that period was the dramatically elevated status of the Virgin Mary to an exalted position virtually equal to that of Christ. One of the most popular and influential American Catholic organizations founded in the postwar period was the Blue Army of Fatima, a group devoted to promoting the vision of the Blessed Mother claimed by three Portuguese children in 1917. The Blue Army was created by a layman, John Haffert, after he visited the sole surviving witness of the apparition in Portugal in 1946. After becoming a nun, the witness, Sister Lucia, only gradually disclosed the message given her by the Blessed Virgin. During the Spanish Civil War she reported that Mary,

in addition to a general appeal for prayer and reparation, had taken a political stand on world Communism and the Russian threat to Christianity. According to Sister Lucia, Mary in 1917 had asked for the consecration of Russia to her Immaculate Heart, and for Catholics to receive Communion on the first Saturday of five consecutive months. Fulfilling these requests would lead to the conversion of Russia and world peace, while ignoring them would result in war, hunger, and the persecution of the Church.

The Blue Army concentrated entirely on the anticommunist implications of Lucia's claims, and in so doing it established a typology of gentle Catholic suffering and humility in the face of barbaric Soviet power. As Haffert wrote: "The first recorded Bolshevik terrorism in Russia directed by Lenin took place at noon, May 13, 1917 . . . THE VERY HOUR OF THE FIRST APPARITION OF FATIMA. It was an attack on a Moscow Church where Maria Alexandrovna was teaching Catechism. The Sacrament was desecrated and several children were trampled beneath the hooves of Bolshevisti horses."[55]

Catholic anticommunism can never be fully understood without taking into account the meaning of this antitriumphalist language. American Catholicism was supposed to have reached unprecedented heights of power and influence by the late 1940s. In 1949 Paul Beecher Blanshard, the liberal Protestant, published his *American Freedom and Catholic Power*, which quickly sold over one hundred thousand hardcover copies, including many bought by leading secular academics and intellectuals. As mentioned in Chapter 3, Blanshard was essentially a neonativist, and he argued (in a manner not so unlike the nineteenth-century divine who inspired his middle name) that the church hierarchy was bent upon imposing its authoritarian model on American society. This was not an altogether dishonest book; American clerics had provided Blanshard with ample evidence to bolster his claims. But he mistook a discourse of cranky defensiveness and insecurity for an aggressive design of conquest. His argument was also crippled by a large contradiction. In his attack on the cult of Fatima and other miraculous apparitions, Blanshard argued that the hierarchy exploited such events to maintain their control over the masses of laity. Yet the "cultural schizophrenia" which resulted from Catholics' being denied their rightful role within a rationalized, scientific society was precisely the force which *prevented* Catholics from reshaping America in the historical image of their church: mysticism, now more than ever, was tantamount to defeatism. As late as the 1950s a significant proportion of American Catholics continued to be moved by the same impulse and circumstance which, according to historian Thomas Kselman, prompted the nineteenth-century renewal of Marian piety in France: "[T]he revived popularity of these ideals can be seen as the result of a dialectical process in which the values denied by the secular establishment are affirmed by religion."[56]

Catholics concerned not only with communism and their place in American life but also their own immortal souls looked to Mary for consolation and hope. On November 5, 1945, twenty-five thousand people gathered at a vacant lot in the Bronx where a nine-year-old boy and his friends had "built a crude shrine on the spot where he saw an apparition of the Virgin Mary last Monday." The boy, Joseph Vitolo, Jr., insisted that the vision was unlike that featured in the popular motion picture he had recently seen, "The Song of Bernadette" (for which Jennifer Jones won an Academy Award for her portrayal of the poor French girl who was visited by the Blessed Virgin at Lourdes). Following the failure of a well to appear on the spot of the visitation—as the Blessed Mother had promised Joseph—interest in the event began to wane, but not before Julia Porcelli of the *Catholic Worker* wrote: "One of the wonderful things about the whole story is that thousands left their homes, their movies, their parties, to stand for hours in all kinds of weather because a little boy claimed to see the Blessed Mother. People can make sacrifices if they are interested."[57]

A more dramatic spectacle occurred on a late summer morning in 1950, when "approximately 100,000 Catholic pilgrims gathered at the farm of Fred and Mary Ann Van Hoof in Necedah, Wisconsin. They had come hoping to witness a miracle that would confirm reports that Mary, the mother of Jesus, had on several occasions during the past few months appeared to Mrs. Van Hoof and given her messages warning of dangers threatening America and the Catholic Church."[58] Historians Thomas A. Kselman and Steven Avella's study of "Marian Piety and the Cold War in the United States" showed that Marian devotion in America was rooted in nineteenth-century European Catholicism, but it also uncovered dissimilarities which were clearly a product of the American environment. Mrs. Van Hoof was a Spiritualist as well as a Catholic; in her address to the multitudes she related this message from Mary: "Those of not the Catholic faith, those that's just Christians, remember your Lord in your way." This hope may well have been prompted by tensions between Catholics and Protestants in Necedah, which had been growing since the opening of a dam on the nearby Wisconsin River led to the influx of many Catholics in need of work. Since the apparitions were heavily promoted by a group of local Catholic businessmen, the same kind of internal anxieties which helped explain Father Coughlin's appeal may have been at work here as well. Kselman and Avella could not precisely locate the cultural source of the events at Necedah, in part because of a lack of prior studies of the American-Catholic mentalité, but also because the model of peasant Catholicism which served Kselman well in his study of nineteenth-century France was inapplicable to the Wisconsin setting. In fact, the local hierarchy discouraged devotion to Our Lady of Necedah while warmly embracing the touring statue of Our Lady of Fatima when it was brought to the city of LaCrosse in 1950, as if in recognition of the volatility of local anxieties. For the Necedah episode featured a potentially explosive complex of fears over Soviet communism as well as personal well-being.[59]

Several of the businessmen sponsoring the Necedah proceedings were residents of nearby Appleton, the hometown of Sen. Joseph R. McCarthy. Kselman and Avella noted that "no historian has yet addressed the supernatural dimension of Catholic anti-communism," and while their critique included the standard work on McCarthy and American Catholicism—Donald F. Crosby's *God, Church, and Flag*— this latter work did provide evidence of the special quality of the distinctly Catholic support for the senator. Although Crosby claimed that Catholics were almost as divided over McCarthyism as other Americans, he also showed how—in a striking echo of the Coughlin years—pro-McCarthy Catholics viewed their hero as "a kind of crucified Christ figure" once he came under sharp attack in 1954. In *A Conspiracy So Immense*, McCarthy biographer David M. Oshinsky noted that, as McCarthy grew closer to censure by the Senate, the language of his supporters in letters to his chief antagonist, Sen. Ralph Flanders, became "more abusive, more religious, more conspiratorial in tone ('You have the Lord against you' . . . 'I put horns and tail on you and you look like Satan')." A correspondent to the *Brooklyn Tablet* wrote, of McCarthy's tribulations (in a tone of weary resignation, as though Catholics had been through it all before): "[I]t is the same story today as it was during the time of the Prophet from Galilee."[60]

If the cold war signaled the rise of Catholic power, what accounts for the persistence of this language of sorrow and lamentation? Was it merely an anachronistic habit, or did it indicate a continuing ambivalence about the role of Catholics in American life? The character of McCarthy himself provides ample material for speculation on these questions. In his book, the most well rounded study of the senator to date, David Oshinsky suggested that McCarthy was essentially a nihilistic wildman who only belatedly came to believe in the veracity of his own claims about Communist subversion of the American government. McCarthy's Catholicism was an integral yet totally unself-conscious aspect of his makeup. Oshinsky quoted a witness to a McCarthy escapade from his early senatorial career, when his status as a favorite of the real estate lobby landed him a speaking engagement in Columbus, Ohio:

> It was disgusting to see this great public servant down on his hands and knees, reeking of whiskey, and shouting, "Come on babies, Papa needs a new pair of shoes." He did stop long enough between rolls to look over the gals his aides brought to him: on some, he turned thumbs down, but if one suited his fancy, he'd say, "That's the baby, I'll take care of her just as soon as I break these guys." . . . Be that as it may, Mr. McCarthy was up bright and early on Sunday morning, looking none the worse for wear and tear, and inquiring about the best route to the nearest Catholic church.[61]

By the time McCarthy came to believe in himself, it was too late for him to begin acting in a fashion more becoming of a United States senator ("You don't understand," he told columnist Jack Anderson at the conclusion of a 1953 congressional hearing in which he had accused the Voice of America and the International Information Agency of Communist subversion. "This is the real thing, the *real thing*.") He could never harness what commentator Eric Sevareid called his "manic brilliance." McCarthy was Irish; it is too often forgotten that modern Irish-Catholic culture was the product of a kind of holocaust in which starvation and violent uprooting produced a benumbed people who frequently discarded whatever faith they ever had in the "system."[62]

McCarthy resignedly anticipated his own downfall, and in 1956 he told Tom Dooley that he was in store for the same fate. They met that year shortly after Dooley's return from Vietnam. McCarthy told his compatriot that they were both "a flash in the pan," who, after enjoying "pretty brilliance for a while . . . are heard from no more." The resignation of the Irish was linked to their brooding relationship with martyrdom and the Cross. In 1954 a New York–based group with ties to the old country, the United Irish Counties, passed a resolution "wholeheartedly supporting Joseph McCarthy at a time when 'his opponents were doing everything possible to crucify him.'" In popular culture the Irish were also often typecast as doomed figures. As Daniel Patrick Moynihan wrote, in *Beyond the Melting Pot*, Hollywood often depicted the "tough American, up from the streets," as an Irishman (often played by James Cagney): "fists cocked, chin out, back straight, bouncing along on his heels. But also doomed: at the end of the movie he was usually dead."[63]

The Irish were on the leading edge of American Catholicism's increasing visibility and apparent power; they controlled the hierarchy and the diocesan media. But the conflict between Catholic and American values transcended ethnicity: when the Irish evaluated the sources of their displeasure, religion was always at the heart of the issue. And if Catholicism appeared increasingly "Americanized" in the late 1940s, perhaps those Catholic mores least susceptible to assimilation likewise grew more prominent, as surviving signs of contradiction.

This was particularly true of sexuality. Many of the most volatile conflicts between Catholics and others during the 1940s and 1950s concerned some aspect of sexuality, from birth control to salacious films. While the American church had—since at least the turn of the century—been viewed as extremely conservative, if not prudish, regarding sexuality, the rhetoric grew more intense after 1940. In that year a priest in Springfield, Massachusetts charged that birth control crusader Margaret Sanger was "coming to interfere with the laws of our Commonwealth. She is coming to enlist the aid of dog-loving women in

changing the fundamental laws of our state." The announced appearance of
Sanger in nearby Holyoke that fall provoked an outbreak of sharp conflicts
between the Catholic and Protestant communities.[64]

While conflicts over standards of morality often reflected broader tensions
within communities, sex-related issues became increasingly visible *within* the
church during the 1940s. The end of the depression also meant the end of the
many informal dispensations granted impoverished Catholics barely able to
feed their existing children, let alone new ones. The authority of the celibate
clergy over sexuality now became an issue of renewed concern, just as more
and more Catholics were finally achieving that middle-class status which
usually required some degree of control over fertility. Until the very end of the
1950s, the laity completely refrained from public criticism of the church's
policies toward sexuality and birth control (which helps explain the fury of that
eventual assault); all the *Integrity* group could do by way of heroism was to
exceed the church's already stringent demands. Priests wrote marriage manuals
and received clarification of their teachings not from married couples but from
the clerical authorities at the *Ecclesiastical Review*, who routinely condemned
"bathing beauty contests," the use of hot baths with contraceptive intent, and
gum chewing at Mass, all in surgically scholastic language.

But if discourse on sexuality was denied Catholics, this only intensified the
obscure relationship between sexuality and worldview. The graphic, even sensual Catholic anticommunist rhetoric of the postwar years suggests that many
Catholics may have unconsciously blended their own sexual feelings—which
they were discouraged from accepting as legitimate—not only with the crucified Christ and the long-suffering Blessed Mother but with the image of
Communist violence as well. Cardinal Spellman, the most vociferous anticommunist among the hierarchy, was also the most vigorous champion of
efforts to purge any expressions of sexuality from popular culture. His biographer asserted that Spellman "was a prim and prissy man who was uncomfortable with the subject of sex." Shortly before condemning the immorality of a
Greta Garbo film, Spellman had linked sexual suffering with the war in Europe.
"'All of us,' he said, 'are victims of war, the war of the flesh.'"[65]

A strong undercurrent of sexual tension ran throughout Tom Dooley's *Deliver Us from Evil*, particularly evident in the passages concerning torture.
Dooley had written to his mother: "They took this old priest and hung him
from a beam overhead in the mission by his feet. Then they beat him with short
bamboo rods, with the emphasis on his genitals. Into his head they stuck

thorns (so he could be like the Christ of whom he spoke)." Dooley wrote of a priest whom the Communists had left "a mass of blackened flesh from the shoulders to the knees. The belly was hard and distended and the scrotum swollen to the size of a football." The assault on a priest's sexual organs seemed the ultimate violation of his sanctity and served to emphasize the lascivious character of the Communists. Dooley often repeated the charge (discredited by most observers) that Ho Chi Minh had launched his regime in Vietnam by "disembowelling" thousands of women.[66] Such language helped solidify American and Catholic support for Ngo Dinh Diem, who was a Benedictine oblate and, like Dooley, a single and presumably chaste male. Dooley acknowledged to his mother that the authoritarian, uncompromising Diem might be "a bit too pure" to succeed as an Asian strongman. Diem was but the latest in an uninterrupted series of celibate Catholic heroes. The sponsor of Diem's 1953 retreat to Maryknoll seminaries in New Jersey and New York was Francis Cardinal Spellman.[67] Msgr. Fulton J. Sheen had become a national celebrity as a result of his charismatic television performances. One of the most celebrated books of the late 1940s was Thomas Merton's *The Seven Storey Mountain*, in which a former Ivy League rake detailed his rejection of the things of the flesh in favor of a Trappist monastery in Kentucky. Dorothy Day described her victory over worldliness in *The Long Loneliness* (1952). Even Joseph McCarthy remained a single man until the fall of 1953.

An important element of Catholic chastity was the intense devotion to the Virgin Mary in the 1940s and 1950s, across all lines of class and education. More than half of the students at Notre Dame reported making weekly visits to the Grotto of Our Lady during this period (one quarter prayed daily at the shrine). In *Deliver Us from Evil*, Dooley wrote that Notre Dame was his "favorite Lady." He would also later report his love of nuns, "their goodness, the sweetness of their soap and starch, the softness of their reprimands."[68] But there was more to cold war Mariolatry than chivalric romanticism or parochial school nostalgia. The exaltation of Mary was generally linked with women's special, and superior, vocation to suffering and self-martyrdom: in her virginity she invited both men and women to mortify their own sexuality in emulating herself and her Son. This is why antitriumphalism—with all its emphasis on worldly failure and suffering—carried such a powerful erotic charge. As Thomas Kselman wrote of Mrs. Van Hoof of Necedah: "Like many of the most prominent visionaries of the nineteenth and twentieth centuries, she was poor, humble, uneducated, and female. It was precisely these traits that were attractive to Mary, according to the literature on Bernadette of Lourdes and Melanie of La Sallette. One priest in attendance on August 15 claimed that Mrs. Van Hoof's humility alone was sufficient proof of the apparitions."[69] The most notorious Catholic separatist of the late 1940s, Father Leonard Feeney, convinced a group of students at Harvard and Boston College that all those who lived outside the church were condemned to eternal damnation. He has thus been viewed as an arrogant triumphalist. But in 1954 the Newark diocesan paper warned that a group of the now-excommunicated Feeney's disciples were selling Catholic literature in the North Jersey area. Members of the group, who dressed in black clerical garb, called themselves "Slaves of the Immaculate Heart of Mary."[70]

By the early 1950s the notion of the church as the Mystical Body of Christ had come to serve the same sensually consoling role as Dorothy Day had envisioned in the late 1930s. This symbol was absolutely crucial, for it clearly distinguished the culturewide emphasis on self-abnegation from a merely imitative Catholic puritanism. The Mystical Body linked the vocation to suffering with a warming dissolution of the self; it became, more than ever, the central metaphor of Catholic estrangement within American culture. When Cardinal Stritch of Chicago warned Catholics in 1954 to avoid "religious unity assemblies or conferences with other faiths," he reminded the faithful that the church "is now as she always has been, the one and only Spouse of Christ, the one and only Mystical Body of Christ." *Deliver Us from Evil* was welcomed into American Catholic discourse as a work which wedded a concrete experience of suffering to fidelity to the Mystical Body. In the *Ecclesiastical Review* Father James A. Murphy wrote that the book offered an "eyewitness account of the terrible struggle raging between communism and Christianity. In military and medical jargon the author paints the portrait of Christ crucified in Indo-China. Before the readers [sic] eyes the members of Christ's Mystical Body are called up, here in huddled masses, there in wretched loneliness. Inhuman outrages: a priest crowned with thorns in imitation of Christ, but the thorns were nails hammered into his head." A nun writing in the Carmelite journal *Spiritual Life* similarly viewed Dooley's work as a model realization of practical theology: "The reading of a book like Doctor Dooley's *Deliver Us from Evil* shocks us into the reality of the application of the doctrine of the Mystical Body as we learn of the Christlike ministrations of American sailors to the persecuted Vietnamese."[71]

Dooley's assistant Teresa Gallagher recalled in 1982 that he frequently spoke to her of "the Mystical Body of Christ, all the members of His church, living and dead, who are able to help each other with their prayers." His own early writings displayed only an intuitive grasp of this basic tenet of both popular and scholarly Catholic identity. In *Deliver Us from Evil* Dooley's religious rhetoric was crudely designed to satisfy his various audiences; never a student of Catholicism to begin with, he had grown even more out of touch during his overseas tour of duty. The disparity between his public and private expression reveal the depth of his uncertainty, his inauthenticity. He assumed his mother wanted to hear about "the strong Catholic Church, and the true meaning of the Church Militant" in Vietnam. Dooley did genuinely believe that he was performing an important mission for the church by educating American servicemen: "When a sailor understands what he is working for, and why the people are as they are, the refugee instead of being a dirty foul smelling, sickly person dirtying his deck, becomes a true refugee, a true escapee from the terrors of red rule. When I tell the boys of the priest who was hung by his feet from an overhead, and beaten with short bamboo rods (and then brought by another priest to me) they understand what is meant by the Church Militant."[72]

He thus identified triumph with suffering in the same contradictory fashion as so many of his fellow Catholics back home. There was an effortless quality to it all; he could easily have become an anticommunist hack without ever having to return to Southeast Asia. But something was happening to Dooley, something which belied the crude ignorance of Asia and Asians he could still display, as when he wrote to his mother: "[T]hese Vietnamese are a grateful people, in spite of being Oriental."[73] The origins of this turning are difficult to locate precisely, but according to his brother Malcolm, Dooley "had become completely entranced by everything Oriental" even before he arrived in Vietnam. When Malcolm appeared in Yokosuka in May 1954, Tom drove him to the shrine of the Buddha at Kamakura: "I marvelled at Tom's complete preoccupation with the magnificence of the huge statue and the pagan beauty of the shrine. Here we were, both young Catholics, and both feeling a sense of awe in the presence of this memorial." Tom then wanted to get a drink, and over sake and a dinner of eel, rice, and shrimp Malcolm suddenly "realized how deeply preoccupied Tom was with the Oriental mind, customs and religion. By talking privately with the owner when Tom was out of the room, I learned that he came here often, asked many questions, and spoke better Japanese after each visit."[74]

When Dooley wrote to his mother from Vietnam in request of books about Southeast Asia, he emphasized the strategic importance of the region, its "important role in the security of the rest of the world." But Mrs. Dooley was sufficiently alarmed to send along a book on Catholic philosophy, prompting her son to write in reassurance: "I can see you puzzled and concerned for fear I might become an apostate and join the local order of Buddhist bonzes. Have no fear." But if Dooley truly was a product—however privileged—of the Catholic ghetto, many of his phrases and gestures indicated an almost gleeful awareness that his world was being turned upside down. "If you notice," he wrote to his mother in a note attached to a holy card obtained from a Vietnamese priest, "the Blessed Virgin is depicted as being an oriental, with the typical Vietnamese national dress and shoes. . . . [I]t is quite lovely."[75]

6

A Catholic Errand in the Wilderness

Tom Dooley in Laos and America, 1956–1961

Within the first few months of 1956, Tom Dooley signed contracts with *Reader's Digest* and the publishing firm of Farrar, Straus and Cudahy; was reassigned to the Navy Surgeon General's Office in Washington; spoke before a number of high-level military agencies including the Joint Chiefs of Staff and two psychological warfare groups; lectured in dozens of cities on behalf of his corporate benefactor, Charles Pfizer and Company; and spoke movingly at an assemblage of the American Friends of Vietnam, a prestigious pro-Diem lobby whose membership included Sen. John F. Kennedy, Angier Biddle Duke, and Arthur Schlesinger, Jr.[1]

An Irish-Catholic woman employed by the Surgeon General's office recalled that "he was always in a hurry, and the consensus in the Navy Department was that if Dooley kept up this pace he was headed for a breakdown, either mental or physical." She also remembered: "[H]e was the snappiest, best looking naval officer I had seen in a long time, and he was blessed with a keen sense of humor and all the charm of his Irish ancestry." Navy publicists "could not get enough of him" because "he was in great demand and always made good copy." Dooley seemed well on his way toward his avowed ultimate goal, the Surgeon General-ship of the Navy. Thus it was no small shock when one evening in February 1956 he told his mother: "'I'm resigning from the Navy, and I'm going to Laos.' It was as simple as that."[2]

Dooley's abrupt resignation from the Navy—effective March 28, 1956—was linked to his sexuality. He was apparently charged with involvement with a group of homosexual officers stationed at Yokosuka in 1954 and 1955. People who knew him as an adolescent report that he began having sexual relations with men, at the latest, while a student at St. Louis University High School. Amidst the insular, conformist atmosphere at Notre Dame, he was widely perceived as "queer," although that term did not necessarily indicate active homosexuality. Homosexuality was obviously not considered an appropriate topic for conversation among Catholics; in clerical journals it was gingerly treated as a perversion of natural law; what Dorothy Day termed the "most loathsome" of sins. One of Dooley's St. Louis classmates recalled that his own Irish-Catholic mother, an educator, believed that homosexuality was something which "only happened in hell."

In 1959 the FBI began an inquiry into the circumstances surrounding Dooley's resignation from the Navy. An FBI memorandum of December 11, 1959, reported that the Office of Naval Intelligence "had conducted an investigation of Dooley while Dooley was in the Navy and that Dooley had been permitted to resign from the Navy for the good of the service in order to avoid a general court-martial. . . . Dooley had been interviewed concerning allegations of homosexuality at which time he admitted to ONI a long history of that trait."[3]

In a March 9, 1960, memorandum concerning an invitation to J. Edgar Hoover to appear at an interfaith gathering honoring Dooley and others, a bureau agent explained that "Dooley was discharged from the Navy because of homosexuality" and concluded that "certainly the Director would not desire to appear on a program with Dooley." Hoover readily concurred.[4]

The Navy had provided Dooley with an alternative to the sometimes stifling influence of his family and his Catholic education. His first enlistment coincided with a period of profound change in America's homosexual subculture. In *Sexual Politics, Sexual Communities*, historian John D'Emilio argued: "[O]ne can scarcely overestimate the significance of the 1940s in restructuring the social expression of same-sex eroticism. The war years allowed the almost imperceptible changes of several generations, during which a gay male and lesbian identity had slowly emerged, to coalesce into a qualitatively different form. A sexual and emotional life that gay men and women previously experienced mainly in individual terms suddenly became, for the war generation, a widely shared collective phenomenon."[5]

Dooley was too well known and too closely tied to his family to simply disappear into the "urban gay subculture" which emerged after the war. He had also undergone what was later described as a conversion experience in Vietnam. Although the dramatic quality of the experience was greatly exaggerated both by Dooley and his supporters, he had undoubtedly left Southeast Asia with fervent convictions as to the personal and political uses of medicine in the developing world. With the publication of a second book, *The Edge of Tomorrow* (1958), Dooley expanded his vocation as an anticommunist mystic. In Vietnam, he wrote, "We had witnessed the power of medical aid to reach the hearts and souls of a nation. . . . To me that experience was like the white light of revelation. It made me proud to be a doctor. Proud to be an American doctor who had been privileged to witness the enormous possibilities of medical aid in all its Christlike power and simplicity."[6]

At a Washington dinner party in February 1956, Dooley described his dream of an independent medical mission to the Laotian and Cambodian ambassadors to the United States. In distinctly unmystical terms he explained that his team would comprise "plain Americans working among the plain people of the country, wherever we were needed, in paddy fields and villages, in jungles and mountains." In *The Edge of Tomorrow* Dooley reported that the Laotian ambassador, while interested, wanted to know what the young American doctor expected to gain from such a venture. Dooley's response set the tone for the second stage of his international career: "Suddenly, I remembered something that big, hardboiled Boatswain's Mate Norman Baker had once said in answer to a somewhat similar question. Gambling on my ability to translate Baker's homespun American into French, I explained how Baker had groped for words to explain our motives, and then blurted out: 'Aw, hell, sir, we just want to do what we can for people who ain't got it so good!'"[7]

According to Dooley, the Laotian ambassador accepted his proposal on the spot. The prospectus for "Operation Laos" confirmed Dooley's genius for linking personal need with the current state of the American mood. President Eisenhower had been promoting the renewed importance of voluntarism, of those "person-to-person" programs through which Americans could demonstrate their essential good will. In Laos there would be no Catholics to save from communism; just Buddhists and the members of various animistic sects. Dooley thus invoked his pure, transcendent, and eminently *pragmatic* Americanism: "We want to take positive steps for America, not just denying what the Communists say about us, but getting there and doing something about it. We shall try to translate the democratic ideals we DO possess into Asian realities they CAN possess. Our influence in this shall be medicine."[8] Dooley then borrowed in paraphrase the slogan of Father James Keller's Christophers, an influential Catholic fraternity which, like so many other religious institutions from this period, stressed positive thinking and cheerful patriotism: "Rather than curse the darkness, perhaps we can light a few candles."

Dooley received the noncommittal approval of the State Department and, to achieve legal status, agreed to operate under the aegis of the International Rescue Committee, a group dedicated to aiding refugees from totalitarianism (the IRC, which promoted a strongly anticommunist line during the cold war, had aided considerably in the resettlement of North Vietnamese refugees during the Passage to Freedom). He received additional support from CARE and many of the pharmaceutical companies that had supplied the Navy in Vietnam. Three of the Navy corpsmen (none with medical backgrounds) he had worked with in Vietnam agreed to accompany him to Laos. During the spring and early summer of 1956 Dooley went about raising funds for his mission from private and corporate sponsors. In this role he was always remarkably successful: "Tom was one helluva fund raiser," according to a former executive director of CARE. "He'd walk in the room and you'd have to hide the gold in your teeth." There was a somewhat comical, class-bound innocence in Dooley's method: he acquired his outdoor equipment not through military surplus but from Abercrombie and Fitch, a very fashionable New York retailer (where, after explaining his cause, the bill was "slashed to a fraction of the original amount").[9]

Dooley wanted to establish a village hospital as close to the Chinese border as possible, preferably in the province of Nam Tha, which was adjacent not only to China but to the provinces of Phong Saly and Sam-Neua, strongholds of the procommunist Pathet Lao insurgents. But after failing to win the approval of United States ambassador Graham Parsons, he settled on a clinic at Vang Vieng, some 120 miles north of Vientiane, the capital of Laos. The project gave Dooley ample opportunity to exercise his virtually limitless passion for healing, while fulfilling an equally urgent need to promote his own vision of America to a "primitive" and vulnerable people: a vision which rejected the heavy-handedness of earlier political and missionary enterprises. "We will treat the people," he wrote, "learning the characteristics of their honest and gentle Buddhist life. We have no intention of trying to foist our way of life on them, nor convert them. The only aim is 50% medicine and 50% contact with Americans who want simply to help." Dooley was highly conscious of the mediative role he might play between two very different cultures, seeing himself uniquely qualified for the mission: "Living in a village with them, being completely saturated with their life, their religion, their aches and pains . . . yet being an Irish American at heart and in my reasoning, I am thrust in a peculiar position. I have to explain some of the churlish world to my Asians, and when I return I am going to try to explain something of Nam Tha to America."[10]

Although he claimed to transcend politics, Dooley's mission was too important to be overlooked by the United States government. Secretary of State John Foster Dulles, after learning that Dooley was to be involved in the production of a motion picture account of his Vietnam experience, advised that the "Department desires insure most favorable results from U.S. point of view are obtained from Dooley medical mission to Laos and motion picture production Viet Nam." In 1957 a State Department official who had monitored some of Dooley's taped broadcasts over KMOX radio, St. Louis, wrote that Dooley's jungle talks "have a calculated literary style" which could easily be translated into books which would "effectively dramatize the willingness of Americans to meet Asians on their own terms with no motive except that of selfless service."[11] The CIA was more immediately concerned with Dooley's project. "Operation Laos" was explicitly modeled after "Operation Brotherhood," a CIA brainchild through which pro-American Filipinos led by Oscar Arrellano used medicine to win the loyalty of Vietnamese refugees. Dooley wrote in September 1956 that "Arrellano thinks my plan is great. . . . [H]e should, I plagiarized it from Operation Brotherhood." The shadow of Edward Lansdale continued to darken Dooley's career. Arrellano was one of the many Filipinos Lansdale recruited to front his operations in Vietnam. The CIA was of course highly active in both overt and covert operations in Laos during this period as well; a great many embassy and United States Information Agency personnel were obviously CIA functionaries. Dooley most likely served in a more informal role, similar to that of journalists and others on the scene, reporting "little bits of information" to intelligence personnel.[12]

Yet almost from the start, Dooley took a less rigid view of the political situation in Laos than did his government. In a November 1956 communication Assistant Secretary of State Walter Robertson sternly warned Dooley not to view the Pathet Lao as "misunderstood," but to remember that they were "merely an appendage of the Viet-Minh." Dooley was much more hostile to the remote Chinese Communists than to the Laotian left and its leader, Prince Souvanovong, with whom he became friendly. He was even closer to the neutralist prince Souvanna Phouma, who sought to include the Pathet Lao within a coalition government. Dooley was an internationalist with an affinity for such vigorous, Democratic champions of well-spent foreign aid as Sen. John F. Kennedy. But the Laotians represented something to Dooley which transcended politics. He was able to win from them the kind of unqualified affection previously missing from his life, and to satisfy his romantic nature in a manner—as he tenuously came to understand—American experience could, given the circumstances, never equal. He frequently visited Vientiane, where he kept a small cottage behind the Continental Hotel. Walking in that city he would often happen upon a "Laotian 'love court' going on. . . . I had often heard of this unique Lao entertainment which chants of the art of courtship. It is sheer poetry, improvised on the spot. The boy extols the beauty, grace, virtue of the courted maiden; the girl sings of the boy's nobility, charm, bravery. The audience listens raptly, applauding an inspired passage with an enthusiasm that Americans reserve for touchdowns or home runs."[13]

Dooley enjoyed a shamanistic power over his patients, but it was exercised less in the service of American imperialism than in the name of his own highly personal mission. Each night he showed the Laotians a Walt Disney film projected against a sheet stretched between village trees. While they watched the movie, he watched them:

> My boys love to sit with me on the porch and look into the faces of the hundreds of kids who sit on their haunches as close to the screen as they can get. The light reflected in their eyes is wonderful. There is fascination and charm, poignancy and yes, sadness too. You can see it in their eyes as they watch the world of wonder that our movies show them. We have decided against explaining some of the 16 millimeter stories to them, those that don't have a Laotian soundtrack. We do not translate but let the children build their own little delusional castles. And how they must dream, after they see the fantasy of love and lollipops, the sugarcane world of Disneyland.[14]

For all his eccentricity Dooley continued to enjoy the enthusiastic support of American corporations and such groups as the Junior Chamber of Commerce, which named him one of the ten "Outstanding Men" for 1956. Dooley was finally achieving the status of "regular guy" which had eluded him at home. He promoted this image by identifying with the small-time goodness and humility embodied in the Jaycees and by regularly criticizing the "brighter kinds of people," who claimed that "this America of ours is going to pot"; that it had become "a nation of bribes and payola." A part of Dooley longed for approval among solid, "normal" Americans, and through his books and lectures he succeeded in this to an extravagant degree. Upon the 1958 publication of *The Edge of Tomorrow*, William Hogan of the *San Francisco Chronicle* wrote: "The tall, good-looking, idealistic Tom Dooley emerges as a kind of 'Mister Roberts' of classic tradition. He is a good guy with a good cause—and the privately financed cause is working." Dooley was such a booster of common-sense, bottom-line Americanism that he even charged each of his Laotian patients for services rendered: they paid in chickens, coconuts, or with their own labor.[15]

Dooley's accomplishment was the more remarkable for the underlying turmoil which increased throughout his first mission in Laos. When the three former Navy corpsmen decided to return home in late 1956, he recruited three Notre Dame undergraduates to replace them. Dooley had gone to extremes to downplay his Catholicism in the early Laotian period (although one of the original corpsmen, speaking in 1982 on behalf of efforts to have Dooley canonized, claimed—in sharp contrast to the doctor's hard-earned reputation for precocious ecumenism—that "he was totally committed to the Catholic Church, spoke of it more often than any priest I ever met and even tried to convert me on a weekly basis").[16] The selection of the Catholic students reflected his growing confidence: he no longer feared that the Laotians (and even some skeptical Americans) might view him as a Jesuit in disguise. But shortly before the men left for Laos, their parents began receiving phone calls from individuals who claimed that Dooley was a homosexual. One of the students was subsequently dissuaded by his parents from going, while the other two joined Dooley, having been convinced that the phone calls were part of a Communist plot to stop his mission. On February 14, 1957, Dooley wrote a highly emotional letter to his family from Vientiane in which he depicted himself as a victim and martyr of Communist intrigue.

He now sought refuge in both the church and in Catholic sources of consolation. He reported that Sen. Joseph McCarthy (toward whose politics "I have no great point of view") "called me in for several sessions while in D.C. and warned me of such an attack that may sometime come." McCarthy had suggested that Dooley, like himself, would be used, then unceremoniously discarded by an unnamed power elite. To Dooley, the motives behind the attacks were "obvious. To stop my mission. For me to collapse because of no new men." In response to fears that the rumor might spread to Notre Dame, Dooley advised a friend there to "skip it. Don't talk of it. I am not in the least concerned about it at Notre Dame. Neither is Our Lady in the Grotto."[17]

Dooley had muted his Catholicism in order to promote the transcendent Americanism of his vocation. He had been unable to face up to his sexuality at all. Now the two were linked as sources of his alienation: the latter more secretive and obscure, of course, but together they formed a volatile component of his personality which could remain submerged only at great personal cost. Yet he also seemed to sense how much he meant to American Catholics, how important his saintliness was to a community faced with the day-to-day compromises required by a money-driven culture. Dooley's evasions protected a myth whose power revealed much about the underlying travail of postwar Catholic culture.

Celebrity Sainthood

By 1958 Tom Dooley was in full command of his seemingly magical powers. After returning home the previous autumn, he had established MEDICO ("medical international co-operation"). MEDICO was designed to enshrine Dooley's vision on a global scale, sending teams of physicians and volunteers to developing nations lacking in medical care. Following a February 1958 press conference launching MEDICO, Dooley went on a whirlwind lecture tour (188 speeches in seventy-nine days over a five-month period) in which he detailed his success at winning hearts and minds in Laos and emphasized the urgency of his growing "person-to-person, heart-to-heart program." In April the *Edge of Tomorrow* was published to enthusiastic popular acclaim; it quickly became a best-seller. Harry Hansen wrote in the *Chicago Tribune*: "His book reflects a radiant personality that must have influenced the villagers to accept him as their big brother." In September the *New York Times* magazine published his brief essay, "Foreign Aid—The Human Touch," in which Dooley concisely summarized his small-is-beautiful ideology. That same month saw the publication of *The Ugly American*, a book coauthored by Dooley's old friend, Bill Lederer, and Eugene Burdick.[18]

The Ugly American did not explicitly treat Dooley and his work, but its enormous popularity (seventy-eight weeks on the *New York Times* best-seller list, over 3 million copies ultimately sold) marked a turning point in his career. The book was a "slashing" indictment of indolent American Foreign Service personnel who partied behind the embassy gates of a Southeast Asian nation ("Sarkhan") while Russian agents won peasant loyalties by pretending to actually care about them. The "ugly American," a compassionate engineer who works right alongside the vulnerable "natives," was actually one of several heroes in the book. Another protagonist was that old master of black magic, Edward Lansdale (barely disguised this time as "Colonel Hillandale"). But the first exemplary American introduced by the authors was an Irish-American priest, John X. Finian, S.J. Burdick and Lederer located him in Burma, but the character was largely inspired by Lederer's idealized vision of Dooley's work in Laos. Finian, like Dooley, is an ardent anticommunist who—virtually alone among the American community—wins the natives' love and loyalty by learning their language and encouraging their dreams. He allows one of *them* to explain to *him* that "the thing we want is a country where any man can worship any god he wishes; where he can live the way his heart says." This same native had told the priest: "I think it would not be possible to be a good Catholic and a good Communist. Somehow, in some way that I cannot tell you clearly, they are not things that can be mixed."[19]

Since Finian works for the Jesuits, he is less independent than was the real-life Dooley. Lederer's portrait of Finian was closer to the by now familiar Catholic anticommunist archetype than to Dooley's more complex stance, but it helps account for the nature of his appeal at the end of a decade of cold war. Far from the intriguing, authoritarian figure of the stereotyped Jesuit, Finian resembles the ideal but all too rare take-charge American executive. He is "a practical, tough-minded, and thoughtful man." Realizing that the Communists had "duplicated the ritual, faith, dedication, zeal, and enthusiasm of the Church," he resolves to fight them on their own level through black "psywar" (by starting a newspaper called *The Communist Farmer* which printed articles by Marx attacking the stupidity of the peasants along with Stalin's rationalization for the slaughter of the kulaks). "When Americans do what is right and necessary," the priest concludes, "they are also doing what is effective."[20]

Partly in response to Paul Blanshard's earlier attacks, a number of prominent American Catholic intellectuals of the 1950s were espousing a similarly aggressive line regarding the new character of the American church. The brilliant Jesuit Walter Ong could write in 1957 of a cheerful Catholic "apostolate" to the business world. Ong argued that the "religious roots" of American capitalist optimism (best exemplified for him by Dooley's Protestant sponsors, Mr. and Mrs. De Witt Wallace of *Reader's Digest*, the "missioner of cheery do-goodism") were shared by Catholics. "The plain fact," he wrote, "is that, paradoxically, the Church which must preach Christ crucified has found this optimism one of her ready points of entry into the American sensibility." In fact, the Catholics' "less somber theology" and their view of human nature as less than totally depraved might, Ong hinted, make them more comfortable in the commercial milieu which, in the presumably new eyes of the church, was "not to be neglected, but redeemed."[21]

Ong believed that Catholic success in America was a "minor miracle," considering that the church still taught that "poverty, both of spirit and in reality . . . is a blessing." That this situation should "give rise to tensions is to be expected." Yet Ong, like virtually all other Catholic intellectuals of the 1950s, downplayed these tensions in an effort to define the church's place within the great American consensus. Along with John Tracy Ellis (author of the 1955 essay, "American Catholics and the Intellectual Life," which generated intense debate over the disparity between Catholic and secular education), John Courtney Murray, and Gustave Weigel—sophisticated theorists of church-state relations—Ong was a liberal cleric who had established closer ties with the secular academic mainstream than would ever have been thought possible before the Second World War (among his good friends was the great scholar of Puritanism, Perry Miller). Yet he was still a priest in a culture wary of priestcraft; as the Notre Dame historian-priest Thomas McAvoy wrote at the time: "[G]iven this very important American tradition, there is a special work for the Catholic layman to defend and perhaps extend the Catholic faith and culture where the clergyman is unwelcome." In American Catholicism's first true "Era of the Layman," Tom Dooley—for all his transdenominational appeal—was a prototypical figure.[22]

He meant a great deal to hard-headed, anticommunist realists as well. In 1959 Burdick and Lederer dropped the fictional veneer and paid explicit tribute to Dooley in their article for *Life*, "Salute to Deeds of Non-Ugly Americans." They credited him with a firsthand understanding of "the iron-hard link between malnutrition, ill health and ignorance on one side and the appeals of Communism on the other." A year later Henry Cabot Lodge, United States representative to the United Nations, remarked: "One feels that if there were an unlimited number of Dr. Dooleys, this country would have practically no foreign relations problems." Such enthusiastic high-level support—coupled with his enormous popularity among Catholics and millions of other "ordinary" Americans—obscured Dooley's growing alienation from American policy, a condition aggravated by his inability to precisely locate the source of his disaffection. At the beginning of *The Edge of Tomorrow* Dooley referred to his discovery, during the Passage to Freedom, of the "Christlike power and simplicity" of medicine, and then asked: "Was that why the foreign-aid planners, with their billion dollar projects, found it difficult to understand?"[23]

In the post-McCarthy climate of *The Ugly American* and the fervent anticommunism of such liberal Democrats as John F. Kennedy and Adlai Stevenson—whom Dooley admired—this critique could serve the purposes of a tough yet spiritually informed new breed of internationalism (in accepting an award from the American Junior Chamber of Commerce in 1958, Dooley exclaimed: "[T]his is a new world—we need a new kind of man—a man spiritually and morally tough"). Dooley was appalled by the attitude of most American Foreign Service personnel and their families in Laos, complaining to his mother of their shallowness and jealousy toward him. Yet his hostility was usually fueled by personal rather than strategic or ideological considerations. He was particularly critical of members of the American Woman's Club in Vientiane: "a group of rather worthless women who are consumed in internecine wars, staggering under servant duplicities, digestive troubles, PX inabilities to get the best wines, and general complaining about being stationed in Laos. Not one can speak Lao, nor is there a class for it; not one woman rolls bandages for the hospital, much less for me."[24] Dooley was distrustful of women generally, with the exception of his mother (he wrote on one occasion, "[she is] all I have"). For a number of years he allowed a woman in St. Louis to believe he would someday return and marry her if he could learn to "love [her] a little more." His jungle mission provided refuge from such a commitment (he once joked, when asked why he rejected female volunteers: "[I]f I took over with me three young, healthy, normal American girls and lived up there with them, the Pope would never believe me"). Several of his corpsmen were in fact married; one was even a newlywed who left his expectant wife behind in New Hampshire. Dooley described one of these women—who continually expressed her longing for her husband—as "worthless. . . . She should realize that she has a part in the operation too. . . . [H]er job is at home, like Milton said, 'to stand and wait.'"[25]

Dooley did not disclose his hostility to women in his published works. But, beginning with *The Edge of Tomorrow*, he expressed a vague estrangement from life in his native land, which stood in such stark contrast to the primitive spirituality of Laos. "In college we were taught the ubiquity of God," he wrote, "But to see God in all things when you are plunged into bleating materialism is sometimes hard. I certainly cannot see God when I look at a Mercedes Benz convertible. But in the jungle it is easier. Here we can know God a little better. Perhaps it is because of solitude. We can see God in the tropic rain, in the monsoon mud, in the tangy sweet smell of the earth that comes upon us as we walk amongst the mountains. . . . We ought to shut up a few minutes and seek Him."[26]

Critiques of American materialism during the late 1950s were, of course, neither uncommon nor necessarily controversial. The mildness of Dooley's complaint, coupled with its homely religiosity ("often, late at night, Bob, John and I would kneel beside our cots and pray the family rosary out loud"), prevented readers from feeling threatened by his growing unorthodoxy. In the early days of the Laos mission Dooley's letters to his mother affirmed his continuing devotion to the church. After attending Mass in Vientiane he marveled at "the universality of the Church. Put a pin through the globe at Washington and it will come out in Laos." No matter where one worshipped, the church offered "the same hymns, the same quiet joy from receiving communion." Yet by November 1958 he was compelled to assure his mother—always acutely conscious of even the most subtle changes in her son's tone—that he remained in the fold: "I am sorry you do not think I am still a Catholic. I am." Still, Dooley never explicitly linked his modest estrangement from America's imperial mission with his personal religiosity. Several of his later critics would actually attribute his allegedly blind, chauvinistic anticommunism precisely to his religious background. According to the journalist Nicholas von Hoffman, who condemned Dooley's propagandism, "there was no contradiction involved in what he was doing because he was a Catholic, American boy doing good and right things."[27]

Dooley went to great lengths to domesticate his ethno-religious inheritance into a familiar American idiom. He often portrayed Laos as a new frontier for the extension of ecumenical brotherhood. At Easter, 1957, he was visited by two Seventh Day Adventist missionaries who accompanied him on rounds which included the circumcision of several Pakistanis living in Nam Tha. "Far after dark we crawled back to the house and just collapsed. Only to hear Pastor Currie laughing loudly. 'Think of it,' he said, 'Irish Catholics eating lunch with Seventh Day Adventists, on Easter Sunday, performing an ancient Hebrew rite on Moslem children in the Buddhist Kingdom of Laos!'" Dooley subsequently intervened with the Laotian government to allow the Protestant missionaries to continue to operate in that country.[28]

The strategy worked. *Christian Century*—an organ of the liberal Protestant establishment and a tireless antagonist of Cardinal Spellman and Catholic efforts to modify the absolutist strictures against state aid to parochial school students—issued an editorial in 1959 praising Dooley for standing in "the succession of Albert Schweitzer and Gordon Seagrave and the other great Christian physicians of our time." Since the journal, as late as 1961, could still characterize the Catholic church as "an instrument of power ready to serve its own ends at public expense," Dooley served as a model for an acceptable, "Christian" Catholic. Yet Dooley's quest for transdenominational appeal was contrived and awkwardly forced. He resorted to stage Irish clichés to avoid looking beneath the surface of his charming personality: "[L]ike most Irishmen I think I'm practically faultless." Dooley's upper-class childhood had not made him immune to a historical tendency among the American Irish described by author John Corry: "[T]hey often fight so hard to be accepted that they can never be themselves at all." Dooley was remarkably ignorant of and indifferent to his heritage, partly because his class position distinguished him so from the mass of Irish Americans (his father, as he recalled in a letter to his mother, was notorious for his hostility toward labor unions). Dooley's dramatic conversion experience in 1954 supplied the justification for his cavalier attitude toward personal history. "Listening to Tom Dooley," a Catholic journalist wrote in 1958, "you might easily get the impression that he was born at the age of 28 aboard the USS Montague in Vietnam's Haiphong Bay." In filling out passport applications between 1947 and 1958, Dooley listed as his father's birthplace four different cities in Missouri, and as many different dates of birth. And, as mentioned in Chapter 5, he also claimed to have been in the "Pacific Theater of War" between 1944 and 1946.[29]

Dooley's alienation from the truth and his confusion regarding his identity led to an unexpected result: by the end of his first year in Laos he had developed an impassioned affinity for the people he originally merely expected to "save" from communism. As late as January 1957 he had professed uncertainty as to his future and expressed a distaste for the Laotian environment, complaining of "the filth, the humidity, the mustiness of everything, the flies, the constant odor of decomposition. . . . I am here only because I believe it is the right thing that I should be doing." But the Laotians responded warmly to his mission, in contrast to the reception accorded such highly organized agencies as CARE and the National Catholic Welfare Conference (both groups were expelled by the government in 1958). Like Dooley, the Laotians were groping for a sense of autonomy and a stable identity; they resented the

Dr. Tom Dooley and Laotian villagers, 1959. Courtesy Western Historical Manuscript Collection, University of Missouri–St. Louis.

lingering paternalism of most Westerners just as Dooley half-consciously resented (even as he courted) the expectations of his sponsors, his government, even his family. His first description of Lao religion employed a familiar analogy, but it suggested too a wry, double-edged insight that they shared some common ancestral ground: "Buddhism in Laos has a strong admixture of ancient animism; and for people like Chai there are more spirits and phantoms in Laos than there are fairies and leprechauns in Ireland."[30] The mountain people Dooley worked with were not ethnically "Laotian" (the majority of whom actually lived in Thailand); for the most part they were members of the Meo, the Yao, or a number of smaller ethnic groups. The montagnards had historically been neglected by the dominant lowland Lao; only now were they being courted by rival political groups. Yet "family and clan" remained "the only important social groups" for these people, and they continued to "look to shamans for supernatural assistance, protection, and augury." Dooley was moved by their gentleness just as he grew aware that conventional American foreign policy had precious little to offer them.[31]

He was also developing a sense of genuine outrage and impatience with some of his countrymen. In the spring of 1957 Dooley wrote of several

American anthropologists ("first class asses") who were stranded in Nam Tha because of monsoon rains.

> They are studying this and that, buying a lot of native costumes for the museum[,] . . . but they go about it in such an infuriating way, bargaining over and over again for a matter of eight kip, which to the Lao is perhaps a day's earning, but to the America [*sic*] is eight cents. When I voice objection they say that the people enjoy the argument (I know a bit better). . . . They bought a complete Yao outfit, beautifully made, all hand embroidered, taking months. The man sold it literally off his back . . . asked the equivalent of twenty dollars which is not too much considering the panels of embroidering, the silver necklace and bracelet, a Chinese silk veston. . . . [T]he anthropologists argued him down to 15, which was okay, but then for the next forty five minutes (I timed them) they embarrassed me, humiliated the old man by showing the dirt, the slight tears, and the seams not being straight . . . and finally got it for $14.50. Was it worth it?[32]

As "Thanh Mo (Doctor) America," Dooley was beginning to receive the kind of unqualified love and admiration he had never found at home. His immersion in the Laotian jungle led to unsettling experiences accessible to precious few of his countrymen. The Laotians were periodically afflicted with what the "witch doctors" called "kia atomique" ("atomic flu"). More than one hundred and fifty villagers appeared at Dooley's morning sick call one day with "bizarre symptoms" the shamans ascribed to lingering effects of the bombings of Hiroshima and Nagasaki. While blaming Communist propaganda for the scare in *The Edge of Tomorrow*, Dooley privately confessed: "[I] don't know if I'm getting brainwashed . . . but sometimes I wonder about that bomb."[33]

Dooley's 1958 American fund-raising tour for MEDICO netted over three hundred thousand dollars in cash donations along with over a million dollars' worth of medicines furnished by such corporations as Charles Pfizer, Mead Johnson, and Eli Lilly. "Everywhere I went in America," he wrote, "people showed their warm admiration towards our program—warm admiration portrayed by cold cash." On the lecture circuit Dooley exploited the "charm which he could turn off and on as with a spigot" to elicit support as well as to dispel doubts that there was anything peculiar about a young physician spurning lucrative American opportunities for service to Asians. He told *Life* magazine,

"Heck, I really don't want to spend the rest of my life rotting in the jungle. I want to drive snappy convertibles, pinch pretty girls and drink bourbon on the rocks" (he was also featured in such this-worldly publications as *Vogue*). *His* very uncertainty and confusion lent a ring of authenticity to such statements, but for all his love of American glamour and his growing celebrityhood, Dooley resented being a "public relations object." During his first tour in Laos he had frequently complained to his mother of the pressures exerted upon him by his various promoters: *Reader's Digest*, KMOX radio in St. Louis (for whom he did a weekly jungle broadcast), and assorted agencies and individuals. This anger partly reflected his own vulnerability; he craved fame but was unable to admit it to himself. Nor could he express his anger toward his mother. When KMOX failed to receive several tapes on time, Mrs. Dooley grew concerned, and the station contacted the State Department for information, supposedly on behalf of his worried mother. Dooley blamed the radio station, but the relatively minor incident stung him because "they are still talking in Vientiane about how 'Dr. Tom is so busy with his slant eyes that he doesn't write his mommy.'" But Laos at least afforded Dooley occasional moments of self-understanding and deep religious experience. He now considered his permanent vocation ("the root of the tree of me") to be that of jungle physician. By June 1958 he was, in his mother's words, "home again in Laos."[34]

Dooley and the new corpsmen established a village hospital at Muong Sing, which, only five miles from the Chinese border, was even closer to "the rim of red hell" than the outpost at Nam Tha. The year 1959 was to be the most critical year of Dooley's life. In February he embarked on a trip down the Mekong River with corpsman Earl Rhine and several Laotian assistants. The previous year Dooley had discovered the value of going out into the jungle, performing medical services in villages along the banks of the Mekong. In his final book, *The Night They Burned the Mountain*, Dooley movingly described the personal benefits of such a trip. In the course of treating the malnourished and vulnerable peasants, he attained a greater "awareness of God, of the great pattern of the universe, the similarity of all the world, the magnificence of the dense green jungle, the majestic cathedral-like colors of the rain-forest." He reiterated the contrast between the materialism of America and the raw spirituality of Asia: "All this cries of a Creator; this speaks of God. For me it is harder to know God in the tumult of plenty, in city traffic, in giant buildings, in cocktail bars, or riding in a car with body by Fisher. But just as a maker is stamped on America's products, so is His stamp on all the universe."[35]

Dooley spent a great deal of time on the trip talking with "my boys" about "fundamental questions." He concluded, from his experience in the misery of the Mekong, that "poverty and malnutrition and wretchedness, which make health impossible, are not God-made, but wholly man-made, but the cure for the scourges, the compassion to want to cure, this also comes from God." On the first night of the return trip upriver, Dooley stopped in a village to ask the chief if his team could spend the night there. On the way back to his canoe, he tripped over an untied boot lace and plummeted down the steep river bank, severely bruising his chest. In *The Night They Burned the Mountain*, Dooley wrote of the incident, "I did not of course realize it, but that fall was to become a pivotal point in my life." The pain never went away; in July Dooley asked a visiting American surgeon to remove a cyst which had developed in the affected area. A black tumor was excised, which the surgeon preserved in formalin so as to have it analyzed in a Bangkok hospital. The tumor was diagnosed as malignant melanoma, a rare form of skin cancer which, at that time, proved fatal to more than half its victims within the first year after contracting the disease. On August 15, 1959, Dooley was called back to New York to undergo surgery at the famed Memorial Hospital.[36]

Dooley's flair for drama may have been responsible for the widespread belief that the fall had *caused* the cancer; he certainly did nothing to discourage that notion (and in a letter to a supporter he bluntly asserted: "I contracted the cancer in Asia, probably from a fall on the side of a river bank"). Even his surgeon admitted that the etiology of melanoma was a "controversial subject" in medicine generally, although he concluded, "I don't think Dr. Dooley's fall caused his disease" (melanoma, as doctors knew even then, originates in a pigmented mole in the skin). Regardless of its origins, Dooley's illness was the dominant motif of his final eighteen months of life. His illness, like everything else that ever happened to him, became a vehicle for self-promotion, but as always he was uncertain as to its essential meaning. His cancer also provided American Catholics with the final text through which his sainthood was assured; a fate he would ultimately resist.[37]

An Uncertain Martyrdom

The Night They Burned the Mountain (1960) was the most introspective and revealing of Dooley's published works. He wrote to his mother, "I think this is probably the best I have ever written . . . but the book has a touch of poignancy that may not be too good to read." The personal power which accompanied his evolving quest for identity made it harder for him to satisfy his various American constituencies, a source of no little anxiety. What had begun as a project in support of American empire and Catholic anticommunism had either ascended or sunk—depending on one's perspective—to a search for the self-understanding so painfully and glaringly lacking in the earlier Tom Dooley. As he wrote in *The Night They Burned the Mountain*: "I realized that I had become more aware of myself and my life's adventure in the material of Asian life." But once back in the United States, it became clear both how far he had yet to go and, more importantly, how his drive for an integrated identity could become short-circuited in a culture of celebrity which he both courted and feared. He wasted no time in returning to the American limelight, arranging to have his cancer surgery filmed for a documentary which aired over the Columbia Broadcasting System on April 21, 1960.[38]

In "Biography of a Cancer" Dooley explained his willingness to allow the entire nation to witness the operation. "There's a certain amount of ignorance in America," he said, "about this word 'cancer.'" He compared that ignorance to that of Laos, where "the people fall into witchcraft and into sorcery." The documentary also gave Dooley an opportunity to supply his own interpretation of the illness, lest he be prematurely consigned to a tragic, untimely death. "I'm scared to death of this thing becoming maudlin," he explained. "I don't want anyone to get sloppy over this. You know, I don't like anything that says—a dying doctor's anguish bit. That's—that's stupid." Yet Dooley was still unequipped to treat the disease as something which had happened to him, Tom Dooley, as opposed to the jungle doctor or the American Catholic hero. He was now given to fantasies of discorporation. In *The Night They Burned the Mountain* he described an experience he had on the flight back to America prior to his surgery: "I felt a cloudy out-of-touchness with everything. I had a pleasant disembodiment from my own self. . . . My mind put me somewhere else where I could look back at the body of Tom Dooley." His surgeon was concerned with Dooley's attitude. In "Biography of a Cancer" his comments were recorded even as he removed cancerous tissue from Dooley's chest. "I've felt a great deal of pity for this young guy," he remarked. "He's—he has a malignant disease. He knows it. And he's been trying to act as though it didn't bother him in the slightest. . . . Today, for the first time, he admitted that he was beginning to be worried a little bit, and I told him that I was very happy that he was appearing so normal."[39]

Following the apparently successful operation and a very brief period of recuperation, Dooley embarked on an exhausting lecture tour to raise much-needed funds for MEDICO. Talking about himself was clearly the best therapy. In "Biography of a Cancer" he frankly admitted that he welcomed the publicity from the program not only in order to allay people's fears of cancer but because he wanted to serve notice that he fully intended to return to Laos, and he needed support: "For the next few weeks that you're going to photograph every part of me, I welcome you here, because maybe this will give me a chance to tell Americans how we need help . . . how we at MEDICO believe that the Brotherhood of Man does indeed transcend the sovereignty of nations, and that we want to use MEDICO as a supra national thing—as people in America helping people in Asia—on a heart-to-heart basis—through the hands of medicine." Early in the course of his lecture tour it became clear that many of Dooley's Catholic followers took a view of his illness which differed markedly from his own. His suffering was now interpreted as a final, even an essential confirmation of his spiritual greatness; his superiority over purely secular heroes. In November 1959 Dooley was awarded an honorary degree by the College of the Holy Cross, in Worcester, Massachusetts. In conferring the degree the Jesuit president of Holy Cross, William A. Donaghy, contrasted Dooley's gift of pain with the prevailing unholy attitude: "Modern man has lost the old concept of pain as a sacramental mystery, a participation in the Passion, a means whereby the member can become more like the thorn-crowned Head. In the Christian scheme of things pain was not merely to be anesthetized but canonized. It was not only a cause of misery but a chance for merit. Saints prayed for it and received it with resignation and even rejoicing in the dear ingenuous old days before aspirin so largely supplanted aspiration."[40]

During the fall of 1959 Dooley received over five thousand letters a day. Many admirers now expressed an urgent desire to join his team (although they were not always sure precisely where he worked), and they often equated his illness with holiness. "When I read of your suffering," a woman wrote, "I thought how close you are to God. Please help me to come closer to God through the people of Viet Nam." This was a view with deep roots in American, particularly Irish-American, Catholicism. In 1961 a nun vividly described Dooley's exalted place within this tradition, noting that he had "suffered at a young age so poignantly—realizing so deeply that as we are rewarded down here for our efforts, how much more is the reward later for the silent sufferings of the soul known only to the God who permits them—and truly shows His love for us—because without chastisement—suffering—loneliness and last but not least sickness how seldom we would give Him a thought—and never does He forget or stop thinking of us—truly God loved Tom." For all his ostentatious patriotism, Dooley had increasingly encouraged his followers to see him as a victim of faithless American bureaucrats and policy makers. In *The Night They Burned the Mountain* he asked: "Were those who criticized me in southeast Asia as powerful and vitriolic in their anti-Dooley ideas as they had been in the past? Would those who could think only in terms of multi-million dollar projects snigger at my paltry efforts, or would they see that if the darkness is black enough a small candle can give a brilliant light?" Dooley often reminded his readers that "several of the critics of what we are trying to do are in high places." As in the latter days of the Coughlin and McCarthy periods, many Catholics now experienced a conflict between their tendency to exalt, even demand, martyred heroes, and a deep resentment at the obscure secular forces who had brought that martyrdom about. Much of Dooley's mail was crude yet pointed:

> Dr. Dooley is a man who deserves much respect
> But criticize they must
> Loafer, com. (communist) and derelict
> Way out in Laos jungles
> Where no man dares to tread
> He starves himself
> to help keep the people fed.[41]

Dooley actually manipulated Catholic resentments in order to disarm his growing body of critics. As a correspondent for *Life* wrote in 1960: "[T]he fact that Dr. Tom Dooley is a controversial figure in Asia astonishes most American visitors. The fact that he is not controversial in the U.S. astonishes their compatriots in southeast Asia." Some of the critics objected to Dooley's practice of establishing a village clinic and then, after a year or so, placing it in the hands of untrained Laotian personnel. This had led to disastrous results at Nam Tha, where the clinic was closed soon after Dooley's departure. But the more important source of friction between Dooley and the American contingent in Laos concerned his lifestyle and personality. The jungle doctor spent an inordinate amount of time in places like Vientiane, Bangkok, and Saigon, ostensibly in search of supplies and medicines. Rumors about his sexual behavior were a staple item within the American community in those locales; for that and for other reasons, Dooley was widely viewed as a hypocrite, if not a downright fraud. He continued to apply the *Ugly American* diagnosis to his compatriots in Asia. The Americans in Vientiane, he wrote in 1959, "are such selfish jackasses that they always have some excuse why they can't lend me a jeep."[42]

Dooley's illness thus provided him with an opportunity to solidify his relationship with American Catholics. He readily supplied the text they required in order to reconcile his suffering with the greater plan of salvation. Although he talked at first of his "black" cancer, he soon found more appropriate words which were widely disseminated through the Catholic press: "God has been good to me. He has given me the most hideous, painful cancer at an extremely young age. It's a gift. He wants me to use it. Thousands of people know me. They follow me in what I do. Now I have cancer. That's not important. It's how I react to cancer. These people will see how I react. . . . Maybe they will say, 'well, Tom Dooley is going back to the stinking jungle. Maybe I can do the dishes.' That's my new gift."[43]

Although Dooley rarely addressed his appeal explicitly to Catholics, this message uncovered the roots of his popularity among his coreligionists. While it indicated his resignation to God's will, it also stressed the necessity to bear one's burden unto the world as a means of lessening the suffering of others by embracing one's own. Suffering and beauty, suffering and majesty, were thus inextricably linked. Yet at the same time Dooley's illness further undermined his Catholic identity, just as it increased his chances for achieving a more usable personal one. At first this caused a great deal of confusion. On returning to Laos late in 1959, Dooley decided to visit Lourdes, but was only made more uneasy there. As he wrote to Robert Copenhaver, his press agent and one of his few close friends: "No one knew anything about it except Dooley and, I hope, the Blessed Virgin. Don't know how much good it is going to do, but one can never tell. It is my personal mind and my personal taste that, if someone was going to work a miracle for Dooley, it would not be dependent upon whether or not he went to Lourdes."[44]

The possibility of a cure at Lourdes seemed particularly improbable because his pilgrimage to the mecca of peasant faith came right on the heels of a two-month fund-raising tour in which he made forty-nine speeches in thirty-seven cities. In raising nearly a million dollars for MEDICO, Dooley fully utilized the most modern public relations methods, generating national interest in his dramatic public appearances (creating, in Daniel Boorstin's phrase, "pseudo-events"). Mostly, though, Dooley relied upon his own charismatic powers. He raised $10,000 from "a single impassioned appearance on Dave Garroway's 'Today' show." His appeal was strategically calculated. After deciding it would be a good idea to appear on Ralph Edwards's "This Is Your Life" program (in which celebrities—purportedly to their complete surprise—were brought face to face in a studio with old friends and loved ones), Dooley supplied careful instructions, from the jungle, to his mother in St. Louis. He did not want any representatives of the Navy on the show. Nor did he want any mention of "love affairs, old girls, horses, or anything that smacks of my being a rich man's son. I am. But I do not wish the world to know I've a rich widow mother, a substantial bank account, and no financial worries . . . lest lots of young kids say 'I couldn't do what he does, look at the wealth behind him.'"[45]

Dooley also wrote that it was "preposterous" for one of his most devoted supporters—a priest of the Oblate of Mary Immaculate order—to expect him to speak for less than his customary fee. "I want $1,000 per speech, and there are those that will pay it." Twenty-five years after his death Dooley's former adviser William Lederer angrily wrote: "What was good for Dooley was good for the world." During Dooley's lifetime his critics were more temperate, but his controversial status increased markedly during his final eighteen months. Almost all of the criticism focused on his egocentrism, but the more specific, if underlying, complaint was that his behavior seemed inappropriate for a Catholic hero. It was difficult for Catholics and non-Catholics alike to reconcile the selfless Dooley ("Blessed Thomas of Laos," as his secretary would later call him), with the Dooley of the "Tonight" show, the highly stylish Dooley who kept a suite at the Waldorf Astoria and sported the latest in fashion. Carl Wiedermann, a physician who met Dooley after his surgery, once asked him why he did not give up his career and spend his remaining days "savoring the good things of life" at a place like the Isle of Capri, where Wiedermann had once lived. He was startled when "Dooley asked me about a certain dancer and about a number of people in the international set on Capri. . . . [T]hen he spoke quite familiarly about people who travel in this fast crowd, a group you can only meet in places like Capri." Even those who knew him well were often impressed with his conviviality and zest for the good life. Publisher Robert Giroux recalled that "*after* his surgery" he and his colleague Roger Straus took

Dooley to dinner at the Lotos Club in Manhattan, "then on to '21' Club (at his request) for a nightcap. He had tremendous vitality."[46]

The problem, for Dooley's Catholic followers, was that so much of his appeal was founded upon his rejection of American materialism. In 1960 the Newark diocesan newspaper awarded third prize for a "Past and Future" contest to Phyllis Lombardi, a fourth grader from St. Aloysius parish, West Caldwell, New Jersey. The contestants had written a brief essay on their "favorite American." Phyllis wrote:

> My favorite American is Dr. Tom Dooley. He was a graduate of Notre Dame. After he graduated he knew we had many doctors in the United States and he thought about the people in Asia. He knew they were helpless when it came to medical care. So he went to Asia to help the people there. I think that was a great thing to do. He could have opened an office here in the U.S. and probably he would have become a very wealthy doctor, but, no, he gave up his friends and the pleasures of home to help the Asians. To me he is one American who can make Americans proud.

Dooley's blend of self-aggrandizement and selfless mysticism presented Catholics with an unprecedented conflict of interpretation. As Shirley Feltmann wrote in *Today*, a monthly aimed at bright Catholic adolescents: "Perhaps the most surprising paradox about Dr. Dooley is the public relations aura which seems to hang over him like a Madison Avenue halo." Even the highly optimistic Walter Ong, in his essay on the "Apostolate of the Business World," admitted that Catholics were not yet "explicitly aware" of the compatibility between their faith and modern American life. Dooley's mother made a revealing comment on her son's unusual nature: "Tom's genes are definitely Irish—but every once in a while his calm, almost cold, American executive and business judgment amazes people, so unexpected and not quite Irish. He has courage, stamina, and sentiment, a mixture of his heritage." Yet if Dooley thus represented a new American hybrid, it was a blend of radically disparate traditions. As one of his female admirers exclaimed, Dooley embodied "a mixture of "The Man in the Grey Flannel Suit and Mother Cabrini."[47]

Dooley's response to the controversy was typically blunt: "If you're gonna be a humanitarian today, you've gotta run it like a business. You've gotta have Madison Avenue, press relations, TV, radio . . . and of course you get condemned for being a publicity seeker for it. But from '54 to '58, I took care of

100 people a day. Now MEDICO treats 2,000 people a day." He confronted the religious issue with one of his wittily pointed asides: "I know of but one meek, humble man who accomplished anything. That was more than 1,900 years ago, and I'm not so sure he was meek and humble." In a 1959 letter to his mother from Laos, he dismissed his critics in direct, if melodramatic terms: "I am coming home for the cold calculating business of making money. Money for medicines for men who are wretched."[48]

Yet after his cancer surgery Dooley never really resumed his career as a full-time jungle doctor. His illness surely played a role, although it did not prevent him from conducting an exhausting public life on an international scale. While he claimed that the ever-expanding MEDICO program (by 1960 there were fourteen projects around the world, all modeled after Dooley's Laotian hospitals) demanded his personal attention, much of his time was spent tending his public image, defending himself and his programs from damaging attacks. Shirley Feltmann described an elaborate press conference held during the spring of 1960 at the Waldorf Astoria, at which Dooley announced the opening of a MEDICO clinic in Malaya and briefed reporters on the state of his own health. But, Feltmann wrote, "neither of these reasons seemed at the core of the conference, which appeared rather to be an antidote to a critical article about Dr. Dooley which *Life* had carried a few weeks before." The *Life* article, a pictorial with a brief essay by Scott Leavitt, was the most damaging critique of Dooley's work and character published during his lifetime. Leavitt charged: "He has identified himself completely with MEDICO. Since MEDICO is a worthy and unassailable cause, Dooley feels that anything he is doing—or wants to do, or has done—is equally worthy and unassailable. The question is: how much of what Dr. Tom Dooley does is done because he wants to serve MEDICO, and how much because he wants to serve Dr. Tom Dooley?" Leavitt went on to describe Dooley's inconsiderate methods of dealing with his subordinates ("they are here to do just exactly as I tell them, not to ask questions"), his rudeness, and his egotism (at a Saigon party he cut a woman short "in mid-anecdote by announcing there was 'room for only one extrovert'"). Leavitt's more serious allegations concerned criticisms of Dooley's medical performance by unnamed physicians who complained that "he is too quick on diagnosis and prescription," and that he did not spend sufficient time at his hospital, where he was, after all, the only physician. Leavitt also exposed Dooley's mania for public relations coups. In anticipation of a visit by some American physicians, Dooley had circulated a "military-style order to his forces at Muong Sing," which demanded that the hospital wards be full and that the "bear-mauling man" be prominently exhibited. The "bear-mauling man" and the miraculous reconstructive surgery Dooley performed upon him was featured in *The Night They Burned the Mountain* as well. Leavitt concluded by raising the religious issue. "It is too bad that Dooley and his supporters have tried to depict him as a saint. He is not. It may be that only a man like Dooley, with an unyielding, belligerent faith in himself, could have accomplished what he has done in Laos. And it may be that only a real saint could have done it without exasperating and angering so many people."[49]

The article was an enormous public relations defeat for Dooley. Before its publication he had warned his secretary, Teresa Gallagher, from Laos that Leavitt might not "write all 'God Bless' about us." His request that she attempt to see the article prior to publication in order that she might "cool it down" was poignant in its futility (as James Monahan of *Reader's Digest* wrote: "[T]he truth is that Dooley was really a babe-in-arms where publicity was concerned"). Dooley had been made by publicity, now he would suffer from it. The article provoked a brief flurry of attacks upon Dooley by individuals who heretofore had remained silent. The respected French scholar of Indochina, Bernard Fall, wrote the editor at *Life*: "I congratulate you for displaying rare courage—deflating the Tom Dooley myth. I can vouch for all the assertions you make about Dr. Dooley's record." A former Dooley corpsman wrote that Dooley was "a tremendous character, doing a decent job against terrifying obstacles," but he added: "[I]n Dooley's life, there is no room for people as people; only people to be used as tools." While many others rallied to his defense, Dooley was hit hard by the criticisms. Ironically, his own desire to project himself as a "regular guy" ("I like my blondes and bars as much as the next . . . maybe a bit more") backfired in this case. He had allowed himself to be photographed—wearing an alligator shirt and a wide grin—giving a young woman a ride on a motor scooter in Vientiane. The reaction of a Massachusetts high school student to the photograph was not atypical: "We sent you money to help you take care of the poor and sick people in Asia," she wrote, "and not to enable you to take pretty girls riding on the back of your fancy motor scooter."[50]

The fallout from the *Life* article also provided an indication of the marginality of Dooley's mission in terms of the reality of Laotian life and politics. His staunchest, largely Catholic supporters now sensed a conspiracy. In a letter to Teresa Gallagher, Dooley's mother quoted a Notre Dame trustee and influential attorney who had told her "it all hinges on backing 'The Great White Fleet,' and

Tom not being in accord with it, has undoubtedly antagonized *Life*, so there may be more to this than meets the eye." In fact the United States government, by 1958, was supplying virtually the entire budget of Laos, which had come into being as a nation only in 1954, as a buffer state between North Vietnam and pro-Western Siam (later Thailand). Dooley had helped promote the fiction that a nascent Laotian democracy was under constant threat by the Communist-backed Pathet Lao. In reality the conflict was a largely internecine struggle involving members of the same family, many of whom at one time or another oversaw the mismanagement, if not thievery, of millions of dollars of American aid. Dooley actually had personal relationships with leading figures within all of the major competing factions, but he most closely identified with a group of pro-Western, CIA-backed "young turks" known as the Committee for the Defense of National Interests. In 1958 the CDNI helped undermine the fragile coalition government of Prince Souvanna Phouma, who was the best hope for a genuinely "neutralist" regime in Laos. As indicated earlier in the chapter, Dooley claimed a friendship with Souvanna Phouma, just as he did with Kong Le, a paratroop captain who engineered a coup in the summer of 1960 (Kong Le was a nationalist who hoped to eliminate American influence and convince "Laotians to quit killing other Laotians"), but he was probably closest of all to Phoumi Nosavan, the army colonel who led the American-backed counter-revolution later that year.[51]

For all his love for the Laotian people, Dooley could not thus claim that an American power elite was punishing him for obstructing American goals in the region. What was worse, from the point of view of his morale, was his irrelevance to the situation. At the height of the 1960 crisis he wrote from Laos (after boasting of his friendships with the various combatants), "So you see, mother, if there is such a thing as a 'man above politics' it is your son, Tom." Yet he was also below and outside of politics as well. The crisis of the summer of 1960 simply meant that he could not get supplies flown in from Vientiane; the rebels had seized all available aircraft, including his own small Piper Apache. Dooley decided to leave Laos for a mission of "diplomacy" which entailed trying to clear supply lines from outside of Laos as well as touring other MEDICO facilities in East Asia. (Cable communications from outside of Laos were cut off following Kong Le's takeover of Vientiane. Dooley did, however, receive one perfectly translated message from America. Twentieth Century Fox wanted to know if he preferred Jack Lemmon or Frank Sinatra for the lead role in the Hollywood version of the "Tom Dooley Story.") In Dooley's last hurrah in

Dr. Tom Dooley with Laotian child, Muong Sing, Laos, 1960. Courtesy Western Historical Manuscript Collection, University of Missouri–St. Louis.

Southeast Asia, he managed to smuggle a planeload of supplies to the outposts at Ban Houei Sai and Muong Sing.

In October he returned to New York for a series of medical tests. Following the tests, which he claimed proved negative for further spread of the cancer, Dooley embarked on his last journey to Asia. After stops in India and Thailand he reached Laos in early November, only to be stranded at the Vientiane airport when the war-weary air traffic controllers refused to provide clearance for his flight to Muong Sing. A physician who accompanied Dooley on the trip recalled that after Dooley successfully pleaded over the phone with Souvanna Phouma to gain clearance for takeoff, he slumped back in his seat and grumbled, "[W]hy do they do this to me? They know I am only here to help them." "That night," his associate recalled, "I had the feeling that Tom Dooley saw the end of MEDICO in Laos." He also saw the end of his own life. The cancer had metastasized in his blood, and he was dying. After performing his last acts of surgery in Muong Sing, he began the final long journey back to America.[52]

Tom Dooley died in New York on January 18, 1961, the day after his thirty-fourth birthday. Two days later John Fitzgerald Kennedy became America's first Roman Catholic president. Most accounts of Dooley's death stressed its highly spiritual character. En route to New York Dooley stopped in Bangkok, where

Father John Boucher, a Redemptorist priest, gave him Extreme Unction. Father Boucher recalled telling Dooley: "You're not really dying yet but I don't have to tell you about your condition. Maybe Extreme Unction might help you." Father Boucher also reported that while Dooley was still urgently concerned over the fate of MEDICO, he accepted the idea of his own death in a heroically Christian spirit: "[S]omehow I feel resigned and peaceful. If this is the way God wants it to be, this is the way I want it, too." As Boucher listened to Dooley speak, it occurred to him that "a couple of thousand years ago a Man of the same age spoke almost the same words in the Garden of Gethsemane." (The eulogist at Dooley's St. Louis funeral Mass similarly proclaimed: "[T]he greatest life that was ever lived was in 33 years. Dr. Dooley was thirty-four.")[53]

At the end of the long and agonizing flight to New York, Dooley was determined to walk off the airplane under his own power. It was snowing heavily in New York, and there were only a few of his closest associates waiting at the airport. For an international celebrity, there was something very lonely about his final days: it was as though he had already outlived his own legend. Teresa Gallagher recalled that while waiting for his plane to arrive she bitterly "resented the nonchalance of the ambulance driver and his assistant who were just sitting there talking and smoking as if nothing were wrong." In Dooley's last days at the hospital he was consoled mainly by Catholics, the most notable being Francis Cardinal Spellman of New York. On the night of his death a priest gave him last rites, concluding: "Son, go now and meet thy God." Teresa Gallagher and a male nurse then stood vigil over Dooley. As a result of the sacrament, Gallagher thought he seemed "so much more peaceful and at rest." A few moments later Dooley was dead. "There had been no gasping, no thrashing, nothing. There was just a quiet, peaceful slipping away." Gallagher's "immediate reaction" to his death was: "God is good."[54] Dooley did not go to his death in a spirit of resignation. On December 5, 1960, he wired his mother from Hong Kong: "Cannot let this destroy me. With orthopedic corset I can return to my work and adhere former schedule." In death as in life Dooley, for all his "egocentrism," functioned more as a cultural symbol than as a fully realized human being with an integral voice of his own. *The Night They Burned the Mountain* represented a departure from the pious simplicity of most of his earlier work, but it ended on a note of false bravado, with Dooley—in his "regular guy" persona—getting a free ride from a New York cab driver who told him (after asking, "You've seen a lot of Communism, aintcha?") to "keep that buck and get back as soon as possible to your kingdom of Laos." Dooley wrote:

"I smiled and felt warm and good inside and turned to my fellow American and said, 'O.K., Mac. Shall do.'" But Dooley planned to write another book, to be entitled "The Night of the Same Day" (as his editor Robert Giroux put it, "Dooley liked poetic titles"). Although the book was never completed, an astonishing selection of manuscript fragments exist. They demonstrate beyond any doubt that by the end of his life Dooley was obsessed with gaining an understanding of himself which transcended the shallow labels he had allowed others to apply to him during his career. The fragments are of the same form as Dooley's consciousness: they offer, as he put it, "brief glimpses, flashes, snatches, fragments . . . but not yet the total experience."[55]

Most importantly, the fragments disclose the extent of Dooley's alienation from his public image, from the masses of his supporters, and, more subtly, from orthodox Catholicism. Among the sources of Dooley's dawning enlightenment was Kahlil Gibran, who had not yet attained anything like the cult status he would (posthumously) enjoy in the 1960s and who, indeed, was virtually unknown to American readers during Dooley's lifetime. An undercurrent of Eastern spirituality runs throughout these writings (in his later radio broadcasts Dooley even appeared to be speaking English with Laotian inflections). He clearly perceived the sharp dichotomy between Western values and his own idealized vision of an emerging non-Western consciousness. "Two sets of eyes scan the world," he wrote. "Two minds measure the result of years of effort. Yet their judgments of accomplishment are as different as New York is from Muong Sing." Yet his appreciation of Eastern thought was never entirely free of the Manichean tendencies of his own religiocultural inheritance: "The filth of the body cannot reach a pure soul."[56]

For all his flirtation with exotic mysticism Dooley's last fragments reveal, above all, that he was a romantic in a classically American sense. Given his background, that may have been the most exotic and dangerous of all possible leaps of faith. Dooley was an avowed admirer of Robert Frost, but if there is any single spirit that hovers over the fragments, it is that of Walt Whitman. In *The Night They Burned the Mountain* Dooley had paraphrased Whitman (without acknowledgment) in describing the vision-lending power of his experience at Haiphong in 1954. "I saw it," he wrote, "I was there." In the fragments he wrote: "I can only be true to my own personal vision. Whether it coincides with that of my friends or not." Dooley seemed to understand what his personalism entailed in terms of what it supplanted. He was, he wrote in one of the most richly cryptic passages from the fragments, "hardly a self-abnegating character." He also wrote, as if in response to those who had exalted his suffering as an essential propaedeutic to sainthood: "Not to reject pain instantly is not to be human."[57]

Although Dooley quoted repeatedly from Thomas Wolfe in the fragments, Whitman remains the guiding spirit because of Dooley's sexuality. In a large sense the fragments represent his embrace of a romantic homosexual American poetic which runs from Whitman through Hart Crane to Dooley's contemporary Allen Ginsberg. The fragments are addressed to an unnamed young American man. "America's greatness," he wrote, "is not the splendor of sun-tanned summer vacationists, not the temple of the supermarket . . . nor the ribboned freeways of our land . . . not the sweet smell of excess in opulent hotels, soft carpeted clubs, prestige cars, and gadgets. Our country's beauty is the spirit of YOU . . . young men."[58]

"I force a lad into experience," he wrote, "and the more unpleasant it is the more he must face up to his own weakness and overcome it." Dooley's jungle mission thus provided the vehicle for overcoming his estrangement from American life by bringing a select part of it with him. "The deepest need of man is the need to overcome his separateness, to leave his prison of aloneness." From Laos he hoped to generate a new transnational identity born out of his own visionary experience. Dooley had traveled to the far border of generally understood "rational" consciousness by 1960. "TRANSMIGRATION," he mused: "Medico can be a corner stone of such a concept." He also suggested that "interplanetary living" would become an option for the young people of his era. Dooley's personality continued to oscillate between a gentle mysticism and grandiose self-aggrandizement. "God has been tender and loving with me," he wrote, adding, in words which would have startled his Catholic disciples, "showing Himself to me often." And he continued to view himself as a victim of inferior sensibilities occupying positions of influence: "The original man is misunderstood, misinterpreted, criticized, ridiculed, envied, smirched, vilified, defamed, harassed, hounded, deserted, tormented and a few more."[59]

The surviving fragments of "The Night of the Same Day" call for a redefinition of Dooley's significance as a central figure of the 1950s. The facile piety of Dooley's early career, with its glibly ecumenical appeal, evoked theologian Will Herberg's portrayal of mid-century American religious culture as a bland "Triple Melting Pot." Herberg argued that a religious identity—even if it was as a Catholic or Jew—was acceptable and even essential in an era which rejected ethnic identities as divisive. The descendants of immigrants had gladly shed those ancient tribal identities, but their Americanization had "been purchased at a heavy price, the price of embracing an idolatrous civic religion of Americanism." In fact, Dooley's willingness to please a variety of constituencies, his exaltation of American corporations (and groups such as the Junior Chamber of Commerce), and his anti-intellectualism combined to make him, on the surface, the prototypical 1950s American so carefully scrutinized in the best-selling works of David Riesman, William H. Whyte, and a host of others. All of these works—which have assumed a kind of normative power as definitive studies of the period—were concerned with the erosion of American individualism in the postwar period. As Philip Gleason argued, the defeat of totalitarianism in the Second World War had merely led to continuing anxieties about mass society, particularly on the part of the many refugee intellectuals who played such a crucial role in postwar American intellectual life.[60]

One of those refugees, Erik Erikson, provided the central symbol for the period. As cultural historian Warren Susman wrote: "From the end of the 1940s to almost the end of the 1950s, the problem was fundamentally redefined as that of personal identity. Who would object to seeing this as the age of Erik Erikson?" Erikson explicitly linked his psychoanalytical work with the unique situation of American culture. "We begin to conceptualize matters of identity," he wrote in 1950, "at the very time in history when they become a problem. For we do so in a country which attempts to make a super-identity out of all the identities imported by its constituent immigrants." From the perspective of Erikson's criteria for an integrated personal identity—"to experience one's self as something that has continuity and sameness, and to act accordingly"—Dooley might seem the classic fragmented personality: other-directed, anxiety-ridden, lonely. Yet the fragments from "The Night of the Same Day" suggest that Dooley was involved in an intense, even desperate search for just that kind of identity so valued by the nervous critics of 1950s American culture.[61]

The central problem was that the critics were simply looking in the wrong places. In reality the postwar years witnessed fervent individual quests for meaning, creativity, and authenticity, but they emanated from cultural precincts beyond the pale of the scholarly discourse which passed for authoritative knowledge at the time. A cultural revolution had been emerging, for instance, within black culture since the early years of World War II, launched primarily by jazz musicians who thought the war was merely "a grotesque show staged by sick old men who had succeeded in turning America into a huge prison camp." The wartime recording ban made big bands—with their lush orchestrations oriented toward white listeners—obsolete; in their place emerged more streamlined combos which placed greater emphasis on solo voices. The leading figure in the resulting movement soon to be known as "bebop" was Charlie Parker, a native of Kansas City who had migrated to New York in 1939 to complete his jazz education. At nineteen already a veteran of thousands of late night Kansas City jam sessions, Parker was constantly seeking fresh approaches for alto saxophone improvisation. One night he experienced an epiphany which he later verbalized:

> I was jamming in a chili house on Seventh Avenue between 139th and 140th. It was December, 1939. Now I'd been getting bored with the stereotyped changes that were being used all the time at the time, and I kept thinking there's bound to be something else. I could hear it sometimes but I couldn't play it. Well, that night, I was working over "Cherokee," and as I did, I found that by using the higher intervals of a chord as a melody line and backing them with appropriately related changes, I could play the thing I'd been hearing. I came alive.[62]

Parker's straightforwardly personal testimony joined a tradition of confessional discourse rooted in Puritan conversion narratives. The critics of postwar culture all shared a vision of American selfhood which—regardless of their own commitments—was rooted in the type of Protestant individualism and its attendant anxieties so brilliantly dissected by Alexis de Tocqueville. Yet by the 1950s America was well into what church historian Winthrop Hudson called "the post-Protestant age," a product not only of the massive immigration of Catholics and Jews since the late nineteenth century but of a crisis within Protestantism itself. As Alfred North Whitehead wrote in 1932, Protestantism's "dogmas no longer dominate; its divisions no longer interest; its institutions no longer direct the patterns of life." Postwar academic critics—among them many non-Protestants involved in their own struggle for acceptance—labored to fill the void left by the demise of Victorian intellectual gentility. They were thus horrified by bebop and even more so by the "beat generation" writers—notably Allen Ginsberg and Jack Kerouac—who rejected the security of their Ivy League educations in the name of just that type of freedom and spontaneity which Parker and his comrades embodied. There was a major irony in all of this. The members of the postwar underground, or nascent "counterculture," actually revived, consciously or otherwise, the antinomian tradition which was a fundamental component of American Protestant romanticism. As the French-Canadian Catholic Jack Kerouac put it, the beats were searching for a way to enunciate the "unspeakable visions of the individual." A major revival of American romanticism was thus underway, driven largely by individuals who had to discover and assimilate the tradition entirely on their own in the course of less than a generation.[63]

There was no tradition of personal "vision quests" in American Catholicism; moreover, ethnic Catholicism was as alien to classic American spiritual adventurers as to their less daring counterparts. While on the one hand Henry David Thoreau had demonstrated his kinship with Walden's merchants by making a careful accounting of his thrifty venture in the wild, on the other he portrayed an Irish farmer as hopelessly foreign to the gospel of productivity. "But alas," he wrote, after describing the hapless state of one John Field, "the culture of an Irishman is an enterprise to be undertaken with a sort of moral bog hoe." Thoreau also remarked, some years later: "I am not sure but this Catholic religion would be an admirable one if the priest were quite omitted." The only really heroic role model available to Dooley, initially, was that of the priesthood. To Catholic interviewers he often paid obeisance to this ideal; in so doing he was forced to denigrate his own vocation. "Dr. Dooley admits that he has been mulling over a religious vocation for years," wrote R. J. Allen in the *Catholic Digest*. "'I'd like very much to be a priest,' he says. 'If I felt I was halfway worthy, I would be one tomorrow. Think of the double blessing my work would have if I were a priest.'" In truth Dooley felt doubly damned for his mockery of the priestly commitment to celibacy, a problem aggravated by the great esteem in which priests were held, and the lack of sexual options for lay people. Occasionally some bitterness over this flared up in Dooley. "Strangely," a friend noted, "he was particularly hard on Catholics and others with pronounced religious training or convictions. He was determined that proselytizing must never become a part of Medico's field operations."[64]

Dooley's last fragments suggest his affinity with the emerging post-Protestant American avant-garde. He was something of a poet, and as the following, admittedly incoherent excerpt indicates, he was attuned to the kind of new language championed by Ginsberg and other beats:

Gentle sweetness
Keyhold of his eye
A cartoon moon shines overhead.
Red traffic lights give a sense of rain . . .
Green give a sense of distance, snow, sand,
Wild restless travel
I love you, and dig your greatness . . .
haunted in the mind by you
What is the amount of awe.
Great moon blue eyes of a saint.
Sad heap of the night
The huge unbelievable Lao nightland.[65]

Early in his career Dooley had provided hints that he was more than just a conventional Catholic boy from Notre Dame. He touched off a minor incident in 1956 by telling a reporter that he enjoyed the music of Elvis Presley. In the early morning hours of December 3, 1959, after appearing at a St. Louis Junior Chamber of Commerce banquet in which he was presented with a check for $18,000, Dooley escorted a visiting Laotian prince to the Chase Club, where they heard the Kingston Trio perform their best-known song, "Hang Down Your Head, Tom Dooley." Although the song was a traditional Irish ballad transmuted into a folk song concerning a desperado of the American West, many people mistakenly assumed the tune was directed at the newly famous jungle doctor of Laos. Dooley took it all in good humor, although one of his Catholic biographers later argued that the song was part of a Communist plot to "'get even' with Dr. Tom. They would use a song and make him look foolish. . . . It was about a man named 'Tom Dooley' who was being hung for doing wrong. . . . This is how the Communists work." Unlike many of his admirers, Dooley was far too sophisticated to believe such a thing. But by 1960 the effort to maintain his public image was beginning to take its toll. On a plane flight between Bangkok and Vientiane in November, he conversed with the wife of a fellow physician. She "seemed to be probing Tom's sincerity and motivations. She was a formidable verbal antagonist for him and he seemed puzzled. During the flight Tom made a couple of remarks which might go well only in a very 'Bohemian' group."[66]

Dooley's secret affinity for the bohemian or beat movement of the 1950s was probably rooted more deeply in his sexuality than in aesthetics or ideology. As

John D'Emilio wrote: "[T]he beats offered a model that allowed homosexuals to view their own lives from a different angle. Through the beats' example, gays could perceive themselves as nonconformists rather than deviates, as rebels against stultifying norms rather than immature, unstable personalities." At the same time, Dooley's vaguely bohemian romanticism was an unacknowledged source of his appeal to many Catholics perhaps growing slightly disillusioned with the uniformity of parish life. Teresa Gallagher organized a group of volunteer stenographers known as the "Dooley Disc Girls" at the Metropolitan Life Insurance Company in New York. Consisting mostly of Irish Catholics, the Disc Girls transcribed correspondence which Dooley sent from Laos on tape. He in turn introduced them to a very strange new world: "Tom's descriptions of the living conditions of the typical Lao home were fascinating to us." They found Dooley charming and elegant, and they admired the ease with which he moved through the society of largely non-Catholic New York sophisticates. Gallagher recalled that Dooley had "exquisite taste, particularly in jewelry." On his frequent trips to New York Teresa Gallagher witnessed an aspect of Dooley unknown to the public:

> Then there are the wonderful nights when I prowl like the beast . . . in the brooding silence of the city's night. Often Teresa comes with me, and we walk through the merciful anodyne of dark. I am not walled by the night. I can reach out to the ends of the earth, only at the night. In my hunger I can eat the very streets, my eye can see the hundreds of cities I have seen, my ear can hear the cacophony [*sic*] of languages I hear, my brain can gulp in huge draughts the visions of the millions I have seen suffer and suffer and suffer.[67]

Dooley brought a new appreciation to Gallagher and others of the Mystical Body of Christ—which she claimed was the central tenet of his program's philosophy. Dooley was also, as she later astutely pointed out, "an early worker in the ecumenical movement." In October 1960 Dooley returned from Laos bearing gifts for the Disc Girls. He presented Teresa Gallagher with a scroll from the walls of an ancient Buddhist temple, "explaining that these were to the Buddhist what a Station of the Cross was to a Catholic." Several years before the Second Vatican Council would modify the church's traditional teaching that there could be no salvation outside the church, Dooley had remarked, of his Buddhist patients: "I doubt if God will hold that against them." But Dooley was never primarily interested in renewing American Catholicism, although his concerns were often congruent with those of the liberal laity. His desire to interest American youth in the type of work he did led to his sympathetic criticism of alienated teenagers and their "age of the shrug." While he briefly succeeded in providing an alternative role model for Catholic and other youth, they quickly forgot him once he was dead. In *Strangers in the House*, a 1961 study of Catholic youth, Andrew Greeley quoted "a young friend" who had observed: "When Dooley died, a lot of people wept, but there weren't many who wanted to take his place." Even Teresa Gallagher—if inadvertently— indicated the nature of Dooley's competition when she wrote of one of his final campus appearances: "[T]he cheering could only be compared to the kind of rapturous cheering the Beatles arouse."[68]

MEDICO nearly went out of business during the years following Dooley's death. It had never outgrown its total identification, in the public mind, with his own work and personality (despite belated efforts by Dooley to place it on a sounder foundation). In 1962 MEDICO was virtually swallowed up by CARE. Dooley's closest followers had been quarreling among themselves since shortly after his death, and now they were exiled from any work connected with his name. The executive director of CARE at the time recalled thinking of Dooley's associates and volunteers: "'My God, what a crew.' There was a lot of bitterness in those days among Dooley's followers." A surgeon named Verne Chaney— who had worked briefly for MEDICO in Cambodia and Vietnam—launched the Tom Dooley Foundation in 1961. He soon alienated Teresa Gallagher and others close to Dooley by straying from the small scale personalism of MEDICO, conducting surveys and other expensive programs. Gallagher told him: "'Tom never wanted to do any surveys.' But Chaney would say, 'We're not in the bandaid business anymore, Teresa. We're big time.'" In 1970 Gallagher established the Tom Dooley Heritage, a voluntary agency which constructed a hospital in northeast Thailand to treat Laotian refugees, mainly Hmong tribes- man who had aided the United States in its "secret" war against the Viet Cong in Laos. Tom Dooley Heritage was thus involved in precisely the sort of work which launched the career of its inspirator and honoree in 1954, but although the Hmong had fled the Communist Pathet Lao—and a number of them converted to Catholicism—there was little likelihood the program would cap- ture the American imagination.[69]

The acrimony and dissension which beset Dooley's survivors presaged the dissolution of a distinct Catholic culture in the years following the heady triumphs of the Second Vatican Council, 1962–65. While for some Dooley remained a crucial link to a lost era (as Verne Chaney unkindly remarked of a number of Dooley's former volunteer secretaries: "[T]hey get together and they practically have seances with Tom"), others now saw him as a ludicrous figure from the Catholic Dark Ages. Writing for a Catholic magazine in 1969, journalist Nicholas von Hoffman suggested that Dooley would go down in history as "too preposterous a figure for youth to identify with or to use as a model to imitate in their own lives." Dooley was even condemned, in the late 1960s, in the pages of Notre Dame's student newspaper. The rapid shift in Catholic opinion toward Dooley only indicated the fragility of that culture's foundations, *before* as well as after the shocks of the 1960s. More than a tragic, transitional figure between Joe McCarthy and John F. Kennedy, Dooley was a genuinely American character who offered a variety of mystical self-expression which had never before been seen within American Catholicism and which, by the time of his death, could no longer be contained within Catholic culture. For all his popularity he was, in his last years, stranded without a constituency he could feel comfortable with. He was surprisingly close in spirit to the beat movement, but he remained too thoroughly Irish Catholic to feel fully at home there. Dooley generated his own vision of what productive work in the world entailed, but in the end his own medical work was actually relevant only insofar as it provided him with the raw experiential materials needed to fashion a story of his own life. While he cured many among the sick of Laos, he did his patients no favor by abandoning several hospitals in search of greater adventure. As Dooley often stated, he identified himself most intimately as a physician of a special sort. "This kind of medicine is my salvation, my hold on life. It is my means of expression. . . . I must treat patients with my own hands, reach out and give personal help every day." But one of the surprising aspects of the fragments from "The Night of the Same Day" is the extent to which Dooley saw his authorial identity as directly linked to his medical vocation. His publisher, he wrote, "slaps me right up against the naked facts of self and work . . . and there is nothing beyond me that can help me. . . . [T]he strength must be in me, words must pull out of me . . . there can be no substitute. For me . . . a time of stress and torment." This is what lay behind his "passionate desire to tell others of this work, of this kind of medicine, of this life."[70]

In the end his actual work was largely irrelevant to American anticommunism or the fate of American influence in Southeast Asia. But as a self-described "old romantic" he managed to move Catholic personalism close to the sources of classic American selfhood and self-expression, a not inconsiderable achievement. The title of *The Night They Burned the Mountain* referred to the Lao mountain tribesmen's custom of setting fire to the hillsides just before the rainy season, so that the soaked ashes would provide rich fertilizer for their poor mountain rice fields. Dooley was at first terrified at the sight of the mountain on fire, until a Lao assistant appeared by his side and said, "Do not fear, Thanh Mo America, this is the night they burn the mountain." Later that year, as he recuperated from cancer surgery in New York, Dooley dreamed of the mountain: "My boys were with me, and some of my Lao students. And in the vivid flash of the moment, in my dream, I saw a century-old pagoda that nestles on the mountain slope.The pagoda is made of mud stones and is crowned by a high spire. Hanging from the spire are long white banners, the streamers of Buddhist prayers." In the dream Dooley then saw the Laotians planting rice seedlings into the "burnt soil" of the mountain. Upon waking, he "knew the meaning of my dream." "After Communion that morning, Tuesday, the first of September, my God and my dream commanded me. I must, into the burnt soil of my personal mountain of sadness, plant the new seedlings of my life—I must continue to live." The product of a startlingly disparate variety of forces, Dooley's self-evasions protected his inspirational mission until it could no longer be sustained by temperament or circumstance. He was the last Catholic hero of the preconciliar years, and while his legacy was shattered by the subsequent, intertwined history of his church and his country, he provided an obscure, fragmentary model for a new Catholic identity in which the story of one's soul could be told as part of an American adventure.[71]

Jack Kerouac and Thomas Merton,

the Last Catholic Romantics

The strange career of Dr. Tom Dooley offered up a species of Catholic romanticism that threatened to outgrow its separatist origins to play a more engaged role in the national culture. Yet by the end of his life Dooley was expressing his Catholicity in such an unprecedented manner that there was little chance his example would soon be widely emulated. His identity as celebrity mystic was the product of diverse ethnic, religious, sexual, educational, and class influences all related in varying degrees to the special experience of Catholic immigrants in America. The early strength and ultimate weakness of the personalism of Dorothy Day lay precisely in her resistance to the impact of American experience on Catholic culture. American Catholics of the 1930s had plenty to fear from their host culture; American Catholics of the 1950s felt they had everything to gain. The "reverse pilgrimage" of the alienated convert was now challenged by the thrill of discovery for postimmigrant "cradle Catholics." It was not, however, a process without great price in pain, both to converts seeking eternal truth through the church and lifelong Catholics whose attraction to secular culture often resulted in severe crises of identity. The disparity between the two traditions narrowed in the 1950s and early 1960s, as evidenced by the experience of the two most vulnerable Catholic romantics of the postwar era.

In the epigraph to his spiritual diary, *The Sign of Jonas* (1953), the Trappist monk Thomas Merton wrote: "I find myself traveling toward my destiny in the belly of a paradox." The son of artists (his mother was from Ohio, his father from New Zealand), raised in Europe and America, Merton converted to

Catholicism in 1938 and entered the Trappist's Monastery of Our Lady of Gethsemani in Kentucky three days after the bombing of Pearl Harbor. He took vows of obedience as well as silence: when his abbot suggested he need not entirely forsake the writing career he had begun in "the world," Merton dutifully produced devotional works, along with an autobiography (*The Seven Storey Mountain*, 1948) which became one of the great success stories in the history of American publishing. Having turned his back upon the world, Merton became a great American Catholic celebrity.[1]

That was one paradox, but an even larger one centered around Merton's role as an "official" Catholic romantic at a time when a kindred spirit and native child of American Catholicism—the "beat" novelist, Jean-Louis Lebris de Kerouac—was ignored or reviled in his own search for grace.

Jack Kerouac was born in the mill town of Lowell, Massachusetts, on March 12, 1922, the son of Leo Alcide and Gabrielle Ange Levesque Kerouac. They were Catholic immigrants from Quebec who grew up in Nashua, New Hampshire. Kerouac was the couple's third and final child; he had a brother, Gerard, and a sister, Caroline, or "Nin." Kerouac grew up in the separate world of the Franco-American subculture: until he entered a public junior high school at the age of eleven (his family having moved to the Pawtucketville section of Lowell, Jack was now considered by the administrators of St. Joseph's School to be living "outside the official zone" encompassed by the school), he spoke little English. He was called "Ti Pousse" (little thumb) as a baby, and "Ti Jean" forever after by his mother, whom he called Memere.[2]

All of Kerouac's biographers have duly noted his Catholicity, but it is generally viewed as an unfortunate anachronism colored by the defensive, anti-intellectual Franco-American culture of his boyhood. Kerouac's religiosity has often been depicted as a destructive force which finally triumphed over the tolerant, libertarian bohemianism he espoused as spokesman for the beat generation. Historian Richard Sorrell was among those few who sensed that Kerouac's "life and literature can best be understood in terms of his ethno-religious background, which was heavily Franco-Catholic."[3] Sorrell, along with the French-Canadian novelist Victor Lévy Beaulieu, provided the cultural-historical background for Kerouac's mystical, intensely "gloomy" Catholicism. Franco-Americans in New England were closely linked to the continuing traumas of their coreligionists in Canada, where British conquest had created enormous anxieties about the survival of French-Catholic culture in North America. Those who immigrated to the United States between 1860 and the

1920s—in search of work in the textile mills and factories of New England—brought with them an especially pressing anxiety about their role in promoting "la survivance." Most of those whom Sorrell termed the "Franco-American elite"

> carried the concept of a providential mission with them from French Canada: past and future, heritage and destiny, were linked together by a divine union of nationalism and Catholicism. They were the pure Catholic nationality which would expand the kingdom of God and expose the false material values of Protestantism. Religion thus became a way of life, rather than just a part of life, as Catholicism became increasingly associated with nationalism in Quebec, and with conservative and even reactionary theological and social views.[4]

In Woonsocket, Rhode Island, in the 1920s, an episode known as the "Sentinelle affair" brought the issue of "survivance" to the forefront of Catholic life and revealed the complexity of intraethnic Catholic relationships as well as the relationship of the church to American culture. The Sentinelles were militant Franco-Americans who resented the efforts of the Irish-controlled diocese of Providence to coerce Americanization through the primary use of English in secondary schools. The issues recalled the nineteenth-century Cahensly affair and a variety of other conflicts rooted in the desire of non–Irish-Catholic immigrants to control their own national parishes and schools. Despite the papal condemnation of the "phantom heresy" of Americanism in 1899, the proassimilationist wing of the Irish hierarchy was clearly in control of the church by the 1920s. One of the revealing aspects of the Sentinelle affair was the hierarchy's use of a "Franco woman, Rose Ferron, celebrated for her stigmata, to pray for the wayward sinners and force them into submission." Victor Lévy Beaulieu claimed that, although Jack Kerouac was but a small child during the affair, his "mother often told him about Rose's religious epic and her role in the affair that had Monsignor Hickey opposing the Sentinellists."[5]

Kerouac was thus introduced from the cradle to antitriumphalist immigrant mysticism; its effect on his life and work would be enormous. The death of his beloved "saintly" nine-year-old brother Gerard (when Jack was four) provided him with an additional spiritual burden. He was indelibly marked with the image of "the nuns at Gerard's bedside to take down his dying words because they'd heard his astonishing revelations of heaven delivered in catechism class." Influenced perhaps by the exalted status of martyrs such as Marie-Rose

Ferron, Jack "gleefully ran to tell his father" upon learning of his brother's death. For this and other reasons he developed an increasing sense of guilt toward his late brother and his parents. According to Kerouac biographer Dennis McNally: "For the rest of Jean's childhood, tales of Gerard's goodness would be the staple of Memere's lessons in behavior, lessons that reminded him endlessly of his inferiority and suggested that he was somehow responsible for his brother's death."[6]

Kerouac's 1963 novel, Visions of Gerard, was cited in a scholarly article on Franco Americans and family therapy for its depiction of the maudlin Jansenism he absorbed in Catholic school: "But you bumbling fool you're a mass of sin, a veritable barrel of it, you swish and swash in it like molassess—you ooze mistakes through your frail crevasses." Yet the relics of Jack's boyhood religion became, in time, a rich source of inspiration. Like no Catholic before him, Kerouac was able to blend mystical imagery with materials from the American popular culture he adored with equal fervor. In Dr. Sax he wrote of "the statue of Ste. Thérèse turning her head in an antique Catholic twenties film with Ste. Thérèse dashing across town in a car with W. C. Fieldsian close shaves." He wrote more hauntingly of "the cross in my mother's room, a salesman had sold it to her in Centralville, it was a phosphorescent Christ on a black-lacquered Cross—it glowed the Jesus in the Dark, I gulped for fear every time I passed it the moment the sun went down, it took that own luminosity like a bier, it was like Murder by the Clock the horrible fear-shrieking movie about the old lady clacking out of her mausoleum at midnight."[7]

Kerouac's early love for the Three Stooges and the Shadow, Krazy Kat, and Harpo Marx reflected an early desire for experience beyond the limits of immigrant Catholicism. His parents faced the same dilemma as millions of other immigrants: how to improve their lives without doing violence to a cultural inheritance which viewed undue ambition and mobility with suspicion. Gabrielle and, especially, Leo Kerouac tended—more than most of their compatriots—to instill in their children (Jack more than Nin) a nascent success ethic. The family struggled to live apart from "Little Canada," the most conspicuously Franco-American neighborhood in Lowell. For all that Catholicism meant to these immigrants, Kerouac's early years were actually spent amidst an environment in which the church was at once venerated and derided; suspiciously viewed as an obstacle to American success as much as a source of communal strength. Leo Kerouac's "intransigent Catholicism" was not without the anticlerical streak common to many non-Irish immigrants. As Kerouac biographer Gerald Nicosia wrote: "Leo was not about to serve what he saw as a money making enterprise. Not only did he refuse to attend Mass; but when Gabrielle asked a priest to come and speak with him, he told the priest to 'get lost' right in front of the neighbors. In a French-Canadian neighborhood at that time, such an act was shocking."[8]

Kerouac neatly captured this earthy irreverence in *Dr. Sax*, his "Gothic fairy tale" of a Lowell childhood. Recalling the "poor priest LaPoule DuPuis" ("the last unmarried son of a huge Quebec family that according to tradition felt it would be damned if someone in the house didn't belong to the priesthood so madcap sexfiend LaPoule was retired piously behind the cloistral wall"), he wrote: "One Saturday night he got dead drunk after pirouetting with all the ladies at a big roaring party and passed out before midnight (woulda stopped drinking at midnight anyway, as he was saying Mass in the morning). Come morning Joe's father hauls LaPoule into the shower, shoves black coffee down his throat, then calls the whole gang to come see the fun at eleven o'clock Mass—."[9]

This was Kerouac's remembrance of 1930s Lowell, written from the bathroom of William S. Burrough's Mexico City apartment in 1952. Kerouac's bittersweet, nostalgic evocation of bygone ethnic neighborhoods was but one of the many highly conservative aspects of his work. Although he was fairly oblivious to the history of American Catholicism, it was the dual ascendance of liberal, "Americanist" clerics and "radical" converts that helped obliterate the often bawdy, brawling aspects of immigrant life by the 1950s. By then Catholicism was increasingly acceptable—even, in some rarefied precincts, surprisingly fashionable—while manifestations of ethnicity were virtually taboo. In his best (and, until 1973, unpublishable) book, *Visions of Cody*, Kerouac presented a long series of surreptitious observations of New Yorkers which demonstrated his persistent appreciation of ethnicity. He wrote of

the Irish gentleman all bundled tightly in a dark greenslick raincoat, collar up, tight at his raveled chin, hat, no umbrella, a little anxious as he proceeds somewhat slowly to his objective and lost in thought of his job or wife or by God anything including feelings of homosexual deterioration or that Communists are secretly controlling his life at this very moment by thought-waves from a machine projecting from a submarine five miles offshore, maybe a teletype operator at U.P., thinking this he goes down Sixth Avenue the name of which was changed to Avenue of the Americas some years ago to his complete disgust.

In a similar vein he described "the sharp little Jewish lady in a fur coat who lofts an umbrella that catches the eye it's so expensive and designed (red on brown) so beautifully, cutting along with that surefooted bandy legged gazotsky waddle that distinguishes her from other ladies."[10]

Kerouac's attentiveness to ethnicity—however pointed and perhaps even unsavory at times—was an aspect of his resistance to the growing conformity of American culture after the Second World War. The secretive nature of the sketches in Visions of Cody reflects Kerouac's knowledge that his insights led in nearly forbidden or at least unpopular directions. Coupled with the seeming formlessness of the work, his anachronistic preoccupations were often inaccessible to even his most ardent contemporary supporters. In 1952 Allen Ginsberg wrote to their mutual friend, Neal Cassady (the "Cody" of the title): "Jack's book arrived and it's a holy mess—it's great allright but he did everything he could to fuck it up with a lot of meaningless bullshit I think, page after page of surrealist free association. . . . I don't think it can be published anywhere, in its present state. . . . [W]hy is he tempting rejection and fate?" By 1972 it was clear to Ginsberg that the book, like so much of Kerouac's work, was largely concerned with the loss of community in America, and that Jack's fascination with human variety reflected his "tender brooding compassion for bygone scene and personal Individuality oddity'd therein."[11] Kerouac could recall a time when Catholicism was an integral part of community life; by the late 1940s he was estranged from the church in large part because the Lowell of his boyhood now existed only as a powerful goad to the imagination. Official Catholicism was as uninterested in ethnic diversity during this period as academic social critics; this helps explain, in part, why Kerouac was not taken seriously as a Catholic writer. For one of the main components of Kerouac's beat sensibility was a jeremiadic obsession with the loss of immigrant culture: "The sins of America are precisely that the streets . . . are empty where their houses are, there's no sense of neighborhood anymore, a neighborhood quarter or a neighborhood freeforall fight between two streets of young husbands is no longer possible except I think in Dagwood Bumstead and he ain't for real—he couldn't— beyond this old honesty there can only be thieves."[12]

While Kerouac mourned the loss of a culture in the late 1940s, Thomas

Merton celebrated his discovery of one. But the Catholicism of *The Seven Storey Mountain* was nothing like that of Kerouac's 1930s Lowell. Although Merton would grow, painfully, into engagement with the suffering of the world, he owed his initial fame to an account of leaving that world for the timeless peace of monastic life. His Kentucky monastery might well have been located anywhere in the world, for all its detachment from temporal life.

Merton's rootlessness made his preconversion life all the more fascinating to the readers of *The Seven Storey Mountain*. His father, Owen Merton, was an accomplished though financially insecure New Zealand painter who met his wife, Ruth Jenkins Merton, at the Paris atelier of Percyval Tudor-Hart. Ruth Jenkins, who was also a student of Percyval-Hart, was the daughter of Martha Baldwin and Samuel Adams Jenkins. Jenkins eventually "became important in the life of his grandson to a degree Thomas Merton was sometimes reluctant to admit." Nominally Episcopalian, ("[M]y grandparents were like most other Americans," Merton wrote. "They were Protestants, but you could never find out precisely what kind of Protestants they were"), Jenkins was from pioneer stock (a member of the "Sons of Ohio") and became a successful salesman in the 1890s for the publishing firm of Grosset and Dunlap. Later he achieved financial independence through, among other things, the sale of picture books "which would tell the story of a popular film using stills from the movie."[13]

Jenkins—who provided for Thomas Merton's needs throughout most of his youth—was similar to Dorothy Day's father in his unabashed Philistinism and his "freely expressed prejudices against foreigners and Jews." Moreover, "Catholicism had become associated, in his mind, with everything dishonest and crooked and immoral." Merton grew up with a "deep, almost subconscious aversion from the vague and evil thing, which I called Catholicism." Even more than Dorothy Day, Merton identified Catholicism with the deepest prejudices of an adult he resented but could not reject directly. Conversion presented at least in one sense an opportunity for retribution. Of his grandfather he wrote: "Pop was very well liked. The term 'live-wire' was singularly appropriate for him. He was always bristling with nervous energy, and most people were happy when he came shouting through their departments, snapping his fingers and whacking all the desks with a rolled-up copy of the *Evening Telegram*."[14]

Ruth Jenkins was encouraged to pursue an artistic career ("in an era when this was a social asset in a daughter and a social disaster in a son"), but her father was not pleased by either her decision to study in Paris or her marriage to an impoverished painter. According to Merton biographer Michael Mott,

Jenkins blamed himself for having taken his family on "restless European tours," during which he sometimes scattered "small change in showers from the car as he passed through villages in France." Yet despite her mildly "modernist" airs Ruth Jenkins was simply modern: she reared her son Tom (his given name; she resolutely rejected the more formal Thomas) after the fashion of a well-educated secularist from a distinctly Protestant background. She was extraordinarily observant of each stage of his development, keeping a journal to chart his progress. Merton later showed some bitterness toward what he considered his mother's "cerebral" approach to child-rearing: "[A]t home, my education was progressing along the lines laid down by some progressive method that Mother had read about in one of those magazines." He noted that his grandmother had to teach him the Lord's Prayer: "The only explanation I have is the guess that Mother must have had strong views on the subject. Possibly she considered any organized religion below the standard of intellectual perfection she demanded of any child of hers."[15]

Like Kerouac, Merton had an important relationship with a brother; in this case a younger one, John Paul (born in 1918, he would die in the crash of a Canadian Air Force plane over the English Channel in 1943, less than a year after going to Gethsemani to be baptized). Although he never described John Paul as exactly "saintly," Merton wrote that his brother "was a child with a much serener nature than mine, with not so many obscure drives and impulses." In *The Seven Storey Mountain* Merton recorded his guilt over having mistreated John Paul when they were children. He recalled an incident when he and some friends threw rocks at the younger boy to scare him away. John Paul had simply stood by impassively under the assault. "Many times it was like that. And in a sense, this terrible situation is the pattern and prototype of all sin: the deliberate and formal will to reject disinterested love for the purely arbitrary reason that we simply do not want it." Michael Mott suggested a more mundane reason for the hostility: Merton's jealousy of the attention his mother paid to her new child:

> For three and a half years Ruth had found everything Tom did important enough to write down. Now she was writing about John Paul. This baby took his rests. This baby had no temper tantrums. Tom now had tantrums enough for any number of children, yet these did not draw his parents' attention to him for long, and they went into no notes. There was no mirror, no reflection back: above all, there was no written record. This did

not take from him the impression that all he did was important, only that all the important things he did and saw and said were being wasted for want of a recorder.[16]

This sense of rejection provided a source of Merton's creativity; he turned to books and cultivated the life of his imagination. Then his mother became ill and died when he was six years old. He later wrote that "her sickness probably accounts for my memory of her as thin and pale and rather severe." His mother's death provided an early lesson about impermanence and loss and precipitated a life "on the road" with an artist father seeking fresh landscapes inside and out.[17]

Merton's remark, "mother's death had made one thing evident: Father now did not have to do anything but paint," suggests both that his parents were not particularly close (Merton's biographers avoid the subject, but a pervasive feeling of distance and coolness emerges just the same), and a sense that his father viewed him as something of a burden. Owen Merton was anxious for his sons to be well educated, but this entailed periods of separation and a general uprootedness which saw Tom spending brief periods in Bermuda, Long Island, and France before he was finally taken to England in 1928. The following year, being ineligible for "front rank schools like Eton or Harrow" by virtue of his erratic schooling, he enrolled at Oakham, a small and fairly undistinguished "public" school. Shortly thereafter his father became seriously ill; in 1931, at the age of fifteen, Merton became an orphan.[18]

Accounts of Merton's adolescence stress his extensive travel and his growing appreciation for the high culture of European Catholic tradition. Surprisingly, his privileged status has rarely been considered of special importance, nor has the fact that his education and wanderings were largely made possible by the American grandfather who would fare quite poorly in Merton's authorial estimation. That is not to say that he lived luxuriously, but that he enjoyed a style that only members of the leisure class could take for granted. Merton clearly identified instead with the impoverished refinement of his parents: "[F]rom both I got capacities for work and vision and enjoyment and expression that ought to have made me some kind of a King, if the standards the world lives by were the real ones. Not that we ever had any money: but any fool knows that you don't need money to get enjoyment out of life."[19]

In 1933 Merton received a scholarship to Clare College, Cambridge; under the influence of his British guardian, he decided to prepare for a career in the

Foreign Service. Merton's brief stint at Cambridge was a disaster and a turning point. His prep school friends later reported that he "went right off the rails . . . mucked in with the wrong set. . . . [D]ebauchery is not too strong a word." The Trappist censors of *The Seven Storey Mountain* made certain that Merton's readers could only speculate what he meant when he wrote that "my soul and all its faculties were going to seed because there was nothing to control my appetites—and they were pouring themselves out in an incoherent riot of undirected passion." Merton's evasions only spurred heightened interest in his misdeeds: the most common rumor was that he had impregnated a young woman who subsequently (after Merton had left England) was killed along with their child in the German blitz of 1940. Merton's biographers are in agreement that there was an involvement with a woman that resulted in the threat of legal action against him. His guardian simply told Merton not to return to Cambridge for his second year. Biographer Monica Furlong wrote that "it was common enough then for a 'gentleman' to father a child by a 'lower class' girl and then disown her." Merton's friend Ed Rice plainly stated that "it was a serious, complicated situation and in retrospect clearly one that had a lot to do with his eventual conversion and vocation." According to Michael Mott, there is also "a good deal of circumstantial evidence" that Merton agreed to "be nailed (or pretend he was being nailed) to a cross" at a drunken Cambridge party. Like Dorothy Day, then, Merton's preconversion life seems to have featured not just unconventional but "blasphemous" behavior, for which he was later more than anxious to atone. Merton's upper-class Cambridge "decadence" was even more alien to the experience of most American Catholics than Dorothy Day's; thus the great interest which so many of them found in his confessions.[20]

Merton's trust fund remained intact despite his various Cambridge scandals since his grandfather was probably not informed as to the reasons why Tom left the university. He enrolled instead at Columbia College, commuting by train from the Jenkins's Long Island home. Merton graduated from Columbia in 1938, two years before Jack Kerouac—a highly recruited high school football player—began his brief but memorable career there. Columbia ("this big sooty factory") represented a step down in class for Merton, but he felt liberated by the "genuine intellectual vitality in the air—at least relatively speaking." To the Kerouac family Columbia stood for opportunity: Jack would become a professional man and rescue his parents from a life of drudgery. He had chosen Columbia over Boston College despite the fact that his father had been assured of lucrative printing contracts should Jack enroll there. But in *Vanity of Duluoz* Kerouac recalled: "I had not wanted to go to a Jesuit school, let's put it flatly. Not only did I want to go to Columbia College so I could dig the city . . . but I didn't like the idea of being told what to think by professors in big black robes."[21]

The differences between Merton and Kerouac went beyond class and ethnic background. Ironically, it was the slight, relatively unathletic Merton who went on to become a "big man on campus," while Kerouac (despite having achieved a ninety-two average during his year at the prestigious Horace Mann school, where he had been sent to prepare for Columbia academics) failed to take his schoolwork or campus life very seriously. Merton became editor of the yearbook and art editor of a campus humor magazine. "He was invariably dressed like a businessman, in a neat suit and a double-breasted chesterfield topcoat, carrying a leather briefcase full of papers, articles, books and drawings." Five years later, on the same campus, Kerouac "cut classes and stayed in [his] room and slept in the arms of God." He did become briefly prominent after breaking his leg in a game against the Army freshmen. "Jack had become so popular as the injured football hero, hobbling around campus on his crutches, that someone started a campaign to get him elected vice-president of next year's sophomore class." But Kerouac failed chemistry and lost much of his enthusiasm for football. Some of Kerouac's Lowell friends had worried that "Jack wouldn't be able to handle that Ivy League world. Jack didn't seem as brilliant as the others, and he always appeared more comfortable in the Pawtucketville gang than with people as literate as himself." In September 1941, as America grew closer to entering the war, Kerouac "cut himself off from traditional achievement forever" by quitting school and hitting the road.[22]

A great deal transpired between 1935 and 1941 to partially account for the very different experiences Merton and Kerouac knew at Columbia. Political activism was at its peak during Merton's years there; he even briefly joined the Communist party (taking the name "Frank Swift"), despite being even less interested in Marxism than Dorothy Day. By the time the *Seven Storey Mountain* was published, a prior flirtation with communism was virtually obligatory for converts to Catholicism. Merton wrote that "there were, at that time, quite a few Communists or Communist sympathizers among the undergraduates, and especially in Columbia College where most of the smartest students were Reds." At the same time he described the bulk of the faculty as "liberals." By the time Kerouac arrived at Morningside Heights the campus Left was fairly dormant, yet he wrote, in *Desolation Angels*: "[W]hen I went to Columbia all they tried to teach us was Marx, as if I cared." But rather than viewing communism as Merton later did, as heretical, Kerouac linked it with psychoanalysis and all the other rationalist ideologies which he viewed as illusory distractions from the romantic business of self-expression. The real difference between Merton and Kerouac—both in their Columbia days and for years thereafter—was that the former was oriented toward scholasticism, despite being a bit of a "character," while Kerouac was a thoroughgoing antinomian.[23]

Merton's conversion was a largely intellectual affair. In February 1937, with "five or ten loose dollars burning a hole in my pocket," he walked into Scribner's bookstore in Manhattan and purchased a copy of Etienne Gilson's *The Spirit of Medieval Philosophy* (he was taking a course at the time on French medieval literature). It was only as he rode on the train toward home that he discovered the imprimatur signifying that this was a "Catholic book." "I felt as if I had been cheated . . . you must understand that while I admired Catholic culture, I had always been afraid of the Catholic Church." But as he grudgingly read the book Merton grew fascinated with the French scholastic's discussion of "aseitas":

> In this one word, which can be applied to God alone, and which expresses His most characteristic attribute, I discovered an entirely new concept of God—a concept which showed me at once that the belief of Catholics was by no means the vague and rather superstitious hangover from an unscientific age that I had believed it to be. . . . Aseitas—the English equivalent is a transliteration: aseity—simply means the power of a being to exist absolutely in virtue of itself, not as caused by itself, but as requiring no cause, no other justification for its existence except that its very nature is to exist. There can be only one such Being: that is God.[24]

Merton's movement toward the certitudes of Catholic thought did not actually estrange him from secular academic life: if anything it drew him closer to an important segment of the literary and philosophical establishment of the late 1930s. His favorite professor at Columbia was Mark Van Doren, the renowned litterateur. Merton wrote that "Mark's temper was profoundly scholastic in the sense that his clear mind looked directly for the quiddities of things, and sought being and substance under the covering of accident and appearances." Van Doren was friendly with the American neo-Thomists Mortimer Adler and Richard McKeon, who "had started out at Columbia but had to move to Chicago, because Columbia was not ripe enough to know what to make of them." Neo-Thomism provided the sense of order which Merton craved. His celebrated frenzied search for meaning was actually not so unusual nor extreme in itself; it only seemed so to Merton and his readers because underneath lay a rather cautious sensibility. Even the "nervous breakdown" he describes in *The Seven Storey Mountain* sounds more like a case of simple exhaustion caused by Merton's far-flung campus activities. The stuffy tone in which he later described his experience of New York nightlife was surely not the product of monasticism, but rather rooted deeply in his temperament:

> Three or four nights a week my fraternity brothers and I would go flying down in the black and roaring subway to 52nd Street where we would crawl around the tiny, noisy, and expensive nightclubs that had flowered on the sites of the old speakeasies in the cellars of those dirty brownstone houses. There we would sit, for hours, packed in those dark rooms, shoulder to shoulder with a lot of surly strangers and their girls, while the whole place rocked and surged with storms of jazz. . . . It was not that we got drunk. No, it was this strange business of sitting in a room full of people and drinking without much speech, and letting yourself be deafened by the jazz that throbbed through the whole sea of bodies binding them all together in a kind of fluid medium. It was a strange, animal travesty of mysticism, sitting in those booming rooms, with the noise pouring through you, and the rhythm jumping and throbbing in the marrow of your bones. You couldn't call any of that, per se, a mortal sin. We just sat there, that was all.[25]

In the 1950s and thereafter, Merton was occasionally viewed as a progenitor of the beat generation. His Columbia friend Ed Rice wrote, in 1958: "Some people think that Thomas Merton was the prototype of all the beat young men 'hung up in this sad world.' Obliquely and in confusion, with many false starts and up countless blind alleys he finally worked his way out of the modern trap and found a measure of peace in the silence and solitude of Gethsemani. Others of course are still looking." Yet it was precisely the triumphalistic outcome of his search that legitimated Merton's experience, in the view of a Catholic intellectual culture still convinced that "outside scholasticism there seems to be nothing but intellectual chaos and despair." Merton's conversion, as the antidote to the random uncertainty of experience, worked analogically within the broader trajectory of American Catholicism. As historian William

Halsey argued: "To achieve success, Thomism was used, some would say abused, to maintain a hold on reality where the value of stability triumphed over flux even while restlessness and movement were ever-present forces in American Catholic life." There is a singularly grim quality to Merton's account of his preconversion, pseudobohemian existence. The author of a 1949 *Life* article in praise of the Trappists wrote of Merton, with perhaps inadvertent bluntness: "[H]e became thoroughly disgusted with himself and joined the Catholic Church." Only as Merton matured and grew more interested in personal spirituality would he chafe against monastic discipline and authority. Beginning in the 1950s, many Catholic intellectuals outside the monastery gates would experience similar feelings. Merton's career would chart that evolution toward a more personalist Catholicism; he would always remain an official, highly representative Catholic figure.[26]

Jack Kerouac had identified intimately with a personal Christ since early childhood; doctrinal formalities paled before his desire to have "God show me his face." The young protagonist of his first novel, *The Town and the City*, thought of the church as the home of "Jesus suffering and heroic, dark, dark, Jesus and his cross, dear great sacrificial Jesus the hero and the Lamb. . . . [H]e had wept at the spectacle of that heroic sorrow." The intensity of the relationship proceeded apace: "Then the boy looked up at the altar manger and saw that he too must suffer and be crucified like the Child Jesus there, who was crucified for his sake, but who also pointed out what was going to happen to him, for he too was a child with a holy mother, therefore he too would be drawn to Calvary and the wind would begin to howl and everything would get dark."[27]

In his childhood mysticism Kerouac often imbued social outcasts or "deviant" characters with saintly and even Christlike attributes. In *Dr. Sax* he recalled a figure known as "Zaza:" "[H]e had a maniac laugh he was an idiot, underdeveloped mentality, sweet and kind, tremendously dirty, saintly, goofy, hard-working, willing, did chores I guess, a monster idiot Frenchman from the woods." At Columbia Kerouac may unconsciously have come to see himself in a similar way, and he sought the same qualities in his friends. After brief stints in the Merchant Marine and the Navy (where he was discharged as an "indifferent character": in *Vanity of Duluoz* he remembered explaining to the Navy psychiatrist: "I'm only Samuel Johnson, I was the nut of the Columbia campus, everybody knew it. . . . [I]t's not that I refuse Naval discipline, not that I WONT take it, but that I CANNOT"),[28] Kerouac returned to the campus in

1943 but left school for good after one last attempt to rejoin the football team. He soon grew close to the individuals who comprised the literary and inspirational nucleus of the beat generation: Allen Ginsberg, William S. Burroughs, and Lucien Carr, among others. He also met his first wife, Edie Parker, a wealthy art student from Detroit.

Most of Kerouac's intellectual friends came from "better" circumstances, a fact which often made him insecure. Lucien Carr "sorta looked at me as some kind of lout which was true." One night Carr and another friend ripped a suitcoat off the back of William S. Burroughs (Harvard graduate and disowned scion of a wealthy St. Louis family) and tore it into ribbons. "And of course to a Lowell boy like me, destroying a coat was strange but to them . . . they all came from well-to-do families." Yet Burroughs and the others introduced Kerouac to the mysterious night world of Times Square and environs, and he responded to that world as though he had rediscovered a lost universe of immense human variety and color.[29]

In a 1959 essay, "The Origins of the Beat Generation," Kerouac responded to the concerted attack on his work and the beat phenomenon by locating its roots in a spiritual revival he first discovered among the outcasts of Times Square. "One of them, Huncke of Chicago, came up to me and said 'Man, I'm beat.' I knew right away what he meant somehow. . . . [T]he hipsters, whose music was bop, they looked like criminals but they kept talking about the same things I liked, long outlines of personal experience and vision, night-long confessions full of hope that had become illicit and repressed by War, stirrings, rumblings of a new soul (that same old human soul). And so Huncke appeared to us and said 'I'm beat' with radiant light shining out of his despairing eyes."[30] Before he fully grasped the religious significance of the broken yet knowing inhabitants of the demimonde, Kerouac celebrated the pure variety of the scene, as though it represented a surrogate Lowell in its working-class albeit bohemian vitality. In his first and most "conventional" novel, the Wolfe-inspired *The Town and the City*, he wrote of

> soldiers, sailors, the panhandlers and drifters, the zoot-suiters, the hoodlums, the young men who washed dishes in cafeterias from coast to coast, the hitch-hikers, the hustlers, the drunks, the battered lonely young Negroes, the twinkling little Chinese, the dark Puerto Ricans, and the varieties of dungareed young Americans in leather jackets who were seamen and mechanics and garagemen everywhere. . . . [N]owhere was it

so dense and fabulous as on Times Square. All the cats and characters, all the spicks and spades, Harlem-drowned, street-drunk and slain, crowded together, streaming back and forth, looking for something, waiting for something, forever moving around.[31]

From the very start of his literary career, then, Kerouac's work was antithetical to the experience-denying scholasticism of official Catholicism, although the challenge was as much unintended as it was unacknowledged.

At the same time, Kerouac's nascent bohemianism estranged him from his parents, who continued to dream of the comfortable retirement which Jack's Ivy League education was supposed to provide. Leo and Gabrielle had followed him to New York in search of work in the early 1940s, so they witnessed his transformation firsthand. In *Vanity of Duluoz* Kerouac recalled his father asking, "[C]an't you find good young friends anymore?" In August 1944 Lucien Carr stabbed to death a man who had been pursuing him for years, much to Carr's own amusement. Although it was ultimately treated as an "honor slaying," Kerouac—who helped Carr dispose of the knife—was briefly jailed as an accessory after the fact. When Jack called his father in search of bond money, Leo stormed: "No Kerouac ever got involved in a murder. I told you that little mischievous devil would get you in trouble. I'm not going to lend you no hundred dollars and you can go to hell." Kerouac felt the sting of his parents' disappointment for the rest of his life. He was unable even to honor his father's request—as he was slowly dying from cancer in 1946—that he provide for his mother. His inability to fulfill the dreams of his immigrant parents accounts for much of the guilt and the profound sense of loneliness which permeates his work. Kerouac was a most reluctant rebel. His dismissal from the Navy— treated humorously in his writing—haunted him to such an extent that, when, almost twenty years later, Timothy Leary gave him a dose of psilocybin, Kerouac "regressed back to his Navy discharge, still trying to understand and justify his failure to take Navy discipline." His ethnoreligious and class background rendered his literary vocation terminally problematic. "I wonder what working people think of me," he wrote in *Visions of Cody*,

when they hear my typewriter clacking in the middle of the night or what they think of when I take walks at 2 A.M. in outlying suburban neighbor- hoods—the truth is I haven't a single thing to wr—feel foolish. . . . How I wish I could grow corn tomorrow morning! . . . Instead of that I give myself tremendous headaches and I am also less paid than a Mexican in

New Mexico, and at least the Mexican in New Mexico has the right to get angry and to feel truly righteous in his heart. If I went for righteousness at the face of God on what grounds could I make such a claim?[32]

Kerouac's ambivalent attitude toward success was also evident in his early relationship with the literary establishment. He often boasted that he "got an A from Mark Van Doren in English at Columbia (Shakespeare course)." He also credited Van Doren with bringing *The Town and the City* to the attention of a publisher. According to his biographer Gerald Nicosia, Kerouac approached Van Doren in March 1949, with "a Chinese parable that ended with the imperative 'Do what you will when you think of it, at once.' Van Doren immediately telephoned Harcourt Brace," to recommend the book. Yet unlike Thomas Merton, whose relationship with Van Doren was grounded in a compatible sensibility, Kerouac sought "paternal approval" from the literary statesman. Such approval was difficult to maintain, particularly once Kerouac and his friends became notorious around Columbia for their decidedly unacademic lifestyles. When Allen Ginsberg was arrested for his naive involvement with a burglary ring in 1948, it was Van Doren, among others, who suggested he be placed in a psychiatric institution rather than face the disgrace of a trial. While Kerouac was frightened by the "compulsive lawbreaking" of the Times Square crowd, William Burroughs (his nonacademic mentor) now condemned Van Doren and the others as "old women." [33]

Kerouac's letters from the middle to the end of the 1940s show that he was still desirous of a career as a traditional literary gentleman. He compared his relationship with Van Doren to that of Thomas Wolfe and his editor, Maxwell Perkins. But he was not fully aware of the degree to which Van Doren guarded a vision of literary orthodoxy. A bohemian lifestyle was one thing, but once Kerouac began his experiments in verbal sketching and "spontaneous prose" around 1949, he virtually cut himself adrift from the arbiters of taste. In 1954 he brought Van Doren several of his numerous unpublished manuscripts to read. Of Kerouac's personal favorite, *Dr. Sax*, the verdict was harsh: "monotonous and probably without meaning in the end." Just prior to that, Kerouac had written to Allen Ginsberg that Van Doren "is nowhere, face it." He had to countenance the rejection of a well-connected father figure, and with it the hope of acceptance in the literary world he had fantasized about as a child. Those who dismissed Kerouac as an iconoclastic bohemian completely overlooked the enormous influence of his mill-town Franco-American background in shaping his expectations. He had to make the difficult choice between searching for his own true voice and "making it."[34]

Kerouac went unmentioned in Mark Van Doren's lengthy autobiography. Thomas Merton, though, figures prominently. Van Doren was responsible for selecting the poems for Merton's first book. He recalled that as early as 1941 he discovered "how excellent a poet Merton had become, how passionate, how rich, and in a subdued, deep fashion how witty too; for his wit, I knew at last, would never die." Van Doren also noted the "unbounded" literary ambition which was presumably "laid aside" when Merton entered the monastery. Yet a former student of Merton's at Gethsemani stated plainly that he and his teacher both "aspired to fame as writers." What Norman Mailer later wrote of Kerouac and other writers of the 1950s was true for Merton as well: "[H]e has been running for President as well as sticking at his work." Kerouac and Merton were above all writers with serious religious interests. Although they played for much greater stakes than the championship of Catholic romanticism, there is an unconscious complementarity about their work which illustrates like nothing else the ironic character of Catholic literary culture in the final years of its special mystique.[35]

From the time of his conversion, Merton, like Dorothy Day, pursued a vision of a universal Catholicism which inevitably clashed with the reality of American Catholic life. More than a year before joining the Trappists, he wrote in his journal of the need to distinguish between "cultural" and "religious" definitions of Catholicism: "You say so and so is a Catholic. Maybe you just mean he has an Irish name, and was once baptized, and when he blasphemes he blasphemes the name of Christ without giving the impression at all that he really knows what he is saying or doing. Or when you say Catholic, maybe you mean someone who reads a lot of rather messily got up little magazines written in bad English and full of sentimental illustrations. You are still talking about Catholics in the cultural and not the religious sense." Merton went on to discuss a "fairly devout Italian woman (I say she is fairly devout because at least she has a lot of those awful chromos insulting the Sacred Heart and the Blessed Virgin on the walls of her apartment)" who read a book about a nun falling in love with an Indian and mistook it for a "devotional work." In his convert's zeal Merton wanted the purest faith attainable; like Dorothy Day, he concluded that this entailed a complete renunciation of his former life. His departure for Kentucky occurred immediately after spending a very brief time at the Harlem branch of Friendship House, a lay apostolate founded by Day's friend and sometime rival, the Russian baroness Catherine de Hueck. He soon realized, "I would have to renounce more in entering the Trappists. That would be one place where I would have to give up *everything*."[36]

Merton soon found that he did not have to give up that which meant the most to him, his writing. But he was now under the discipline of the Cistercian abbot; along with his poetry and memoirs he was directed to produce numerous devotional and historical works commissioned by the order. Among these was *What Are These Wounds?*, a hagiographical account of a thirteenth-century Cistercian nun and mystic, Saint Lutgarde of Aywieres. This work had more in common with the type of pious literature Merton scorned than the elegant scholastic works which attracted him to the church. He wrote of the saint's achievement of the stigmata: "One night, then, she had gone to the dormitory and was praying . . . when the thought of martyrdom came to her. . . . Then suddenly a vein near her heart burst, and through a wide open wound in her side, blood began to pour forth, soaking her robe and cowl. As she lost her senses and sank to the floor, Christ appeared to her, in glory, His face radiant with joy." "As the years went by," Merton wrote later in the book, "and as her desire for death and suffering grew stronger with each day, Christ did not deny her the opportunities she desired. . . . [B]roken with sickness, she was finally visited with a terrible trial. Eleven years before she died she became stone blind."[37]

Not surprisingly, Merton later regretted having written *What Are These Wounds?*, which he considered his poorest work. Merton biographer Michael Mott argued that "he knew the difference between pious and religious poetry, but had plunged into near-parody in an attempt to match his prose to pious models." Merton himself later explained, "[T]hat was the way I thought a monk was supposed to write, just after I had made simple profession." Yet in 1945 writing of this kind signified more than that. The lurid accounts of exalted suffering worked for Merton just as they did for Huysmans and for Dorothy Day, ritually vindicating the self-punishment conversion both offered and demanded. Beyond that, Merton's pious writings served as a counterweight to freer expressions of self found in his more widely read books such as *The Seven Storey Mountain* and the *Sign of Jonas*. Merton projected a dual image as romantic and as obedient monk. By the late 1940s the external rationale for the intense authoritarianism of the American church was greatly diminished, but signs of greater autonomy among the faithful were few. Merton's monastic career provided a striking if tentative model for a new Catholic selfhood still firmly embedded within the bosom of the church.[38]

Yet even Catholics often found it hard to believe Merton could freely embrace monastic authority. He was regularly reported seen at bars, race tracks and "at rectory and convent doors asking for help and claiming to be Merton and just out of Gethsemani." This was during the period when Jack Kerouac was actually "on the road," pursuing in blessed anonymity the experiences which were featured in his more notorious novels. In 1947 he met Neal Cassady, the son of an Irish-Catholic derelict and sometime barber from Denver, Colorado. Over the next several years these soul brothers traveled widely in the United States and Mexico; as Kerouac characteristically explained in 1968: "We had more fun than 5,000 Socony gas station attendants can have." He also noted, of the legendary Cassady: "He's a Jesuit by the way. . . . He was a choir boy in the Catholic churches of Denver. And he taught me everything that I now do believe about anything that there may be to be believed about divinity."[39]

Kerouac had such a difficult time persuading critics and readers to regard him as primarily a religious writer that his later comments were often suffused in an alcoholic, sadly comical irony. After being asked by a *Paris Review* interviewer who noted his interest in Buddha, "How come you've never written about Jesus?" he exploded, "I've never written about Jesus? In other words, you're an insane phony who comes to my house . . . and . . . all I *write* about is Jesus. I am Everhard Mercurian, General of the Jesuit Army." So much of Kerouac's reputation was based on misreadings of *On the Road* that his more explicitly spiritual works were overlooked. The final version of *On the Road*, as literary historian Tim Hunt and others have demonstrated, was actually but one of several: Kerouac regarded *Visions of Cody* as the authentic version. The discrepancy is significant because *Visions of Cody* is the best example of the "spontaneous prose" method Kerouac pioneered.[40]

Spontaneous prose was Kerouac's way of creating a form to harmonize with the spiritual content of his work. It was inspired by the high-energy ramblings of his friend Neal Cassady, the improvisational virtuosity of saxophonist Charlie Parker and other bebop musicians, and his own highly confessional temperament. It also reconciled his enormous energy with a contemplative orientation: "[W]riting at least is a silent meditation even though you're going 100 miles an hour." The poet Allen Ginsberg located Kerouac's art within the broad context of American literary personalism: "There is a tradition of prose in America, including Thomas Wolfe and going through Kerouac, which is personal, in which the prose sentence is completely personal, comes from the writer's own person—his person defined as his body, his breathing rhythms, his actual talk."[41]

Kerouac did not initially attribute his literary experimentation to the Catholic mystical tradition. His new creative freedom drove him further from the church, for his vision seemed irreconcilable with the demands of orthodoxy. In Lowell he discussed his feelings with a sympathetic priest, Father Armand "Spike" Morrisette. "He told Spike that he loved to sense the mysterious, to tremble; to him such feelings were an experience of God. He found mystery everywhere, not just in Church." Gerald Nicosia argued that "Jack's own experience of Christianity was a longing to fly out into endless space," but he added that "in such total liberation he feared the loss of identity." By the early 1950s Kerouac was looking for a new theology to support those flights.[42]

He settled upon Buddhism, but not before at least considering alternatives closer to his own tradition. In the early 1950s Kerouac became friendly with Robert Lax, a poet who had converted from Judaism to Catholicism two years after Thomas Merton, his closest friend, entered the monastery. Lax had been a classmate of Merton's at Columbia; after graduation he embarked on a wandering career throughout the world which would go on for decades. When Lax (who Kerouac called a "goodsaint") discovered the depth of Kerouac's spiritual interests, he invited him to visit a monastery called L'Eau Vive, at Soissy-sur-Seine, thirty miles north of Paris. Kerouac explained in a November 1953 letter to Allen Ginsberg that L'Eau Vive was not a conventional monastery but a retreat house where Buddhists, Christians, and spiritual wanderers of all kinds gathered together. Thus began Kerouac's fascination with monasticism, which would last for the rest of his life. Yet as of 1953 he was highly ambivalent about any restrictions on his freedom of movement and experience. In a rare reference to the by now famous Thomas Merton, he hinted that the religious life inhibited authentic literature as much as it did adventure. In praising William S. Burroughs's manuscript, *Junkie*, he suggested that Burroughs was a more genuinely spiritual writer than professional religionists like Merton, confined as he was to a life of monastic domesticity.[43]

The gulf between Kerouac and Merton is evident in their transitional works from the period. In 1951 Merton published *The Ascent to Truth*, a study of the mystical theology of St. John of the Cross. As early as 1947 he had determined to write a systematic work on the "dark" path of the Spanish contemplative, who approached God via the negation of all conceptual notions of the divine. The book, in Michael Mott's words, "contains Merton's most extreme statements concerning the authority of the Catholic Church." In a chapter on false mysticism Merton proclaimed that the church desired to "protect her faithful against a superstitious popular passion for marvels and wonders"; events such as those at Fatima, he explained, were accorded "a place of extraordinary prominence in the Catholic life of our time . . . only after a long and careful investigation." One of the key signs of false mysticism, he argued, was its repudiation of "the dogmatic authority of the teaching Church."[44]

The Ascent to Truth was Merton's last fully triumphalist work: in its strained neo-Thomism it demonstrated the inadequacies of Catholic formalism, particularly in the hands of a still slightly anxious convert like Merton. Jack Kerouac's *The Subterraneans*, on the other hand, was the least religious and most "bohemian" of his novels. Written over the course of three long days and nights in 1953 (fueled by benzedrine as much as Kerouac's vaunted athleticism), the book described his brief affair with a black woman he called "Mardou Fox." For the first time Kerouac located himself, if somewhat sheepishly, amidst the bohemian intellectual community, with its interests in existentialism and sexology: "to show how abstract the life in the city of the Talking Class to which we all belong, the Talking Class trying to rationalize itself I suppose out of a really base almost lecherous lustful materialism—it was the reading, the sudden illuminated glad wondrous discovery of Wilhelm Reich, his book *The Function of the Orgasm*, clarity as I had not seen in a long time . . . you can't be happy without normal sex love and orgasm."[45]

In an introduction to the Norwegian edition of *The Subterraneans*, Kerouac argued that "the prose is what I believe to be the prose of the future, from both the conscious top and the unconscious bottom of the mind, limited only by the limitations of time flying by as your mind flies by with it." For all his proud claims that "not a word" of the book had been changed from his original creative performance, *The Subterraneans* contained hints of the severe emotional suffering he was undergoing. Kerouac's unhappiness with himself was reflected in his oft-stated wish to be something other than a "white man." In *The Subterraneans* he described his "old dream of wanting to be vital, alive like a Negro or an Indian or a Denver Jap or a New York Puerto Rican." He was disgusted with the intellectual self-consciousness of his life in literature. *The*

Subterraneans concludes: "And I go home having lost her love. And write this book" (Kerouac told an interviewer in 1968 that he had taken sexual advantage of the heroin-addicted Mexican protagonist of his novel, *Tristessa*: "She said, 'remember, I'm very weak and sick.' I said, 'I know, I've been writing a book about how you're weak and sick.'").[46]

Kerouac's sudden turn to Buddhism in 1953–54 was due in large part to this sickening with himself. He became an extremely ardent student of the teachings found in Dwight Goddard's *The Buddhist Bible* and other works which preached the unreality of the self. He was particularly moved by the first of the Buddha's Four Great Truths: "All life is suffering." To a deeply frustrated author (by 1956 he had at least ten unpublished manuscripts), these preachments made consoling sense; to a thoroughgoing, if alienated Catholic, they evoked memories of intense childhood piety. (Kerouac claimed that the motto on his family's coat of arms read: "Love, work, and suffer.")

Kerouac became as aggressive in his devotion to Buddhism as the most militant parish priest. His new faith caused fissures in his most intimate relationships. Neal Cassady's enthusiasm for the occultist Edgar Cayce drew a scornful rebuke from Kerouac: "he [Cassady] being a life-proud American . . . thinking that misery is grand . . . life is suffering, this you've got to understand, if you think it is anything but suffering you have lost completely the significance of even the need for emancipation." Although Neal and his wife Carolyn (with whom Kerouac occasionally lived during these years) dismissed his Buddhism as "a nihilistic evasion," he continued to harangue them. He went so far as to tell Carolyn that "Jesus should have gone to Asia, where Buddha would have saved him from his messiah complex."[47]

While many of his friends later made the connection between Kerouac's Buddhism and his Catholicism, there is little evidence that they did so in the 1950s except in the most negative of ways. Kenneth Rexroth, a venerable litterateur who was well connected with the emerging community of Buddhist scholars and practitioners in 1950s San Francisco, wrote at the time that Kerouac "calls himself a Buddhist, but he is certainly the most excited Buddhist I ever heard of." The first book Kerouac wrote after the sensational publication of *On the Road* was *The Dharma Bums*, an account of his experiences with the West Coast poet and Buddhist, Gary Snyder. Nearly a decade later Kerouac complained to his bibliographer: "Malcolm Cowley made me take out the best part of *Bums*, an argument with Gary Snyder. Gary said, 'you old son of a bitch, you're going to end up asking for the Catholic rites on your death bed.' I said, 'How did you know, my dear? Didn't you know I was a lay Jesuit?' He got mad at me."[48]

The Dharma Bums is an exuberant tribute to Snyder's combination Buddhist-Wobbly anarchism and old-fashioned Western independence. It also contrasted Kerouac's religious personalism with the formalism of his inherited faith. A television broadcast of a midnight mass from St. Patrick's Cathedral he viewed from his mother's house featured "bishops ministering, and doctrines glistening, the priests in their lacy snow vestments not half so great as my straw mat beneath a little pine tree I figured." Yet the novel also revealed the extent to which Buddhist nostrums could warp Kerouac's innate sensitivity. In one of the most disturbing scenes of all his novels, he describes his attempt to prevent the suicide of one of Neal Cassady's numerous mistresses. She had grown convinced that a "big new revolution of police" was imminent. Kerouac—who usually called himself "Jack Duluoz" in his books, but was "Ray Smith" in the *Dharma Bums*—responded to her distress by yelling, "Why don't you listen to me? . . . [Y]ou're getting these silly convictions and conceptions out of nowhere, don't you realize all this life is just a dream? Why don't you just relax and enjoy God? God is you, you fool." The woman killed herself that night. Kerouac's new faith—a sign of his longing for a more ordered way of life—was thus practiced in a way that sometimes parodied Catholic authoritarianism. The depth of his spiritual unease belied the insistence in his Buddhist work, *The Scripture of the Golden Eternity*: "When you've understood this scripture, throw it away. If you cant [sic] understand this scripture, throw it away. I insist on your freedom."[49]

Kerouac's Buddhism was related to his ambivalence toward success as well as the frightening intensity of his personal experience. His close friend, the novelist John Clellon Holmes, argued: "The *On the Road* experience, all the eruptive books in between, so disturbed him that he—I believe, kept saying to himself, 'Why are you doing this?' His faith—his religious faith—put it down or made it easy for him to say, 'stop doing it,' but he did it anyway, and that's where Buddhism comes in. All faiths are the same, really. They're just stages." Holmes perceptively noted that "Jack's ground was always Catholicism. . . . Jack's youth, Jack's sense of continuity, Jack's sense of family, Lowell, all the rest of that, is totally Catholic." The poet Philip Whalen argued: "When push came to shove, what he was hung up on was the Little Flower of Jesus, St. Thérèse of Lisieux, various other Catholic saints, and that's what he really believed in and got the most out of and kept returning to."[50] Yet the role that Catholicism played in his literary and spiritual careers is not so easily ascertainable as such remarks might suggest. Kerouac turned to Buddhism as a justification for his fear of success and the world because there was no usable Catholic alternative available to him. Knowing that his intense anti-authoritarianism disqualified him from an official monastic vocation, he swung wildly for the rest of his life between efforts at complete solitude and renunciation and the frantic, even desperately affirmative experience of the world which provided the vitality for the *On the Road* period. The power of his writing stems in no small part from his intuitive sense that complete surrender to his very powerful otherworldly instinct was an inauthentic choice, for all the claims it made upon him. The dialectical beauty of Kerouac's work embodied the major struggle of American Catholics with creative gifts: how to work in the world without doing violence to the mysticism of a Catholic childhood.

Kerouac's Buddhist period thus made an inadvertent contribution to the growing struggle between scholasticism and Catholic personalists. Alienated from the rigidities of his own tradition, Kerouac declined—unlike such other beat cronies as Gary Snyder—to enter into a formal master-disciple relationship, preferring to interpret texts freely and write his own "scripture." His Buddhist phase extended a process begun in the 1930s when Kerouac had plunged headlong into an American popular culture derided for its "pagan materialism" by the scholastics. Buddhism worked for a time in the absence of an explicitly personalist Catholic ethos.

For Thomas Merton, Eastern religions served not as a surrogate faith system but as a sign of his gradual rejection of Catholic triumphalism. Although he had been friendly with a Hindu monk at Columbia, it was not until the 1960s that he began publishing works on Eastern spirituality. Coupled with and informed by his activity in the peace movement, Merton's turn to the East signaled a new era of personal force and maturity. As Buddhist scholar Rick Fields wrote: "Merton believed that however much the contemplative traditions of both East and West might differ, they both took as their primary aim the transformation of man's consciousness through the practice of spiritual disciplines—something that was desperately needed in a world drifting towards war and destruction. He sought therefore to open communication between contemplatives who had so far remained divided along religious and monastic lines." Merton's pursuit of Eastern wisdom freed him from his role as exemplar of selfless Catholic obedience. In *The Seven Storey Mountain* he had made it clear that his life was now permanently in the hands of God and the Cistercian authorities. The willful Merton of his earlier years had become "my double, my shadow, my enemy, Thomas Merton, the old man of the sea." He insisted that he would now write only by order of the abbot. In a preface to the revised edition of one of his less dogmatic early works, *Seeds of Contemplation* (1949), Merton solemnly proclaimed: "If there is anything in these pages that cannot be reconciled with the teaching of the Church, it is to be considered as automatically deleted."[51]

He soon discovered, though, that monastic life was far from the ideal environment for cultivating his new being. He desired much more solitude than was available at overcrowded Gethsemani, in the midst of various construction projects in those years (by 1951 so many novices had flocked to the monastery—many of them inspired by Merton's writings—that they had to be housed in tents). Merton was able to defuse this potentially serious conflict by insisting that he merely wanted to become *more* of a monk, to live in even greater austerity and darker solitude. Throughout the 1950s he regularly petitioned for a transfer to the Carthusians or the Camaldolese, an order of monks who lived in isolated hermitages. They had no foundations in the United States. Merton's abbot, Dom James Fox, persistently rejected his pleas, because he felt Merton was not fully stable, and his writings provided a major source of the monastery's income. In 1956 Gregory Zilboorg, a psychiatrist and recent convert to Catholicism, met Merton at a workshop on "psychiatry and its practical application to the religious life," held at St. John's University in Minnesota. Merton had been permitted to make this, his first extended trip outside the monastery, because as master of novices he needed to be aware of signs of psychological disturbance. Zilboorg had already "psychoanalyzed" Merton through his writings, and he now proceeded to deliver numerous devastating blows to the monk-author who was causing such turmoil with his constant requests for transfer.

Zilboorg told Merton that he was profoundly neurotic: "[Y]ou like to be famous, you want to be a big shot, you keep pushing your way out—into publicity—megalomania and narcissism are your big trends." In front of Dom James, Merton's abbot, Zilboorg further charged: "You want a hermitage in Times Square with a large sign over it saying 'Hermit.'" According to Michael Mott, Merton "flew into a fury and cried tears of rage. . . . [T]hese were the most damaging ten minutes since he had left the world for the monastery." Merton was later inclined to agree with the diagnosis. He wrote to his literary

Thomas Merton at the Monastery of Our Lady of Gethsemani, Kentucky, early
1950s. Courtesy Thomas Merton Studies Center, Bellarmine College, Louisville,
Kentucky.

agent: "I will never give anyone any trouble about vocation or stability again, as
long as I am in my right mind."[52]

Merton was forty-one years old at the time. He could have walked away from
the monastery at any time to pursue his quest for solitude. He could have lived
in a cave. He appealed to so many American Catholics during the 1950s
precisely for his refusal—or inability—to walk away. That he was often sorely
tempted was evident to readers of his more intimate works, such as his

remarkable journal, *The Sign of Jonas* (1953). Much of the book concerns his preparations for ordination into the priesthood in 1949. He frankly admitted his fear of the priestly state but concluded: "[U]ltimately the only solution to that problem is obedience. If my Superiors want me to be a priest, it is at least safe. God wants it and He will do me good by it although it may contain an unimaginable death." He then confessed: "Sometimes I want to run away and be a tramp and hang around on the roads without anything, like Humble George or Saint Benedict Joseph Labre."[53]

Merton's sophisticated resignation to authority appealed to the many Catholics who no longer reflexively followed the dictates of the church but were far from ready to risk the ostracism which might result from direct questioning of authority. The jarring transformation of postwar society—particularly the suburban exodus—hit Catholics particularly hard because they had been overwhelmingly located in urban ethnic enclaves prior to the war. The centralizing power of a transcendentally "Catholic" identity as opposed to the myriad of "ethnic" identities left many confused as to the meaning of "Catholicity." Garry Wills argued that in the 1950s a "Catholic liberal was, in fact, a kind of honorary convert. He tried, for quite understandable reasons, to cast himself out of the ghetto of his upbringing and come back at the church from some entirely new direction, sacred or secular, or both alternately." Wills traced Merton's appeal to postimmigrant Catholics who were seeking a more "universal" and intellectually respectable basis for their faith.[54]

Wills overestimated the self-confidence of those "liberal Catholics." He described Catholics who blithely enjoyed "interesting experiences as a weekend monk with Tom Merton" (of Merton's condemnation of radio and newspapers, Wills wrote: "[I]t was the voice of a theological Dwight Macdonald, at war with spiritual Mid-Cult"). Far from smug, many American Catholics were as yet uncertain as to their place in a middle-class culture. Greater social status required new forms of behavior which were not always pleasant. As Daniel Patrick Moynihan argued of the ascendance of the American Irish: "Most Irish laborers died penniless, but they had been rich one night a week much of their lives, whereas their white-collar children never know a moment of financial peace, much less affluence. A good deal of color goes out of life when a group begins to rise. A good deal of resentment enters."[55]

Along with their traditional obedience to the church, many Catholics now enlisted in a corporate culture with demands of its own. Merton's works implied that obedience, though not always enjoyable or even understandable, had to serve as a counterweight to more individualistic desires. Yet small gestures of autonomy, muted protests, were acceptable and even necessary for the preservation of one's sensitivity. In Merton's case this could mean the writing of a book such as *The Silent Life* (1957), which exalted the eremetic monastic orders he was forbidden to join.

Merton's measured sophistication served as a model for many aspiring Catholics, both those he touched directly in the monastery as well as many more in "the world." Among his students at Gethsemani was John Stanley, a young veteran of the Second World War from an Irish-English background. Stanley suffered a nervous breakdown in 1951, left the monastery, and settled at the New York Catholic Worker house before leaving the church completely. Although he became somewhat preoccupied in later years with what he saw as Merton's contribution to the cold war rhetoric of the 1950s, he could still write:

> TM was a delight, tho' I knew him but briefly at Gethsemani; you knew you were running with the smart set when you were with him; even the way he said mass, swift, elegant, gentle, considerate—to an awkward acolyte like me. When I sat next to him in the refectory for the infirm, he'd give me his egg, sweetly. Without doubt he is the brightest man I ever knew and a paragon of a teacher. My, he was yare, as Katherine Hepburn said about her yacht in the "Philadelphia Story"; moving his great power around deftly, easily, without splash, flash or shudder.[56]

Merton possessed just enough of an air of puckish irreverence, along with his inexorable spiritual gifts, to make him an ideal hero for a generation of Catholics anxious to show secular intellectuals that their church embodied more than "a mass of Irish pastors truckling to Italian cardinals." His close ties to Mark Van Doren, James Laughlin, Robert Giroux, and other important literary and publishing figures provided Merton's readers with a surrogate connection to the aesthetic mainstream of high culture. As Garry Wills wrote: "A fussy concern with taste was, of course, as much a part of America at large in the Forties and Fifties as was the spread of religiosity. It was the time of Trilling and Tate and Ransom, of Brooks and Wimsatt and Wellek." It was also a time when conversion to Catholicism was a move admired by many of the taste-makers. Merton was an important figure in the spiritual life of Clare Boothe Luce and numerous other elegant fellow converts, including his own literary agent, Naomi Burton Stone, an Englishwoman who joined the church in the early 1950s after Merton advised her to "put all [her] problems in God's hands and take the step toward the Church bravely." Meeting Merton and his fellow "Catholics who were, surprisingly, intellectuals," helped her overcome her prejudice that Catholics had stopped thinking in the sixteenth century.[57]

The growing sophistication of Catholics in the 1950s was evident in the pages of *Jubilee*, a magazine of "the Church and her people" edited by Merton's Columbia classmate and drinking companion, Ed Rice. In many respects *Jubilee* was the upscale successor to *Integrity*. Merton was an early contributor to Carol Jackson and Ed Willock's fledgling publication. In a 1948 article, "Contemplation in a Rocking Chair," he had provided additional inspiration for lay apostolic selflessness: "We must do what St. Francis did: strip ourselves of everything and run away naked. And that means a very real, not merely metaphorical interior and exterior poverty: a poverty that includes hardship and privation and blind dependence on God."[58]

In contrast, *Jubilee*, founded in 1953, featured glossy pictorial layouts on interesting Catholics regardless of their material circumstances. Rice's magazine was particularly noteworthy for its promotion of "tasteful," meaning simple, or even—in the modernist sense—minimalist religious art. This was a special cause of Merton's; in *The Sign of Jonas* he confessed: "It is not much fun to live the spiritual life with the spiritual equipment of an artist." This condition was exacerbated by the tastelessness, he felt, of American Catholic culture. "At all these pontifical functions," he wrote in his journal in 1947, "they have been playing some weird music on the organ. It reminds me of the stuff you used to hear at the movies before the silent movies went out and the talkies came in. Now I discover it is the hymn that the faithful sing at Fatima. Mother of God, why do you let these things happen?"[59]

It turned out that the high-culture aspirations of *Jubilee* were difficult to sustain. Rice lived in near or real poverty throughout the magazine's career. He blamed the low standards of Catholics themselves; the wealthy ones he approached for money "said the magazine wouldn't sell, that Catholics are dopes and don't read." In the late 1950s *Jubilee* became a mildly avant-garde Catholic periodical, even printing several short stories by Jack Kerouac, who sometimes visited the magazine's New York offices after becoming a tormented celebrity (he apparently aroused little interest among the readership, however; in the only published response to his pieces, a woman from Jersey City called him a charlatan). Robert Lax, the best mutual friend shared by Merton and Kerouac, was the magazine's "roving editor"; along with Rice and such others as Wilfrid Sheed and the poet Ned O'Gorman, he encouraged a vision of *Jubilee* as the

home of wry Catholic quasihipsters at the end of the decade. The magazine's
annual Christmas greeting offered a virtual "who's who" of the Catholic avant
garde, extending warm greetings to Merton, Kerouac, and Dorothy Day alike.
But a heavy overtone of Catholic "tastefulness" persisted.[60]

Jack Kerouac was the bane of the tastemakers. He was also the complete fool
for Christ, hauntingly echoing the experience of Dorothy Day's imaginary
hobo-personalist, Ben Joe Labray. Like Ben Joe he traveled the backroads and
railyards of America, communing among "bums of the black" with the sort of
natural ease that had eluded the various Catholic apostles to these "ambassadors of Christ." Like many of them, Kerouac had become a confirmed alcoholic
by the middle of the 1950s; he was thus more inclined to participate in than
judge this aspect of the lifestyle. Few realized at the time that Kerouac was
pursuing the kind of self-dissolution which would follow from an effort to
bridge the gap between the detached, sophisticated piety of a Dorothy Day or a
Merton and the more literal self-destruction of less detached postimmigrant
Catholics. It was an untenable choice for living, but it produced the most
revealing literature written by an American Catholic.

Kerouac even had his own monastic experience. In 1956 he arranged to
spend the summer working as a fire lookout atop Desolation Peak, in Washington's Mount Baker National Forest (the year before, at "the height of the
stability crisis," Thomas Merton had been approached by his abbot with the
idea that he become a full-time fire lookout and hermit atop a tower on
monastery property. Merton ultimately declined the position, in part, Michael
Mott argued, because "Merton was not on good enough terms [with himself] to
live in solitude on the top of the fire tower on Vineyard Knob or anywhere
else"). In *Desolation Angels* (the first section of which was written in 1956,
though it was not published until 1965) and "Alone of a Mountaintop" (from
Lonesome Traveler, 1960) Kerouac described "an experience men seldom earn
in this modern world: complete and comfortable solitude in the wilderness,
day and night, sixty-three days and nights to be exact." Since he had just come
from his stay with Gary Snyder, he was still meditating more on the Buddha
than on Christ, but his ecumenism showed through as always: "For those who
believe in a personal God who cares about good and bad are hallucinating
themselves beyond the shadow of a doubt, tho God bless them, he blankly
blesses blanks anyway—."[61]

Bored and lonely, Kerouac learned something of the vast indifference of
nature to human existence. Into the rocks and gorges he yelled, "'What is the

meaning of the void?' The answer was perfect silence, so I knew." Above all was the realization, "I didn't have to hide myself in desolation but could accept society for better or worse." "Desolation in Solitude" was followed, appropriately, by "Desolation in the World," in which Kerouac described his descent from the mountain ("But what a joy, the world! I go!"). The most vivid scene from the section found Kerouac in a Seattle burlesque house, where in the midst of a wine drunk he experienced a vision:

> The whole world . . . roaring right there in that theater and just beyond I see files of sorrowing humanity wailing by candlelight and Jesus on the Cross and Buddha sitting neath the Bo tree and Mohammed in a cave and the serpent and the sun held high and and all Akkadian-Sumerian antiquities and early sea-boats carrying courtesan Helens away to the bash final war and broken glass of tiny infinity till nothing's there but white snowy light permeating everywhere throughout the darkness and sun—.[62]

To sanctify the world from the most "profane" perspectives was a major part of Kerouac's artistic goal. "I wake up in the morning with my cross around my neck," he wrote in *Desolation Angels*. "I realize what thicks and thins I'll have to wear this through, and ask myself, 'what would Catholics and Christians say about me wearing the cross to ball and drink like this?'—but what would Jesus say if I went up to him and said 'May I wear your cross in this world as it is?'" Kerouac's frenetic side increasingly held sway against his contemplative interests, so that his religious interests became colored by a desperate longing. This was especially troublesome because there were no Catholic models upon which to base his adoration of the visible everyday world. Nor was there any precedent for his frighteningly direct treatment of many of the darker themes in the Catholic consciousness. In *The Dharma Bums* he announced: "I'd also gone through an entire year of celibacy based on my feeling that lust was the direct cause of birth which was the direct cause of suffering and death and I had really no lie come to a point where I regarded lust as offensive and even cruel." Lacking the official vocation to celibacy, Kerouac's fears of the flesh and sex could sound truly disturbed. Of an elderly forest ranger he wrote: "And is Blacky less a man because he never married and had children and did not obey nature's injunction to multiply corpses of himself?"[63]

Merton's celibacy was of course taken for granted in the 1950s. Sophisticated Catholics also knew that his celebrated friend, the neo-Thomist philosopher Jacques Maritain, had taken, along with his wife Raissa, a vow of chastity decades earlier. In 1958 Merton's old friend, Catherine de Hueck of Friendship House, told him that she and her journalist husband Eddie Doherty had done likewise in 1954. Celibacy continued to be the most exalted state for Catholics in the 1950s, even married ones, but Kerouac's boisterous ruminations on this as on other issues never became part of Catholic discourse.[64]

After Kerouac became a celebrity in 1957, he frequently invoked his Catholicism against those who accused him of barbarism, rebellion, and immorality. In his essay, "The Origins of the Beat Generation," Kerouac noted the sudden explosion of interest in the beat phenomenon. "People began to call themselves beatniks, beats, jazzniks, bopniks, bugniks and finally I was called the 'avatar' of all this. Yet it was as a Catholic," he wrote,

> it was not at the insistence of any of these 'niks' and certainly not with their approval either, that I went one afternoon to the church of my childhood (one of them), Ste. Jeanne d'Arc in Lowell, Mass., and suddenly with tears in my eyes and had a vision of what I must have really meant with 'Beat' anyhow when I heard the holy silence in the church . . . the vision of the word Beat as being to mean beatific. . . . There's the priest preaching on Sunday morning, all of a sudden through a side door of the church comes a group of Beat Generation characters in strapped raincoats like the I.R.A. coming in silently to 'dig' the religion. . . . I knew it then.

Having been ignored and then condemned, Kerouac retreated into the familiarly defensive posture of Catholic antitriumphalism. His religiosity—no longer joyous or affirmative—became the sign of contradiction with which he held off his assailants. In "The Origins of the Beat Generation" he complained that every publication save, oddly enough, the *New York Times* had erased a large crucifix he had worn for a photography session with several of his fellow beat writers. "I am not ashamed to wear the crucifix of my Lord," he wrote. "It is because I am Beat, that is, I believe in beatitude and and that God so loved the world that he gave his only begotten son to it." He concluded: "I am sure no priest would've condemned me for wearing the crucifix outside my shirt everywhere and no matter where I went, even to have my picture taken in *Mademoiselle*. So you people don't believe in God. So you're all big smart know-it-all Marxists and Freudians, hey? Why don't you come back in a million years and tell me all about it, angels?"[65]

Kerouac now invoked suffering Catholicism in much the same way that the disciples of Coughlin and McCarthy had in the days of their heroes' decline: to

Jack Kerouac, New York City, 1959. Photograph by Fred W. McDarrah.

legitimize his rage and frustration (in *Vanity of Duluoz* Kerouac recalled that his uncle in Brooklyn—with whom he lived while attending Horace Mann School —told him: "When you have more time I tell you some more about Father Coughlin." Later, Kerouac would bitterly tell friends that Senator McCarthy had "the dope on all the Jews and fairies.") He also now blamed his failure to publish on Jewish publishers who preferred the works of Malamud and Bellow to his own. Kerouac's friend Lucien Carr often told him: "You have a barrel full of apples, and you got a few rotten ones in there. . . . [Y]ou're ruining your soul." Kerouac's occasional tantrums reflected self-doubt more than active hostilities; as Carr also remarked, "he was a man without hate—without hate." Disoriented by his new role as a celebrity, Kerouac now played the fool for Christ with a manic intensity.[66]

He performed in a manner calculated to earn the ridicule of his secularist critics. At a Hunter College symposium on "Is There a Beat Generation?," Kerouac appeared on a panel with James Wechsler of the *New York Post*, the anthropologist Ashley Montagu, and British novelist Kingsley Amis. Hunter student Jack Newfield recalled that most of the audience had come to see Kerouac, who promptly "disappointed his disciples": "Gulping brandy compulsively, dragging poet Allen Ginsberg out of the wings like a donkey, reciting doggerel about Harpo Marx and clowing with Wechsler's hat, Kerouac seemed more in harmony with the clown spirit of his 'beloved Harpo' than with the merchandised image of the creative, adventuristic, iconoclastic Beats."[67]

Criticism from the Left was one thing, but Kerouac was also vulnerable to attacks from Catholics. Dennis McNally claimed that Catholic intellectuals were "the only writers in America who half-defended" the beats, applauding "Beat antimaterialism and its sense of morality, although they cringed at its actual application." The authors McNally cited offered only the most qualified approval for the beats, seeing them as somewhat confused seekers after God. None of them discussed Kerouac's Catholicism. Probably more typical was the position of Father Bernard P. Donachie, who in 1958 called the beats "quitters in the game of life" from the pulpit of St. Patrick's Cathedral. In a study of the church and suburbia, the young priest-sociologist Andrew M. Greeley quoted Kerouac's definition of the beats from *The Subterraneans*: "[H]ip without being slick . . . they are very quiet, they are very Christlike." Greeley assured his readers that the beats were "not, by the way," Christlike at all.[68]

Kerouac's natural constituency would have included the personalists of the Catholic Worker movement. As late as 1966 Allen Ginsberg suggested to

Dorothy Day that she publish one of Kerouac's poems "(presuming it's Catholic anarchist) (or Sacred Heart somewhere in the anarchy)," but according to the paper's editor at the time, Robert Steed, Day was not interested. When Kerouac came to the attention of the Catholic Workers, it was as a libertarian bohemian, not as a Catholic.[69]

As he grew more notorious, Kerouac continued to startle his audience with the bluntness of his religious pronouncements. He told a television interviewer that his whole purpose in life was to have "God show me His face." Reporter Mike Wallace asked him, "Why are so many members of the Beat Generation bums and tramps?" Kerouac's reply echoed Peter Maurin: "Oh, you see, Christ says go out and find the bums. . . . Find the blind and the cripples." His final comment demonstrated his profoundly antitriumphalist worldview: "Christ invites everyone, including the outcasts. So there's no contradiction at all between Christ and a bebopper and a hipster."[70]

Kerouac's unprecedented attempt to reconcile his love of sensation and popular culture with mysticism drew angry and even violent reactions. "Kerouac," wrote a *Playboy* reader (the magazine published "Origins of the Beat Generation" in its June 1959 issue) "in one breath extolls the virtues of physical filth and free love, and in the next, the beauty of a crucifix and Catholicism. His long-winded jumble . . . established that 'beat' is synonymous with immaturity and confusion." Since numerous writers extolled "free love," it was the juxtaposition that rankled most. There were only certain places, like monasteries, where Catholics were expected to unabashedly pursue God. As Catherine de Hueck wrote to Merton in 1941, on his vocation: "How wonderful, how perfect! A Trappist and a priest! High is your calling dear friend, and wonderful to behold the Face of God in silence."[71]

Kerouac's career as "a priest of life" (a term he initially applied to his hero, Neal Cassady) was greatly abetted by the exploding culture of celebrity. But his public appearances were a source of great discomfort and self-doubt. Just as the hero of Myles Connolly's *Mr. Blue* fantasized about starting a film company to publicize the end of the world, Kerouac's often drunken performances seemed bent on hastening his own destruction. Though passive when sober, he became involved in several violent incidents in and around New York taverns. After receiving a brutal beating in the spring of 1958 he was taken to a hospital where he repeatedly mumbled "cauterize my wounds" to the attending physician. For all his frantic posturing about accepting the world, Kerouac's underlying attitude was obviously quite ambivalent. Shortly after the success of *On the*

Road he bought a home for his mother and himself in suburban Northport, Long Island. For the last decade of his life he alternated between the solitude of his home life and his public role as "King of the Beats." The effort to integrate an active life with a life of contemplation was ultimately a spectacular failure. Kerouac saw the implications of this for his claims as a Catholic priest of life. After years of being protected by his mother from himself and the demands of his fame, he told a friend: "I'm a Jesuit. I live in a house with my mother. It's a monastery, and I'm a monk and she's a reverend mother."[72]

The depth of Kerouac's suffering was captured in *Big Sur* (1962), the "comeback" novel which, along with *Visions of Cody*, is his most significant work. The novel describes his attempt to rediscover his identity and his voice in the wake of his sudden fame and subsequent breakdown. The work is pervaded by his unique religiosity from the start: "The church is blowing a sad windblown 'Kathleen' on the bells in the skid row slums as I wake up all woebegone and goopy, groaning from another drinking bout and groaning most of all because I'd ruined my secret return to San Francisco by getting silly drunk while hiding in the alleys with bums and then marching forth into North Beach to see everybody." In *Big Sur*, "Jack Duluoz" has made the trip from Northport to the West Coast after "finally realizing [he] was surrounded and outnumbered and had to get away to solitude again or die." His friend "Lorenzo Monsanto" (Lawrence Ferlinghetti)—poet and proprietor of a renowned San Francisco bookshop—had invited him to stay at his isolated cabin at Bixby Canyon overlooking the beach at Big Sur. At first Jack finds peace amidst the solitude, reexperiencing his childhood piety far from the sources of his worldly undoing. He tells himself: "Go back to childhood, just eat apples and read your Catechism—sit on curbstones, the hell with the hot lights of Hollywood." He begins writing down the sounds of the sea at night. But soon he gets bored; deprived of alcohol, he becomes depressed. When he tries to take a "huge deep Yogic Breath" of sea air he nearly faints, "only it isn't an ecstatic swoon by St. Francis, it comes over me in the form of horror an eternal condition of sick mortality in me." The sea now seems to cry out: "GO TO YOUR DESIRE DON'T HANG AROUND HERE."[73]

In San Francisco Jack learns that his beloved cat has died in Northport; seeing this as another horrible omen, he goes on a binge with a variety of beat characters. He returns to Big Sur with Monsanto, "Cody Pomeray" (Neal Cassady), and others. On a side trip to the hot baths located on the future grounds of Esalen Institute, he becomes suspicious of some homosexuals bathing nearby: "It's very typical of me and Cody that we won't undress in this situation (we were both raised Catholics?) supposedly the big sex heroes of our generation."[74]

Religion becomes one of the main sources of his growing paranoia. Suffering from delirium tremens, Jack concludes that his friends are plotting against him. He admits that he has for long "conceived of [himself] as a special solitary angel sent down as a messenger from Heaven to tell everybody or show everybody by example that their peeking society was actually the Satanic Society and they were all on the wrong track." At the height of his suffering he concludes that his friends at the cabin are trying to poison him because he is "a Catholic: it's a big anti-Catholic scheme, it's Communists destroying everybody." Hearing voices in the night, he endures a titanic struggle between God and the devil, his soul at stake: "For a moment I see blue Heaven and the Virgin's white veil but suddenly a great evil blur like an ink spot spreads over it, 'The devil!—the devil's come after me tonight! tonight is the night! that's what!'—but angels are laughing and having a big barn dance in the rocks of the sea, nobody cares any more—suddenly as clear as anything I ever saw in my life, I see the Cross." The vision of the Cross results in a reaffirmation of Kerouac's Catholicism. "I say through all the noise of the voices 'I'm with you, Jesus, for always, thank you.'" He is no longer a Buddhist: "I lie there in cold sweat wondering what's come over me for years my Buddhist studies and pipesmoking assured meditations on emptiness and all of a sudden the Cross is manifested to me—My eyes fill with tears—'We'll all be saved.'"[75]

Although the novel ends on an optimistic note, the Cross remained primarily a sign of contradiction for Kerouac, a personal cross he shouldered in the depths of loneliness and alcoholic despair. It did not really provide him with a way back into the world. He continued to reflexively associate Catholicism with sadness, withdrawal, and resignation to suffering. In *Big Sur* he describes his affair with a woman named Billie. As his emotional distress tears the relationship apart, he responds positively to her suggestion that they go to a monastery together: "'Billie you might go to a nunnery at that, by God get thee to a nunnery, you look like you'd make a nun, maybe that's what you need. . . . [Y]ou could become a big reverend mother someday with not a worry on your mind tho I met a reverend mother once who cried . . . ah it's all so sad.'"[76] He could no longer sustain the hope that "makes me proud to love the world somehow."

Kerouac declined rapidly in the 1960s. As his alcoholism worsened, he made a final effort to find himself by moving back to Lowell with his mother. But his old friends either resented or pitied him, and the community as a whole was largely indifferent to his presence. In 1969 he moved to St. Petersburg, Florida, with his mother and his third wife, whom he had married partly in order that she would care for the now invalid Memere. On October 20, 1969, while watching the "Galloping Gourmet" television program, he collapsed and was rushed into emergency surgery to stop his internal bleeding. After twenty-six blood transfusions, he died the next day of hemorrhaging esophageal varices, "the classic drunkard's death." In one of his last public appearances, on the "Firing Line" program of William F. Buckley, a fellow Catholic and prep school acquaintance whom Kerouac now professed to admire greatly, he denied any connection with the hippies or even the beat generation. He was particularly angry at being linked with such notions as "beat mutiny," or "beat insurrection," phrases he would never utter, "being a Catholic."[77]

In the late 1950s Thomas Merton overcame the fussy scrupulosity which had bedeviled his early monastic years and began renewing his interests in world literature and Asian religion (in *The Seven Story Mountain* he recanted his flirtation with "Oriental mysticism," describing it as "simply more or less useless, except when it is mixed up with elements that are strictly diabolical"). He also became interested both in a deeper spirituality which transcended denominational boundaries and in the implications of mystical awareness for promoting world peace. In all of these concerns he was, as always, just a half step or so ahead of many American Catholic intellectuals. Merton now became highly appreciative of and receptive to influences associated with the beat movement. One of his correspondents was a Dominican monk named Brother Antoninus (formerly William Everson). Antoninus was also a poet highly favored by beat patron Kenneth Rexroth and others in San Francisco; for that and other reasons his archdiocese forbade him in 1960 from making public appearances. In December of that year he wrote an insightful letter to Merton prompted by his rereading of *The Seven Storey Mountain*. He now perceived "[a] vast split between your personal reactions and religious meditations, the latter convert-like, pedantic, pedagogical. I suspect this still troubles you. Your great books are your personal ones— *Seven Storey*, *Sign of Jonas*." Antoninus sensed in Merton's recent work a "freeing from the religious superego," and he hoped he could evade the "digested quality about so much theological writing today. Thomistic especially. Insufferable stuff."[78]

Merton indicated his attraction to Catholic personalism in a 1958 letter to

Catherine de Hueck. He confessed that after "boldly advertising to the world that I ought to become a saint," he had learned that it was not as simple as that. "Maybe I have a call," he continued,

> to that peculiarly Russian form of sanctity—yurodivestuo—to be a fool for Christ and really enjoy it. It is certainly a wonderful thing to wake up suddenly in the solitude of the woods and look up at the sky and see the utter nonsense of everything including all the solemn stuff given out by professional asses about the spiritual life: and simply to burst out laughing, and laugh and laugh, with the sky and the trees because God is not in words, and not in liturgical movements, and not in 'contemplation' with a big C or in asceticism or in anything like that, not even in the apostolate.[79]

Merton became a strong supporter of the Catholic Worker movement in the early 1960s. He told psychoanalyst Erich Fromm that the movement was "tolerated" as "a sign that we can find a mansion for beats in the church as well as for the respectable." Dorothy Day was compelled to correct Merton's perception of her movement: "[I]n your letters you associate us with 'beats' of whom there have been, thank God, but a few." Even after developing a critical social conscience and an affinity for the beats, Merton remained an enormously influential Catholic, and he knew it. In a letter to Ethel Kennedy—a fervent admirer—he expressed the hope that she might encourage her brother-in-law, President John F. Kennedy, to read his latest works on the immorality of nuclear warfare. Yet his continuing struggle with the Trappist censors over such "controversial" writings helped rekindle the independent side of Merton's nature, and for the remainder of his life he grew more and more fascinated with such unchurched figures as Lenny Bruce, Bob Dylan, and the great saxophonist John Coltrane.[80]

A onetime student of Merton's wrote: "[A]s a companion he was the most charming of men, but as a monk hardly the ideal." By the middle of the 1960s "the monastery had become a background for his work rather than the subject." In 1965 he was finally given permission to establish a hermitage in a small cinderblock cabin some distance from the monastery itself. He was spending more and more time on his Buddhist studies. He began receiving visitors fairly often; they were instructed to bring plenty of liquor. He also initiated a love affair with a young student nurse he met at a Louisville hospital in 1966. As to the inevitable question of whether Merton relinquished his celibate commitment, Michael Mott wrote that after one of their secret trysts, Merton wrote an account which made it quite clear he was "in trouble with his vow." Although he apparently gave the woman some reason for hope that he might abandon monastic life to marry her, he finally decided the relationship had to end. Mott wrote that when his friends were later told of the affair, they congratulated him for being human: "as if a monk could not be human; as if there were any mystery at all that Thomas Merton was human. He had been working to turn himself from the pious, rigid, opinionated young monk into a vulnerable human being for twenty years."[81]

To Merton, as to many Catholics in the 1960s, it became quite difficult to reconcile being human with the authority of a church which was once the ground and center of their identity. As nuns and priests defected in droves, Merton characteristically maintained a tenuous link with the church while becoming for all practical purposes a "free lance monk." In 1968, with a new abbot recently installed at Gethsemani, he was granted permission for a lengthy trip to Asia to participate in a Bangkok conference on monastic renewal. He had become a recognized authority on the links between Eastern and Christian spirituality, and was even considered by some in Asia to be the truest Western interpreter of Zen Buddhism. Before leaving for Asia, Merton indicated to his old friend Ed Rice that "he did not intend to return to Gethsemani"; yet others have cited a letter to the community in which Merton reaffirmed that he was "a monk of Gethsemani and intend to remain one all my days" as evidence of his intention to return to Kentucky. Rice argued that Merton could have remained associated with Gethsemani while living in an Asian hermitage. It all became academic when, on December 10, 1968, Merton was electrocuted in Bangkok. Stepping out of the shower, he touched an electric fan which may have been faultily wired. He fell to the floor and the fan fell on top of him, leaving a deep burn in his chest. Though apparently accidental, some continue to argue either that Merton was murdered or that he committed suicide. His death did eerily recall the closing lines of *The Seven Storey Mountain*, where Merton had imagined Jesus's wish that he "may become the brother of God and learn to know the Christ of the burnt men."[82]

In 1967 Merton had sought poems for his new little magazine, *Monk's Pond*. He wrote to Robert Lax: "Send prose poetries send anything . . . get Kerouac send . . . get everybody send some ideas visions hallucinations and sundries." Lax wrote back: "Here is from old Jack Kerouac two poems; first treats of the wry condition of man himself, second, lyric and hibernal, refers obliquely to the bow of krishna and the arrows of Suzuki." In another letter he wrote: "J-L Kerouac sends always his best; from him is much prayers, he haths the drinks to fight." Merton replied: "Thanks also the Kerouac velumplines, valentine. Will print in the prints. Thanks to Kerouacs." Merton's gesture of sympathetic interest toward Kerouac symbolically closed a thirty-five-year chapter in the history of American Catholicism. "Bohemian Catholicism" had always been an oxymoron despite the longings of numerous Catholic Workers for the romantic and unchurched life of Greenwich Village. In his essay, "The Beat Movement Concluded," critic Wilfrid Sheed claimed that the "years of Beat gestation" coincided with Thomas Merton's Columbia period, and that the sensibility he and his college friends promoted "needed only missionaries to take it on the road and blend it. In this sense, Kerouac might loosely be called St. Paul as farce." Sheed cited the language of the Lax-Merton correspondence as evidence of the affinity between the successive generation of Columbia bohemians. "Merton's private letters," he wrote, "are written in a speed shorthand directly related to Kerouac's bop prosody." But Merton did not write that way for publication; not, at least, during the 1950s. Michael Mott made the dubious claim that Merton's 1956 poem "White Pastures," represented a free-form experimental poetic "before Ginsberg and others" had discovered a similar method. Ginsberg had in fact been emulating Kerouac's spontaneous sketching technique since very early in the 1950s. In that decade Merton had, at least publicly, renounced his youthful independence in the name of Christian perfection and discipline. By the 1960s he had "come full circle to certain passions of his teens and college years. His life was becoming more complicated and complex, and the tensions increased." He had broken free of the notion that monasticism somehow entailed a vertical ascent to perfection.[83]

The poems Kerouac dedicated to Merton in Monk's Pond show that he continued to integrate sacred and worldly themes in his work, as he juxtaposes mystical themes with allusions to Jimmy Durante. By this time Kerouac's powers were greatly diminished and Merton's use of the poems was an act of compassion. But it was also a kind of tribute. Kerouac had done everything that Dorothy Day and Peter Maurin could ever have asked of a fool for Christ, in answering for himself the question, "[W]hat would Jesus say if I went up to him and said 'May I wear Your cross in this world as it is?'" Kerouac's poverty earned him precisely the freedom they claimed would follow from a transcendence of materialism. "Everything belongs to me," he wrote in Visions of Cody, "because I am poor." As an "independent educated penniless rake going anywhere,"

Kerouac was obviously not affiliated with the lay apostolate, but only the profoundly naive can any longer argue that, during her lifetime, the Catholic Worker was not primarily a vehicle for Dorothy Day's powerful journalism, just as monasticism greatly facilitated Merton's career in literature. After Marycrest, Catholic romantics could only really hope to provide a model for personal spirituality. Day and Merton merely had the weight of authority on their side, however much they sometimes chafed under it. Conversion was supposed to simplify a quest for perfection which was rooted not in Catholicism but in the Protestantism of their forebears.[84]

Kerouac embodied the cyclical nature of traditional Catholicism, as he recapitulated all too dramatically the passage from "sin" to redemption and back again. He was the "natural" Catholic Day and Merton knew they could never become without mighty and conspicuous works of self-abnegation. When Kerouac wrote about the "fellaheen," or peasantry, with which he so strongly identified, he demonstrated none of the impatience with which Day and later Merton viewed their benighted fellow Catholics. To them the immigrant, peasant consciousness prevalent in Catholic culture was a circumstance of history; to Kerouac it was the essence of faith. At his best he offered hope that the religion of immigrants might provide the basis for an American catholicity in the radical, original sense of the word. As he wrote of the "fellaheen" Mexicans he befriended, smoked dope, and attended Mass with: "[I]t amazed me to remember that we were all Catholics."[85]

Epilogue

One night late in the 1950s, Kieran Dugan, a *Catholic Worker* editor and former seminarian from Notre Dame, encountered Jack Kerouac at a bar in New York. Dugan was with a woman named Norma Melbourne. When a drunken Kerouac was introduced to her he remarked, "Norma Melbourne, the suede jacket champion of Australia?" Kerouac then fell to his knees and hugged Dugan around the legs, whereupon Dugan said, "Cool it, Jack."[1]

Twenty-five years after the incident Dugan told the story with such vigor and warmth that it was clear the moment was epiphanic; he had upstaged the ultimate Catholic hipster. That meant a lot around the Catholic Worker during this period: the young men and women of the movement—unlike their counterparts from the 1930s and 1940s—were finding it very difficult to sustain their undivided loyalty to the church, even Dorothy Day's church. Day had a custom of sending the paper's editors to Mass before she would bring the copy to the printer. By the late 1950s it was common for the editors to walk out of the Chrystie Street House of Hospitality in the direction of the church, only to change course and repair to the White Horse Tavern or another watering hole once they were out of visual contact with Day. Another Catholic Worker, "remarkable for the brilliance and passionate intensity with which he confronted his own existential dilemmas," decided, on his way to a Friday Mass in 1957, to eat a cheeseburger instead. He never went to Mass again. Several years later a vice-president of the Grail, while stationed in Paris, decided to start smoking and going to movies, activities which boldly contradicted the Grail's "haughty goodness."[2]

Events like these became commonplace by the 1960s. It has often been assumed that the Second Vatican Council (1962–65) was ultimately responsible for the massive defections which beset the church during that decade and after. Developments coming in the wake of the Council—such as the institution of the vernacular Mass—had an unsettling effect on many Catholics who thought of the church as the one bastion of eternal order and truth left in the world. "Humanae Vitae," the 1968 encyclical reaffirming the church's opposition to artificial birth control, furthered tensions between the Vatican and the American church. Many Catholics now ceased regarding the church as authoritative in teaching, and as William F. Buckley's celebrated response to an encyclical of Pope John XXIII ("mater si, magistra no") demonstrated, conservatives were as likely as liberals to reject that authority. Daniel Bell neatly summarized the plight of the church in the 1960s: "The paradox of the post-conciliar Church—a paradox which Tocqueville pointed out about the nature of revolution—is that as the authority grows progressively weaker, the protest against it intensifies. Persons who were acquiescent under the rigid pre-conciliar regime now declare authority repressive even though the new system is more liberal."[3]

Yet for those Catholics who had been involved in the various lay apostolates, the Council signaled an end more than a beginning. None of the liturgical experimentation of the postconciliar period struck the older personalists as particularly innovative, especially compared to the rites performed at the Catholic Worker farms or Marycrest in the 1940s. Michael Harrington (who "left" the church in the 1950s) argued that the "death of God" was as instrumental in American Catholicism's crisis as "the breakup of the Catholic ghetto." The latter is certainly more easily discernible as a causative factor; it wasn't so much the death of God as the sudden irrelevance of doctrinal authority that produced such massive confusion and bitterness (a story as yet unwritten). Harrington also made the important point that Pope John XXIII was compelled to call a council in spite of the dim hopes for a genuine renewal of Catholicism, at least in North America. "The historic moment could not long have been deferred; the choice was between a slow death and a desperate attempt at life."[4]

This study has argued that to an elite group of Catholics, at least, the institutional church was of secondary importance as early as the 1930s. Dorothy Day provided a sophisticated mystique for those Catholics ready to break out of their immigrant parishes. But because she was embarked on a reverse pilgrimage it was only a matter of time before her followers, like other Catholics, would reject the world-denying aspects of mystical self-abnegation and suffering in the name of experience or opportunity. Those of a romantic bent, like Tom Dooley or Jack Kerouac, would move toward a native tradition of spiritual self-expression without ever resolving what that meant for their profoundly Catholic temperaments. Day herself helped bring this chapter of cultural history full circle. By centering her movement in Lower Manhattan, she ensured that Catholic Workers would not be sheltered from the avantgarde community she had fled in 1927. By the 1950s a new bohemia had arrived and she was unable to shield the Workers from it, just as she was unable to recognize the essentially mystical nature of the beat movement. The night the Jewish beat poet Allen Ginsberg read his "Kaddish" at the New York House of Hospitality, the younger members of the movement responded with tears and warm approval. By the late 1950s, then, the dream of a radically separate Catholic subculture belonged to history.[5]

Regardless of her view of the consequences, Day actually encouraged ecumenism in the 1950s. Her participation in protests against air raid drills brought her in league with such non-Catholic activists as A. J. Muste and the avantgarde dramaturgists, Judith Malina and Julian Beck. Her movement also continued to attract, as it always had and continues to do, people who simply wanted to help the poor and advance the cause of peace. In the 1950s Day brought into the movement a man who turned the sign of contradiction on its head: the one-man revolution, Ammon Hennacy. Hennacy was anything but a fool for Christ. A colorfully eccentric long-time anarchist and pacifist, Hennacy fell in love with Day and moved into the New York Catholic Worker House of Hospitality in 1952. Something of a confidence man, Hennacy allowed himself to be baptized but never ceased his attacks on the hierarchy, in keeping with his rugged antinomianism. He became the most celebrated member of the Catholic Workers after Day herself, conducting a public fast on each anniversary of the Hiroshima bombing, selling the newspaper on the steps of St. Patrick's Cathedral, and conducting spirited exchanges with critics. Day, who considered Hennacy a "present-day prophet," had prayed that he might also become a "perfect Christian" through baptism. She steadfastly resisted whatever physical advances he may have made; nearing sixty, she remained thoroughly Jansenistic: "In any physical expression of . . . love, this body of ours at whatever age is treacherous."[6]

Although Hennacy's vitality was a great addition to the movement, he never embraced any of Day's religious ideology. His *Autobiography of a Catholic Anarchist* reveals both his flair for self-promotion and the rock-ribbed individualism of his Ohio Protestant origins. The book is a minor classic in the tradition of plain speech; in it Hennacy redundantly details his life of travel and manual labor and his single-minded devotion to the cause of peace and anarchism. The work is totally bereft of a sense of interiority. Hennacy's lack of a gift for spirituality actually made him a refreshing character amidst the superheated atmosphere of postwar Catholicism: he could offhandedly write to Thomas Merton to tell him that he had no use for *The Seven Storey Mountain* but was glad to see the monk was becoming interested in nuclear disarmament.[7] Yet Hennacy also introduced a strong note of anti-authoritarianism into the movement: he was a personalist without self-abnegation as a counterweight. His criticisms of priests would have been inconceivable in the old Catholic Worker movement; now they proved highly contagious. In 1961 he left for Salt Lake City, where he established the nonsectarian Joe Hill House and developed a deep enthusiasm for Mormon culture.

Hennacy died in 1970, but not before instructing his young wife, Joan Thomas, to write his biography. The work includes autobiographical fragments Hennacy wrote in 1968. He begins: "Since I wrote my autobiography in 1952–53 many books have been written which deal with sex very frankly. So now I feel that I can add thoughts on this and other things I have overlooked." He proceeds to narrate an explicit if matter-of-fact account of his own sexual initiation, and goes on to make some pointed, even cruel remarks about the sexuality of several former associates in the Catholic Worker movement. Like Caroline Gordon's *The Malefactors*, this text strived, in its peculiar way, to complete the less than fully human textual record compiled by the Catholic personalists. In this as in many other ways, Jack Kerouac was the pioneer. In his novel *Big Sur* he defended his description of the "nervously sad delight of love" and complained: "[I]t's awful, we're stuck with a 50% incomplete literature and drama."[8]

In the early 1960s Dorothy Day was deeply upset by the "promiscuity" of several of the beat-influenced Catholic Workers. She even discovered that poet Ed Sanders's *Fuck You: A Magazine of the Arts* was being run off on Catholic Worker mimeograph machines. Sanders, a non-Catholic, subsequently ridiculed her as "the grand old lady of American pacifism." In 1965 several Catholic Workers gained notoriety for burning their draft cards. That same year a young man from upstate New York named Roger LaPorte set himself afire in front of the United Nations. As he lay dying he announced that he was a Catholic Worker protesting the Vietnam War, but he was a recent arrival to New York City, and few Workers claimed to even know him. His death set off shock waves within what was now known as the "Catholic Left"; Thomas

Merton fired off an anxious telegram demanding to be dissociated from peace groups endorsing such self-violence. Day was not so sure that the act was not yet another sign of contradiction. In her journal she wrote that LaPorte set himself aflame "to suffer with those victims of war in napalm, to be themselves, victims, rather than executioners. Certainly the motive was love." John Leo, a young Catholic intellectual, now charged that Day's movement "had never been well-grounded intellectually."[9]

The Catholic Worker movement survived, although after Day's death in 1980 it resembled more a peace group dedicated to the memory of a charismatic individual than a Catholic movement in the sense Day herself would have insisted upon. There was, to be sure, no longer a mass base of working-class Catholics wary of upward mobility. As Donald Meyer succinctly wrote, in the preface to the revised edition of *The Positive Thinkers*: "The 'individualization' of Catholicism has, of course, swelled the precincts of basic middle-class life immeasurably." By the 1960s and 1970s it seemed that American Catholics were free of the identity concerns which plagued many of their parents. When, in the early 1970s, the soon-to-be pop star Bruce Springsteen related childhood tales of the confessional to his audience, it was in the ironic spirit of recalling ancient phantoms which could no longer threaten. In 1985 the singer Madonna glibly described Catholicism's influence upon her to a *Time* interviewer: her comments occupied a space roughly equivalent to that accorded her views on drugs and "belly buttons." She sang about being a "material girl" with the fervor of a just slightly nervous apostate.[10]

Tom Hayden, the author of the "Port Huron Statement," which launched Students for a Democratic Society in 1962, was a former Catholic. So was Mario Savio, leader of Berkeley's Free Speech movement. So too was Timothy Leary, who urged the use of LSD as a sacrament in the 1960s (in the 1980s he formed one half of a neovaudevillian road show which also featured ex-Catholic G. Gordon Liddy). Viva, one of the "superstars" associated with Andy Warhol's New York pop art "family," claimed that Warhol's scene was "a way for a group of Catholics to purge themselves of Catholic repression . . . and Catholic repression in the Fifties was so extreme that the only way to liberate oneself from it was to react in the completely opposite direction, and then hopefully level off after that." A former altar boy from Cheshire, Connecticut, became the spokesman for the punk rock movement of the mid-1970s; he advised readers of the *Village Voice*: "Don't go out with Catholic girls." And yet the fragmentation of Catholic culture, which began in the late 1950s, was in large part due to the aging of the postimmigrant generation: while their children were certainly not unanimous in their approval of Spockian child-rearing methods, they were surely less inclined to demand the self-abnegation of *their* children that many of their parents demanded of them. At the same time, the events of the 1960s were so tumultuous as to make predictions of the death of Catholic culture premature. Beyond all the aggressive declarations of independence from Catholic dogma lay the many unresolved issues which discontinuities only heighten. As Philip Gleason wrote of the 1960s reaction against immigrant Catholicism: "overlearning things sometimes seems our specialty."[11]

There were still signs of contradiction to be reckoned with. In 1968 a Queens, New York, housewife began receiving visions of the Blessed Mother, "Our Lady of Bayside." Local Catholics promoting the visions became involved in such causes as the right-to-life movement; they also picketed plays and films they believed to be anti-Catholic. In the 1980s Our Lady of Bayside condemned rock music, astrology, and television, but in order that skeptics be ensured of the reality of the visions, "Our Lady has directed that the pictures [of the apparitions] should be taken with Polaroid or other kinds of self-developing cameras, since these pictures develop on the spot and therefore eliminate later accusations of tampering with the negatives." In 1981 John Ibson wrote that the founding generation of American Studies scholars "did not explore the possibility that for some nineteenth-century Americans the Virgin Mary was of more consequence than the Virgin land." The effort of late twentieth-century American Catholics to reconcile the traditions gave promise of continuing and unpredictably creative forms of expression.[12]

Notes

This book was planned and written to appeal to the general reader as well as to the specialist. Accordingly, the scholarly apparatus is presented as simply as possible. To keep the text uncluttered, the sources for quotations and other items are summarized in notes at the end of each paragraph. Sources in each note are given in the order in which the information appears in the text. By matching text and notes, the reader should be able to discern readily the source for any particular item.

Introduction

1. Hatch, *The Sacred Cause of Liberty*; George William Curtis, quoted in Foner, *Free Soil, Free Labor, Free Men*, p. 228; Moore, *Religious Outsiders*, p. 70.

2. Moore, *Religious Outsiders*, p. 51.

3. O'Brien, *The Renewal of American Catholicism*, pp. 80–108.

4. King, *The Iron of Melancholy*; Lears, *No Place of Grace*.

5. Sollors, *Beyond Ethnicity*.

Chapter 1

1. O'Brien, "The Pilgrimage of Dorothy Day," p. 711.

2. Day, *The Long Loneliness*, p. 149.

3. Ibid., p. 17. The best source of biographical information on Dorothy Day is William D. Miller, *Dorothy Day: A Biography*. For his discussion of Day's childhood Miller draws upon materials given to him by Day in 1975 as well as the materials in the Dorothy Day–Catholic Worker Papers at Marquette University (hereafter cited as CW Papers). I was able to obtain access to restricted material for Day's career as head of the Catholic Worker movement (see Chapters 2, 3, and 4), but Miller remains the only scholar to have used the journals and family letters pertaining to Day's life prior to her

conversion. Selections from Day's journals and retreat notes have been edited by William D. Miller and published as *All Is Grace: The Spirituality of Dorothy Day*. Miller's biography of Day is, unfortunately, undocumented, as is his earlier valuable study of the Catholic Worker movement, *A Harsh and Dreadful Love: Dorothy Day and the Catholic Worker Movement*. Like Miller, I believe that Day's novel, *The Eleventh Virgin* (New York, 1924), is the best source of insight into her life before 1920. While it cannot be treated as a factually reliable source, there is not the least doubt that the book conveys with great if subjective accuracy the emotional and spritual travail of Day's early life.

4. William D. Miller, *Dorothy Day*, p. xiii; Day, *The Long Loneliness*, p. 20.

5. James, *The Varieties of Religious Experience*, p. 139; Day, *On Pilgrimage*, p. 47.

6. William D. Miller, *Dorothy Day*, p. 4; Ellsberg, *By Little and By Little*, p. xxii; William D. Miller, *A Harsh and Dreadful Love*, p. 36.

7. Day, *The Long Loneliness*, p. 26; William D. Miller, *Dorothy Day*, p. 312.

8. Day, *The Long Loneliness*, p. 35.

9. William D. Miller, *Dorothy Day*, pp. 17, 25.

10. Jung, *Memories, Dreams, Reflections*, p. 90.

11. Ibid., pp. 12–15, 91; Day, *The Long Loneliness*, p. 18.

12. Day, *The Eleventh Virgin*, p. 41.

13. Thomas à Kempis, *The Imitation of Christ*, pp. 19, 28, 33. In *The Puritan Origins*, Sacvan Bercovitch wrote of Cotton Mather: "Not accidentally, the only 'Popish' work he approved and valued, and the only one published by the seventeenth-century colonial press, was Thomas à Kempis's *Imitation of Christ*. 'It may be of some good consequence for me,' Mather confided in his diary, 'to read a chapter in that Book, the last Thing I do, every Night'" (p. 34). Thus Day was probably able to gain access to this work without having to enter Catholic circles. But more importantly, Bercovitch's discussion of Mather focuses on his triumphalist glorification of John Winthrop's Puritan leadership, for which Christ's perfection served as a typological model. Day valued the work for its emphasis on self-abnegation—that aspect of the text which later supported her distinctly antitriumphalist Catholicism.

14. Day, *The Eleventh Virgin*, pp. 15–19.

15. William D. Miller, *Dorothy Day*, p. 18.

16. Lears, *No Place of Grace*, pp. 34, 259. Paula Marie Kane, in "Boston Catholics and Modern American Culture," discusses several female converts to Catholicism in the early twentieth century. Her subjects, like those of Jackson Lears, tended to be refined aesthetes who were much more attracted to Catholic authority and tradition than was Dorothy Day.

17. Day, *The Long Loneliness*, pp. 35–36, 134; Day, *On Pilgrimage*, p. 126.

18. Day, *The Eleventh Virgin*, pp. 42–43; Day, *Meditations*, p. 82; Day, *The Eleventh Virgin*, p. 59.

19. Day, *The Eleventh Virgin*, p. 20.

20. Ibid., pp. 50–51; Day, *The Long Loneliness*, pp. 32–34.

21. Day, *The Long Loneliness*, pp. 34–35; Day, *The Eleventh Virgin*, pp. 51–52.

22. Day, *The Eleventh Virgin*, p. 22.

23. William James, quoted in King, *The Iron of Melancholy*, p. 169; Denis de Rougemont, *Love in the Western World*, pp. 155, 43, 48.

24. Lears, *No Place of Grace*, p. 123.

25. Day, *The Long Loneliness*, p. 23.

26. Praz, *The Romantic Agony*, pp. 95–286; Swinburne, "Tristram of Lyonesse," in *Swinburne's Collected Poetical Works*, 2:151.

27. Dorothy Day, *From Union Square to Rome*, p. 32.

28. De Rougemont, *Love in the Western World*, pp. 53–54.

29. Day, *The Long Loneliness*, p. 37.

30. Ibid., p. 38; Day, *From Union Square to Rome*, pp. 38–39.

31. *From Union Square to Rome*, pp. 45, 49.

32. Rauschenbusch, "Jesus the Revolutionist," pp. 231–32; Day, *From Union Square to Rome*, p. 40.

33. Daniel Aaron called Day a "rebel girl" in *Writers on the Left*, p. 103; *Call*, December 3, 1916, p. 5; Day, *From Union Square to Rome*, p. 67; Day, *The Long Loneliness*, p. 51.

34. Day, *From Union Square to Rome*, pp. 74–75; *Call*, February 25, 1917, p. 3, February 6, 1917, p. 1.

35. William D. Miller, *Dorothy Day*, p. 103; Day, *The Eleventh Virgin*, pp. 167–69.

36. Floyd Dell, quoted in May, *The End of American Innocence*, p. 287; Fishbein, *Rebels in Bohemia*, pp. 136–37.

37. Day, "Un-Modern Love," pp. 31–32; William D. Miller, *Dorothy Day*, p. 127; Wills, "Dorothy Day at the Barricades," p. 230; Day, *The Eleventh Virgin*, pp. 258–59; William D. Miller, *Dorothy Day*, pp. 136–37.

38. Rideout, *The Radical Novel*, pp. 111–12; Piehl, *Breaking* Bread, p. 16; Day, *The Eleventh Virgin*, p. 293.

39. Slater, *The Pursuit of Loneliness*, p. 4. Like Jesus Christ, St. Augustine, Martin Luther, William James, and numerous other "great people," Day's crisis and conversion experience occurred near her thirtieth year, rather than during adolescence. In *Young Man Luther* Erik Erikson suggested that Luther benefited from the "moratorium" societies often allow young people "after they have ceased being children, but before their deeds and works count toward a future identity" (p. 43). Erikson noted that Luther's tenure as an Augustinian monk provided just such a moratorium (pp. 132–33). His ultimate conversion thus provided the classic model for Protestants in that it brought him back into the world. John King's *The Iron of Melancholy* is largely devoted to conversions which led individuals from the "iron cage" of their neurotic compulsions (or "works" in the sense that Luther defined the prison of Catholic ritual) to meaningful work in the world. Against this background Day's conversion might almost be seen as a negative, or "anti" conversion, in which the process is reversed; the self is deconstructed and experience is negated. King, by the way, cites the reseach of Gerald Moran for conversions in New England prior to the Great Awakening to suggest that "mature" conversions were not an uncommon occurrence in that era (pp. 354–55, n. 16).

40. Day, *From Union Square to Rome*, p. 17.

41. Boulton, *Part of a Long Story*, pp. 40–42, 75.

42. William D. Miller, *Dorothy Day*, pp. 21, 100–118.

43. Hoffman, *The Subversive Vision*, p. 46.

44. Day, "Mary, Mary, Quite Contrary," p. 38; William D. Miller, *Dorothy Day*, p. 311.

45. Day, *The Eleventh Virgin*, p. 53.

46. Day, *The Long Loneliness*, pp. 135–36; William D. Miller, *Dorothy Day*, p. 165; Day, "Having a Baby," pp. 5–6.

47. Day, quoted in Coles, *A Spectacle unto the World*, p. 29; Day, *The Long Loneliness*, p. 139.

48. Day, *The Long Loneliness*, p. 143; Day, *From Union Square to Rome*, pp. 134–38.

49. Day, *The Long Loneliness*, pp. 61, 62–63; Day, "All Is Grace"; Day, *From Union Square to Rome*, pp. 128–30.

50. Day, *From Union Square to Rome*, pp. 128–30; Day, *The Long Loneliness*, p. 150.

51. Day, *The Eleventh Virgin*, p. 198; King, *The Iron of Melancholy*, p. 16.

52. Day, *The Long Loneliness*, pp. 107, 114.

53. Laver, *The First Decadent*, p. 89; Huysmans, *Against the Grain*, pp. 231–49.

54. Laver, *The First Decadent*, pp. 155, 161.

55. Huysmans, *En Route*, p. 109.

56. Praz, *The Romantic Agony*, p. 307; Gilman, *Decadence*, pp. 99–109.

57. Huysmans, *Saint Lydwine of Schiedam*, pp. 54–55; Laver, *The First Decadent*, p. 245.

58. Laver, *The First Decadent*, p. 260. Herbert Mason reported that Huysmans's later works were "now valued very highly in the Church"; see the *Catholic Worker* 27 (March 1961): 5.

59. Day, *The Long Loneliness*, p. 107.

60. Day, *The Eleventh Virgin*, p. 263; Cowley, *Exile's Return*, p. 69.

61. Gordon, *The Malefactors*; Harrington, *Fragments of the Century*, p. 20; William D. Miller, *Dorothy Day*, pp. 453–54.

62. Jack English Interview, CW Papers.

63. Interview with Robert Steed (unless otherwise specified, interviews were conducted by the author; see Bibliography for locations and dates); Wolff, *Black Sun*, pp. 133–42; May, *The End of American Innocence*, p. 194.

64. Gordon, *The Malefactors*, p. 234. The character of "Sister Immaculata" represents a very strange instance of art's imitating the life which was in the process of imitating the artist. In 1966 Sister Mary Bernetta Quinn published *The Metamorphic Tradition*, in which she wrote: "I am indebted to Caroline Gordon Tate for this suggestion of a likeness between Crane's imagery and that of Saint Catherine. In a letter of December, 1950, Mrs. Tate wrote: 'I have been reading St. Catherine of Siena's "Dialogues" and I am much struck by the resemblances between her images of the Bridge (Christ) and Hart's images of the Bridge. I used to think when he was writing the poem that Roebling's bridge was almost too frail to stand up under the imagery he loaded on it. I see now that he had got hold of an archetypal symbol, or image, or rather that it had got hold of him'" (p. 148). Caroline Gordon was—during this period—deeply interested in the Catholic Worker movement and especially in the controversial retreat theology of Day's

spiritual director, Father John Hugo. The attitude toward Hart Crane demonstrated in *The Malefactors* is strongly suggestive of Day's own antitriumphalist vision of a fallen world and the role a drunken homosexual poet might play therein. The meaning of Catholic antitriumphalism is discussed more fully in Chapter 2. Day reportedly admired Gordon's treatment of homosexuality, "the most loathsome of sins" (William D. Miller, *Dorothy Day*, pp. 453–54).

65. Day, *The Long Loneliness*, p. 107; Wilson, *Axel's Castle*, p. 48.

66. Day, *On Pilgrimage*, p. 21.

Chapter 2

1. *Catholic Worker* 1 (December 1933): 4.

2. William D. Miller, *Dorothy Day*, p. 232.

3. Novitsky, "The Ideological Development," p. 53.

4. Day, "Guadaloupe," pp. 477–78.

5. Ibid., p. 478.

6. Day, "East 12th St.," p. 128.

7. William D. Miller, *Dorothy Day*, p. 357.

8. Day, "Spring Festival in Mexico," p. 297.

9. Day, *House of Hospitality*, p. 89.

10. Piehl, *Breaking Bread*, p. 65. Along with Novitsky's work, there are biographies of Maurin by Arthur Sheehan, *Peter Maurin: Gay Believer*, and Marc Ellis, *Peter Maurin: Prophet in the Twentieth Century*.

11. The events of Maurin's life prior to 1933 are so shrouded in mystery that any effort at "biography" is inevitably frustrated. Studies of his life provide an extreme case of Erik Erikson's claim that "the making of legend is as much part of the scholarly rewriting of history as it is part of the original facts used in the work of scholars." From Erikson, *Young Man Luther*, p. 37; Day, *Meditations*, p. 89.

12. E. Weber, *Action Française*, p. 66; Dansette, "The Rejuvenation of French Catholicism," pp. 34–52; Breunig, "The Condemnation of the Sillon," pp. 222–44.

13. *Catholic Worker* 8 (January 1941): 1, 7.

14. William D. Miller, *Dorothy Day*, p. 230.

15. Novitsky, "The Ideological Development," p. 177.

16. *Catholic Worker* 1 (May 1933): 4.

17. Ibid., pp. 1, 8.

18. For the text of "Rerum Novarum," see Pope Leo XIII, "On the Rights and Duties of Capital and Labor"; for "Quadregesimo Anno," see Pope Pius XI, "On Reconstructing the Social Order." For an excellent critique of the "Catholic Social Doctrine" tradition as embodied in these encylicals, see Hebbelthwaite, "The Popes and Politics," pp. 85–99; for a good, brief discussion of the social encyclicals from the point of view of a labor historian, see Freeman, "The Transit Worker's Union," p. 340.

19. *Catholic Worker* 1 (May 1933): 5.

20. Hennessey, *American Catholics*, p. 247; Halsey, *The Survival of American Innocence*, p. 259.

21. King, *The Iron of Melancholy*, pp. 7, 289–322; Meyer, *The Protestant Search*, pp. 99, 122–23.

22. Bercovitch, *The Puritan Origins*, pp. 18, 20.

23. Day, "Peter Maurin," p. 166; *Catholic Worker* 16 (June 1949): 1.

24. Day, "Peter Maurin," 166–67.

25. Breig, "Apostle on the Bum," pp. 9–12.

26. Ibid., p. 9.

27. Ibid., p. 10.

28. Ibid., p. 11.

29. Ibid.

30. *Catholic Worker* 1 (May 1933): 1.

31. Breig, "Apostle on the Bum," p. 12.

32. Day, *Loaves and Fishes*, p. 93.

33. Deverall, "The Way It Was," p. 262.

34. Ellis, *Peter Maurin*, p. 85.

35. William D. Miller, *Dorothy Day*, p. 107.

36. *Catholic Worker* 16 (June 1949): 2.

37. Maurin, quoted in Day, "I Remember Peter Maurin," pp. 34, 36; Maurin, quoted in Sheehan, "Conversations with Peter," pp. 11–12; for Kenkel and the Central Verein, see Gleason, *The Conservative Reformers*.

38. Novitsky, "The Ideological Development," p. 85; see also Novitsky, "The Radical Implications," p. 83. For Day's revision of "man is naturally bad" compare *Catholic Worker* 1 (May 1933): 1, with *Catholic Worker* 3 (December 1935): 1. While Maurin may himself have made the change, Day chose the latter version for inclusion in *The Green Revolution*, a collection of Maurin's writings that "Miss Day and the editors of the *Catholic Worker* believe . . . should represent the ultimate and authoritative edition of Peter Maurin's 'Easy Essays.'"

39. Cort, "The Catholic Worker," p. 636; *Catholic Worker* 3 (February 1936): 4.

40. Day, "Peter Maurin," p. 8.

41. Ibid., p. 163.

42. Dorothy Day to Catherine de Hueck (no date, probably 1936), CW Papers.

43. *Catholic Worker* 3 (July 1936): 2; *Catholic Worker* 3 (May 1936): 3.

44. Corrin, *G. K. Chesterton and Hilaire Belloc*, p. 95; *Catholic Worker* 3 (November 1935): 1, 8.

45. Corrin, *G. K. Chesterton and Hilaire Belloc*, p. 93; *Catholic Worker* 3 (November 1935): 1, 8.

46. Corrin, *G. K. Chesterton and Hilaire Belloc*, p. 98; Piehl, *Breaking Bread*, p. 130.

47. William D. Miller, *Dorothy Day*, p. 299; Day, *Loaves and Fishes*, p. 55.

48. *Daily Worker*, August 18, 1934, p. 7.

49. J. Maritain, "Religion and Politics in France," p. 273; Hellman, *Emmanuel Mounier*, p. 32; see also Rauch, *Politics and Belief.*

50. Hellman, *Emmanuel Mounier*, pp. 12–51.

51. Ibid., pp. 133, 177–78; Mounier, *The Personalist Manifesto*, p. 17.

52. Hellman, *Emmanuel Mounier*, p. 65.

53. *Catholic Worker* 3 (December 1935): 2; *Catholic Worker* 3 (January 1936): 5.

54. *Catholic Worker* 5 (December 1937): 6.

55. Kazin, "The Self as History," p. 32; Day, *On Pilgrimage*, p. 84.

56. *Catholic Worker* 16 (June 1949): 1, 2.

57. Maisie Ward, quoted in a letter, Caroline Gordon to Dorothy Day (no date), Gordon Papers; Ward, *Unfinished Business*, p. 179; Julia Porcelli, quoted in William D. Miller, *A Harsh and Dreadful Love*, p. 90; interview with Robert Steed; interview with John Stanley.

58. Dorothy Day, from a broadcast transcript of "Still a Rebel," *Bill Moyer's Journal*, WNET, 1973, CW Papers.

59. Mersch, *The Whole Christ*, pp. 542–84.

60. Ibid., p. 562.

61. Sheen, *The Mystical Body of Christ*, pp. 24–25; Adam, *The Spirit of Catholicism*, pp. 36–38, 169–86; Mersch, *The Whole Christ*, p. 8.

62. Pope Pius XI, "On the Catholic Priesthood," p. 179; Pope Pius XII, "Mystici Corporis," pp. 7–63.

63. *Catholic Worker* 2 (May 1934): 4.

64. *Catholic Worker* 3 (October 1934): 3.

65. Gleason, "In Search of Unity," p. 190.

66. Piehl, *Breaking Bread*, p. 138.

67. Halsey, *The Survival of American Innocence*, pp. 37–38, 57; Brown, "The Grail Movement" (paper), p. 14.

68. *Catholic Worker* 1 (April 1934): 3.

69. Pope Pius XI, "Rite Expiatis"; *Catholic Worker* 3 (January 1936): 5; *Catholic Worker* 3 (May 1936): 8; *Catholic Worker* 2 (October 1934): 5.

70. Marx, *Virgil Michel*, p. 377; *Catholic Worker* 3 (June 1935): 1; O'Brien, *The Renewal of American Catholicism*, p. 113.

71. Susman, "The Thirties," pp. 179–218; see also Susman, *Culture as History*, pp. 184–210; Shapiro, "Decentralist Intellectuals," pp. 938–57. "I think the people . . . " is quoted by Arthur M. Schlesinger, Jr., in his review of Robert S. McElvaine, ed., *Down and Out in the Great Depression*, *New York Times Book Review*, February 6, 1983, p. 3; John Steinbeck, *The Grapes of Wrath*, p. 374.

72. William D. Miller asserted in *Dorothy Day* that Day sought "a hard contest" (p. 377). Retreats are discussed briefly in Dolan, *Catholic Revivalism*, p. 53.

73. Sharp, "Shall the Diocesan Clergy Conduct Retreats?," p. 338. Figures for female retreatants were not offered.

74. Dolan, *Catholic Revivalism*, Chapter 6, contains a very interesting discussion of Catholic ambivalence toward worldly success as reflected in mission sermons and attitudes toward temperance. For a further discussion of this theme, see Chapter 3. Day discussed her initiation into "the retreat" at length in *The Long Loneliness*, pp. 243–63.

75. Day, *The Long Loneliness*, p. 253.

76. William D. Miller, *Dorothy Day*, p. 338; Day, "All Is Grace," pp. 94–96. An unpublished manuscript, "All Is Grace" consists of several drafts, not all of them consecutively numbered. I have simply cited the page numbers that appear on the version cited. William D. Miller has published selections from the manuscript as *All Is Grace: The Spirituality of Dorothy Day*.

77. Hugo, *The Sign of Contradiction*, pp. 294–95. All of Hugo's works were privately printed, either by the Catholic Workers or by himself.

78. M. Weber, *The Protestant Ethic*, p. 181.

79. Addams, "A Function of the Social Settlement," pp. 194–95.

80. Day, "All Is Grace," p. 9.

81. Hugo, *The Sign of Contradiction*, p. 431.

82. Day, "All Is Grace," p. 41.

83. Ibid., p. 191.

84. William D. Miller, *A Harsh and Dreadful Love*, p. 188. Day may have been the first Catholic to discuss her personal relationship with God in this way, but she was surely not the first American to do so. In *The Protestant Temperament* (New York, 1977), Philip Greven wrote of the most pietisitic American Protestants: "For some evangelicals, one of the most powerful desires of all was for oneness with Christ—a virtual fusing of the self with Divinity, so that there would be no separation or any distinctions between self and God" (p. 85). Day's earliest religious experiences sound very similar to those of, say, Jonathan Edwards's wife Sarah. But the early evangelicals, for the most part, were caught up in the transition that Richard Bushman neatly termed *From Puritan to Yankee*. They never generated a permanent counterculture to resist the increasingly worldly aspirations of their Protestant colleagues. Indeed, Bushman and others argued that the Great Awakening was an integral part of this transition. Moreover, the evangelicals' *systematic* work toward self-dissolution and the breaking of their children's wills was fundamentally contrary to the self-conscious abandon of twentieth-century Catholic radicals. See Greven, *The Protestant Temperament*, pp. 21–61. Dorothy Day and Cotton Mather ultimately share little in common but a religious and national inheritance. Day found in Catholicism a refuge from the very forces the Puritans helped unleash. The quoted passage is from "All Is Grace," pp. 21, 71. One of the few studies of a "Catholic temperament" is Chinnici, "Organization of the Spiritual Life," pp. 229–55. Jay Dolan, in *Catholic Revivalism*, which covers the nineteenth and very early twentieth century, found, as did Chinnici, an emphasis among Catholic preachers on the negative, guilt-inducing character of Catholic piety in America. Against this background Day's rhetoric becomes even more striking, even in its wild ambiguity.

85. Day, "All Is Grace" (unpaginated fragments).

86. Ibid.

87. William D. Miller, *Dorothy Day*, p. 339; Stanley Vishnewski Interview, CW Papers. Vishnewski's account of the retreat theology is eerily reminiscent of the language of such scurrilous nineteenth-century anti-Catholic tracts as Maria Monk's *Awful Disclosures* (1836). It is at least possible that Day heard her father referring to this genre of

literature as part of his rhetorical attacks upon Catholics during her childhood. Since she saw Catholics' persecution as a sign of election, she may have unconsiously parodied anti-Catholic polemics when promoting the retreats (though this does not explain the affinity of the Franco-American Hugo for the same spiritual style).

88. Hugo's retreat notes were privately printed as *Applied Christianity*. He was harshly assailed in a review by Father Francis J. Connell in the *American Ecclesiastical Review* and in a remarkably sharp rebuke by another priest, Joseph Clifford Fenton, in "Nature and the Supernatural Life," also in the *American Ecclesiastical Review*. Fenton concluded that the retreat theology was "definitely pernicious." Day's remarks on the Mystical Body are in "All Is Grace," p. 67. Fathers Connell and Fenton later became the chief antagonists of John Courtney Murray, the Jesuit who gained renown for his efforts to reconcile Catholicism with American political theory. See Cuddihy, *No Offense*, pp. 73–82.

89. Fenton, "Nature and the Supernatural Life," p. 67.

90. Day, *The Long Loneliness*, pp. 258–59; Hugo, *The Sign of Contradiction*, p. 103.

91. "Gloomy Catholicism" is from Sorrell, "The Catholicism of Jack Kerouac," p. 197. The connection between Catholicism and French-Canadian "survivance" is made by Mason Wade in *The French-Canadian Outlook*, Chapters 1, 2, and 4. Father Hugo's critique of the Western democracies is in Hugo, *The Weapons of the Spirit*, p. 23.

92. Veysey, *The Communal Experience*, p. 38; MacDonald, Introduction to *The Catholic Worker*, p. 9.

93. John Cooney, *The American Pope*, p. 90; Day, from "Still a Rebel," *Bill Moyer's Journal*, 1973, CW Papers.

94. Wilfred Parsons to Dorothy Day, November 22, 1933, CW Papers.

95. From a manuscript fragment of a letter from Day to the editor of *Faith Today* (probably 1954), CW Papers.

96. Daly, *Gyn/Ecology*, pp. 98–101; Dorothy Day to Catherine de Hueck, August 9, 1936, CW Papers.

97. Brien, "The Catholic Revival Revisited," p. 716; Day, "Peter and Women," p. 189; Day, "All Is Grace," p. 55.

98. Day, *The Long Loneliness*, pp. 235–36; William D. Miller, *Dorothy Day*, p. 516.

99. Glazer, "A Decade of Transition," pp. 98–99.

100. Day, "All Is Grace," p. 13; p. 4 of a chapter of a 1967 draft, "Beginnings"; Day, *On Pilgrimage*, pp. 57–58.

101. Novitsky, "The Ideological Development," p. 71; *Catholic Worker* 16 (June 1949): 3; Rodgers, *The Work Ethic in Industrial America*, pp. 16–17, 100. For Canon Cardijn and his JOCISTE movement, see Robb, "Specialized Catholic Action," pp. 218–59; *Catholic Worker* 14 (July–August 1946): 1, 2.

102. *Catholic Worker* 6 (May 1938): 2.

103. *Catholic Worker* 7 (July–August 1939): 4.

104. *Catholic Worker* 8 (June 1940): 7.

105. A. Sheehan, *Peter Maurin: Gay Believer*, pp. 152–53; *Catholic Worker* 7 (September 1939): 5.

106. *Catholic Worker* 9 (November 1941): 6.

107. *Catholic Worker* 14 (October 1946): 6.

108. *Catholic Worker* 8 (June 1940): 7.

109. King, *The Iron of Melancholy*, p. 290; Catholic Worker 3 (February 1936): 1. Bethune came from a much more sophisticated background than most of the other Catholic-born Catholic Workers.

110. Dorothy Day to Catherine de Hueck (no date, probably 1936), CW Papers.

111. Hamilton, *Robert Lowell*, p. 100.

112. Ibid., pp. 80–81.

113. Gordon, *The Malefactors*, p. 304.

114. Day, "Peter Maurin," pp. 83–84.

115. Bercovitch, *The American Jeremiad*, p. 160; George William Curtis, quoted in Foner, *Free Soil, Free Labor, Free Men*.

116. Day, "Peter Maurin," pp. 83–84; King, *The Iron of Melancholy*, p. 333.

Chapter 3

1. Sperry, *Religion in America*, p. 199. Blanshard is discussed more fully in Chapters 3 and 5.

2. Thomas, "Nationalities and American Catholicism," p. 161; a good summary of Greeley's sociological life's work is offered in Greeley, *The American Catholic*.

3. Emma Goldman, quoted in O'Brien, "The Pilgrimage of Dorothy Day," p. 712; interview with Kieran Dugan.

4. Brinkley, *Voices of Protest*, p. 83.

5. Interview with Kieran Dugan; Greeley, Foreword to *International Conflict*, p. xi.

6. Piehl, *Breaking Bread*, p. 54.

7. *Catholic Worker* 2 (September 1934): 3.

8. *Catholic Worker* 3 (February 1936): 1.

9. *Catholic Worker* 1 (July–August 1933): 8.

10. Ibid.; *The Brooklyn Tablet*, May 6, 1933, p. 1.

11. *Catholic Worker* 4 (October 1936): 2.

12. *Catholic Worker* 1 (September 1933): 12.

13. *Catholic Worker* 3 (May 1935): 5.

14. Pope Pius XI, "Quadregesimo Anno," pp. 272–73; Coughlin, *Series of Lectures*, p. 22; Editorial Comment, *The Catholic World* 138 (October 1933), pp. 1–7; Coughlin, *Series of Lectures*, p. 15.

15. Coughlin, *Series of Lectures*, p. 44; Brinkley, *Voices of Protest*, p. 145.

16. Coughlin, *Series of Lectures*, pp. 19, 91.

17. Ibid., p. 96.

18. *Catholic Worker* 4 (March 1937): 7.

19. Dolan, *Catholic Revivalism*, pp. 162–63.

20. *Brooklyn Tablet*, August 3, 1935, p. 7.

21. Shenton, "The Coughlin Movement and the New Deal," p. 367; Coughlin, *Series of Lectures*, p. 70.

22. Marcus, *Father Coughlin*, pp. 70, 224.

23. Ibid., p. 228.

24. Glazer and Moynihan, *Beyond the Melting Pot*, p. 230.

25. Shenton, "Coughlin Movement," pp. 368–69.

26. Mrs. Joseph Richter to Dorothy Day, January 26, 1937, CW Papers.

27. J. Gerhard to the *Catholic Worker*, June 3, 1936, CW Papers.

28. Day, quoted in Betten, *Catholic Activism*, p. 53; Mitchell, "Father Coughlin's Children," p. 74.

29. *Brooklyn Tablet*, February 29, 1936, p. 4.

30. Sheen, *The Mystical Body of Christ*, p. 34.

31. Orsi, *The Madonna of 115th Street*, p. 155. For a discussion of the central role of suffering women in popular European-Catholic devotions of the nineteenth century, see Kselman, *Miracles and Prophecies*, esp. pp. 102–6.

32. Orsi, *The Madonna of 115th Street*, pp. 100, 223.

33. Ibid., p. 63; and see also Orsi's manuscript, "The Madonna of 115th Street," p. 115.

34. *Sign* 12 (November 1932): 225.

35. For evidence of Coughlin's early anti-Semitism, see Bennett, *Demagogues in the Depression*, p. 52; see also Athans, "A New Perspective," 224–37. Athans focuses on the influence of the Irish priest Denis Fahey in helping to inspire Coughlin's anti-Semitism after 1938. She stresses Coughlin's devotion to the symbol of the Mystical Body of Christ in defending the church against its alleged enemies, thus further placing his rhetoric, at least, at the center of the new Catholic discourse of the 1930s. It is also interesting to note that Coughlin often referred in letters to Fahey to the "Mystical Body of Satan," anticipating by a decade one of the pet rhetorical devices of Msgr. Fulton J. Sheen in his crusade against communism. See also *Catholic Worker* 10 (July–August 1942): 2; R. Maritain, *We Have Been Friends Together*, pp. 104–40.

36. R. Maritain, *We Have Been Friends Together*, pp. 123–29. *Catholic Worker* 10 (July–August 1942): 2.

37. Stanley Vishnewski, quoted on Maurin and the Jews in M. Ellis, *Peter Maurin*, n. 18, p. 189; *Catholic Worker* 2 (December 1934): 3.

38. *Catholic Worker* 7 (February 1940): 2.

39. R. Maritain, *We Have Been Friends Together*, pp. 123, 125; Bloy, *Pilgrim of the Absolute*, p. 253. Despite the influence of Bloy on his thinking, Maurin "was in favor of opening of doors" to Jewish refugees from Nazism. See A. Sheehan, *Peter Maurin: Gay Believer*, p. 195.

40. Bayor, *Neighbors in Conflict*, p. 99. This work made an extraordinary contribution to our historical understanding of interethnic conflict in New York.

41. *Brooklyn Tablet*, March 25, 1933, p. 5.

42. *Catholic Worker* 7 (June 1939): 5.

43. *New Republic* 97 (December 28, 1938): 233–34.

44. Bayor, *Neighbors in Conflict*, pp. 102–3.

45. Ibid., p. 34; Thernstrom, *The Other Bostonians*, pp. 152–60. Daniel Patrick Moynihan wrote that the "Irish era" in New York did indeed end in the 1930s. "A symbolic point might be the day ex-Mayor Jimmy Walker sailed for Europe and exile with his beloved, but unwed, Betty." Glazer and Moynihan, *Beyond the Melting Pot*, p. 217.

46. *Catholic Worker* 7 (June 1939): 5.

47. *Brooklyn Tablet*, September 14, 1935, p. 6.

48. Ibid.

49. *Brooklyn Tablet*, September 14, 1935, p. 7. Someone suggested to me that correspondents like O'Brien may have had (presumably clerical) "help" in the composition of such letters. This view overlooks the legendary success of Catholic elementary schools in teaching proper grammar and careful sentence construction.

50. Erikson, *Young Man Luther*, p. 142.

51. Howard Meeks to Dorothy Day, October 10, 1939; April 28, 1942, CW Papers.

52. William D. Miller, *Dorothy Day*, p. 266.

53. Jack English Interview, CW Papers; Cogley, *Catholic America*, p. 106.

54. Marx, *Virgil Michel*, p. 124.

55. McCarthy, *Private Faces, Public Places*, pp. 65–132; Michael Mertem to Dorothy Day (n.d., ca. 1930s), CW Papers.

56. Louise Carr to Dorothy Day, April 28, 1941; Vincent C. Allred to Dorothy Day, March 13, 1941; Clarence Carr to Dorothy Day, February 27, 1946, CW Papers.

57. Sister Peter Claver Interview, CW Papers.

58. Barbara Callahan to Day (n.d., ca. 1940s), CW Papers.

59. Dennis Robb, "Specialized Catholic Action," pp. 36–37.

60. Ibid., p. 234.

61. Brown, "The Grail Movement," p. 18.

62. Ibid., p. 46.

63. Lydwine van Kersbergen, quoted in Bill and Dorothy Gauchat Interview, CW Papers; Brown, "The Grail Movement," p. 53.

64. Brown, "The Grail Movement," p. 71.

65. Interview with Dolores Elise Brien; interview with Ned O'Gorman; interview with John Stanley.

66. Brown, "The Grail Movement," p. 208.

67. Connolly, *Mr. Blue*, p. 71.

68. Ibid., pp. 49, 50–65, 114, 118.

69. Ibid., p. 75.

70. Sylvester, *Moon Gaffney*, p. 87.

71. Ibid., pp. 162–65; For a nonfiction sample of Sylvester's critique of Catholic culture, see Sylvester, "Problems of the Catholic Writer," pp. 109–13. For a clerical response, see Gillis, "Problems of the Catholic Writer," pp. 481–86. For a discussion of

Syvester in the context of the quest for "the great Catholic-American novel," see Sparr, "The Catholic Literary Revival," pp. 331–36.

72. Sylvester, *Moon Gaffney*, pp. 207–8.

Chapter 4

1. "Mr. and Mrs. X," "Responsibility in Catholic Marriage," p. 5.

2. Rev. Henry V. Sattler, Letter to the Editor, *Integrity* 10 (November 1955): 6.

3. Robinson, "*Integrity*: The Beginnings," pp. 27–28. For a discussion of *Integrity* in the context of Catholic family issues, see Burns, "American Catholics," pp. 170–212.

4. E. Willock, "Catholic Radicalism," p. 633.

5. William D. Miller, *A Harsh and Dreadful Love*, p. 218; E. Willock, "Catholic Radicalism," pp. 630–31; Day, "The Catholic Worker," p. 19; E. M. Sheehan, "Through Eyes That See," p. 46–47.

6. E. Willock, "Marriage for Keeps," p. 20; *Catholic Worker* 14 (July–August 1946): 1.

7. Hoehn, *Catholic Authors*, p. 261.

8. Ibid., p. 262.

9. Ibid., Robinson, "*Integrity*: The Beginnings," p. 28.

10. Michaels, *Designs for Christian Living*, pp. 27–40; Hoehn, *Catholic Authors*, p. 261; Veysey, *The Communal Experience*, p. 57.

11. Stanley, "In Memory of Ed Willock," p. 80; Brien, "The Catholic Revival Revisited," p. 714; interview with Dolores Elise Brien.

12. Michaels, *This Perverse Generation*, p. 34.

13. Halsey, *The Survival of American Innocence*, p. 152; Michaels, "A Christian Abnormal Psychology," pp. 2–42; Correspondence, *Integrity* 1 (March 1947): 43; Hoehn, *Catholic Authors*, p. 261.

14. E. Willock, "The Cross and the Dollar," p. 45; Stanley, "In Memory of Ed Willock," p. 80.

15. Michaels, "The Frustration of the Incarnation," p. 21.

16. E. Willock, "To Be Specific," p. 16; E. Willock, "Hints for Converting America," p. 43.

17. Carol Jackson to Thomas Reese, December 3, 1946, Seminarian's Catholic Action Papers (herafter cited as SCA Papers); Michaels, "The Unity of the World," p. 17.

18. Michaels, "I'd Rather Be a Menial," p. 33.

19. Jackson, "In Defense of Monica Baldwin," p. 48; Michaels, "A Christian Abnormal Psychology," p. 34.

20. Michaels, "A Christian Abnormal Psychology," p. 27.

21. Ibid., p. 39.

22. Calkins, "Rhythm—the Unhappy Compromise," pp. 3–11; Jackson, "The Tragedy of Modern Woman," p. 5; Stancioff, "The Love Education of Girls," pp. 29–30; Jackson, "The Tragedy of Modern Woman," p. 10.

23. E. Willock, "This Gift Is Ours," p. 37; E. Willock, "To Be Specific," p. 20.

24. E. Willock, "This Gift Is Ours," p. 38; E. Willock, "The Family Has Lost Its Head," pp. 38–39.

25. E. Willock, "Men, Mary, and Manliness," pp. 36–45.

26. Robinson, "*Integrity*: The Beginnings," p. 28; E. Willock, "To Be Specific," p. 19.

27. Cell Minutes, Young Christian Workers, Wilmington, Delaware, August 14, 1946, SCA Papers; Doreen O'Sullivan, personal correspondence, May 12, 1982.

28. Cell Minutes, Young Christian Workers, Wilmington, Delaware, January 30, July 24, November 13, 1946, SCA Papers.

29. Pamphlet from Center for Men of Christ the King, SCA Papers; O'Gorman, "An Education of a Poet," pp. 183–84.

30. E. Willock, "And All These Things," p. 7.

31. E. Willock, "Poverty and Marriage," p. 32; Editorial, *Integrity* 2 (August 1948): 1–2.

32. E. Willock, "The Catholic Politician," pp. 26–36; Michaels, "Man's Providence," p. 37.

33. E. Willock, "The Catholic Politician," pp. 31–32; Robinson, "*Integrity*: The Beginnings," p. 27.

34. E. Willock, "Poverty and Marriage," p. 32; Editorial, *Integrity* 1 (May 1947): 3; E. Willock, "Marriage for Keeps," p. 21.

35. Editorial, *Integrity* 1 (May 1947): 3; Diner, *Erin's Daughters in America*, pp. 6–29; Thoreau, *Walden*, p. 148.

36. Morgan, "Six Aren't Enough," p. 18; interview with Dorothy Willock; Stanley, "In Memory of Ed Willock," p. 81.

37. Ward, "Plea for the Family," p. 43.

38. "Mrs. J.," "The Joy of Poverty," pp. 194–207.

39. Walsh, "The Young Familiar Faces," pp. 116–41.

40. Michaels, "A Christian Abnormal Psychology," p. 18; Walsh, "The Young Familiar Faces," pp. 137–39.

41. Walsh, "The Young Familiar Faces," pp. 123, 139; Echele, "An American Poverello," p. 6; Newland, "Lent and the Family," p. 7.

42. Miller and Nowak, *The Fifties*, pp. 149, 156; E. Willock, "The Family Has Lost Its Head," p. 43.

43. Newland, "From a Letter," p. 27; D. Willock, "Life with Mother," p. 21.

44. Ward, "Plea for the Family," p. 44. See also Ward, *Unfinished Business*. In *Poets in Their Youth*, p. 126, Eileen Simpson quoted an anecdote of Jean Stafford's that suggests the distance between the Sheeds and such of their constituents as the Willocks. The publishers had invited Stafford and her husband Robert Lowell to their home in the country: "I packed a typewriter case, the only thing we had which could pass for luggage, with two pairs of pajamas, unironed, and two toothbrushes. As our taxi pulled into the driveway, the butler came down the stairs, opened the door and before I could stop him, whisked away the typewriter case. After being greeted by the Sheeds, we were shown to our room. There was the typewriter case, open on the luggage rack. The

toothbrushes were in a glass in the bathroom. The two pairs of unironed pajamas were neatly arranged, one on either side of the bed."

45. Interview with John Dermody; interview with Alan Hudson.

46. Ibid., E. Willock, "A Place to Live," p. 13. On the Catholic cooperative movement that was emerging in New York Catholic parishes in the 1940s see LaBossiere, "Saga of Stuyvesant Heights," pp. 4–12. Several of the early members of the Marycrest Association came from a veterans' housing complex known as Shank's Village, located near the Hudson River in Rockland County, New York. By 1954 five hundred families faced eviction from Shanks Village, which indicates that the postwar housing crisis lasted for at least a decade. See the *New York Herald Tribune*, January 3, 1955, p. 13.

47. E. Willock, "A Place to Live," p. 13; Eva Gretz to Dorothy Day, March 24, 1942, CW Papers.

48. Harold Craddock to Dorothy Day, March 25, 1939, CW Papers.

49. Dorothy Day to Msgr. Leo G. Fink, February 20, 1947, CW Papers.

50. William D. Miller, *A Harsh and Dreadful Love*, pp. 202–4.

51. On Borsodi see Shi, *The Simple Life*, pp. 215–47; interview with John Stanley; interview with William Cobb. The paraliturgical celebrations at Marycrest reflected a larger interest among many Catholics of the 1950s in the kind of purified, primitive aesthetic favored by Dorothy Day and the Catholic Workers since the 1930s. See Wills, *Bare Ruined Choirs*, pp. 38–60. Some of the rites favored by the Marycresters are described in Weiser, *Handbook of Christian Feasts*. K. A. Miller's *Emigrants and Exiles* discusses some of the prefamine Irish rituals that Willock sought to revive without being fully aware of their tenuous relationship to orthodox Catholic practice: "[P]re-famine Catholics *were* devout but their piety was expressed primarily in archaic, communal traditions which had originated in pre-Christian times and had since acquired only a thin veneer of medieval Catholicism. For example, rural Catholics prayed and bathed at holy wells once sacred to ancient Catholic deities; on St. John's Eve—formerly Beltaine, the pagan New Year—the drove cattle through hilltop bonfires to protect them from disease and misfortune" (p. 73). Willock was unable to build a positive ideology around these survivals of Irish folk culture because he was so contemptuous of urban Irish-American culture. He regularly condemned drinking, sports, and popular entertainments as decadent and immoral, but as a radical Catholic he could not offer even the meager rewards, in this world at least, that secular reformers held out to those who avoided the tavern or dance hall.

52. Interview with Philip O'Brien; interview with John Dermody; D. Willock, "My Marriage Course," p. 42; Stanley, "In Memory of Ed Willock," p. 81; interview with Frances Hogan.

53. The members of Marycrest did consult with priests to resolve disputes, particularly after Willock became incapacitated. When a founding member decided to leave the community in 1960, the Dominican Father James Mark Egan "decided that A. has a moral obligation to pay his work dues of 144 stones, even though he may have voluntarily contributed more time than this to the Association without receiving credit"; interview with Mary Hudson; interview with Hazel Dermody; interview with Lynn and

William Oswald. For sexual practices at Oneida see Kern, *An Ordered Love*, pp. 235–56. See also Blanshard, *Personal and Controversial*, pp. 223–24. In June 1951 Carol Jackson attended a Carnegie Hall meeting of Blanshard's Protestants and Other Americans United for the Separation of Church and State. She came away feeling that, while Blanshard "wants no moral regulation of sexual conduct . . . he did not seem like a man who had a weakness for sensuality. I got the impression of cold, intellectual hatred for purity and morality." See *Integrity* 5 (June 1951): 40–42. This characterization neatly sums up the *Integrity* group's general opinion of liberal Protestantism. The early years at Marycrest were extremely difficult and generated conflicts and bitter feelings that have not yet fully abated. Yet members of at least six founding families continue to live in the community, which now resembles an eclectic middle-class neighborhood. The men and women I spoke with were without exception remarkably interesting and generous: they bear the mark of survivors of an experiment many now admit to never having quite understood. To those living in the surrounding community of West Nyack, Marycrest is primarily associated with the vast numbers of children who lived there. As to the current religious convictions of those long-since grown children, estimates by their parents suggest that between 60 and 90 percent are no longer "practicing" Catholics; yet as one parent argued, the same might be true for children of other Catholic neighborhoods of the 1950s and 1960s. Many Marycresters believe the 1960s simply arrived there somewhat early, certainly well before the dawn of the Second Vatican Council. The independence (some would even say contrariness) of the founding members undermined the utopian hopes for radical Christian community and brought home a lesson in pluralism and the need for tolerance of diversity that millions of Catholics would struggle with during the 1960s. In 1958 a founding member wrote to Ed Willock: "A much greater broadness in attitude and attitudes (within the wide-ranging, far-reaching Christian norms) must be fostered. Our unanimity, our one-ness, exists in Dogma only. After that let the green revolutionists and the idlers-in-taverns, the devotees of the Catholic Worker and those of the financial pages of the dailies, those who wish to attend school budget meetings and those who don't; not necessarily go their separate ways but perhaps sit at table and behold how good and how pleasant it is for brethren to dwell together in unity. That's the only revolution I shall ever again be interested in!"

54. Robinson, "*Integrity*: The Beginnings," p. 60; Michaels, "Christ with Us," p. 44; Michaels, "Religious Fanaticism," p. 20.

55. E. Willock, "Not Enough Fools to Go 'Round," p. 14; E. Willock, "Suffering and Spiritual Growth," pp. 23–26.

56. *Advocate*, December 29, 1960, p. 7; Day, "In Memory of Ed Willock," pp. 549–51.

57. Interview with Dorothy Dohen; Dorothy Dohen to Thomas Merton, May 13, 1967, Merton Collection; Editorial, *Integrity* 6 (April 1952): 1.

58. E. Willock, "Marriage for Keeps," p. 22.

59. Editorial, *Integrity* 6 (September 1952): 1; Editorial, *Integrity* 7 (October 1952): 1; Editorial, *Integrity* 8 (July 1954): 1.

60. "Mr. X," Letter to the Editor, *Integrity* 9 (November 1955): 6.

Chapter 5

1. Halsey, *The Survival of American Innocence*, p. 173.

2. The most extensive Dooley biography is the highly unreliable work of his mother, Agnes W. Dooley, *Promises to Keep*; for the presumed source of his grandfather's fortune, see Crowell and Wilson, *How America Went to War*, pp. 156, 179.

3. A. W. Dooley, *Promises to Keep*, pp. 7–10; Selsor, *Sincerely, Tom Dooley*, pp. 25–26; Seifert, "The Untold Story of Tom Dooley," p. 60.

4. Allen, "The Amazing Dr. Dooley," p. 28; A. W. Dooley, *Promises to Keep*, pp. 8; *Portrait of a Splendid American*, Side One; A. W. Dooley, *Promises to Keep*, p. 13.

5. Jencks, *Tom Dooley, American Saint?*, p. 5.

6. Harrington, *Fragments of the Century*, pp. 4–14.

7. Interview with Michael Harrington; Seifert, "The Untold Story of Tom Dooley," p. 60; A. W. Dooley, *Promises to Keep*, pp. 14–15.

8. A. W. Dooley, *Promises to Keep*, pp. 18–22.

9. Leader, "How the Landscape Has Changed," p. 23.

10. Gleason, "In Search of Unity," p. 197.

11. Stritch, "The Foreign Legion of Father O'Hara," p. 27.

12. Connelly and H. J. Dooley, *Hesburgh's Notre Dame*, p. 37.

13. Woodward, "The Lessons of the Master," p. 15; Gleason, "In Search of Unity," p. 189; Woodward, "The Lessons of the Master," pp. 17, 18, 19; Francis L. Kunkel, Letter to the Editor, *Notre Dame Magazine*, Summer 1984, p. 2.

14. Richard Hofstadter, *Anti-Intellectualism in American Life*, p. 136.

15. Woodward, "The Lessons of the Master," p. 19; Brashler, "The Hard Fate," pp. 34–37.

16. Dooley's passport application is dated January 28, 1957. His applications were included among declassified papers obtained from the U.S. Department of State. See also the Notre Dame yearbook, *The Dome* 38 (1947): 312; Geyer, "A Small Place in the Sun," p. 15.

17. Allen, "The Amazing Dr. Dooley," p. 28; A. W. Dooley, *Promises to Keep*, pp. 25–28.

18. A. W. Dooley, *Promises to Keep*, p. 41.

19. Ibid., p. 47; *Portrait of a Splendid American*, Side One; Matthews, "The Navy Sent Him," p. 5; A. W. Dooley, *Promises to Keep*, p. 50.

20. Seifert, "The Untold Story of Tom Dooley," p. 62; Selsor, *Sincerely, Tom Dooley*, p. 55–61; *Portrait of a Splendid American*, Side One.

21. A. W. Dooley, *Promises to Keep*, pp. 56–57.

22. Ibid., p. 81.

23. Matthews, "The Navy Sent Him," p. 6; Tom Dooley to Agnes Dooley, September 29, 1954; October 1, 1954; August 26, 1955, Dooley Papers.

24. U.S. Department of Defense, "Failure of the Geneva Settlement," p. 11; informative accounts of the exodus of Catholics from North Vietnam include Fall, *The Two Viet-Nams*, pp. 153–55; Haas and Nguyen Bao Cong, *Vietnam: The Other Conflict*, pp. 20–

24; Karnow, *Vietnam: A History*, pp. 220–22. Lansdale is discussed further later in the chapter.

25. Tom Dooley to Agnes Dooley, August 26, 1955, Dooley Papers.

26. A. W. Dooley, *Promises to Keep*, pp. 161–70; William J. Lederer, personal correspondence, March 16, 1986.

27. Andrews, "Tom Dooley's Testament," p. 105.

28. T. A. Dooley, *Deliver Us from Evil*, p. 23.

29. Durdin, "Mission of Mercy Accomplished," p. 19; T. A. Dooley, *Deliver Us from Evil*, p. 32.

30. T. A. Dooley, *Deliver Us from Evil*, pp. 71–72; von Hoffman, "Hang Down Your Head, Tom Dooley," p. 22.

31. "Lansdale Team's Report," pp. 59–60; Halberstam, *The Best and the Brightest*, p. 157; FitzGerald, *Fire in the Lake*, p. 104; Karnow, *Vietnam: A History*, pp. 220–22. Cecil B. Curry's *Edward Lansdale, the Unquiet American* appeared as this book was going to press. Curry learned that Lansdale's father had been raised a Catholic but that he yielded to his wife's staunch faith in Christian Science wherever matters of child rearing were concerned.

32. Drinnon, *Facing West*, p. 378; Lansdale, *In the Midst of Wars*, pp. 105–6, 151.

33. Winters, "Tom Dooley: The Forgotten Hero," p. 11; Greene, *The Quiet American*, p. 157.

34. FitzGerald, *Fire in the Lake*, pp. 127–28.

35. Fall, *The Two Viet-Nams*, pp. 246–52. As indicated in Chapter 2 of this work, John Hellman's study, *Emmanuel Mounier and the New Catholic Left*, offers the best historical interpretation of Personalism.

36. Drinnon, *Facing West*, pp. 421–24. See also Lansdale, *In the Midst of Wars*, pp. 244–312, for his account of the battle against the sects. The citation from Diem to Dooley is reprinted in A. W. Dooley, *Promises to Keep*, pp. 151–52. Robert Scheer stated that the award was "inspired" by Lansdale in Scheer, "The Genesis of United States Support," pp. 255–56. Dooley's reaction to the award is from his letter to Agnes Dooley, May 12, 1955, Dooley Papers. Dooley became an important figure in the "selling" of Vietnam orchestrated not only by Lansdale, the former advertising executive, but through an elaborate publicity campaign led by the American Friends of Vietnam, a pro-Diem lobbying group formed in 1955 which included a broad variety of political, religious, and academic leaders, from Cardinal Spellman to Arthur Schlesinger, Jr. The pro-Diem network is discussed in Scheer, "The Genesis of United States Support," pp. 246–64.

37. Halberstam, *The Best and the Brightest*, p. 158.

38. U.S. Department of Defense, "Failure of the Geneva Settlement," p. 12; Gallagher, *Give Joy to My Youth*, p. 18.

39. Tom Dooley to Agnes Dooley, May 12, 1955, Dooley Papers; *St. Louis Post-Dispatch*, May 16, 1955, p. 5B; "Letter of Father Dominique Pham Quang-Phuoc of the Diocese of Haiphong directed to the Catholics of Haiphong," February 24, 1955, Dooley Papers.

40. Fall, *The Two Viet-Nams*, p. 154; T. A. Dooley, *Deliver Us from Evil*, pp. 182–83; Tom Dooley to Agnes Dooley, February 24, 1955, Dooley Papers.

41. Scheer, "Hang Down Your Head," p. 26; Lansdale, *In the Midst of Wars*, pp. 152–53; Tom Dooley to Agnes Dooley, November 28, 1954, Dooley Papers.

42. The Pentagon Papers include an account of a 1956 Washington meeting of the American Friends of Vietnam, a diverse group that included Sen. John F. Kennedy. At that meeting "Dr. Tom Dooley described emotionally the plight of the refugees from North Vietnam, and sketched in graphic terms Viet Minh terrorism." See the *Advocate* (a Newark, New Jersey, diocesan paper), from February 1954 through May 1955, for a good sampling of attitudes toward Vietnam in the Catholic press. Although coverage of local issues would obviously differ greatly in different parts of the country, most national and international stories were supplied to the entire Catholic press by the National Catholic News Service. The Reverend Patrick O'Connor supplied most of the articles from Vietnam. See also the *New York Herald Tribune*, January 2, 1955, p. 2. For Spellman's relationship to Dooley and his role in the pro-Diem lobby, see Cooney, *The American Pope*, pp. 242–45.

43. Federal Bureau of Investigation Memorandum, December 12, 1959, from Dr. Thomas A. Dooley's FBI file, obtained through the Freedom of Information Act; see also Winters, "Tom Dooley: The Forgotten Hero," p. 17.

44. Crosby, *God, Church, and Flag*, pp. 22–23.

45. *Catholic Worker* 14 (July–August 1946): 7–8.

46. Gornick, *The Romance of American Communism*, p. 126.

47. Glazer and Moynihan, *Beyond the Melting Pot*, p. 271; Caute, *The Great Fear*, p. 108.

48. Crosby, *God, Church, and Flag*, p. 122.

49. Brashler, "The Holy Terrors," p. 30; Caute, *The Great Fear*, p. 109.

50. Liddy, *Will*, pp. 12–13.

51. Ibid., pp. 23–24.

52. Agee, *Inside the Company*, pp. 13–17.

53. McGehee, *Deadly Deceits*, pp. 1–2.

54. Van Devanter, *Home before Morning*, pp. 26–27.

55. Kselman and Avella, "Marian Piety and the Cold War," p. 409; see also "The Vision of Necedah," pp. 21–23; Haffert, *Russia Will Be Converted*, pp. 46–47.

56. Blanshard, *American Freedom and Catholic Power*, pp. 223–39; Kselman, *Miracles and Prophecies in Nineteenth-Century France*, p. 107.

57. Blanshard, *American Freedom and Catholic Power*, pp. 225–26, based his description of the event on the account in *PM*, a left-liberal New York daily; cf. Julia Porcelli's article in the *Catholic Worker* 13 (December 1945), pp. 1–2.

58. Kselman and Avella, "Marian Piety and the Cold War," p. 403.

59. Ibid. pp. 403–24.

60. Crosby, *God, Church, and Flag*, p. 176; Oshinsky, *A Conspiracy So Immense*, p. 487; *Brooklyn Tablet*, October 16, 1954, p. 6; Kselman and Avella, "Marian Piety and the Cold War," p. 419 n. 46.

61. Oshinsky, *A Conspiracy So Immense*, p. 69.

62. Ibid., pp. 285, 505; This aspect of Irish culture has often been treated, from a variety of perspectives. An interesting brief discussion of the Irish-American character that focuses on their historical distrust of a predominant modern "system"—psychotherapy—is McGoldrick, "Irish Families," pp. 310–39.

63. Tom Dooley to Agnes Dooley, February 14, 1957, Dooley Papers; *The Irish World* (September 4, 1954): 6; Glazer and Moynihan, *Beyond the Melting Pot*, pp. 246–47.

64. The priest is quoted in Blanshard, *American Freedom and Catholic Power*, p. 144; a more dispassionate analysis of community religious conflict is presented in Underwood, *Protestant and Catholic*.

65. Answers to Questions, *American Ecclesiastical Review* 117 (November 1947): 387–90; 119 (October 1948): 304–5; 122 (May 1950): 386; Cooney, *The American Pope*, pp. 108–9.

66. Tom Dooley to Agnes Dooley, November 28, 1954, Dooley Papers; T. A. Dooley, *Deliver Us from Evil*, pp. 177–78.

67. Tom Dooley to Agnes Dooley, November 1, 1954, Dooley Papers; for examples of the Diem lobby in the Catholic press, see the *Brooklyn Tablet*, July 31, 1954, p. 1, and the *Advocate*, May 18, 1957, p. 3.

68. Kselman and Avella, "Marian Piety and the Cold War," pp. 407–8; T. A. Dooley, *Deliver Us from Evil*, p. 167; T. A. Dooley, *The Edge of Tomorrow*, p. xxxi.

69. Kselman and Avella, "Marian Piety and the Cold War," p. 420

70. *Advocate*, March 20, 1954, p. 5.

71. *Advocate*, July 10, 1954, p. 1; Murphy, review of *Deliver Us from Evil*, pp. 214–15; Sister Mary Francille, "The Mystical Body of Christ," p. 15.

72. *Newsletter*, Dr. Thomas A. Dooley Cause (Christmas, 1982), p. 2; Tom Dooley to Agnes Dooley, October 27, 1954, November 18, 1954, Dooley Papers.

73. Tom Dooley to Agnes Dooley, January 7, 1955, Dooley Papers.

74. A. W. Dooley, *Promises to Keep*, pp. 61–63.

75. Tom Dooley to Agnes Dooley, November 16, 1954; December 1, 1954; February 2, 1955, Dooley Papers.

Chapter 6

1. Dooley's itinerary for early 1956 is contained in documents obtained from the Medical Command of the United States Department of the Navy; see also U.S. Department of Defense, "Failure of the Geneva Settlement," pp. 31–32.

2. A. W. Dooley, *Promises to Keep*, pp. 163–64, 167.

3. Memorandum from A. H. Belmont to J. Edgar Hoover, Federal Bureau of Investigation, December 11, 1959.

4. Memorandum from C. D. DeLoach to Mr. Mohr, Federal Bureau of Investigation, March 9, 1960.

5. D'Emilio, *Sexual Politics, Sexual Communities*, p. 38.

6. T. A. Dooley, *The Edge of Tomorrow*, pp. 17–18.

7. Ibid., pp. 18–19.

8. A. W. Dooley, *Promises to Keep*, p. 171.

9. Levenstein, *Escape to Freedom*, pp. 206–9; Winters, "Tom Dooley: The Forgotten Hero," p. 12; T. A. Dooley, *The Edge of Tomorrow*, p. 21.

10. A. W. Dooley, *Promises to Keep*, p. 173; Gallagher, *Give Joy to My Youth*, p. 28.

11. Cable from John Foster Dulles to American embassies in Saigon and Vientiane, July 30, 1956, from U. S. Department of State central decimal file for Thomas A. Dooley, 032; Memorandum from John W. Henderson to Mr. Kocher, February 21, 1957, State Department Dooley file, 032.

12. Drinnon, *Facing West*, pp. 411–13; Tom Dooley to Agnes W. Dooley, September 5, 1956, Dooley Papers; Winters, "Tom Dooley: The Forgotten Hero," p. 16.

13. Walter Robertson to Thomas A. Dooley, November 21, 1956, Dooley Papers; T. A. Dooley, *The Edge of Tomorrow*, pp. 30–31.

14. *Portrait of a Splendid American*, Side Two.

15. Dooley, "That Free Men May Live," radio broadcast, KMOX, St. Louis, July 5, 1960; William Hogan, quoted in A. W. Dooley, *Promises to Keep*, p. 197.

16. Dimond, "Tom Dooley's Memory Honored," May 2, 1982, p. 8.

17. See memoranda from FBI file on Dr. Thomas A. Dooley, February 1, 2, 8, 11, and 12, 1957; Tom Dooley to Agnes W. Dooley, Clare Murphy, and Erma Konrye, February 14, 1957. The following excerpt from Jack Lait and Lee Mortimer's best-selling *Washington Confidential*, p. 90, provides a glimpse into popular attitudes toward homosexuality from the period: "The good people shook their heads in disbelief with the revelation that more than 90 twisted twerps in trousers had been swished out of the State Department. Fly commentators seized on it for gags about fags, whimsy with overtones of Kinsey and the odor of lavender. . . . The only way to get authoritative data on fairies is from other fairies. They recognize each other by a fifth sense immediately, and they are intensely gregarious."

18. Harry Hansen, quoted in A. W. Dooley, *Promises to Keep*, p. 197; T. A. Dooley, "Foreign Aid—The Human Touch," April 20, 1958, pp. 12, 96.

19. Lederer and Burdick, *The Ugly American*, pp. 51, 55; for a discussion of Lansdale's inspirational role see Drinnon, *Facing West*, pp. 374–79.

20. Lederer and Burdick, *The Ugly American*, pp. 46–65.

21. Ong, *Frontiers in American Catholicism*, pp. 24–34.

22. Ibid.; J. T. Ellis, "American Catholics," pp. 351–88. One of Ellis's assumptions was that Catholics must inevitably judge their intellectual and cultural achievements by secular American standards. McAvoy, "Catholic Minority Today," pp. 189–90.

23. Lederer and Burdick, "Salute to Deeds of Non-Ugly Americans," pp. 156, 158; *New York Times*, June 24, 1960, p. 15; T. A. Dooley, *The Edge of Tomorrow*, pp. 17–18.

24. Tom Dooley speech, January 26, 1957, tape in possession of Ms. Teresa Gallagher.

25. Tom Dooley to Rose Gilmore, April 9, 1955, Dooley Papers; Tom Dooley, speech

delivered at Mutual of Omaha Auditorium, Omaha Nebraska, November 9, 1959, Dooley Papers; Tom Dooley to Agnes W. Dooley, November 6 and January 20, 1957, Dooley Papers.

26. T. A. Dooley, *The Edge of Tomorrow*, pp. 104–5.

27. Tom Dooley to Agnes W. Dooley, October 1, 1956 and November 8, 1958, Dooley Papers; von Hoffman, "Hang Down Your Head, Tom Dooley," p. 18.

28. T. A. Dooley, *The Edge of Tomorrow*, p. 85.

29. "The Ballad of the Good Tom Dooley," p. 132; "Priest Takes Illinois," pp. 70, 315–17; Allen, "The Amazing Dr. Dooley," p. 28. Dooley's passport applications were obtained from the U.S. Department of State under the Freedom of Information Act; they are dated January 30, 1948; May 7, 1952; January 28, 1957; and October 7, 1958.

30. Tom Dooley to Agnes W. Dooley, January 10, 1957, Dooley Papers; T. A. Dooley, *The Edge of Tomorrow*, p. 32.

31. Morechand, "Many Languages and Cultures," pp. 29–34.

32. Tom Dooley to Agnes W. Dooley, May 15, 1957, Dooley Papers.

33. Tom Dooley to Agnes W. Dooley, July 2, 1957, Dooley Papers.

34. T. A. Dooley, *The Night They Burned*, p. 28; Jeff Cheek, quoted in Monahan, *Before I Sleep*, p. 138; "Do-It-Yourself Samaritan," p. 78; Tom Dooley to Agnes W. Dooley, May 15, 1957; A. W. Dooley, *Promises to Keep*, p. 199.

35. T. A. Dooley, *The Night They Burned*, p. 113.

36. Ibid., p. 116–18.

37. Tom Dooley to Paulette Revotte, July 7, 1960, Dooley Papers; "Biography of a Cancer."

38. Tom Dooley to Agnes W. Dooley, February 11, 1960, Dooley Papers; T. A. Dooley, *The Night They Burned*, p. 20.

39. "Biography of a Cancer"; Dooley, *The Night They Burned*, pp. 20–21.

40. "Biography of a Cancer"; Father William A. Donaghy, quoted in *Before I Sleep*, p. 30.

41. Louise Hersted to Dr. Tom Dooley, August 30, 1959, Dooley Papers; Sister "K" to Teresa Gallagher, February 27, 1961, Dooley Papers; T. A. Dooley, *The Night They Burned*, pp. 38, 101.

42. Leavitt, "Tom Dooley at Work," pp. 121–22; Tom Dooley to Teresa Gallagher, May 29, 1959, Dooley Papers.

43. *Brooklyn Tablet*, January 28, 1961.

44. Tom Dooley to Robert Copenhaver, January 1, 1960, Dooley Papers.

45. Tom Dooley to Agnes W. Dooley, August 8, 1959, Dooley Papers; Winters, "Tom Dooley: The Forgotten Hero," p. 10. Ironically, Daniel Boorstin, along with many others, viewed Dooley as one of the few genuine throwbacks to a time when heroism, not celebrity, was central to our culture. In *The Image*, p. 54, Boorstin wrote: "There are still, of course, rare exceptions—a Dr. Albert Schweitzer or a Dr. Tom Dooley—whose heroism is intelligible. But these only illustrate that intelligible heroism now occurs almost exclusively on the field of sainthood or martyrdom."

46. Tom Dooley to Agnes W. Dooley, August 8, 1959, Dooley Papers; William J.

Lederer, personal correspondence, March 16, 1986; Carl Wiedermann, quoted in Monahan, *Before I Sleep*, p. 116; Robert Giroux, personal correspondence, June 17, 1985.

47. *Advocate*, June 23, 1960, p. 12; Feltmann, "Doctor of Humanity," p. 3; Ong, *Frontiers in American Catholicism*, p. 24; Agnes W. Dooley, quoted in Gallagher, *Give Joy to My Youth*, p. 44; Allen, "The Amazing Dr. Dooley," p. 29.

48. Winters, "Tom Dooley: The Forgotten Hero," p. 11; Tom Dooley to Agnes W. Dooley, August 8, 1959, Dooley Papers.

49. Feltmann, "Doctor of Humanity," p. 3; Leavitt, "Tom Dooley at Work," pp. 221–22.

50. Tom Dooley to Teresa Gallagher, April 2, 1960; Monahan, *Before I Sleep*, p. 102; Bernard B. Fall and Robert E. Waters, Letters to the Editor, *Life*, May 9, 1960, p. 20; Gallagher, *Give Joy to My Youth*, p. 30.

51. Agnes W. Dooley to Teresa Gallagher, April 21, 1960, Dooley Papers. The leader of the CDNI, Sisouk Na Champassak, dedicated his 1961 book, *Storm over Laos*, to the recently deceased Dooley. For Kong Le and his coup see Fall, *Anatomy of a Crisis*, pp. 184–99.

52. Tom Dooley to Agnes W. Dooley, August 17, 1960, Dooley Papers; Monahan, *Before I Sleep*, pp. 154, 194.

53. Monahan, *Before I Sleep*, pp. 231, 234; Jencks, *Tom Dooley*, p. 22.

54. Gallagher, *Give Joy to My Youth*, pp. 191, 203, 205.

55. Telegram, Tom Dooley to Agnes W. Dooley, December 5, 1960, Dooley Papers; T. A. Dooley, *The Night They Burned*, p. 192; Robert Giroux, personal correspondence, June 17, 1985; T. A. Dooley, "The Night of the Same Day."

56. T. A. Dooley, "The Night of the Same Day."

57. Ibid.; T. A. Dooley, *The Night They Burned*, p. 37.

58. T. A. Dooley, "The Night of the Same Day."

59. Ibid.

60. Herberg, "Religion and Culture," p. 15; see also Herberg, *Protestant-Catholic-Jew*; Gleason, "Identifying Identity," pp. 910–31.

61. Susman, *Culture as History*, p. 284; Erikson, *Childhood and Society*, p. 282; Gleason, "Identifying Identity," p. 930.

62. Russell, *Bird Lives*, p. 180; Charlie Parker, quoted in Shapiro and Hentoff, *Hear Me Talkin' to Ya*, pp. 354–55.

63. Hudson, "Protestantism in Post-Protestant America," pp. 20–27; see Chapter 7 for further discussion of the beats.

64. Thoreau, *Walden*, p. 148; Willson, "Thoreau and Roman Catholicism," p. 159; Allen, "The Amazing Dr. Dooley," p. 31; Monahan, *Before I Sleep*, p. 112.

65. T. A. Dooley, "The Night of the Same Day."

66. Monahan, *Promises to Keep*, pp. 38–40, 189; Selsor, *Sincerely, Tom Dooley*, pp. 78–80.

67. D'Emilio, *Sexual Politics, Sexual Communities*, p. 181; Gallagher, *Give Joy to My Youth*, pp. 44, 64; T. A. Dooley, "The Night of the Same Day."

68. Gallagher, *Give Joy to My Youth*, pp. xiii, 169, 175–76; Andrews, "Tom Dooley's Testament," p. 107; Greeley, *Strangers in the House*, p. 20.

69. Winters, "Tom Dooley: The Forgotten Hero," pp. 12–15.

70. Ibid.; von Hoffman, "Hang Down Your Head, Tom Dooley," p. 17; T. A. Dooley, *The Night They Burned*, p. 21; T. A. Dooley, "The Night of the Same Day."

71. T. A. Dooley, *The Night They Burned*, pp. 183–84.

Chapter 7

1. The now-standard biography of Thomas Merton is Mott's *The Seven Mountains*. It is one of the most elegant books ever written about an American Catholic. Mott is particularly strong on the relationship of Merton's inner life to his poetry. He does not, however, provide any but the most cursory interpretation of American Catholic culture, particularly during the crucial period of the late 1940s and 1950s. Another good biography is Monica Furlong's *Merton: A Biography*. This work suffers by comparison with Mott's mainly because Furlong did not have the access to Merton's restricted papers that Mott (as the "official" biographer) enjoyed. Merton has become in recent years the source of a major academic industry that is as significant as it is virtually impossible to keep pace with. There are dozens of specialized studies of Merton's work, thought, and spiritual life, but again, he is rarely treated in the context of the culture into which he converted.

2. Nicosia, *Memory Babe*, p. 32. Nicosia's sprawling study is the largest and best-researched of the numerous Kerouac biographies. McNally's *Desolate Angel* features the best sense of history of the biographical studies. Charters's 1973 work, *Kerouac: A Biography*, remains somehow the most moving account. Although I am aware of criticisms that Kerouac's biographers use his novels as documentary sources for real events, it can be safely stated that his books generally describe actual events as he, of course, perceived them. "Jack Duluoz," the narrator of most of the books (Kerouac hoped in his old age to insert a uniform set of names in all his novels) is as real, when it comes to understanding Kerouac, as his creator.

3. Sorrell, "The Catholicism of Jack Kerouac," p. 190.

4. Sorrell, "Sentinelle Affair," p. 72.

5. Ibid., pp. 67–79. Cahensly was a German whose 1883 visit to the United States—on behalf of an immigrant-aid group—rekindled conflicts over the role of "national" parishes within American Catholicism. Irish-American prelates such as Cardinal Gibbons opposed what they saw as undue European influence over the American church. A brief account of the Cahensly issue is presented in Hennessey, *American Catholics*, pp. 195–96; Cross, *The Liberal Tradition in American Catholicism*, remains a standard account of the late-nineteenth century "Americanism" controversy; see also Beaulieu, *Jack Kerouac*, p. 25.

6. Kerouac, *Visions of Gerard*, p. 7; Nicosia, *Memory Babe*, p. 27; McNally, *Desolate Angel*, p. 6.

7. Langelier and Quintal, "French Canadian Families," p. 231; Kerouac, *Dr. Sax*, pp. 3–4, 39.

8. Nicosia, *Memory Babe*, p. 24; Nicosia also suggested that Gerard's death further embittered Leo Kerouac's attitude toward the church.

9. Kerouac, *Dr. Sax*, p. 54.

10. Kerouac, *Visions of Cody*, p. 21.

11. Gifford, *As Ever*, p. 130; Ginsberg, "The Great Rememberer," p. vii.

12. Kerouac, *Visions of Cody*, p. 261.

13. Mott, *The Seven Mountains*, p. 12; Merton, *The Seven Storey Mountain*, p. 25.

14. Mott, *The Seven Mountains*, p. 12; Merton, *The Seven Storey Mountain*, pp. 20, 25–26.

15. Merton, *The Seven Storey Mountain*, pp. 9–10; Mott, *The Seven Mountains*, pp. 12–13.

16. Mott, *The Seven Mountains*, p. 16; Merton, *The Seven Storey Mountain*, p. 23.

17. Merton, *The Seven Storey Mountain*, p. 14.

18. Ibid., p. 16; Furlong, *Merton: A Biography*, p. 30.

19. Merton, *The Seven Storey Mountain*, p. 4.

20. Ibid., p. 124; Furlong, *Merton: A Biography*, pp. 58–61; Rice, *The Man in the Sycamore Tree*, p. 19; Mott, *The Seven Mountains*, pp. 78–79.

21. Merton, *The Seven Storey Mountain*, p. 137; Kerouac, *The Vanity of Duluoz*, p. 47.

22. Rice, *The Man in the Sycamore Tree*, p. 25; Kerouac, *Desolation Angels*, p. 285; Nicosia, *Memory Babe*, pp. 77, 87.

23. Merton, *The Seven Storey Mountain*, pp. 141–42; Kerouac, *Desolation Angels*, p. 285.

24. Merton, *The Seven Storey Mountain*, pp. 171–72.

25. Ibid., pp. 140, 157.

26. Editorial, *Jubilee*, July 1958, p. 1; Halsey, *The Survival of American Innocence*, pp. 166–67; "Trappist Monastery," p. 90.

27. Kerouac, *The Town and the City*, pp. 121, 177–78.

28. Kerouac, *Dr. Sax*, p. 47; Kerouac, *Vanity of Duluoz*, pp. 166–67.

29. Kerouac, *Vanity of Duluoz*, p. 222.

30. Kerouac, "The Origins of the Beat Generation," pp. 31–32, 42, 79.

31. Kerouac, *The Town and the City*, pp. 361–62.

32. Kerouac, *Vanity of Duluoz*, pp. 224, 243; Charters, *Kerouac: A Biography*, p. 364; Kerouac, *Visions of Cody*, pp. 259–60.

33. Kerouac, *Lonesome Traveler*, p. iv; Nicosia, *Memory Babe*, pp. 267, 284.

34. Nicosia, *Memory Babe*, p. 465; Jack Kerouac to Allen Ginsberg, circa May 1954, Ginsberg Collection.

35. Van Doren, *The Autobiography of Mark Van Doren*, pp. 268–69; Groves, "The Gregarious Hermit," p. 89; Mailer, *Advertisements for Myself*, p. 425.

36. Merton, *The Secular Journal of Thomas Merton*, pp. 38–39, 269–70.

37. Merton, *What Are These Wounds?*, pp. 127, 131.

38. Mott, *The Seven Mountains*, p. 236; Merton's self-evaluation was published post-

humously in Merton, *Introductions East and West*, pp. 126–27.

39. Rice, *The Man in the Sycamore Tree*, p. 79; Kerouac, "The Art of Fiction," p. 77.

40. Kerouac, "The Art of Fiction," p. 85; Hunt, *Kerouac's Crooked Road*.

41. Kerouac, "The Art of Fiction," p. 68; Ginsberg, *Allen Verbatim*, p. 153.

42. Nicosia, *Memory Babe*, p. 86.

43. Jack Kerouac to Allen Ginsberg, circa May 1954, and November 8, 1952, Ginsberg Collection.

44. Mott, *The Seven Mountains*, p. 239; Merton, *The Ascent to Truth*, pp. 171–73.

45. Kerouac, *The Subterraneans*, p. 64.

46. Ibid., pp. 96, 152; Kerouac, quoted in Charters, *A Bibliography*, p. 23; Kerouac, "The Art of Fiction," pp. 90–91.

47. McNally, *Desolate Angel*, p. 182; Jack Kerouac to Allen Ginsberg, circa 1954, Ginsberg Collection.

48. Rexroth, "San Francisco's Mature Bohemians," p. 161; Kerouac, quoted in Charters, *A Bibliography*, p. 25.

49. Kerouac, *The Dharma Bums*, pp. 107, 86–90; Kerouac, *The Scripture of the Golden Eternity*, Scripture 45.

50. Gifford and Lee, *Jack's Book*, pp. 217–19.

51. Fields, *How the Swans Came*, p. 296. Fields also briefly discusses Kerouac's Buddhism, pp. 210–16; Merton, *The Seven Storey Mountain*, p. 188; Merton, *Seeds of Contemplation*, p. 8.

52. Mott, *The Seven Mountains*, pp. 290–97.

53. Merton, *The Sign of Jonas*, p. 109.

54. Wills, *Bare Ruined Choirs*, p. 48.

55. Ibid., pp. 40, 48; Glazer and Moynihan, *Beyond the Melting Pot*, p. 262.

56. John Stanley, Letter to J. L. Barber, May 16, 1984, John Stanley personal archives.

57. Wills, *Bare Ruined Choirs*, pp. 41–44; Burton, *More Than Sentinels*, pp. 245, 253.

58. Merton, "Contemplation in a Rocking Chair," p. 23.

59. Merton, *The Sign of Jonas*, pp. 61, 235.

60. Edward Rice to Thomas Merton, June 23, 1950, Merton Collection; Kerouac, "The Statue of Christ," pp. 20–23; "A Merry Christmas from the editors of *Jubilee*," *Jubilee* 7 (December 1958): 1; "*Jubilee's* Merry Christmas," *Jubilee* 8 (December 1959): 1.

61. Mott, *The Seven Mountains*, pp. 286–88; Kerouac, *Lonesome Traveler*, p. 122.

62. Kerouac, *Lonesome Traveler*, p. 128; Kerouac, *Desolation Angels*, pp. 108–10.

63. Kerouac, *Desolation Angels*, pp. 152, 60; Kerouac, *The Dharma Bums*, p. 25.

64. Kernan, *Our Friend, Jacques Maritain*, p. 46; Catherine de Hueck Doherty to Thomas Merton, February 17, 1958, Merton Collection.

65. Kerouac, "Origins of the Beat Generation," pp. 31–32, 79.

66. Kerouac, *Vanity of Duluoz*, p. 29; McNally, *Desolate Angel*, p. 186; Gifford and Lee, *Jack's Book*, pp. 255, 319.

67. Newfield, *A Prophetic Minority*, pp. 43–45.

68. See Herron, "The New Barbarians," pp. 39–45; Hazo, "The Poets of Retreat," p.

33; Barbeau, "The Plight of the Beat," pp. 210–12; cf. *New York Times*, September 8, 1958, p. 21; Greeley, *The Church and the Suburbs*, p. 136.

69. Allen Ginsberg to Dorothy Day, September 20, 1966, letter in possession of Robert Steed.

70. "Beat Mystics," *Time*, February 3, 1958, p. 56.

71. *Playboy*, September 1959, p. 9; Catherine de Hueck to Thomas Merton, December 13, 1941, Merton Collection.

72. McNally, *Desolate Angel*, p. 249; Jack Kerouac, quoted in Sorrell, "The Catholicism of Jack Kerouac," p. 189.

73. Kerouac, *Big Sur*, pp. 3, 5, 24, 41.

74. Ibid., p. 107.

75. Ibid., pp. 117, 203–6.

76. Ibid., p. 189.

77. McNally, *Desolate Angel*, p. 338.

78. Brother Antoninus to Thomas Merton, December 8, 1960, Merton Collection.

79. Thomas Merton to Catherine de Hueck Doherty, September 18, 1958, Merton Collection.

80. Thomas Merton to Erich Fromm, Cold War Letter, 5 (1962); Dorothy Day to Thomas Merton, (June 4, circa 1962), Merton Collection. Ethel Kennedy to Thomas Merton, September 4, 1961, Merton Collection; Merton to Edward Rice, August 8, 1967, Merton Collection.

81. Rice, *The Man in the Sycamore Tree*, p. 98; Mott, *The Seven Mountains*, pp. 435–54.

82. Rice, *The Man in the Sycamore Tree*, p. 124; Merton, *The Seven Storey Mountain*, p. 423.

83. Thomas Merton to Robert Lax, December 13, 1967; Lax to Merton, n.d.; Lax to Merton, n.d.; Merton to Lax, February 14, 1968, Merton Collection; Sheed, *The Good Word*, pp. 117–20; Mott, *The Seven Mountains*, p. 292; Rice, *The Man in the Sycamore Tree*, p. 135.

84. Kerouac, "Two Poems Dedicated to Thomas Merton," p. 2; Kerouac, *Desolation Angels*, p. 152; Kerouac, *Visions of Cody*, p. 33.

85. Kerouac, *Lonesome Traveler*, p. 29.

Epilogue

1. Interview with Kieran Dugan.

2. William D. Miller, *Dorothy Day*, p. 450; interview with John Stanley; interview with Dolores Brien.

3. Bell, "Religion in the Sixties," p. 171.

4. Harrington, *Fragments of the Century*, pp. 27–32.

5. The Ginsberg reading was described by Robert Steed in an interview of March 12, 1984.

6. William D. Miller, *Dorothy Day*, pp. 423–26.

7. Hennacy, *Autobiography of a Catholic Anarchist*; Ammon Hennacy to Thomas Merton, circa 1962, Merton Collection.

8. Thomas, *The Years of Grief and Laughter*, pp. 272–336; Kerouac, *Big Sur*, pp. 147–48.

9. William D. Miller, *Dorothy Day*, pp. 482–86; Day, "All Is Grace," CW Papers.

10. Donald Meyer, *The Positive Thinkers*, p. xii; When the author asked Springsteen backstage at a New Jersey concert in 1974 if Kerouac had inspired him, he replied: "Yeah, I know that man." See also "Now: Madonna on Madonna," *Time*, May 27, 1985, p. 83.

11. Jacobson, "Teenage Hipster in the Modern World," p. 25; Gleason, "In Search of Unity," p. 205.

12. *Our Lady of the Roses, Mary Help of Mothers: An Introductory Booklet on the Apparitions of Bayside* (Bayside, N.Y.: N.p., n.d.); Ibson, "Virgin Land or Virgin Mary?" p. 286.

Bibliography

Manuscript Sources

Louisville, Kentucky
  Thomas Merton Studies Center, Bellarmine College
    Thomas Merton Collection
Milwaukee, Wisconsin
  Memorial Library, Marquette University
    Dorothy Day–Catholic Worker Papers
    Seminarian's Catholic Action Papers
New York, New York
  Butler Library, Columbia University
    Allen Ginsberg Collection
Princeton, New Jersey
  Firestone Library, Princeton University
    Caroline Gordon Papers
St. Louis, Missouri
  Western Historical Manuscript Collection, State Historical Society of Missouri
  Manuscripts, Thomas Jefferson Library, University of Missouri–St. Louis
    Tom Dooley Papers

Interviews

Bryn Mawr, Pennsylvania
  Dolores Elise Brien, May 17, 1983
Jersey City, New Jersey
  Kieran Dugan, March 29, 1984
New York, New York
  Dorothy Dohen, September 18, 1981

Michael Harrington, January 28, 1984
Mary Hudson, July 28, 1982
Ned O'Gorman, November 8, 1984
John Stanley, August 5, 1983
Robert Steed, March 12, 1984
Pearl River, New York
Alan Hudson, May 23, 1985
West Nyack, New York
Hazel and John Dermody, September 1, 1984
Frances Hogan, July 27, 1984
Mr. and Mrs. Philip O'Brien, December 8, 1987
Lynn and William Oswald, September 20, 1984
Dorothy Willock, June 14, 1982
Telephone Interview
William Cobb, September 12, 1984

Books, Articles, and Dissertations

Aaron, Daniel. *Writers on the Left.* New York: Harcourt, Brace and World, 1961.
Adam, Karl. *The Spirit of Catholicism.* 1924. Reprint. Garden City, N.Y.: Doubleday, 1954.
Addams, Jane. "A Function of the Social Settlement." In *The Social Thought of Jane Addams,* edited by Christopher Lasch. Indianapolis: Bobbs-Merrill Co., 1965.
Agee, Phillip. *Inside the Company: CIA Diary.* New York: Stonehouse, 1965.
Allen, Robert J. "The Amazing Dr. Dooley." *Catholic Digest* 22 (October 1958): 27–31.
Andrews, Robert Hardy. "Tom Dooley's Testament." *Catholic Digest* 29 (April 1965): 105–7.
"Answers to Questions." *American Ecclesiastical Review* 117 (November 1947): 387–90.
"Answers to Questions." *American Ecclesiastical Review* 119 (October 1948): 304–5.
"Answers to Questions." *American Ecclesiastical Review* 122 (May 1950): 386.
Athans, Mary Christine, BVM. "A New Perspective on Father Charles E. Coughlin." *Church History* 56 (June 1987): 224–37.
"The Ballad of the Good Tom Dooley." *Christian Century* 76 (September 9, 1959): 132.
Barbeau, Clayton C. "The Plight of the Beat." *America* 104 (November 12, 1960): 210–12.
Bayor, Ronald. *Neighbors in Conflict: The Irish, Germans, Jews, and Italians of New York City, 1929–1941.* Baltimore: Johns Hopkins University Press, 1978.
"Beat Mystics." *Time,* February 3, 1958, p. 56.
Beaulieu, Victor Lévy. *Jack Kerouac: A Chicken Essay.* Translated by Sheila Fischman. Toronto: Coach House Press, 1975.
Bell, Daniel. "Religion in the Sixties." In *Religion American Style,* edited by Patrick H. McNamara, pp. 170–77. New York: Harper and Row, 1974.

Bennett, David H. *Demagogues in the Depression: American Radicals and the Union Party, 1932–1936.* New Brunswick, N.J.: Rutgers University Press, 1969.

Bercovitch, Sacvan. *The American Jeremiad.* Madison: University of Wisconsin Press, 1968.

_____. *The Puritan Origins of the American Self.* New Haven, Conn.: Yale University Press, 1975.

Betten, Neil. *Catholic Activism and the Industrial Worker.* Gainesville: University of Florida Press, 1976.

Biography of a Cancer. Reporter Howard K. Smith. Producer Albert Wasserman. Executive Producer Fred W. Friendly. CBS Reports, April 21, 1960.

Blanshard, Paul. *American Freedom and Catholic Power.* Boston: Beacon Press, 1950.

_____. *Personal and Controversial.* Boston: Beacon Press, 1973.

Bloy, Léon. *Pilgrim of the Absolute.* Selection by Raissa Maritain. Translated by John Coleman and Harry Lorin Binsse. New York: Pantheon, 1947.

Boorstin, Daniel J. *The Image: A Guide to Pseudo-Events in America.* New York: Harper and Row, 1961.

Boulton, Agnes. *Part of a Long Story.* Garden City, N.Y.: Doubleday, 1958.

Brashler, William. "The Hard Fate of a Zealous Man." *Notre Dame Magazine*, October 1983, pp. 34–37.

_____. "The Holy Terrors." *Notre Dame Magazine*, October 1982, pp. 30–33.

Breig, Joe. "Apostle on the Bum." *Commonweal* 28 (April 29, 1938): 9–12.

Breunig, Charles. "The Condemnation of the Sillon." *Church History* 26 (September 1954): 222–44.

Brien, Dolores Elise. "The Catholic Revival Revisited." *Commonweal* 106 (December 21, 1979): 714–16.

Brinkley, Alan. *Voices of Protest: Huey Long, Father Coughlin, and the Great Depression.* New York: Alfred A. Knopf, 1982.

Brown, Alden. "The Grail Movement: American Catholic Lay Women and the Conversion of the World." Paper delivered to the annual meeting of the American Catholic Historical Association, Washington, D.C., December 29, 1982.

_____. "The Grail Movement: American Catholic Lay Women and the Conversion of the World." Ph.D. dissertation, Union Theological Seminary, 1982.

Burns, Jeffrey. "American Catholics and the Family Crisis: The Ideological and Organizational Response." Ph.D. dissertation, University of Notre Dame, 1982.

Burton, Naomi. *More Than Sentinels.* Garden City, N.Y.: Doubleday, 1964.

Bushman, Richard L. *From Puritan to Yankee: Character and the Social Order in Connecticut, 1690–1765.* Cambridge: Harvard University Press, 1967.

Calkins, Hugh, O.S.M. "Rhythm—The Unhappy Compromise." *Integrity* 2 (June 1948): 3–11.

Caute, David. *The Great Fear: The Anti-Communist Purge under Truman and Eisenhower.* New York: Simon and Schuster, 1978.

Charters, Ann. *A Bibliography of Works by Jack Kerouac, 1939–1975.* Rev. ed. New York: Phoenix Bookshop, 1975.

————. *Kerouac: A Biography*. New York: Warner Books, 1973.

Chinnici, Joseph P. "Organization of the Spiritual Life: American Catholic Devotional Works, 1791–1866." *Theological Studies* 40 (June 1979): 229–55.

Cogley, John. *Catholic America*. New York: Dial, 1973.

Coles, Robert. *A Spectacle unto the World: The Catholic Worker Movement*. New York: Viking Press, 1973.

Connell, Francis J. Review of *Applied Christianity*, by John J. Hugo. *American Ecclesiastical Review* 113 (July 1945): 69–72.

Connelly, Joel R., and Howard J. Dooley. *Hesburgh's Notre Dame: Triumph in Transition*. New York: Hawthorn Books, 1972.

Connolly, Myles. *Mr. Blue*. Garden City, N.Y.: Doubleday, 1954.

Cooney, John. *The American Pope: The Life and Times of Francis Cardinal Spellman*. New York: New York Times Books, 1984.

Corrin, Jay P. *G. K. Chesterton and Hilaire Belloc: The Battle against Modernity*. Athens, Ohio: Ohio University Press, 1981.

Corry, John. *Golden Clan: The Murrays, the McDonnells, and the Irish-American Aristocracy*. Boston: Houghton Mifflin, 1977.

Cort, John C. "The Catholic Worker and the Workers." *Commonweal* 55 (April 4, 1952): 636.

Coughlin, Charles E. *Series of Lectures on Social Justice*. Royal Oak, Mich.: The Radio League of the Little Flower, 1935.

Cowley, Malcolm. *Exile's Return: A Literary Odyssey of the 1920s*. New York: Viking Press, 1951.

Crosby, Donald F. *God, Church, and Flag: Senator Joseph R. McCarthy and the Catholic Church, 1950–1957*. Chapel Hill: University of North Carolina Press, 1978.

Cross, Robert. *The Emergence of Liberal Catholicism in America*. Cambridge: Harvard University Press, 1958.

Crowell, Benedict, and Robert Forrest Wilson. *How America Went to War: Demobilization*. New Haven, Conn.: Yale University Press, 1921.

Cuddihy, John Murray. *No Offense: Civil Religion and Protestant Taste*. New York: Seabury Press, 1978.

Curry, Cecil B. *Edward Lansdale, the Unquiet American*. Boston: Houghton Mifflin, 1988.

Daly, Mary. *Gyn/Ecology: The Metaethics of Radical Feminism*. Boston: Beacon Press, 1978.

Dansette, Adrien. "The Rejuvenation of French Catholicism: Marc Sangnier's Sillon." *Review of Politics* 15 (January 1953): 34–52.

Day, Dorothy. "All Is Grace." Unpublished manuscript, Dorothy Day–Catholic Worker Papers.

————. "The Catholic Worker." *Integrity* 1 (November 1946): 16–21.

————. "East 12th Street." *Commonweal* 17 (November 30, 1932): 128–29.

————. *The Eleventh Virgin*. New York: A. C. Boni, 1924.

————. *From Union Square to Rome*. Silver Spring, Md.: Preservation of the Faith Press, 1938.

————. "Guadaloupe." *Commonweal* 11 (February 26, 1930): 477–78.

————. "Having a Baby." *New Masses* 4 (June 1928): 5–6.

————. *House of Hospitality*. New York: Sheed and Ward, 1939.

————. "In Memory of Ed Willock." *Commonweal* 73 (February 24, 1961): 549–51.

————. "I Remember Peter Maurin." *Jubilee* I (March 1954): 34–39.

————. *Loaves and Fishes*. New York: Harper and Row, 1963.

————. *The Long Loneliness*. New York: Harper and Row, 1952.

————. "Mary, Mary, Quite Contrary." *The Masses* 9 (August 1917): 38.

————. *Meditations*. New York: Paulist Press, 1970.

————. *On Pilgrimage*. New York: Catholic Worker Press, 1948.

————. "Peter and Women." *Commonweal* 45 (December 6, 1946): 188–89.

————. "Peter Maurin." Unpublished manuscript, Dorothy Day–Catholic Worker Papers.

————. "Spring Festival in Mexico." *Commonweal* 12 (July 16, 1930): 296–97.

————. "Un-Modern Love." *The Masses* 9 (September 1917): 31–32.

D'Emilio, John. *Sexual Politics, Sexual Communities: The Making of a Homosexual Minority in the United States, 1940–1970*. Chicago: University of Chicago Press, 1983.

Deverall, Richard L. G. "The Way It Was." *Social Order* 11 (June 1961): 259–64.

Dimond, Joseph. "Tom Dooley's Memory Honored." *National Catholic Register*, May 2, 1982, pp. 1, 8.

Diner, Hesia R. *Erin's Daughters in America*. Baltimore: Johns Hopkins University Press, 1983.

"Do-It-Yourself Samaritan." *Life*, March 17, 1958, pp. 75–78.

Dolan, Jay P. *Catholic Revivalism*. Notre Dame, Ind.: University of Notre Dame Press, 1978.

Dooley, Agnes W. *Promises to Keep: The Life of Dr. Thomas A. Dooley*. New York: Farrar, Straus, 1962.

Dooley, Thomas A. *Deliver Us from Evil*. New York: Farrar, Straus and Cudahy, 1956.

————. *The Edge of Tomorrow*. New York: Farrar, Straus and Cudahy, 1958.

————. "Foreign Aid—The Human Touch." *New York Times Magazine*, April 20, 1958, pp. 12, 96.

————. *The Night They Burned the Mountain*. New York: Farrar, Straus and Cudahy, 1960.

Drinnon, Richard. *Facing West: The Metaphysics of Indian-Hating and Empire Building*. Minneapolis: University of Minnesota Press, 1980.

Durdin, Peggy. "Mission of Mercy Accomplished." Review of *Deliver Us from Evil*, by Thomas A. Dooley. *New York Times Book Review*, August 19, 1956, p. 19.

Echele, Cyril T. "An American Poverello." In *Peter Maurin, Christian Radical*. St. Louis: Pio Decimo Press, 1950.

Ellis, John Tracy. "American Catholics and the Intellectual Life." *Thought* 30 (Autumn

1955): 351–88.

Ellis, Marc. *Peter Maurin: Prophet in the Twentieth Century*. Ramsey, N.J.: Paulist Press, 1981.

Ellsberg, Robert, ed. *By Little and By Little: The Selected Writings of Dorothy Day*. New York: Alfred A. Knopf, 1983.

Erikson, Erik H. *Childhood and Society*. 1950. Reprint. New York: W. W. Norton, 1963.

———. *Young Man Luther: A Study in Psychoanalysis and History*. 1958. Reprint. New York: W. W. Norton, 1962.

Fall, Bernard. *Anatomy of a Crisis: The Laotian Crisis of 1960–1961*. Garden City, N.Y.: Doubleday, 1969.

———. *The Two Viet-Nams: A Political and Military Analysis*. New York: Praeger, 1963.

Feltmann, Shirley. "Doctor of Humanity." *Today* (January 1961): 3–7.

Fenton, Joseph Clifford. "Nature and the Supernatural Life." *American Ecclesiastical Review* 114 (January 1946): 54–68.

Fields, Rick. *How the Swans Came to the Lake*. Boulder, Colo.: Shambhala, 1981.

Fishbein, Leslie. *Rebels in Bohemia: The Radicals of the Masses, 1911–1917*. Chapel Hill: University of North Carolina Press, 1982.

FitzGerald, Frances. *Fire in the Lake: The Vietnamese and the Americans in Vietnam*. New York: Random House, 1972.

Foner, Eric. *Free Soil, Free Labor, Free Men. The Ideology of the Republican Party before the Civil War*. New York: Oxford University Press, 1970.

Francille, Sister Mary. "The Mystical Body of Christ and the Spiritual Life." *Spiritual Life* 3 (March 1957): 10–15.

Freeman, Joshua B. "The Transit Worker's Union in New York City, 1933–1948." Ph.D. dissertation, Rutgers University, 1983.

Furlong, Monica. *Merton: A Biography*. New York: Harper and Row, 1980.

Gallagher, Teresa. *Give Joy to My Youth*. New York: Farrar, Straus and Giroux, 1965.

Geyer, Georgie Anne. "A Small Place in the Sun." *Notre Dame Magazine*, Summer 1985, pp. 14–17.

Gifford, Barry, ed. *As Ever: The Collected Correspondence of Allen Ginsberg and Neal Cassady*. Berkeley, Calif.: Creative Arts, 1977.

Gifford, Barry, and Lawrence Lee. *Jack's Book: An Oral Biography of Jack Kerouac*. New York: St. Martin's Press, 1978.

Gillis, James. "Problems of the Catholic Writer." *Atlantic Monthly* 181 (January 1948): 109–13.

Gilman, Richard. *Decadence: The Strange Life of an Epithet*. New York: Farrar, Straus and Giroux, 1979.

Ginsberg, Allen. *Allen Verbatim: Lectures on Poetry, Politics, Consciousness*. Edited by Gordon Ball. New York: McGraw-Hill, 1974.

———. "The Great Rememberer." Introduction to *Visions of Cody*, by Jack Kerouac. New York: McGraw-Hill, 1972.

Glazer, Nathan, and Daniel Patrick Moynihan. *Beyond the Melting Pot: The Negroes,*

Puerto Ricans, Jews, Italians, and Irish of New York City. Cambridge, Mass.: MIT Press, 1964.

Glazer, Penina Migdal. "A Decade of Transition: A Study of Radical Journals of the 1940s." Ph.D. dissertation, Rutgers University, 1970.

Gleason, Philip. *The Conservative Reformers: German-American Catholics and the Social Order.* Notre Dame, Ind.: University of Notre Dame Press, 1968.

————. "Identifying Identity: A Semantic History." *Journal of American History* 69 (March 1983): 910–31.

————. "In Search of Unity: American Catholic Thought, 1920–1960." *Catholic Historical Review* 65 (April 1979): 185–205.

Gordon, Caroline. *The Malefactors.* New York: Harcourt, Brace, 1956.

Gornick, Vivian. *The Romance of American Communism.* New York: Basic Books, 1977.

Greeley, Andrew M. *The American Catholic: A Social Portrait.* New York: Basic Books, 1977.

————. *The Church and the Suburbs.* Rev. ed. New York: Sheed and Ward, 1963.

————. Foreword to *International Conflict in an American City: Boston's Irish, Italians, and Jews, 1935–1944,* by John F. Stack, Jr. Westport, Conn.: Greenwood Press, 1979.

————. *Strangers in the House: Catholic Youth in America.* New York: Sheed and Ward, 1961.

Greene, Graham. *The Quiet American.* 1955. Reprint. New York: Penguin Books, 1973.

Greven, Philip. *The Protestant Temperament: Patterns of Child-Rearing, Religious Experience, and the Self in Early America.* New York: Alfred A. Knopf, 1977.

Groves, Gerald. "The Gregarious Hermit." *American Scholar* 49 (Winter 1979–80): 89–93.

Haas, Harry, and Nguyen Bao Cong [pseud.]. *Vietnam: The Other Conflict.* London: Sheed and Ward, 1971.

Haffert, John M. *Russia Will Be Converted.* Washington, N.J.: AMI Press, 1950.

Halberstam, David. *The Best and the Brightest.* Greenwich, Conn.: Fawcett, 1972.

Halsey, William M. *The Survival of American Innocence: American Catholicism in an Era of Disillusionment, 1920–1940.* Notre Dame, Ind.: University of Notre Dame Press, 1980.

Hamilton, Ian. *Robert Lowell: A Biography.* New York: Random House, 1982.

Harrington, Michael. *Fragments of the Century.* New York: E. P. Dutton, 1973.

Hatch, Nathan. *The Sacred Cause of Liberty: Republican Thought and the Millenium in Revolutionary New England.* New Haven, Conn.: Yale University Press, 1977.

Hazo, Samuel. "The Poets of Retreat." *Catholic World* 198 (October 1963): 33.

Hebblethwaite, Peter. "The Popes and Politics: Shifting Patterns in 'Catholic Social Doctrine.'" *Daedalus* 111 (Winter 1982): 85–99.

Hellman, John. *Emmanuel Mounier and the New Catholic Left, 1930–1950.* Toronto: University of Toronto Press, 1981.

Hennacy, Ammon. *The Autobiography of a Catholic Anarchist.* New York: Catholic Worker Press, 1954.

Hennessey, James. *American Catholics: A History of the Roman Catholic Community in the United States*. New York: Oxford University Press, 1981.

Herberg, Will. *Protestant-Catholic-Jew: An Essay in American Religious Sociology*. Garden City, N.Y.: Doubleday, 1955.

———. "Religion and Culture in Present-Day America." In *Roman Catholicism and the American Way of Life*, edited by Thomas T. McAvoy, C.S.C., pp. 4–19. Notre Dame, Ind.: University of Notre Dame Press, 1960.

Herron, William G. "The New Barbarians." *Cithera* 1 (November 1961): 39–45.

Hoehn, Matthew, O.S.B., ed. *Catholic Authors: Contemporary Biographical Sketches, 1930–1947*. Newark, N.J.: St. Mary's Abbey, 1948.

———. *Catholic Authors: Contemporary Biographical Sketches*. Newark, N.J.: St. Mary's Abbey, 1952.

Hoffman, Michael J. *The Subversive Vision: American Romanticism in Literature*. Port Washington, N.Y.: Kennikat Press, 1972.

Hofstadter, Richard. *Anti-Intellectualism in American Life*. New York: Alfred A. Knopf, 1963.

Hudson, Winthrop. "Protestantism in Post-Protestant America." In *Roman Catholicism and the American Way of Life*, edited by Thomas T. McAvoy, C.S.C., pp. 20–27. Notre Dame, Ind.: University of Notre Dame Press, 1960.

Hugo, John J. *Applied Christianity*. New York: Privately printed, 1944.

———. *The Sign of Contradiction*. New York: Privately printed, 1947.

———. *The Weapons of the Spirit*. New York: Catholic Worker Press, 1943.

Hunt, Tim. *Kerouac's Crooked Road: Development of a Fiction*. Hamden, Conn.: Shoe String Press, 1981.

Huysmans, Joris-Karl. *Against the Grain*. Translated from the French by C. Kegan Paul. New York: H. Fertig, 1976.

———. *En Route*. Translated from the French by C. Kegan Paul. London: Kegan Paul, Trench, Trubner, and Co., 1908.

———. *Saint Lydwine of Schiedam*. Translated from the French by Agnes Hastings. New York: E. P. Dutton, 1911.

Ibson, John. "Virgin Land or Virgin Mary? Studying the Ethnicity of White Americans." *American Quarterly* 33 (Bibliography Issue, 1981): 284–308.

Jackson, Carol. "In Defense of Monica Baldwin." *Integrity* 4 (July 1950): 48.

———. "The Tragedy of Modern Woman." *Integrity* 3 (November 1948): 3–10.

Jacobson, Mark. "Teenage Hipster in the Modern World." *Village Voice*, August 7, 1978, pp. 1, 19–25.

James, William. *The Varieties of Religious Experience*. 1902. Reprint. New York: Longmans, Green, 1929.

Jencks, Barbara C. *Tom Dooley, American Saint?* Providence, R.I.: Privately printed, 1961.

"*Jubilee's* Merry Christmas." *Jubilee* 8 (December 1959): 1.

Jung, C. J. *Memories, Dreams, Reflections*. 1961. Reprint. New York: Random House, 1965.

Kane, Paula Marie. "Boston Catholics and Modern American Culture, 1900–1920."
Ph.D. dissertation, Yale University, 1988.

Karnow, Stanley. *Vietnam: A History*. New York: Viking Press, 1983.

Kazin, Alfred. "The Self as History: Reflections on Autobiography." In *The American
Autobiography: A Collection of Critical Essays*, edited by Albert E. Stone, pp. 31–43.
Englewood Cliffs, N.J.: Prentice-Hall, 1981.

Kern, Louis J. *An Ordered Love: Sex Roles and Sexuality in Victorian Utopias—The Shak-
ers, the Mormons, and the Oneida Community*. Chapel Hill: University of North Carolina Press, 1981.

Kernan, Julie. *Our Friend, Jacques Maritain*. Garden City, N.Y.: Doubleday, 1975.

Kerouac, Jack. "The Art of Fiction XLI." *Paris Review* 43 (Summer 1968): 60–105.

———. *Big Sur*. New York: Farrar, Straus and Cudahy, 1962.

———. *Desolation Angels*. New York: G. P. Putnam's Sons, 1965.

———. *The Dharma Bums*. New York: New American Library, 1959.

———. *Dr. Sax*. New York: Ballantine Books, 1973.

———. *Lonesome Traveler*. New York: McGraw-Hill, 1960.

———. *On the Road*. New York: Viking Press, 1957.

———. "The Origins of the Beat Generation." *Playboy*, June 1959, pp. 31–32, 42, 79.

———. *The Scripture of the Golden Eternity*. New York: Corinth Books, 1960.

———. "The Statue of Christ." *Jubilee* 6 (June 1958): 20–23.

———. *The Subterraneans*. New York: Grove Press, 1971.

———. *The Town and the City*. New York: Harcourt, Brace, 1950.

———. "Two Poems Dedicated to Thomas Merton." *Monk's Pond* 2 (Summer 1968): 2.

———. *Vanity of Duluoz: An Adventurous Education, 1935–1946*. New York: Coward-
McCann, 1968.

———. *Visions of Cody*. New York: McGraw-Hill, 1972.

———. *Visions of Gerard*. New York: McGraw-Hill, 1976.

King, John Owen, III. *The Iron of Melancholy: Structures of Spiritual Conversion in
America from the Puritan Conscience to Victorian Neurosis*. Middletown, Conn.: Wes-
leyan University Press, 1983.

Kselman, Thomas A. *Miracles and Prophecies in Nineteenth-Century France*. New Brunswick, N.J.: Rutgers University Press, 1983.

Kselman, Thomas A., and Steven Avella. "Marian Piety and the Cold War in the United
States." *Catholic Historical Review* 72 (July 1986): 403–24.

LaBossiere, Cecilia. "Saga of Stuyvesant Heights." *Torch* (July–August 1943): 4–6.

Lait, Jack, and Lee Mortimer. *Washington Confidential*. New York: Crown, 1951.

Langelier, Regis. "French Canadian Families." In *Ethnicity and Family Therapy*, edited
by Monica McGoldrick, John K. Pearce, and Joseph Giordano, pp. 229–46. New
York: Guilford Press, 1982.

Lansdale, Edward Geary. *In the Midst of Wars: An American's Mission to Southeast Asia*.
New York: Harper and Row, 1972.

"Lansdale Team's Report on Covert Saigon Mission in '54 and '55." In *The Pentagon Papers as Published by the New York Times*. New York: Bantam Books, 1971.

Laver, James K. *The First Decadent: Being the Strange Life of J. K. Huysmans.* London: Faber and Faber, 1954.

Leader, Robert. "How the Landscape Has Changed." *Notre Dame Magazine* (Spring 1984): 22–25.

Lears, T. J. Jackson. *No Place of Grace: Antimodernism and the Transformation of American Culture, 1880–1920.* New York: Pantheon, 1981.

Leavitt, Scot. "Tom Dooley at Work." *Life*, April 18, 1960, pp. 113–22.

Lederer, William J., and Eugene Burdick. *The Ugly American.* New York: W. W. Norton, 1958.

————. "Salute to Deeds of Non-Ugly Americans." *Life*, December 7, 1959, pp. 148–63.

Levenstein, Aaron. *Escape to Freedom: The Story of the International Rescue Committee.* Westport, Conn.: Greenwood Press, 1983.

Liddy, G. Gordon. *Will: The Autobiography of G. Gordon Liddy.* New York: Dell/St. Martin's Press, 1980.

McAvoy, Thomas T. "The Composition of the Catholic Minority Today." *Commonweal* 77 (October 14, 1962): 189–90.

McCarthy, Abigail. *Private Faces, Public Places.* Garden City, N.Y.: Doubleday, 1972.

Macdonald, Dwight. Introduction to *The Catholic Worker.* Greenwood Reprints Edition. Westport, Conn.: Greenwood Press, 1970.

McGehee, Ralph. *Deadly Deceits: My 25 Years in the CIA.* New York: Sheridan Square Press, 1983.

McGoldrick, Monica. "Irish Families." In *Ethnicity and Family Therapy*, edited by Monica McGoldrick, John K. Pearce, and Joseph Giordano, pp. 310–39. New York: Guilford Press, 1982.

McNally, Dennis. *Desolate Angel: Jack Kerouac, the Beat Generation, and America.* New York: McGraw-Hill, 1979.

Mailer, Norman. *Advertisements for Myself.* New York: G. P. Putnam's Sons, 1976.

Marcus, Sheldon. *Father Coughlin: The Tumultuous Life of the Priest of the Little Flower.* Boston: Little, Brown, 1973.

Maritain, Jacques. "Religion and Politics in France." *Foreign Affairs* 20 (January 1942): 266–81.

Maritain, Raissa. *We Have Been Friends Together.* New York: Longmans, Green, 1942.

Marx, Paul B. *Virgil Michel and the Liturgical Movement.* Collegeville, Minn.: St. John's Abbey–Liturgical Press, 1957.

Matthews, Davida. "The Navy Sent Him to His Life's Work." *All Hands* (November 1977): 4–8.

Maurin, Peter. *The Green Revolution.* Fresno, Calif., 1961.

May, Henry. *The End of American Innocence: A Study in the First Years of Our Own Time, 1912–1917.* New York: Alfred A. Knopf, 1959.

"A Merry Christmas from the Editors of *Jubilee*." *Jubilee* 7 (December 1958): 1.

Mersch, Emile. *The Whole Christ: The Historical Development of the Doctrine of the Mys-*

tical Body in Scripture and Tradition. Milwaukee, Wisc.: Bruce Publishing Co., 1938.

Merton, Thomas. *The Ascent to Truth*. New York: Harcourt Brace Jovanovich, 1981.

————. "Contemplation in a Rocking Chair." *Integrity* 2 (August 1948): 15–25.

————. *Introductions East and West: The Foreign Prefaces of Thomas Merton*. Edited by Robert Daggy. Greensboro, N.C.: Unicorn Press, 1981.

————. *The Secular Journal of Thomas Merton*. New York: Farrar, Straus and Giroux, 1959.

————. *Seeds of Contemplation*. New York: Dell, 1953.

————. *The Seven Storey Mountain*. Garden City, N.Y.: Garden City Books, 1951.

————. *The Sign of Jonas*. Garden City, N.Y.: Doubleday, 1956.

————. *The Silent Life*. New York: Farrar, Straus and Giroux, 1975.

————. *What Are These Wounds? The Life of a Cistercian Mystic, Saint Lutgarde of Aywieres*. Milwaukee, Wisc.: Bruce Publishing Co., 1950.

Meyer, Donald. *The Positive Thinkers: Religion as Pop Psychology from Mary Baker Eddy to Oral Roberts*. 2d ed. New York: Pantheon, 1980.

————. *The Protestant Search for Political Realism, 1919–1941*. Berkeley: University of California Press, 1960.

Michaels, Peter. [Carol Jackson.] "A Christian Abnormal Psychology." *Integrity* 1 (January 1947): 2–42.

————. "Christ with Us." Review of *The Dry Wood*, by Carryl Houselander. *Integrity* 2 (December 1947): 48.

————. *Designs for Christian Living*. New York: Sheed and Ward, 1947.

————. "The Frustration of the Incarnation." *Integrity* 1 (October 1946): 13–23.

————. "I'd Rather Be a Menial." *Integrity* 1 (March 1947): 27–37.

————. "Man's Providence." *Integrity* 1 (May 1947): 34–39.

————. "Religious Fanaticism." *Integrity* 8 (July 1954): 8–20.

————. *This Perverse Generation*. London: Sheed and Ward, 1949.

————. "The Unity of the World." *Integrity* 4 (December 1949): 15–21.

Miller, Douglass T., and Marion Nowak. *The Fifties: The Way We Really Were*. Garden City, N.Y.: Doubleday, 1977.

Miller, Kerby A. *Emigrants and Exiles: Ireland and the Irish Exodus to North America*. New York: Oxford University Press, 1985.

Miller, William D. *All Is Grace: The Spirituality of Dorothy Day*. Garden City, N.Y.: Doubleday, 1987.

————. *Dorothy Day: A Biography*. San Francisco: Harper and Row, 1982.

————. *A Harsh and Dreadful Love: Dorothy Day and the Catholic Worker Movement*. New York: Liveright, 1972.

Mitchell, Jonathan. "Father Coughlin's Children." *New Republic* 88 (August 26, 1936): 72–74.

Monahan, James, ed. *Before I Sleep: The Last Days of Dr. Tom Dooley*. New York: Farrar, Straus and Cudahy, 1961.

Monk, Maria. *Awful Disclosures of the Hotel Dieu Nunnery of Montreal*. Facsimile of

1836 edition. Hamden, Conn.: Archon Books, 1962.

Moore, R. Laurence. *Religious Outsiders and the Making of Americans.* New York: Oxford University Press, 1986.

Morechand, Guy. "The Many Languages and Cultures of Laos." In *Laos: War and Revolution,* edited by Nina S. Adams and Alfred McCoy, pp. 29–34. New York: Harper and Row, 1970.

Morgan, Bill. "Six Aren't Enough." *Integrity* 2 (June 1948): 12–18.

Mott, Michael. *The Seven Mountains of Thomas Merton.* Boston: Houghton Mifflin Company, 1984.

Mounier, Emmanuel. *A Personalist Manifesto.* Collegeville, Minn.: St. John's University Press, 1938.

"Mr. and Mrs. X." "Responsibility in Catholic Marriage." *Integrity* 10 (October 1955): 3–9.

"Mrs. J." "The Joy of Poverty." In *Be Not Solicitous: Sidelights on the Providence of God and the Catholic Family,* edited by Maisie Ward, pp. 194–207. New York: Sheed and Ward, 1953.

Murphy, James A. Review of *Deliver Us from Evil,* by Thomas A. Dooley. *American Ecclesiastical Review* 157 (September 1957): 214–15.

Newfield, Jack. *A Prophetic Minority.* New York: New American Library, 1966.

Newland, Mary Reed. "From a Letter." *Integrity* 4 (February 1950): 27.

––––––. "Lent and the Family." *Integrity* 6 (March 1952): 3–8.

Nicosia, Gerald. *Memory Babe: A Critical Biography of Jack Kerouac.* New York: Grove Press, 1983.

Novitsky, Anthony. "The Ideological Development of Peter Maurin's Green Revolution." Ph.D. dissertation, State University of New York at Buffalo, 1977.

––––––. "Peter Maurin's Green Revolution: The Radical Implications of Reactionary Social Catholicism." *Review of Politics* 37 (January 1975): 83–103.

O'Brien, David J. "The Pilgrimage of Dorothy Day." *Commonweal* 107 (December 19, 1980): 711–15.

––––––. *The Renewal of American Catholicism.* New York: Oxford University Press, 1972.

O'Gorman, Ned. "An Education for a Poet." In *Generation of the Third Eye,* edited by Daniel Callahan. New York: Sheed and Ward, 1965.

Ong, Walter J., S.J. *Frontiers in American Catholicism: Essays on Ideology and Culture.* New York: Macmillan Co., 1957.

Orsi, Robert A. *The Madonna of 115th Street: Faith and Community in Italian Harlem, 1880–1950.* New Haven, Conn.: Yale University Press, 1985.

––––––. "The Madonna of 115th Street: Faith and Community in Italian Harlem, 1880–1950." Ph.D. dissertation, Yale University, 1982.

Oshinsky, David M. *A Conspiracy So Immense: The World of Joe McCarthy.* New York: Free Press, 1983.

Our Lady of the Roses, Mary Help of Mothers: An Introductory Booklet on the Apparitions of Bayside. Bayside, N.Y.: N.p., n.d.

Piehl, Mel. *Breaking Bread: The Catholic Worker and the Origin of Catholic Radicalism in America*. Philadelphia: Temple University Press, 1982.

Pope Leo XIII. "On the Rights and Duties of Capital and Labor." In *The Church Speaks to the Modern World*, edited by Etienne Gilson, pp. 200–244. Garden City, N.Y.: Doubleday, 1954.

Pope Pius XI. "On Reconstructing the Social Order." In *The Church and the Reconstruction of the Modern World*, edited by Terence P. McLaughlin, pp. 218–78. Garden City, N.Y.: Doubleday, 1957.

———. "On the Catholic Priesthood." In *The Church and the Reconstruction of the Modern World*, edited by Terence P. McLaughlin, p. 179. Garden City, N.Y.: Doubleday, 1957.

———. "Rite Expiatis." In *The Papal Encyclicals*. Vol. 3, *1903–39*, edited by Claudia Carlen, pp. 293–304. Wilmington, N.C.: McGrath Publishing Company, 1981.

Pope Pius XII. "Mystici Corporis." In *Foundations of Renewal*, pp. 7–63. Glen Rock, N.J.: Paulist Press, 1961.

Portrait of a Splendid American: A Documentary Tribute to Dr. Tom Dooley. Columbia Records, ML 5709.

Praz, Mario. *The Romantic Agony*. 1933. Reprint. New York: World Publishing Company, 1965.

"Priest Takes Illinois." *Christian Century* 78 (January 18, 1961): 70.

Quinn, Sister Mary Bernetta. *The Metamorphic Tradition in Modern Poetry: Essays on the Work of Ezra Pound, Wallace Stevens, William Carlos Williams, T. S. Eliot, Hart Crane, Randall Jarrell, and William Butler Yeats*. New York: Gordian Press, 1966.

Rauch, R. William. *Politics and Belief in Contemporary France*. The Hague: Hartinus Nijhoff, 1972.

Rauschenbush, Walter. "Jesus the Revolutionist." In *The Cry for Justice: An Anthology of the Literature of Social Protest*, edited by Upton Sinclair. New York: Lyle Stuart, 1964.

Rexroth, Kenneth. "San Francisco's Mature Bohemians." *Nation* 184 (February 23, 1957): 159–62.

Rice, Edward. *The Man in the Sycamore Tree: The Good Life and Hard Times of Thomas Merton*. Garden City, N.Y.: Doubleday, 1970.

Rideout, Walter. *The Radical Novel in the United States, 1900–1934*. Cambridge: Harvard University Press, 1956.

Robb, Dennis. "Specialized Catholic Action in the United States, 1936–1949." Ph.D. dissertation, University of Minnesota, 1972.

Robinson, Carol Jackson. "*Integrity*: The Beginnings." *Catholic Press Annual* 3 (1962): 27–34, 60.

Rodgers, Daniel T. *The Work Ethic in Industrial America, 1850–1920*. Chicago: University of Chicago Press, 1978.

de Rougemont, Denis. *Love in the Western World*. Translated from the French by Montgomery Belgion. 1940. Reprint. New York: Fawcett, 1956.

Russell, Ross. *Bird Lives! The High Life and Hard Times of Charlie (Yardbird) Parker*. New York: Charterhouse, 1973.

Scheer, Robert. "Genesis of United States Support for Ngo Dinh Diem." In *Vietnam: History, Documents, and Opinion on a Major World Crisis*, edited by Marvin E. Gettleman, pp. 246–64. New York: Fawcett, 1965.

―――. "Hang Down Your Head, Tom Dooley." *Ramparts* 4 (January–February 1965): 23–28.

Seifert, Shirley. "The Untold Story of Tom Dooley." *Coronet* (August 1961): 58–64.

Selsor, Lucille. *Sincerely, Tom Dooley*. New York: Twin Circle, 1969.

Shapiro, Edward S. "Decentralist Intellectuals and the New Deal." *Journal of American History* 58 (March 1972): 938–57.

Shapiro, Nat, and Nat Hentoff, eds. *Hear Me Talkin' to Ya: The Story of Jazz as Told by the Men Who Made It*. New York: Dover, 1955.

Sharp, John K. "Shall the Diocesan Clergy Conduct Retreats?" *Ecclesiastical Review* 83 (October 1930): 337–46.

Sheed, Wilfrid. *The Good Word and Other Words*. New York: E. P. Dutton, 1978.

―――. *Frank and Maisie: A Memoir with Parents*. New York: Simon and Schuster, 1985.

Sheehan, Arthur. "Conversations with Peter." In *Peter Maurin, Christian Radical*, pp. 11–12. St. Louis: Pio Decimo Press, 1950.

―――. *Peter Maurin: Gay Believer*. Garden City, N.Y.: Doubleday, 1959.

Sheehan, Elizabeth M. "Through Eyes That See." Review of *On Pilgrimage*, by Dorothy Day. *Integrity* 3 (March 1949): 46–47.

Sheen, Fulton J. *The Mystical Body of Christ*. New York: Sheed and Ward, 1935.

Shenton, James P. "The Coughlin Movement and the New Deal." *Political Science Quarterly* 83 (September 1958): 352–73.

Shi, David E. *The Simple Life: Plain Living and High Thinking in American Culture*. New York: Oxford University Press, 1985.

Simpson, Eileen. *Poets in Their Youth: A Memoir*. New York: Random House, 1983.

Sisouk Na Champassak. *Storm over Laos*. New York: Praeger, 1961.

Slater, Philip. *The Pursuit of Loneliness*. Boston: Beacon Press, 1970.

Sollors, Werner. *Beyond Ethnicity: Consent and Descent in American Culture*. New York: Oxford University Press, 1986.

Sorrell, Richard S. "The Catholicism of Jack Kerouac." *Studies in Religion* 11 (Spring 1982): 190–200.

―――. "Sentinelle Affair (1924–1929)—Religion and Militant Survivance in Woonsocket, Rhode Island." *Rhode Island History* 36 (August 1977): 67–79.

Sparr, Arnold J. "The Catholic Literary Revival in America, 1920–1960." Ph.D. dissertation, University of Wisconsin, 1985.

Sperry, Willard R. *Religion in America*. New York: Macmillan, 1946.

Stancioff, Marion Mitchell. "The Love Education of Girls." *Integrity* 3 (August 1949): 29–30.

Stanley, John. "In Memory of Ed Willock." *Commonweal* 74 (April 14, 1961): 80–81.

Stein, Jean. *Edie: An American Biography*. Edited with George Plimpton. New York: Alfred A. Knopf, 1982.

Steinbeck, John. *The Grapes of Wrath*. 1939. Reprint. New York: Bantam Books, 1964.

Stritch, Thomas. "The Foreign Legion of Father O'Hara." *Notre Dame Magazine*, October 1981, pp. 23–27.

Susman, Warren I. *Culture as History: The Transformation of American Society in the Twentieth Century*. New York: Pantheon, 1984.

_____. "The Thirties." In *The Development of an American Culture*, edited by Stanley Coben and Lorman Ratner, pp. 179–218. Englewood Cliffs, N.J.: Prentice-Hall, 1970.

Swinburne, A. C. *Swinburne's Collected Poetical Works*, vol. 2. London: W. Heinemann, 1935.

Sylvester, Harry. *Moon Gaffney*. New York: Henry Holt, 1947.

_____. "Problems of the Catholic Writer." *Catholic World* 166 (March 1948): 481–86.

Thernstrom, Stephan. *The Other Bostonians: Poverty and Progress in the American Metropolis, 1880–1970*. Cambridge: Harvard University Press, 1973.

Thomas, Joan. *The Years of Grief and Laughter. A "Biography" of Ammon Hennacy*. Phoenix: Hennacy Press, 1974.

Thomas, John L. "Nationalities and American Catholicism." In *Catholic Church, U.S.A.*, edited by Louis Putz, pp. 155–76. Chicago: Fides, 1956.

Thomas à Kempis. *The Imitation of Christ*. Edited by Harold Gardiner, S.J. Garden City, N.Y.: Doubleday, 1955.

Thoreau, Henry David. *Walden and Civil Disobedience*. New York: Airmont, 1965.

"Trappist Monastery." *Life*, May 23, 1949, pp. 85–90.

Underwood, Kenneth Wilson. *Protestant and Catholic: Religious and Social Interaction in an Industrial Community*. Boston: Beacon Press, 1957.

U.S. Department of Defense. "Failure of the Geneva Settlement." In *United States–Vietnam Relations, 1945–1967*, Book 2. Washington, D.C.: U.S. Government Printing Office, 1971.

U.S. Department of Defense. *United States–Vietnam Relations, 1945–1967*. 12 vols. Washington, D.C.: U.S. Government Printing Office, 1971.

Van Devanter, Linda. *Home before Morning: The Story of an Army Nurse in Vietnam*. New York: Beaufort Books, 1983.

Van Doren, Mark. *The Autobiography of Mark Van Doren*. New York: Harcourt, Brace, 1958.

Veysey, Lawrence. *The Communal Experience: Anarchist and Mystical Counter-Cultures in America*. New York: Harper and Row, 1973.

"The Vision of Necedah." *Life*, August 28, 1950, pp. 21–23.

von Hoffman, Nicholas. "Hang Down Your Head, Tom Dooley." *The Critic* 28 (November–December 1969): 16–22.

Wade, Mason. *The French-Canadian Outlook*. Toronto: McClelland and Stewart, 1964.

Walsh, William. "The Young Familiar Faces." In *Be Not Solicitous: Sidelights on the Providence of God and the Catholic Family*, edited by Maisie Ward, pp. 116–41. New York: Sheed and Ward, 1953.

Ward, Maisie. "Plea for the Family." In *Be Not Solicitous: Sidelights on the Providence of*

God and the Catholic Family, edited by Maisie Ward, pp. 3–54. New York: Sheed and Ward, 1953.

———. *Unfinished Business*. New York: Sheed and Ward, 1974.

Weber, Eugen. *Action Française: Royalism and Reaction in Twentieth-Century France*. Stanford, Calif.: Stanford University Press, 1966.

Weber, Max. *The Protestant Ethic and the Spirit of Capitalism*. Translated by Talcott Parsons. New York: Charles Scribner's Sons, 1958.

Weiser, Francis X. *Handbook of Christian Feasts and Customs: The Year of Our Lord in Liturgy and Folklore*. New York: Harcourt, Brace and World, 1958.

Willock, Ed. "And All These Things Will Be Added." *Integrity* 1 (September 1947): 7.

———. "The Catholic Politician—Alas." *Integrity* 3 (October 1948): 26–36.

———. "Catholic Radicalism." *Commonweal* 58 (October 2, 1952): 630–33.

———. "The Cross and the Dollar." *Integrity* 1 (October 1946): 37–46.

———. "The Family Has Lost Its Head." *Integrity* 1 (May 1947): 38–46.

———. "Hints for Converting America." *Integrity* 1 (July 1947): 38–44.

———. "Marriage for Keeps." *Integrity* 5 (October 1950): 3–30.

———. "Men, Mary, and Manliness." *Integrity* 3 (November 1948): 36–45.

———. "Not Enough Fools to Go 'Round." *Integrity* 8 (July 1954): 13–16.

———. "A Place to Live." *Integrity* 6 (July 1952): 6–14.

———. "Poverty and Marriage." *Integrity* 3 (May 1949): 32–37.

———. "Suffering and Spiritual Growth." *Ave Maria* 88 (July 12, 1958): 23–26.

———. "This Gift Is Ours." *Integrity* 3 (December 1946): 31–39.

———. "To Be Specific." *Integrity* 1 (March 1947): 15–25.

Willock, Dorothy. "Life with Mother." *Integrity* 1 (May 1947): 18–21.

———. "My Marriage Course." *Integrity* 2 (December 1947): 37–42.

Wills, Garry. *Bare Ruined Choirs: Doubt, Prophecy, and Radical Religion*. New York: Dell, 1974.

———. "Dorothy Day at the Barricades." *Esquire*, December 1983, pp. 228–33.

Willson, Lawrence. "Thoreau and American Catholicism." *Catholic Historical Review* 42 (July 1956): 157–72.

Wilson, Edmund. *Axel's Castle*. New York: Charles Scribner's Sons, 1950.

Winters, Jim. "Tom Dooley: The Forgotten Hero." *Notre Dame Magazine*, May 1979, pp. 10–17.

Wolff, Geoffrey. *Black Sun: The Brief Transit and Violent Eclipse of Harry Crosby*. New York: Random House, 1976.

Woodward, Kenneth. "The Lessons of the Master." *Notre Dame Magazine*, Spring 1984, pp. 14–21.

Index